Critical Perspectives
on
Project Head Start

*Revisioning the Hope
and Challenge*

edited by
Jeanne Ellsworth
and Lynda J. Ames

STATE UNIVERSITY OF NEW YORK PRESS

Published by

State University of New York Press, Albany

© 1998 State University of New York

For information, address State University of New York Press,
State University Plaza, Albany, NY, 12246

Production by Marilyn P. Semerad
Marketing by Nancy Farrell

Library of Congress Cataloging-in-Publication Data

Critical perspectives on Project Head Start : revisioning the hope and
    challenge / edited by Jeanne Ellsworth and Lynda J. Ames.
        p.   cm. — (SUNY series, youth social services, schooling, and
    public policy)
        Includes bibliographical references and index.
        ISBN 0-7914-3927-5 (hc : alk. paper). — ISBN 0-7914-3928-3 (pbk :
    alk. paper)
        1. Head Start Program (U.S.)—Evaluation. 2. Head Start programs–
    –United States—Evaluation. 3. Socially handicapped children–
    –Education (Preschool)—United States. 4. Minority students—Education
    (Preschool)—United States. 5. Early childhood education—Parent
    participation—United States. I. Ellsworth, Jeanne, 1951–   .
    II. Ames, Lynda J. III. Series.
    LC4069.2.C75 1998
    372.21'0973—dc21   97-50233
                                                                     CIP

10 9 8 7 6 5 4 3 2 1

Table of Contents

Introduction   vii

1. A Lost Legacy: Head Start's Origins in Community Action
   KATHRYN R. KUNTZ   1

2. The Origins of Head Start and the Two Versions of
   Parent Involvement: How Much Parent Participation in
   Early Childhood Programs and Services for Poor Children?
   POLLY GREENBERG   49

3. Beyond Busywork: Crafting a Powerful Role for Low-Income
   Mothers in Schools or Sustaining Inequalities?
   LINDA SPATIG, LAUREL PARROTT, AMY DILLON, AND KATE CONRAD   73

4. Parent Involvement in a Rural Head Start and the
   Reproduction of Class
   ROSLYN ARLIN MICKELSON AND MARY TROTTER KLENZ   111

5. Head Start Bilingual and Multicultural Program Services
   PATRICIA A. HAMILTON, KATHERINE HAYES, AND HENRY M. DOAN   144

6. High/Scope in Head Start Programs Serving Southeast
   Asian Immigrant and Refugee Children and Their Families:
   Lessons from an Ethnographic Study
   EDEN INOWAY-RONNIE   167

7. Family Literacy Informing Head Start: Lessons from
   Hmong and Latino Families
   ELIZABETH P. QUINTERO   200

8. Reform and Empowerment: Rural Mothers and Head Start
   LYNDA J. AMES AND JEANNE ELLSWORTH   219

v

9. More Than a Job: Reflections of a Former Head Start
   Staff Member
   SUSAN W. GEDDES   242

10. Personal Growth in Head Start
    WENDY L. KIRBY   246

11. Developmentalism Meets Standardized Testing:
    Do Low-Income Children Lose?
    LINDA SPATIG, ROBERT BICKEL, LAUREL PARROTT, AMY DILLON,
    AND KATE CONRAD   260

12. A Bumpy Transition from Head Start to Public School:
    Issues of Philosophical and Managerial Continuity within
    the Administrative Structure of One School System
    STACEY NEUHARTH-PRITCHETT AND PANAYOTA Y. MANTZICOPOULOS 291

13. Inspiring Delusions: Reflections on Head Start's Enduring
    Popularity
    JEANNE ELLSWORTH   318

14. Concluding Thoughts: Hope and Challenge:
    Head Start Past, Present, Future
    JEANNE ELLSWORTH AND LYNDA J. AMES   334

Contributors   343

Index   349

Introduction

Head Start was launched in 1965 with optimism and excitement. Lyndon Johnson asserted that the inauguration of the program signified nothing less than "a landmark—not just in education, but in the maturity of our democracy."[1] The new program was said to "symbolize the new U.S. consensus"[2] about preschool education for the poor. Lady Bird Johnson, an early ally of Head Start, characterized the new program as emblematic of the "hope and challenge" of the crusade against poverty.[3]

But the War on Poverty ended after a few skirmishes, and we approach the end of the century with increasing poverty, particularly among children, and "welfare reform" that is miserly and punitive. As a newly elected president, Bill Clinton called for full funding of Head Start—that is, for a funding increase that would allow *all* (not just the present fraction[4]) of income-eligible children to be enrolled in Head Start. But this proposal was quickly squelched, as issues of "quality," "efficiency," and "cost-effectiveness" were reflexively raised. Naive hopes for full funding look almost ridiculous right now, as commitments to poverty and social injustice have been jettisoned, by liberals as well as conservatives, in the name of balancing the budget, "getting tough," and gaining an edge in global competition. Still, Head Start remains a fixture on the American educational scene.

When Lady Bird talked about hope and challenge, we doubt that she considered the challenge posed by budget priorities or a quickly waning commitment to the poor. Rather, we suspect she was referring to the challenge posed by the poor themselves, whose "cycle" or "culture" of poverty were presumed to be formidable but not unconquerable. And when she talked about hope, we imagine she, like others, hoped for a world little changed except that the poor could sustain themselves rather than depend on others. These conceptions of the hopes and challenges of poverty are entrenched in the literature and in the public imagination.

As we detail later, however, Head Start was founded on a variety of premises and promises, some of which *did not* identify poor people themselves as the sole or primary obstacles to alleviating poverty and which envisioned a more radically changed social order. However, the dominant views of what Head Start is and should strive for are rooted in the former terms, which are in turn deeply rooted in deficit theories of poverty. Both sets of hopes and challenges are subject to critique in this volume, since we are convinced that critical perspectives may open new avenues of discussion about Head Start. We consider the existing research to be largely mired in an "outcomes tradition" and hope that we can, in this volume, move beyond that via critical perspectives, further elaborated later in this introduction.

Our choices in planning and editing this book were influenced both by our scholarly inclinations and by our experiences with Head Start. In the fall of 1992, one of us (Ellsworth) was invited to serve as a community representative to the parent governing body of our local Head Start program. In this position, she saw and heard about poor women who were in apparent control of budgets, of the operations of a federal program, of hiring and firing professional staff. She heard intriguing stories of women's lives in Head Start, of families' successes, even of politicization and empowerment—and she had no trouble interesting her colleague (Ames) in a joint research project. As academics and as women, we were intrigued by and committed to telling women's stories. Together, we embarked on an ethnographic study of this Head Start organization, with a focus on mothers' involvement.[5] At the same time, we were forming friendships, making enemies, and helping where we could, as women struggled to assert themselves—in short, we got involved. We were, and continue to be, impressed with official commitment to parent participation in the program and with the energy and resourcefulness of the mothers we came to know. But we also witnessed the day-to-day experiences of parents—we observed women being silenced, parents disempowered, regulations subverted. Like the mothers with whom we worked, we were sometimes sad or angry or frustrated, but we were not surprised. Nor could we dismiss our experiences as attributable to the work of a few misguided or fiendish individuals. As academics and as women, we knew about the salience of social class, about structures of privilege and professionalism, about barriers to power for women, poor women in particular.

As scholars, we did our obligatory literature searches and we noticed, first, the sheer volume of research, and second, its relative sameness. Head Start has been researched extensively. One certainly that the program has periodically to justify itself for re-funding, making studies of discrete "effects" very valuable. But also, Head Start's nationwide educational and social engineering "experiment" has proven irresistible to researchers—as early as 1979, well over a thousand studies had been published, and large-scale reviews of the research have been conducted since 1970. And the literature continues to grow. So why another book about Head Start? After all, in sources that range from college textbooks to popular literature to massive technical reports, one can read the canon: Head Start produces some positive academic outcomes (as measured in achievement test scores, for the most part) that tend to "fade" and some others (staying out of remedial classes, avoiding repeating a grade, not dropping out of school) that are more lasting. Other reviews of this research are available, and the reader with questions about children's academic or social gains will not find easy answers here.

One refrain heard from Head Start's many admirers is that we must look beyond academic gains for children. Head Start always has claimed and aimed to be a program for parents and families and their communities as well as a preschool program for children. So, first, this book responds to calls for more research about families and communities. But we do not simply intend here to consider a different "subject population," seeking other measures of how Head Start produces one or another outcome. Rather, we wish to move discussions of Head Start into new territories via critical appraisals.

BEYOND THE OUTCOMES TRADITION

The existing Head Start research has tended to focus nearly exclusively on "outcomes," most often measuring and charting quantifiable changes in children. Such changes were, after all, what some of the designers and defenders of Head Start had promised, under the powerful and enduring premise that academic and social changes in children would make them capable of profiting from a public school education and thenceforth capable of moving out of poverty, primarily via paid work (as men) or effective homemaking/parenting (as women). While early attempts to measure changes in children's IQ scores soon were abandoned as naive, the temper of investigations has remained one of trying to determine what combinations of variables will produce desired outcomes, such as improved reading or math scores and increases in behaviors and attitudes thought to contribute to better school achievement. Studies of parents and communities also are entrenched in the same outcomes model and assumptions—for example, measuring increases in "desirable" parent-child interactions, seeking correlations between parent involvement and children's scores and grades, surveying for psychological and social benefits for parents.

This body of research has been and can continue to be of value, in particular as Head Start must continually re-apply for funding and also in regard to broader issues of early childhood education. But we share the concerns of those who fear that such studies often leave practice in and assumptions about education and social problems largely unchallenged and unchanged.[6] As we interpret them, critical approaches challenge the outcomes tradition of the dominant research model, which is often unable to deal with the complexities which educational and social welfare programs present. That is, critical perspectives seriously consider factors such as the dynamics of gender and culture, the interaction of programs with economic and political shifts, the socio-political construction of knowledge about children and schooling, and the traditional role of education as a surrogate for noneducational issues.

In outcomes-based research, for example, children's low-income status is likely to be considered a variable that is related to a presumed set of subject characteristics, perhaps "language deficiencies" or "lack of stimulation in the home environment." In research grounded in critical paradigms, low-income status is important, too, but for very different reasons—for example, because social class shapes the relationships of power between and among participants, determines the characteristics of institutions, and defines behavior and culture as either adequate or deficient. Outcomes-based research rarely questions the premises on which Head Start (and, consequently the research itself) is based, for example that employment markets and schools operate for the most part rationally and fairly and create ample opportunities for all well-prepared individuals to compete and win. In this line of reasoning, failure to succeed economically must be attributable to individuals and families themselves. The authors whose work appears in this volume work from other assumptions—for example, that failure to "make it" cannot be explained simply by failure to achieve in school, that job markets and school structures are fair and rational only to privileged groups, that it is crucial to focus on institutional and structural realities to understand poverty and social programs.

In this volume, we focus a critical eye on Head Start in its roles with other institutions, with parents and diverse communities, as a social institution in changing historical and social contexts. We make no claims to be either comprehensive or impartial. As a nationwide program, Head Start operates in communities large and small, urban and rural, homogeneous and diverse; as a social program, it addresses medical and dental care, nutrition, disabilities screening and assistance, and mental health services as well as being a preschool program that works closely with families. We do not offer here an overview, compendium, or summative evaluation. Rather, we explore a few important topics with critical visions—the chapter authors share a commitment to scholarship that will challenge taken-for-granted assumptions, particularly when they contribute to oppressive and unjust social practices and institutions. We have chosen, in addition, to include not only scholarly research, but also some of the reflections and firsthand accounts of individuals who have been involved with Head Start. In these chapters, individuals speak for themselves in ways that will we hope enrich the reader's sense of Head Start and the lives it has touched.

OTHER HOPES AND DIFFERENT CHALLENGES

Community Action and Radical Change

Initiated in 1965 under the Office of Economic Opportunity, Head Start was the favored child among the controversial antipoverty programs. At first a summer preschool program for poor children—or, in the terms of the day, culturally deprived or disadvantaged children—the program soon was expanded to operate year-round, offering educational, health, and social services with a strong component of parent involvement. A central premise in Head Start's rationale, often touted as "proven," is that poor children come from homes where "appropriate" physical, cognitive, social, and moral habits have not been developed; therefore, poor children need a "head start" in order to compete with their middle-class counterparts in public schools. The appeal and persistence of this central assumption are prodigious—and predictable. Citing the poor and their culture as the culprits in the "cycle of poverty" deflects attention from the unyielding inequities of institutions, the machinations of power and privilege, and unpopular economic redistribution plans.

But there were other ideas at work in the origins of Head Start, other less-known angles to the story. Advocates of Community Action posed different explanations of poverty and shaped parts of the program accordingly. Deeply suspicious of "culture of poverty" theories on grounds which William Ryan later termed "blaming the victim," Community Action proponents believed that it is a lack of power that creates and sustains poverty.[7] The prescription for ending poverty, in Community Action terms, is to hand over control for community institutions to the community—that is, to engage the poor in the construction and reconstruction of institutions. As a Community Action program, Head Start was designed with these principles at least partly in mind—with hopes of a changed social order and recognizing the challenges of existing power structures.

Historian Kathryn R. Kuntz examines some modest early successes in Head Start Community Action. For example, she finds evidence that community control of Head Start had the potential to effect radical change in the public schools and consequently provoked considerable fear and opposition among public school administrators. Kuntz goes on to document what she characterizes as a tragic shift away from Community Action, analyzing this shift in terms of gender and professional politics. Women's activism, she stresses, has been stripped of its political significance by traditional accounts of Head Start's history, robbing present-day Head Start women of this important and empowering legacy.

The radical potential of Community Action in Head Start is best illustrated in the story of the Child Development Group of Mississippi (CDGM) in the 1960s. This grassroots group, along with activist outsiders and professionals, administered Head Start programs in Mississippi and became a center for political and social organizing. When the voices of poor blacks in Mississippi began to rise, when local and state officeholders saw their power subverted, they were enraged. After a bitter but brief conflict, the CDGM ultimately lost its sponsorship of Head Start and disbanded.[8]

Another look at Head Start's early years is provided in a chapter by Polly Greenberg, who offers a rare insider view and a personal reflection on those days of excitement and debate. Greenberg's long association with Head Start began when she was a junior member of the staff that founded Head Start and then went south to work with the Child Development Group of Mississippi. While celebrating the high ideals and promise of Head Start, she also notes the underlying political realities that drove the design of the program. Head Start had, as Greenberg emphasizes, the appeal of serving the most "deserving" of the poor—children. She attests, too, to the fact that the program has deep roots in Community Action and ponders the sincerity of commitment to community control of the program.

Parent Involvement and Empowerment

The surviving element of Community Action resides in Head Start's standards for parent involvement. By 1970, the involvement of parents was codified into the national Head Start Performance Standards. Community Action had become parent involvement and *not* community control, since community control had in a few noisy instances done exactly what Community Action radicals had hoped it would—threatened prevailing power structures. Section 70.2 of the performance standards mandates that parents of children in the program constitute a majority on the policy board and details the ways in which that policy board must, by law, have input and/or decision-making power in different areas of operation. Section 70.2, then, sets Head Start apart from other social services and from the public schools in terms of specific and active roles for parents in matters such as curriculum, finance, hiring and firing, and policy. These parent roles, though perhaps without as radical a potential as community control could have had, do give parents significant official control of programs.

During the 1970s and 1980s, though, parent power was muted by a number of forces, including decentralization of the training and technical assistance that supports parent involvement, along with persistent cuts in funds for parent activities.[9] What does parent involvement in Head Start look like in the 1990s? In the first of a pair of chapters about parent involvement, Roslyn Arlin Mickelson and Mary Trotter Klenz analyze the ways in which the interactions of black women and Head Start staff are conditioned by racist, sexist, insular culture in a rural southern setting. These authors conclude that parent participation in this Head Start organization was seriously undercut by social relations of authority and asymmetries of power and knowledge. These forces quash the radical, Community Action-style hopes for empowerment from which parent involvement sprang. Echoing many of these concerns, Linda Spatig, Laurel Parrott, Amy Dillon, and Kate Conrad write about white Appalachian women's experiences with schooling in a Head Start Follow-Through program. These authors argue that Head Start involvement for some women can be personally rewarding and strengthening, but that overall the experiences were socially reproductive. Because of the specific kinds of involvement that the program fostered, instead of challenging, resisting, or confronting the inequities of the school system, the women wound up maintaining and supporting them.

Increasing Cultural Diversity

One persistent rationale for parent involvement in Head Start has been that it will allow each program to be responsive to the particular needs, concerns, and priorities of communities, as defined by parents and families. In their description of Head Start's multicultural dimensions, Patricia A. Hamilton, Katherine Hayes, and Henry M. Doan make it clear that this responsiveness must be not only to regional variations and local preferences, but to an increasingly ethnically, racially, and linguistically diverse population. As these authors point out, Head Start has mandated broad and pervasive measures for responding to cultural diversity. In theory, then, one might expect that each Head Start program would have rather distinctive elements of curriculum and practice. Eden Inoway-Ronnie, however, notes that many Head Starts are quite firmly bound to "developmentally appropriate" approaches, including the highly touted High/Scope approach. Her work examines the discontinuities between widely accepted preschool practice, which focuses on play and exploration, and Hmong parents' concern about explicit instruction in English, which they often are unable to provide at home. She concludes that the use of a prescribed curriculum can contradict Head Start's articulated commitments to establishing programs that are sensitive to diverse communities.

Elizabeth P. Quintero writes from her extensive experience in family literacy projects that have a critical, participatory focus and include individuals from several marginalized ethnic groups. Quintero stresses that critical family literacy can provide an arena in which Head Start teachers can gain sociocultural insights about participants and families can critique school practices and become empowered actors in schools.

Institutional Pressures from Within and Without

As Kuntz points out, from the beginning, Head Start has been moved from agency to agency, reordered and reorganized. At present under the aegis of the Department of Health and Human Services, the program's local and parental oversight co-exists, often uncomfortably, with various levels of bureaucracy. This co-existence, as described in a chapter written by the editors of this volume, can result in conflict engendered by inconsistencies in vision as well as by gender and social class power imbalances. This chapter is related closely to earlier chapters on parent involvement; it also introduces other themes related to the social contexts of the 1990s. Most recently, in the name of "budget-tightening," "accountability," and "cost-effectiveness," Head Start is threatened by the imposition of increasingly heavy-handed, top-down bureaucratic controls. In our chapter, we describe such developments in the context of one parent policy board's experiences with governance and administrators. We focus on a set of particularly revealing conflicts including the unionization of the Head Start staff, a move that, ironically, was undertaken in large measure for protection from new "letter-of-the-law" management approaches. These conflicts have had fallout for the program, parents, and staff. Wendy L. Kirby, a Head Start parent and veteran of three terms as Policy Council chair, uses excerpts from her journals and other writings to document a personal story of hopes and challenges. Susan W. Geddes, a former Head Start teacher and family worker, writes of the place Head Start has had in her life and career and her subsequent involvement in unionization. Along the way, Kirby and Geddes highlight the ways that Head Start has engendered both fierce loyalties and deep disappointments, without overlooking the dynamics of institutional power that can thwart even the best intentions.

When it is associated with public schools, Head Start feels the pressure of yet another bureaucracy, one well known for its intransigence. Two chapters examine the interface of Head Start and the public schools, along with other issues. In retrospect, it seems quaint and naive to have thought, as some Head Start planners did, that Head Start might change schools and schooling, particularly in low-income and minority communities. In fact, Head Start and the public schools now come together most regularly in programs known as "transition," in which the aim is to help children and families maintain gains as they enter the public schools—the proposal to use Head Start as a lever for change clearly has been surrendered to the assumption, once again, that it is people and not institutions, who need to change. A study of one such transition program is described in a chapter by Stacey Neuharth-Pritchett and Panayota Y. Mantzicopoulos. Through extensive interviews, these researchers saw clear rifts between Head Start's and the public schools' philosophical and managerial orientations toward the transition program. They conclude that Head Start's philosophies run headlong into the priorities, traditions, and hierarchical organizational patterns of the public schools. In this case, they conclude, instead of creating a collaborative culture for provision of valuable services, the intersection of Head Start and schools created a "culture of failed implementation."

Linda Spatig, Robert Bickel, Laurel Parrott, Amy Dillon, and Kate Conrad offer another look inside a transition program. These authors describe the interactions of Head Start's developmental, constructivist approach and the U.S. public schools' intense preoccupation with standardized test scores. This discontinuity, they suggest, may limit the access of low-income children to the dominant culture knowledge that is tapped by standardized tests. They share their worries about whether Head Start actually could be contributing to decreases in Head Start children's test scores in school.

The analyses and experiences recounted in this book are sometimes encouraging, sometimes contradictory, sometimes disturbing, always complex. Despite the confusing findings, both here and in the literature as a whole, though, Head Start has lived what one observer has termed a "charmed life."[10] In a final chapter, one of the editors comments on Head Start's public and political personae and on how the program has come to represent all that's deemed good about social welfare programming. This elevated status is particularly amazing in the context of the 1990s, when the War on Poverty has become a war on the poor, when virtually everything connected with the 1960s has been subject to vigorous attack.

We conclude the book with a discussion that focuses on the threads that wind their way through this book, one of which, as is likely clear even from this introduction, is that Head Start generally has not lived up to its promise in terms of working with parents and communities. The promise as we see it lies in strong official or "on-paper" support for community control and parent empowerment. This support engenders abundant hope but faces considerable challenges. Overall, the authors whose work appears in this book both champion and critically question Head Start's reputation and operations. In the concluding chapter, we also consider the complexities and contradictions of our allegiance to the program, despite our considerable doubt about its ability to make much difference to poverty in the United States.

Project Head Start began as what many considered a bold experiment; entering its fourth decade, it is an established feature on the American educational landscape. And, like the American landscape, it varies tremendously—locally and regionally, program to program, year to year. Rather than being one thing, Head Start is many.[11] We hope that this volume can begin to illuminate what some of those things are and can be for American children, families, and communities.

NOTES

1. "Hopeful Head Start," *Time* 86, (September 10, 1965): 17–18.

2. "Fast Start for Head Start," *Time* 86, (July 2, 1965): 64.

3. Edward Zigler and Susan Muenchow, *Head Start: The Inside Story of America's Most Successful Educational Experiment* (New York: Basic Books, 1992).

4. The percent of income-eligible children who are actually enrolled in Head Start varies widely from community to community. A rough but reasonable national estimate is probably somewhere between one-fourth and one-third. See Hamilton, Hayes and Doan in this volume for details about Head Start demographics.

5. Lynda J. Ames with Jeanne Ellsworth, *Women Reformed, Women Empowered: Poor Women and the Endangered Promise of Head Start* (Philadelphia: Temple University Press, 1997).

6. Jerome Karabel and A. H. Halsey, *Power and Ideology in Education* (New York: Oxford University Press, 1977).

7. William Ryan, *Blaming the Victim* (New York: Pantheon, 1976). For background on Community Action in the War on Poverty, see Saul Alinsky, *Rules for Radicals* (New York: Random House, 1976); Saul D. Alinsky, *Reveille for Radicals* (Chicago: University of Chicago, 1946); Kenneth B. Clark and Jeannette Hopkins, *A Relevant War against Poverty: A Study of Community Action Programs and Observable Social Change* (New York: Harper & Row, 1968); Neil Gilbert, *Clients or Constituents: Community Action in the War on Poverty* (San Francisco: Jossey-Bass, 1970).

8. Greenberg, Polly. *The Devil Has Slippery Shoes: A Biased Biography of the Child Development Group of Mississippi* (London: Macmillan, 1969).

9. Valora Washington and Ura Jean Oyemade, *Project Head Start: Past, Present, and Future Trends in the Context of Family Needs* (New York: Garland, 1987).

10. Peter Skerry, "The Charmed Life of Head Start," *The Public Interest* 73 (1983): 18–39.

11. See Sally Lubeck, Mary DeVries, Julie Nicholson and Jackie Post, "Head Start in Transition," *Early Education and Development* 8, (1997): 219–244.

1

A Lost Legacy:
Head Start's Origins in Community Action

Kathryn R. Kuntz

Head Start looks like a publicist's dream come true. The program serves young children who are picturesque in their innocence. Further, Head Start's apparent mission—to help these adorable preschoolers avoid the fate of their impoverished parents—is beyond reproach. In retrospect, it appears inevitable that such a program would catapult to popularity and that it could survive its association with other, more controversial War on Poverty efforts to become the sort of federal effort that politicians in both parties praise. At first glance, the history of Head Start seems to have an unusual fairy tale quality to it.

The actual history of Head Start, though, is more complex than these first appearances might suggest. This is not simply the story of a popular federal program for children, because, in the beginning, Head Start was not simply a program for children. Initially, Head Start aimed at improving whole communities by giving parents and community members new opportunities to participate in the nurturing and education of their children. In its early years the program showed considerable promise as a community action effort. For a time Head Start represented a unique opportunity for poor parents—and especially for poor mothers—to participate in institutional change on the local level. Indeed, Head Start might have become one of the most significant community-level efforts at institutional reform in the second half of the twentieth century had it not retreated from community action. While Head Start's evolution from community action to child-centered services enabled it to survive hostile forces at the federal level, the shift has tended to obscure some of the initial effects of the program at the local level. This chapter seeks to provide a more comprehensive, gender-sensitive history of the programs origins. To appreciate Head Start's place in U.S. history, one must understand both the program's victories and the cost of those victories.

WAGING WAR ON POVERTY

Head Start was a child of what has become America's frequently scapegoated War on Poverty. The War on Poverty was itself the product of American optimism. Fueling this optimism was an increasing sense among the public that it was immoral for a nation as affluent as the United States to accept poverty in its midst. This idea was the theme of Michael Harrington's influential book *The Other America*. Leading economists reinforced this idea when they asserted that poverty was an economic problem and, as such, it could be controlled through economic policy with statements such as "We can abolish poverty in America in ten years" and "The elimination of poverty is well within the means of Federal, state and local governments."[1] Confidence that poverty could be conquered, combined with the belief that it was immoral to allow it to persist amidst affluence, set the stage for federal action.

On January 8, 1964, in a State of the Union address intended to rally the still-mourning nation, Lyndon Johnson pledged to complete the work John Kennedy had begun. As part of that speech, Johnson declared an "unconditional war on poverty."[2] This domestic war became official with the passage of the Economic Opportunity act in August of that year. The Act set up a special agency within the office of the president—the Office of Economic Opportunity (OEO)—to eliminate poverty in the United States. The decision to create OEO outside the established bureaucracies of the Departments of Labor and of Health, Education, and Welfare (HEW) was deliberate; War on Poverty supporters believed that a significant problem in the past had been the bureaucracies of the federal departments charged with serving the poor. Accordingly, Congress gave OEO great flexibility in its use of funds and authorized the agency to try a variety of approaches from manpower and training programs to community action efforts that promoted the formation of local coalitions among government officials, local professionals and the poor themselves to identify and address local problems.

Although the economists who had been so optimistic about eliminating poverty saw it as primarily an economic issue, OEO programs did not include income transfers from the rich to the poor. Instead, the War on Poverty utilized a mix of theories regarding poverty, some of which assumed individuals needed help coping with society and others that critiqued society itself. The Job Corps focused on preparing (or even reforming) individuals through training, education, and counseling; programs such as the Job Corps assumed, at least implicitly, that the poor were in some way deficient and that these deficiencies, once identified, could be overcome. Alternatively, OEO's community action efforts promised to involve the poor in making institutions and communities more responsive to the needs of the poor and mobilizing new resources on behalf of the underprivileged; these initiatives provided an implicit critique of existing institutions, rather than of the poor. Community action emerged as a central tenet of the War on Poverty. Believing that existing federal and state institutions, "vested interests," only served to exacerbate poverty, War on Poverty planners sought to "encourage local communities to coordinate their own public and private resources, and to plan and propose their own programs" by providing funds to local communities in a way that bypassed the existing bureaucracies.[3] The key to this bypass was locally established community action programs (CAPs) which were to be the catalyst for change. Not only were the CAPs set up outside of the existing welfare structure, but OEO charged that they should encourage maximum feasible participation by the poor in all aspects of their work. Not surprisingly, some CAPs assailed the existing infrastructure; legal assistance services, for example, offered impoverished individuals an opportunity to seek justice from absentee landlords, dishonest merchants, and, in some cases, the local welfare offices that had denied them services. Even when not confronting other agencies directly, community action posed a threat to the existing infrastructure because the community action programs served as a striking alternative to the prevailing model where institutions did things *to* the poor rather than *with* the poor. The community action model suggested that the poor could be involved effectively and, in doing so, prompted a critique of the entire gamut of service agencies—from welfare offices and public hospitals to school systems—where the poor did not have a voice.

OEO's dual approach of addressing both individual and institutional issues reflected conflicting ideas about poverty. While institution changing appealed to activists at the local level and some community action proponents nationally, the media and much of the nation's political leadership believed that the poor were somehow deficient or *culturally deprived* and that these deficits were passed from generation to generation "in the social genes of the slums," resulting in a *cycle of poverty*.[4] The cultural deprivation theory suggested that the poor needed to be educated, to have opportunities to learn the values embraced by middle-class America and that, if introduced to these ideas—most important to the work ethic—the poor would straighten up and act like real Americans. The alternatives seemed clear; the secretary of labor warned that, without such intervention, a disadvantaged youngster's fate—unemployment, violence, and a life in squalor—was "sealed between the ages of three and six."[5]

Emerging research in child psychology reinforced the cultural deprivation theory. Psychologists were becoming increasingly critical of the Progressive Era beliefs that a child's development was predetermined by genetics. Many began paying more and more attention to environmental factors. Indeed, some of these scientists began to argue that IQs were not fixed, that environment could have an impact on a child's IQ.[6] Identifying the first five years of life as "critical" to a child's development, these psychologists suggested that early intervention could reverse a child's destiny. Their ideas were quickly confirmed by research with actual children; Susan Gray conducted one of the most influential experiments at Peabody College in Nashville where children who participated in a child development program showed an increase in IQs when compared to nonparticipating children.[7]

The combination of public support for the cultural deprivation idea with the research emerging from child psychology suggests that some sort of early intervention program was probably inevitable. Accordingly, some identify this as the origin of Head Start. Social historian Michael Katz argues that Head Start was founded on this idea of cultural deprivation,[8] and former Head Start administrator Edward Zigler points to the importance of the work in psychology in his explanation of Head Start's origins. Neither author acknowledges, however, that OEO could enable communities to deliver early childhood services without creating a nationwide program such as Head Start. OEO did not need the Head Start model to fund child-oriented efforts. Indeed, OEO funded preschool education and other services for children prior to the development of Head Start and, in response to congressional interest in these efforts, encouraged communities to develop these kinds of programs for children. OEO's decision to invent Head Start—to make its efforts among children more visible and more deliberate—had different origins.

Within months of the OEO's establishment, the executive director, Sargent Shriver, faced a crisis. Despite its various advantages, OEO could fight poverty only when it was invited to do so by local communities; especially with respect to the community action program, OEO funded the initiatives that originated at the local level. While participating in the War on Poverty brought additional federal dollars into the economy, it also brought new ideas, and, for some, the risk seemed higher than the reward. Headlines about conflicts in Syracuse and elsewhere highlighted the risks associated with the CAPs, which frequently challenged local authorities. Further, the risks looked unavoidable; at the urging of local activists, OEO withheld funds from the New York, Los Angeles, Philadelphia, San Francisco, and Chicago CAPs in 1965 because their structures did not allow for maximum feasible participation by the poor.[9] Many localities, particularly in the South, did not welcome CAPs or OEO, and, as a result, Shriver had more money in his budget than he could hope to spend the first year. He needed to develop a popular OEO program to help the agency establish itself in those regions of the country where community action was not, by itself, welcome.

Shriver realized the potential for a program for children to overcome the resistance to OEO when he tested the idea of a program for children out on a conservative Washington newspaper correspondent over lunch.

> I suddenly realized then that there was another advantage to doing something about children—particularly from a racial point of view. . . . In our society there is a bias against helping adults. The prevalent idea is: "By God, there's plenty of work to be done, and if poor people had any get-up-and-go they'd go out and get jobs for themselves." But there's a contrary bias in favor of helping children. Even in the black belt of the deepest South, there's always been a prejudice in favor of little black children. The old-time term "pickaninny" was one of endearment. It wasn't until blacks grew up that white people began to feel animosity or show actual violence toward them. I hoped that we could overcome a lot of hostility in our society against the poor in general, and specifically against black people who are poor, by aiming for the children.[10]

Somewhat accidentally, Shriver hit on what would become a long-term advantage for Head Start: it avoided much of the ambivalence nonpoor Americans felt about welfare programs. By focusing on innocent young children, the program could avoid questions of worthiness. At the same time, the program circumvented immediate association with the civil rights struggle because it served black children, rather than black adults. By 1965 race was an important issue for OEO; as poverty became increasingly associated with African Americans, white Americans displayed a growing ambivalence about ending poverty. Kennedy's original concern about poverty focused on conditions in Appalachia, not Harlem. By 1965 though, "poverty appeared as an urban problem that most seriously afflicted blacks."[11] The stereotype of the poor changed from the "white yeoman staggered by circumstance" in the 1930s to "black welfare mothers with hordes of illegitimate children" in the 1960s.[12]

As Shriver recognized, a program for preschoolers was an opportunity for OEO to fight poverty while circumventing (at least temporarily) the troubling racial questions that made other aspects of the War on Poverty work increasingly controversial. In conceptualizing Head Start, Shriver took advantage of prevailing biases, particularly about children and adults. Rather than addressing the attitudes and institutions that made antipoverty programs controversial—asserting, for example, that a legitimate part of community action was, indeed, helping blacks register to vote—Shriver conceived a program that would be popular because it focused on an impoverished group who was already considered deserving in the eyes of the public. A program for children would be more difficult for communities to resist, and the effort could serve as a wedge for future OEO-sponsored activities.[13]

According to Shriver, he returned to his office after lunch with the correspondent and began talking to staff about designing a program to prepare poor children for school, to take care of their nutrition and health problems, to give them books and toys, to give them a *head start* on their education. In December he asked Dr. Robert Cooke, a physician, to assemble a group of experts to consider the problem of poor children and to recommend a plan of action to OEO.[14]

In January, Cooke's committee provided Shriver with its recommendations in a memo entitled "Improving the Opportunities and Achievements of the Children of the Poor."[15] In its proposal the planning committee set forth seven major objectives for the preschool program:

A. Improving the child's physical health and physical abilities.

B. Helping the emotional and social development of the child by encouraging self-confidence, spontaneity, curiosity, and self-discipline.

C. Improving the child's mental processes and skills with particular attention to conceptual and verbal skills.

D. Establishing patterns and expectations of success for the child which will create a climate of confidence for his future learning efforts.

E. Increasing the child's capacity to relate positively to family members and others while at the same time strengthening the family's ability to relate positively to the child and his problems.

F. Developing in the child and his family a responsible attitude toward society, and fostering constructive opportunities for society to work together with the poor in solving their problems.

G. Increasing the sense of dignity and self-worth within the child and his family.[16]

Regarding parents the report noted, "Many of them have deep feelings of love and aspiration for their children which can be capitalized upon in this program."[17] The committee recommended parent participation in planning the center's programming, acquainting other residents with Head Start services, helping center staff to understand the neighborhood, learning parenting skills, and supervising the children of other parents who are participating in center activities; it also noted that parents could fill a variety of "non-professional, sub-professional and semi-professional roles necessary" for operating the center.[18] The committee did not recommend that parents participate in the hiring of staff or in the development of curriculums for the program. It also did not suggest that the program could become a catalyst for community action efforts by these parents, although OEO officials quickly identified this as a goal for the program.[19] The committee emphasized education in parenting in its report, yet four members protested to Shriver that the level of parent participation outlined in the report was too broad and needed to be focused more narrowly on educating parents. Alternatively, the community action advocates in OEO called the recommendations regarding parents weak considering the agency's commitment to real citizen participation.[20]

The issue of parent participation is central to Head Start. Head Start researchers Jeanette Valentine and Evan Stark argue that there are several conceptions of how Head Start parents should participate in the program, each reflecting a different perspective on poverty more generally.[21] Program planners who understood poverty as a problem originating in the individual held a child's parents accountable for the child's condition and, accordingly, tended to support programs that either removed the child from the influence of the deficient parents or worked to improve the parents, for the benefit of the child. Within Head Start, the advocates of this perspective emphasized education in parenting skills and household management as the primary kind of parent involvement. At the other end of the spectrum, those who saw poverty as a systemic issue supported parent involvement in the governing of Head Start centers, the hiring of teachers, and the overall operation of the program, because their goal was to change the way institutions worked, rather than to focus on fixing individuals. Those occupying the middle ground in this debate supported a combination of education and participation in decision making. The combination, they argued, would benefit parents on an individual basis while it increased the legitimacy (and hence the overall effect) of the program in the local community. There has been considerable criticism of this middle ground by OEO critics who suggest that OEO co-opted and ultimately silenced the poor by inviting them into the process without giving them full control.[22] The dangers of co-optation are important. In many instances outspoken community activists are less outspoken once they have a job inside the system, and certainly there have been cases where organizations have silenced their critics by putting those critics on the organization's payroll. With respect to Head Start, however, it is equally important to recognize that co-optation represented a middle ground; giving parents limited authority in order to garner their support was less disrespectful than assuming poor children could be saved only if experts intervened to protect the children from their parents.

After the planning committee submitted its report, Shriver and several others met with President and Lady Bird Johnson to discuss the proposal. Immediately taken with the idea, Lady Bird became the national spokeswoman for the program.[23] She launched Head Start at a tea in the Rose Garden following President Johnson's official announcement of fund availability. The tea party—attended by members of the planning committee, leading American women, and a few potential Head Start children—provided the origins for two important Head Start legacies.

First, an aura of respectability surrounded the program. The media covered Lady Bird's tea party on society pages rather than in political columns; from the onset the program was more socially acceptable than OEO's somewhat confrontational community action programs. Wives of congressmen and governors vied for invitations to the tea, and, perhaps prompted by the actions of the First Lady, their interest remained high. Volunteering to assist Head Start was "in" and respectable. Even Donna Reed, who starred as the ideal mother in a popular television series, praised the program and encouraged local women to volunteer their time at centers as part of a promotional campaign.[24]

The second trend developing out of the tea was less positive. Remarks by Lady Bird and others implied that poor parents were incapable of raising children properly and that Head Start could—during a few weeks in the summer—work miracles with these children, undoing the terrible damage caused by the children's parents and the squalid conditions of poverty more generally. Unreasonably high expectations about the ability of Head Start programs to rewrite the lives of children plagued the program for years. Often accompanying these unrealistic expectations was a paternalistic view of poor parents as incapable of doing what was best for their children.

Whether in response to the inherent appeal of a program for children or the respectability and promise of miracles added at the tea, interest in the program exploded as soon as OEO announced the availability of funding. Suggesting the program "captured the Nation's imagination and enthusiasm," OEO called the response to Head Start "unprecedented."[25] Concerned that the best applications would come from areas that did not need the program as much as other areas, OEO officials tried to facilitate grants from the most impoverished counties and from areas not served by a community action program by offering various kinds of technical assistance to those areas. Because OEO planned to channel Head Start funding through local community action programs, Head Start facilitated the creation of those agencies in areas previously inhospitable to OEO; this solved Shrivers original problem in getting communities to accept OEO. These tactics worked. Head Start programs operated in more than two hundred of the nation's three hundred poorest counties during the summer of 1965. Overall the program served more than 500,000 children in over two thousand centers.

The planning committee originally recommended a program serving 2,500 children and had agreed to increase the recommended size to 25,000 children only after long discussions with Shriver.[26] The ultimate size of the program—2,000 percent larger than the committee members thought feasible even under the best of circumstances—astonished them. Shriver likened the explosion of Head Start to the Allied invasion at Normandy; he said OEO saw an opening and "pumped in the money as fast as we could intelligently use it."[27] The quick expansion prompted various planning committee members to become concerned about the quality of the programs across the country. Their concern was legitimate; in the rush of processing applications and assuring that the program would be operational from a logistical standpoint, OEO had neither the staff nor the time to ensure program quality at two thousand centers.

Despite internal concerns about the variation in quality, the program maintained its popularity among the general public and with the president. Before the end of the first summer program, Johnson announced an expansion of Head Start. Beginning in the fall of 1965, OEO funded both summer and year-round Head Start programs, in addition to a follow-up program, which would continue Head Start–style services to some children after they entered the public school system.

COMMUNITY ACTION COLLIDES WITH THE EDUCATIONAL SYSTEM

Reflecting public support for the program, Congress initially paid little attention to the inner workings of Head Start. Those who opposed OEO's efforts found other programs to be easier targets than the respectable Head Start program whose volunteers included the wives of their colleagues in Congress. Besides, charges that urban rioters used OEO-funded legal services to avoid being jailed produced national reactions far more urgent and negative than any anxieties about the inconsistent implementation of Head Start goals. For a time, Head Start seemed safe from OEO's opponents in Congress.

Head Start's honeymoon ended in 1967, however, when public school superintendents from across the nation sought to persuade Congress to modify the structure and authority of Head Start. By that time community action programs (CAPs)—the primary OEO-funded bodies at the local level—exerted significant influence over local Head Start programs, just as the CAP officials played a key role nationally. OEO categorized Head Start as a community action program and channeled Head Start grants through CAPs, wherever they existed. In areas where the Head Start program existed before a CAP, the grant was redirected through the CAP once it was established. In these cases the CAP usually delegated the program back to the group who had been running Head Start previously, which, in many cases, was the local school system. The redirection of monies through the CAP meant that CAPs suddenly had a role in school operations, including the hiring of personnel and program planning. School superintendents across the country chafed over the interference of these community radicals—who lacked educational credentials—and asked Congress to remove the CAPs' authority and move Head Start out of OEO and into the Office of Education where the program could be monitored by educational experts, rather than OEO troublemakers. This effort, and the response it generated from both OEO officials and Congress, is important because it illustrates the existing perceptions about Head Start's potential as a community action program.

In 1967 the House of Representatives entertained an amendment to move Head Start to the Office of Education, and a number of school superintendents testified on behalf of the amendment. The issue also came up repeatedly in the Senate's Examination of the War on Poverty hearings held that same year. The superintendents complained about the difficulties in working with OEO and, more frequently, about inappropriate interference, particularly in hiring decisions, from local CAP personnel; they insisted that Head Start was an educational program and, as such, was the province of educators, not radicals.[28] Some superintendents also expressed concern that Head Start had the potential to lower teacher qualifications and thus threaten the future of the entire educational system.[29] The superintendents' primary concern seemed to be re-asserting the authority of educational experts in the schools.[30]

Shriver's response to proposals to move Head Start was insistence that Head Start was a poverty program and a community action program—not merely an educational program. He and other OEO officials testified that Head Start was as much about providing jobs for local community members and changing institutions—particularly educational institutions—as it was about helping children.[31] Shriver credited the program with creating new alliances on behalf of the poor, noting that "there are people working together who never worked together before, [they] were brought together because of their mutual interest in these children."[32] Reinforcing this position, all OEO publications between 1965 and 1969 included Head Start funding under the Community Action category, along with Legal Aid and various other CAP programs; these publications often referred to Head Start accomplishments in community action terms, measuring, for example, the level of institutional change caused by the program rather than simply the number of children served.[33] Both OEO's testimony and the OEO publications suggest that retaining Head Start was important to OEO officials; as Shriver had hoped, the program was facilitating broader community action efforts at the local level.

While Shriver emphasized Head Start's ability as a catalyst for community action, others interpreted Head Start's effects on the public school systems as direct community action. Repeatedly, members of Congress expressed a hope that Head Start would affect the ways schools operated, and at one point in the hearing a congressman challenged a superintendent to describe what his schools had done to help the poor before OEO came along, implying that all school-related assistance was due to outside pressures, not a commitment to equality among educators.[34] Contemporary evidence reinforced the suspicion that the educational bureaucracy did not support the War on Poverty; OEO's first annual report, *A Nation Aroused*, included a long list of groups supporting their effort, and there was not an educational association on the list.[35] In the 1967 Senate hearings complaints from school superintendents prompted one Senator to comment, "This is becoming more or less a pattern in our hearings across the country and usually defines itself, at least in my mind, as a fight between the poor people and the power structure."[36] For him, the issue was not educational expertise; it was community action. His view lumped the school superintendents' complaints with those from other local bureaucrats who also resented the community action efforts that threatened their authority. This interpretation was echoed in a discussion between Senator Robert F. Kennedy and the Brooklyn, New York, superintendent. Kennedy responded to the superintendent's complaints by noting, "Community action is against the establishment. You and I are part of the establishment, so it is directed against us."[37] When discussing the possible implications of moving Head Start with the Berkeley, California, superintendent, one senator went even further in asserting that the public schools reflected local power structures. Responding to the Berkeley superintendent's assertion that "there is only one Mississippi," the senator suggested that local power structures in various other places, including Philadelphia, could threaten the effectiveness of a school-run Head Start program.[38]

Most school superintendents who testified tried to portray themselves as educational experts who were only concerned about the children in their care, but their lack of concern for the possible complications in moving Head Start suggested other motives to those who viewed public school superintendents as "part of the system" that the War on Poverty sought to change. One of the issues consistently raised in discussions about moving Head Start was the anticipated effect on the programs not operated by public schools. The National Education Association and some members of Congress worried that moving Head

Start to the Office of Education would eliminate the local Head Start programs operated by parochial schools and private institutions.[39] At question was whether an Office of Education–operated Head Start would have to follow the guidelines set up for the Elementary and Secondary Education Act of 1965, which provided money only to public school systems.[40] The question was important, because while public schools operated about two-thirds of the summer Head Start programs in 1967, they operated less than one-third of the full-year programs (which were increasingly popular).[41] Despite the number of programs potentially affected, the superintendents, when faced with this issue, typically asserted that no parochial schools were operating Head Start programs in their district, so the issue was not of concern to them. Such a response tended to reinforce the view that these men were looking out for themselves, not the best interests of the Head Start children across the nation. It also highlighted one of the important differences between the superintendents and Congress; public school superintendents could choose to ignore the issue of parochial schools, but Congress could not.[42]

Congress rejected the amendment to move Head Start out of OEO in 1967 and, in so doing, signaled at least lukewarm support for Head Start as a community action effort aimed at changing the nation's schools. While hardly a call to arms, the action suggested a possible shift in public attitudes toward educational experts. Beginning in the 1870s leading educators sought to centralize U.S. urban schools and to transfer operational authority away from local neighborhood-type school boards and into the hands of "honest and competent" educational experts. Their efforts were largely successful; by 1920 elite-dominated school boards were the norm in most urban areas and the idea that educational experts knew best was firmly in place.[43] Given this history, the school superintendents' concerns about Head Start should not be surprising; they were protesting an emerging threat to their authority over all things educational. In rejecting the superintendents' arguments, members of Congress suggested that the superintendents had much in common with the mayors and local bureaucrats who bristled at community action efforts within "their" domain. What is important, Congress seemed to support the Head Start idea that the community—rather than a small group of experts—needed to be involved in the care and education of its children.

Two examples from Milwaukee, Wisconsin—where both the school system and community-based groups operated Head Start centers—highlight these threats to the experts' authority at the local level. In

1966 OEO began to encourage Head Start grantees to ensure that their facilities were integrated. A Milwaukee study indicated that, like the public schools themselves, the Head Start programs in the public schools were largely *de facto* segregated, often serving only white children or black children rather than both.[44] Although school officials argued that "it is difficult to persuade Negro parents to send their children to schools on Milwaukee's predominantly white south side," their explanations were problematic given that some Milwaukee centers—most notably the one operated by a community-based neighborhood association in an African-American neighborhood—offered what observers considered to be a well-integrated program from the onset. The local Congress on Racial Equality (CORE) chapter criticized the segregation of public school Head Start facilities and threatened a boycott if Head Start did not eliminate the segregation. Within eighteen months the school system was bussing Head Start students to create better integrated classrooms in a district where de facto segregation would continue among all other students into the 1970s.[45] Pressure from OEO and local activists forced the school board to accept integration in its Head Start program even as the board continued to resist pressure from those same activists for wide-scale public school integration.

Even when Milwaukee's professional educators prevailed over the activists and the OEO, the skirmishes were not painless. In 1967 Milwaukee's school superintendent declined an opportunity to apply for Head Start Follow-Through funds which financed primary grade classrooms based on the Head Start model. The event was noteworthy because Shriver first announced the Follow-Through program at a conference held in Milwaukee where he added that Milwaukee would be an excellent place for such a program to begin. True to his word, Shriver included Milwaukee in the one hundred cities invited to apply for Project Follow-Through.[46] Both the local CAP and the Parent Advisory Committee—Milwaukee's official Head Start parent organization—encouraged the school system to apply for the funds. Neither group, however, could force an application; the PAC's influence varied from center to center and was probably weakest at the school-run centers. Still, when Head Start parents learned that the superintendent had not applied due to concerns about space, they were outraged and went to the school board to demand an explanation.[47] An editorial cartoon in a local white paper characterized the situation as a missed opportunity, showing the board and superintendent as village idiots, holding out a tub but missing the Follow-Through funds that fell from thc sky.[48] Board members echoed this assessment, assuring parents that the system would reconsider its position the following year, if funds were still available. However, the PAC was not persuaded that the decision was simply an unfortunate mistake, especially after the board refused to ask OEO for permission to submit a late application.[49]

The PAC and its supporters asserted that the board and superintendent were demonstrating a lack of concern for the city's poor children. Supported by the local CAP, these parents questioned the board's motives at length. One parent asserted, "We ask for things, simple things that the federal government wants us to have. And what do you do? You are either too late in asking for them or else you don't want to do it."[50]

In a city divided over school integration, these charges against the prosegregation board resonated in the black community. Even though the school system eventually got money through the Elementary and Secondary Education Act (ESEA) to operate special kindergartens for low-income children, resentment about the Follow-Through issue lingered. Indeed, when the board announced its plan to pursue ESEA funding, some Head Start parents rejected the plan, asserting that the resulting program would be less comprehensive than a Head Start–type effort.[51] The parents were particularly concerned about the lack of health services under the ESEA version, but it was also true that ESEA funding had fewer requirements about parent and community involvement than the Follow-Through funds from Head Start would have had. By choosing to pursue ESEA funding rather than the Follow-Through dollars the superintendent managed to avoid additional parent "interference" in school functioning.

The House's decision to leave Head Start under OEO's authority in 1967 was all the encouragement OEO officials needed to promote a more activist Head Start model. After 1967 OEO was less sensitive to public school concerns about the program and the lingering desire among some members of Congress to move the program. The fact that schools continued to participate in the program after the 1967 hearings, despite a warning from one superintendent that school boards would withdraw in massive numbers if OEO continued on its current course, also strengthened OEO's position.[52]

One measure of OEO's newfound confidence over Head Start's status as an OEO program is its approach to parent participation. Prior to the hearings, the September 1966 *How to Apply for Head Start Child Development Programs* publication recommended that parents be involved in the hiring of each Head Start program's center director, but officials quietly withdrew this requirement under pressure from school systems.[53] After the hearings in late 1967, however, Head Start published its first policy manual where parent involvement in decision making topped the list of types of parent participation.[54] In keeping with OEO's emphasis on program flexibility the manual outlined specific program requirements but left implementation strategies to the discretion of local programs. Regarding parent participation, however, the manual identified requisite structures, termed Parent Advisory Councils, which grantees and delegate agencies were required to establish and utilize. OEO further clarified this structure in the 1969 parent involvement handbook, which clearly identified parent participation in Head Start as community action.

Despite these publications, it is difficult to characterize the overall position of OEO on parent participation. Certainly there is evidence of a struggle within OEO between community action proponents—who saw Head Start as a school reform and community action program— and the early childhood staff who saw Head Start as an educational program. Various individuals involved in Head Start at the national level under OEO have commented on this conflict.[55] Additionally, early OEO and Head Start publications reflect these conflicting priorities.

Some OEO publications emphasized the role of Head Start parents as community change agents. The 1967 OEO report, *The Quiet Revolution*, proudly reported that Head Start centers were increasingly becoming places where community issues such as housing were discussed.[56] The OEO annual reports consistently emphasized the community action aspects of Head Start, including efforts to change other institutions and involve parents in decision making within the centers. Similarly, the 1969 parent participation handbook suggested that participation in Head Start policy boards should lead parents to involvement in local welfare and school boards.[57]

Other publications, however, characterized parent involvement as observing and learning rather than as actively participating in decision making. In its outline of the procedure for a diagnostic staffing for a Head Start child, for example, one publication indicated that the parent was not to participate in the staffing or diagnostic process at all; instead, staff were instructed on how to prepare the parent for the diagnosis, after the staffing was over. The publication gave no indication that a parent might have something to contribute to the problem-solving process; instead, it stated that diagnoses were the realm of the professional.[58] The early childhood experts within Head Start consistently argued that parents needed education and that educating parents would benefit children. Children, of course, were the focus of the early childhood staff members; while the community action advocates believed Head Start's mission was to improve communities, the early childhood staff in OEO saw the program as a service for children. Prone to view the program as a child-saving—rather than community building—effort, the early childhood experts did not believe parents should run Head Start programs without considerable guidance from experts such as themselves.

HEAD START "PARENTS" WERE USUALLY MOTHERS

Gender adds an important dimension to any analysis of OEO's intentions regarding Head Start. Many Head Start publications used the terms "parent" and "mother" interchangeably; the photos and drawings in these publications typically depicted women and children. Head Start teachers were consistently referred to as "she." In fact, a Head Start booklet on the role of the psychologist was unique in that it included photos of men—meeting with other adults, however, not interacting with children. When OEO officials referred to community action among Head Start parents, then—whether they realized it or not—they were generally speaking of community action among women. The gender of these activists is important because, despite the developing women's movement,[59] ideas about women inside OEO (as in the nation as a whole) were quite traditional. In 1970 Cooke—who led the Head Start planning committee—testified to Congress that taking care of young children "is not a very masculine activity in our society, and I think this would be as degrading for a lower income person as to a middle-income person that their major responsibility is a baby caretaker."[60] None of those present at the hearing remarked on the irony in Cooke's statement, perhaps because they considered him a man who supervised women caring for children, not a man who cared for children directly.

OEO's 1967 "Women in the War on Poverty" conference provides a fascinating glimpse of attitudes toward women within the agency. Several speakers referred to the "natural" role of women in the effort, emphasizing the nurturing that was needed to assist the poor to become full citizens and downplaying activism among women.[61] Jule Sugarman, associate director of Head Start, devoted his presentation at the conference to calling for program volunteers. Sugarman did not discuss the unique role women played in Head Start or the opportunities for women's activism within the program, even though some Head Start programs—like that operated by the Child Development Group of Mississippi—clearly relied heavily on female activists.[62] Still, given the tone of the conference, it is more striking that Sugarman did not talk about Head Start's efforts to improve mothering skills; several other speakers referred to the important role of the mother, one quoting Lady Bird Johnson who said, "When you train a man, you train an individual. When you train a woman, you train a family."[63] The conference acknowledged the problem of poverty among women, but, beyond one speaker's comments regarding the wages of domestic workers, there was little attention to the causes of this poverty. Several speakers referred to the fact that women earned less money than men, but no one noted the systemic issues behind this inequality—one of which might have been that women were assumed to be teachers in Head Start while men were psychologists for the program. Indeed, the official conference proceedings provide no evidence that attendees were aware of sex role stereotyping—an idea being addressed by the newly emerged National Organization for Women, along with various grassroots women's organizations.[64]

One thing that remains unclear, then, is how OEO and Head Start officials perceived the activism of Head Start parents, particularly mothers. Was appropriate activism talking about housing conditions at a Head Start meeting or organizing a march through the city to protest housing segregation? Was it acceptable for women to be activists if their actions were on behalf of their children? Indeed, were women supposed to become activists or merely support the activism of men? Conceivably, OEO officials believed that making Head Start a catalyst for change might encourage more men to participate in the program, as leaders of the community-oriented movements originating from the centers. It is more difficult to believe that OEO officials intended Head Start mothers to organize marches and challenge community institutions, given OEO's traditional view of women. Because OEO officials never publicly acknowledged the issue of gender, however, this is speculative.

Another Head Start feature—the use of volunteers and nonprofessional aides in the program—merits attention here since the individuals recruited as paid and unpaid workers were often Head Start mothers or other women from the local community. As with parent participation, one can interpret the practice of providing career opportunities to adults in the impoverished community in several ways. Some Head Start publications suggest that hiring parents to work in the classroom was a means to demonstrate the effectiveness of "appropriate" child development practices and to convert the parents to Head Start–type parenting. Additionally, officials acknowledged the strategic advantages of hiring community members; they argued that children would be more comfortable with these adults and that the larger community would be more interested in a program that had credible local advocates. For community action advocates, the major benefit of hiring locals was broader. They cited Head Start hiring policies—which essentially created new jobs in low-income areas—as evidence that the program was more than an educational program, that like other CAP efforts it was creating jobs and opportunities for the poor.

The 1968 Head Start policies on career advancement and the Head Start Supplementary Training Program (HSST) reinforced the image of Head Start as a program offering adults new opportunities. The policies required that career plans be developed for each Head Start staff member. HSST promoted college training for Head Start staff members. One of the unique features of HSST was its acknowledgment of special issues facing female employees who sought higher education. HSST negotiated with community colleges to drop entrance requirements (since many Head Start workers lacked a high school diploma), to initiate more flexible degree programs to accommodate single mothers, to give college credit for work experiences, to assist with transportation difficulties, and to experiment with alternative approaches to teaching.[65] Through the HSST, Head Start addressed the poverty of female-headed households by facilitating career development.[66]

Head Start's policy of encouraging the hiring of local women and encouraging mothers to participate in the classrooms is important given existing ideas about the culture of poverty and what Patrick Moynihan called the "pathology" of female-dominated black families.[67] Both sets of ideas assumed that, without outside intervention, poor children would become the impoverished parents of the next generation of the poor. By employing parents and local community members as Head Start agents, the program seemed to implicitly reject these ideas. If the child's environment perpetuates poverty and Head Start's role is to break the cycle, it does not make sense to bring the local poverty environment into the Head Start center, whether as paid staff or as volunteers. It made even less sense to give local black women a role in operating the program since this would reinforce the matriarchy that Moynihan identified as part of the problem. On this point parent involvement in program operations is especially critical. While one could argue that the program did not reject Moynihan's ideas explicitly but rather used poor women as volunteers as a matter of expediency—accepting their labor because it was free—this does not explain why the program allowed poor women to influence overall operating conditions. Head Start—by giving these women a level of authority at a time when "experts" were questioning their authority within the family—was a means of empowerment, regardless of the program's intent. Still, Head Start empowered women only insofar as it assumed that they did not have to be "retrained" in order to work with or on behalf of their children.

Although most Head Start publications emphasized the importance of training for aides, opinions varied among Head Start advocates. Some community action advocates supported the hiring policy in a way that did seem to reject the idea that the poor were in some way defective. Marian Wright, testifying about the experiences of the Child Development Group of Mississippi's experiences with Head Start, argued that programs needed "warm responsive bodies who can help teach kids to be free and happy."[68] Nothing in Wright's testimony suggested that local mothers and nonprofessionals were inherently defective due to their poverty. Indeed, she asserted that these nonprofessionals were better suited than college-trained women, echoing the community action notion that institutions and experts could learn something from the poor. More typical than Wright's view, though, was that of Edward Zigler who criticized OEO's operation of Head Start in 1969, arguing that an "indigenous" person was not going to be effective with children "simply because he or she is poor and therefore understanding and sympathetic."[69] Like the early childhood personnel inside OEO, Zigler argued that poor mothers required training before they could contribute effectively to Head Start centers.

Because even those OEO staff who agreed with Wright's position seemed to accept traditional roles for women, the promotion of opportunities for employment as well as participation in decision making within Head Start was somewhat problematic. In large part, OEO circumvented the controversy by referring to parent activism, without acknowledging the primacy of women. The most important ramifications of this strategy occurred at the local level where OEO's lack of support for mother-led activism ultimately undermined its efforts to make Head Start an effective community action program.

A national study of Head Start's impact on communities affirms that the program was affecting institutional changes at the local level during this time. In the study examples abound of Head Start facilitating the involvement of poor parents in school and community issues.

In some areas the parent activism led to curricular changes in the public schools, and in others Head Start parents (again, usually mothers) created consumer cooperatives and other new services. While the expansion of health services for poor children was a frequent result of Head Start's presence in a community, changes in school policies, especially with respect to staffing issues were also common.[70] Although some of these changes were opposed at the local level, Head Start's overall popularity remained high, which clearly strengthened the program's ability to continue to work for institutional changes. Arguably, Head Start represented OEO's best chance to realize its community action goals, provided federal officials could come to terms with the primacy of mothers in the program's community action efforts at the local level. Like others at the time, however, OEO officials did not see these mothers as activists, despite their local successes.

Evidence from Milwaukee suggests that gender also provided the lens through which some communities viewed and understood Head Start parent activities.[71] In Milwaukee, women used Head Start to institute change, but, because the change was instituted by women, local leaders (such as newspaper editors) tended to discount the importance of the activities. As a result, Head Start mothers sometimes fought their community action battles while also coping with a lack of support from their own communities.

An example can help to illustrate this point. In 1969 Milwaukee's CAP withheld Head Start funds from the school system in order to force the system to implement a staffing change requested by the PAC. While the issue got some attention in the white press, the city's black newspapers largely ignored the fight, even when the school system agreed to the PAC's demands and added staff. While these same black papers covered other community efforts to affect school functioning in great detail, they seemed to see little or no significance in the efforts of Head Start parents, even though the efforts forced a change in school policies.[72] Despite the program's demonstrated ability to change the local school system, Milwaukee's black papers tended to cover Head Start events on the women's page, reserving the front page for black men's political activities.

In cities such as Milwaukee, Head Start was a program of children and, to a lesser extent, women. However, activism was the province of men. Although women involved in the school system's parent council groups had access to the school board, community activists did not take these women's involvement in Head Start seriously. This reflects a larger tendency not to take women's activism seriously. One of

Milwaukee's leading black newspapers, *The Greater Milwaukee Star*, mocked women activists in a 1967 account that described "three fiery-eyed women" who "swooped down with all their fury" on the *Star* staff, generating much "squeak and squalor."[73] Although the papers did not treat all women with this level of condescension, Head Start mothers—women whose interests presumably centered around young children—seem to have been particularly susceptible, perhaps because these women often appeared at meetings with toddlers in tow. While the papers praised the activities of a local black alderwoman, they were unable to recognize Head Start mothers as activists. Reading the *Star*, one gets the sense that while there are some women—Angela Davis and a few others—who are part of the struggle for justice, most women are the type depicted on the *Star*'s "Femininity" page who worry about being pretty. The newspaper editors apparently considered women with young children clinging to their skirts or babies in their arms in that second category and treated their activities accordingly.[74]

Male newspaper editors were not the only ones to discount the activism of Head Start women. Polly Greenberg's biography of the Child Development Group of Mississippi (CDGM) provides a fascinating account of the activities and perceptions of activities in Mississippi. Her history suggests that both staff and participants in CDGM made a similar distinction between the political work of male-dominated efforts and the efforts of women involved in the program. While Greenberg demonstrates convincingly that the women of CDGM were community activists of the first order, she also illustrates how this success created ambivalence among some CDGM staff and supporters who perceived a struggle between the reality of women's successful activism and a community-wide commitment to male-led activism.[75]

Head Start mothers' lack of political credibility is significant because it helped to shape Head Start's transition from a community action program to a preschool education program. Dismissing the actions of Head Start mothers as misguided facilitated a broader dismissal of Head Start's potential for community action and thus facilitated the transition to an emphasis on preschool education, rather than on community action. Even though local Head Start programs successfully changed the way that institutions—most notably the school system—interacted with the poor, and even though, as Edward Zigler points out, Head Start's initial size meant the program had a huge constituency from the onset, the nation's leaders (at both the federal and the local level) neither recognized nor embraced mother-led community action. Public perceptions of women's activism as frivolous or inconsequential considerably constrained this group's power. As late as 1992, Zigler's accounts of early meetings with Head Start supporters tended to focus on the inappropriateness of the women's actions rather than the political significance of their efforts.[76] Despite their numbers and their local successes, Head Start mothers did not seem to qualify as legitimate community activists.

HEAD START IS FOR CHILDREN, NOT COMMUNITIES

OEO felt the full cost of neglecting the women's activism after Richard Nixon assumed the presidency in January of 1969 because Nixon's election marked the end of federally supported community action. While many felt that Johnson's other war—the one in Vietnam—had sapped the War on Poverty of its potential, beginning in 1969 the federal shift away from OEO-style intervention accelerated dramatically. The nation's new president did not like OEO; indeed, Nixon later admitted he would have preferred to eliminate the agency immediately.[77] Since outright elimination was not politically feasible, however, Nixon began dismantling OEO by delegating its programs to other agencies. Officials in the new administration insisted that delegating established programs left OEO free to experiment with new ways of eliminating poverty, without the bother of having to administer programs that were already well established.[78] This strategy also served, of course, to separate OEO from its constituencies.

In conjunction with this new policy, Nixon announced, in February of 1969, that he would move Head Start to the Department of Health, Education, and Welfare (HEW). Pledging that the nation would remain committed to the first years of life, Nixon argued that evaluations of compensatory programs, including Head Start, suggested that current efforts were not as effective as Americans had hoped. The president implied that Head Start probably was not as effective as Americans had assumed it to be and argued that the government needed further research before it expended additional tax dollars on the program. For a time it appeared that Head Start might disappear into other HEW programs entirely, much to the dismay of Head Start proponents across the nation.

The national support for Head Start—and the outcry over Nixon's announcement—likely influenced his final decision about the program; in April Nixon clarified the delegation of Head Start, announcing that HEW would establish a new Office of Child Development to house

Head Start, the Children's Bureau, and other efforts aimed at young children. Although this announcement relieved some advocates who feared Head Start would be delegated to the Office of Education, various Head Start supporters testified in opposition to the delegation at the 1969 House hearings, and committee members received numerous letters from Head Start parents protesting the move.[79]

Those opposing the move asserted that Head Start was not yet fully established and that the program could get lost in the bureaucracy of HEW. Officials from the Nixon administration countered, saying that Head Start was well-established and that OEO needed to focus on experimentation. The administration also argued that it was logical to put all programs for children together. Whereas Shriver had argued that poverty programs belonged together, Nixon's administrators pointed to the common denominator of age, suggesting that all programs for children were inherently similar. They explicitly categorized Head Start as a program for children rather than as a program for whole communities.[80]

While little was said to defend Head Start's role as a community action program, many opponents of the move expressed concern that parent participation would be lost if HEW administered Head Start. HEW's history in the realm of parent participation justified this concern. A 1968 task force reprimanded HEW for not providing opportunities for true parent participation in its programs; the report repeatedly recommended that HEW adopt OEO procedures for involving parents.[81] Whether Head Start advocates had read the report or not, they obviously believed that HEW was not committed to parent participation.

Since the decision to delegate the program did not require congressional approval, some witnesses saw Head Start's move as inevitable, and a few even praised the change. One observer suggested that Head Start would be more secure in HEW, given Nixon's obvious dislike of OEO.[82] Additionally, the old resentments between community action and early childhood advocates resurfaced; Dr. Cooke, the chair of the Head Start planning committee, asserted that the community action focus in OEO had restrained Head Start and even hurt the program because the community action staff was jealous of Head Start's popularity. Commenting in a House hearing after the transfer had occurred, Edward Zigler criticized the Community Action Agencies (now CAAs)[83] suggesting that their operation of Head Start had meant that children "become pawns in the all too frequent power struggles of our Nation's community action programs."[84] Zigler testified that, besides moving Head Start out of OEO, the government should sever the CAA's local ties to the program.

Certainly some advocates of Head Start in OEO feared this move would mean separation of Head Start and CAA programs and, ultimately, death to CAAs. OEO had always given the CAAs preference in administering Head Start, and this had long been a sore spot for local school districts who operated Head Start programs under CAA supervision. During the 1969 House hearings, Congresswoman Green, a longtime critic of community action, asked Secretary of HEW Robert H. Finch to consider eliminating CAA supervision of local programs once HEW controlled Head Start, particularly in cases where CAAs delegated Head Start to school systems. Acknowledging that some believed the move might lead to the elimination of some CAAs, Green noted that "if the community action program has to be propped up with four-year-old Head Start children, maybe it ought to fall down."[85] Her sentiments only exacerbated the concerns of CAA supporters.

In the midst of the 1969 House hearings over Head Start's future, the White House leaked the first national evaluation of Head Start, the Westinghouse/Ohio University study, to *The New York Times*. The leak occurred just days before the Head Start officials planned to make the study public, along with a careful explanation of the study's meaning so that the findings would not be misinterpreted.[86] Rather than guiding the process, however, Head Start officials watched helplessly as the media interpreted the study as evidence that the Head Start experiment had failed.[87] The prevailing public interpretation reinforced Nixon's position that Head Start needed closer examination and, subsequently, that the delegation to HEW was a sensible one.

While the popular press affirmed the president's position, others argued for a different interpretation. Some experts criticized the design of the Westinghouse study, and others viewed it as evidence that the public schools, rather than Head Start, were inadequate.[88] In his testimony before the House committee, Dr. Robert S. Mendelsohn, an American Academy of Pediatrics official and consistent Head Start advocate, charged that the schools needed to change to take advantage of the excellent work performed by the Head Start program.[89] Mendelsohn repeatedly advocated that Head Start challenge the public schools to do a better job of educating children by working in direct competition with the schools.[90]

Although few criticisms of the schools were as frank as Mendelsohn's, various congressional witnesses indicated that the transfer of Head Start to HEW would be tolerable, provided the program was not placed in the Office of Education. Additionally, many of the letters from Head Start parents spoke out against giving educators control of Head Start nationally. Parents seemed convinced that the Office of Education would destroy Head Start's parent participation. Even HEW Secretary Finch spoke out against moving Head Start to the Office of Education; he argued that the spirit of the program—helping poor children—would be lost and that there would be great pressure to serve all children—rather than just the poor—if the Office of Education administered Head Start.[91]

Alternatively, Finch insisted that the focus of Head Start would not change under HEW's new Office of Child Development, although he predicted that HEW would work to improve Head Start's management system and to flesh out some of the program's details. Finch went on to argue that HEW was better equipped—in terms of expertise and experience—to develop the fine points of Head Start's program components.[92] Additionally, Finch asserted that, in keeping with Nixon's perspective on OEO, HEW would work to give states a greater role in the program, although they would not give them the right to approve or deny grant applications.[93] None of the committee members present challenged Finch to explain how Head Start was to achieve its goal of institutional change if it worked through the states, particularly through state education departments.

On July 1, 1969, the Office of Child Development (OCD) assumed responsibility for Head Start. Some months later Nixon appointed Edward Zigler as the first director of the new agency. As Zigler assumed his position, much of the focus regarding Head Start was on IQs. Indeed, "a cottage industry in examining IQ changes in Head Start children" emerged, in part as a result of the Westinghouse study.[94] The testing was encouraged by a Congress intrigued by the easily quantifiable evidence the tests produced. While Head Start advocates argued that the program was comprehensive and, subsequently, results could not be measured by a one-dimensional test, some in Congress speculated about whether one could calculate a unit cost for Head Start based on the gain in IQ points.[95] Perhaps in part as a response to these requests, Head Start officials, led by Zigler, began to emphasize the impacts of other parts of the program on children. Zigler commented repeatedly, for example, that Head Start had become the largest provider of health services to low-income children.[96]

While Zigler directed attention to the other services Head Start provided to children, he did not emphasize Head Start's impact on communities, even though new findings suggested that Head Start had affected institutional change in some communities. Shortly after Head Start was transferred to OCD, researchers released the findings of a second national study, which examined the impact of Head Start on local communities. The Kirschner study convincingly documented that Head Start had—in large part through example—affected the operations of educational and medical institutions in the communities hosting Head Start programs.[97] With regard to the impact of Head Start in one community a researcher noted: 'The way [the school system] developed seems to vindicate the original decision to set up OEO as an organization separate from the existing system. . . . The fact that OEO was free of existing institutional structure allowed it to innovate, and the results of this study show that OEO's innovation of the teachers aide in Head Start paved the way for acceptance of this approach in the city schools.'[98]

By the time this report was issued, the transfer of Head Start was complete. Whether the Kirschner researchers intended these comments as a critique of that transfer (and even of HEW, which had numerous ties to the existing system) is speculative.

Whatever the intention, the Kirschner statements likely added fuel to the on-going struggle between OCD and OEO. Nixon's delegation of Head Start to HEW did not affect Head Start's funding mechanism (which required legislative action) so Head Start funding continued to be channeled through OEO. This meant that the administration's recommended cuts in OEO funding affected Head Start as well. Members of Congress tried in 1969 and 1971 to add supplemental Head Start funds, but HEW officials resisted, saying that they needed to be sure that the existing Head Start programs were effective before they sought to add programs. This attitude was, of course, a stark change from Shriver's during the program's explosive growth in 1965 and 1966.[99] The resistance to additional funding frustrated some members of Congress who indicated that their constituents were angry over reductions in the number of local Head Start slots. These representatives voiced their resentment to the OCD officials, who consistently denied that they could use more money.[100] Members of Congress also expressed frustration at the link between Head Start and OEO funding; it was difficult to reward one program while punishing the other financially. Ultimately, these concerns prompted the establishment of separate Head Start funding.

Rather than seeking expansion money, Zigler's OCD focused on Head Start innovation and management issues, including financial and programmatic audits, new forms of technical assistance to local programs, and rule clarification. Generally the oversight was non-punitive; OCD was not interested in defunding programs so much as ensuring they met appropriate standards.[101] As Finch had promised, OCD did not issue new standards immediately upon assuming responsibility for Head Start. Instead, in 1969 it re-issued OEO's Head Start policy manual noting that the guidelines would remain in effect temporarily, until OCD had time to revise the publication.[102] True to its promise, OCD issued a new policy manual in 1970.

The most significant change in policy, though, did not occur in OCD's manual but rather in a subsequent memo outlining new guidelines for parent participation. The memo contained a matrix that delineated when parents, Head Start center directors, delegate agencies, and grantees had to be involved or merely advised about local decisions; Zigler intended the memo to clarify the role of parents. The policy statement, referred to as 70.2, legitimized the role of parents in hiring Head Start staff and approving grant applications. As a result of the policy several public school systems dropped their Head Start programs.[103]

Despite the dramatic reaction of several school-based Head Start programs to the new guidelines, it would be erroneous to consider the policy a victory for community action advocates. While 70.2 gave parents more authority within the program, it limited the scope of activities for Head Start parents dramatically. The new ruling gave parents authority to help select a site for the Head Start program, but it curtailed broader activities such as working together to ensure families received services from other community agencies. While the 1969 parent involvement handbook had given a variety of examples of ways parents could influence communities, such activities were not listed as a function of Head Start in the next handbook.[104] Essentially, Head Start's support of parent-led community action disappeared; after 1970 OCD approved of parent activities only insofar as they were internal to the program. Parents had more authority after 70.2 but a smaller arena in which to exercise that authority.

The 70.2 statement also restricted membership on the councils significantly. For the first time, Head Start officials distinguished between local residents and parents of Head Start children, reserving seats on the policy councils for parents. This rule ensured that councils were not filled with activists who, in Zigler's view, cared more about systemic change than the opportunities provided to a particular group of young children.[105] Perhaps more than any other change, this one signaled that Head Start would focus on specific children, rather than the broader communities.

As a result of the 1970 guidelines, parent participation in Head Start was institutionalized, albeit in a somewhat restricted form. The guidelines required a series of Parent Councils at local centers which sent representatives to a community-wide Parent Advisory Committee (PAC). Further, Head Start parents seemed to have new powers—at least concerning Head Start staffing decisions.[106] In Milwaukee, parents began to exert their new authority almost immediately to prevent changes in the organizational structure of the local Head Start program.

In response to national events, Milwaukee's CAA initiated a restructuring of its Head Start programs; as the future of CAAs became increasingly uncertain, direct management of Head Start was a means by which Milwaukee's CAA could ensure its survival.[107] A coalition of Milwaukee's Head Start parents, however, consistently opposed the restructuring plans that reduced parent participation in center-level governance. In 1971, after years of behind-the-scenes arguments, Milwaukee's PAC used its new authority to force a showdown with CAA officials by refusing to sign a renewal application unless CAA's Head Start director advocating the restructuring was fired for her demonstrated lack of commitment to parent participation.[108] Unable to negotiate a compromise, the CAA appealed to federal officials who ultimately overruled the local PAC, choosing to fund the program despite the existing guidelines which required PAC endorsement of the grant's renewal and despite the federal officials' concerns about the lack of real parent participation in the program.[109]

Milwaukee's black newspapers' coverage of these events demonstrated, once again, their inability to see Head Start in political terms. The front pages of these papers frequently reported on male-led activist efforts, and the editorial pages praised such efforts, often providing stinging criticisms of the white power structures resisting change. On Head Start, however, the papers reported nothing about the conflict between the PAC and CAA as it evolved between 1969 and 1971. Indeed, the struggle seemed to pop out of nowhere in 1971. Rather than seeing the events as the culmination of a long struggle, the papers presented the standoff as the misguided whim of a few women. Additionally, the stories about the PAC's action focused on the implications for the Head Start program, rather than the struggle for community control of the program.[110] The newspapers consistently noted the number of Head Start children served in their accounts of the struggle but never mentioned Head Start's mission to create a community-controlled system of opportunities for children and their parents. Further, when reporting on Head Start meetings, one paper emphasized the "confusion and chaos," of the meetings, rather than their content.[111] As far as can be gleaned from existing accounts, though, the meetings were no more boisterous than any number of other community-level struggles in Milwaukee at the same time; the difference, of course, was that the Head Start struggle was being waged by women, rather than the usual cast of black men. As the conflict heightened and the possibility of no funding for the fall emerged, the papers characterized the PAC's leadership as a group of particularly opinionated women, rather than legitimately elected representatives of the Head Start parents. Clearly the papers saw the primary issue as the survival of the Head Start program, rather than the nature of parent participation.[112] While one might interpret this as a community's recognition that any program is better than none, the consistent belittling of the mothers' activism suggests a broader conclusion: the editors simply did not take the women's struggle seriously.

Milwaukee's newspaper reactions to the federal officials' decision to fund the program despite parent concerns are telling. One of Milwaukee's major white newspapers noted the disparity between the federal action and the goals of the programs, suggesting that "a valuable process of parental participation lies wounded."[113] One of the black newspapers, by contrast, devoted an editorial to applauding the wisdom and patience of the HEW official who, the paper suggested, cared more about the best interests of Milwaukee's children than did the local mothers on the PAC.[114] The editorial provides a stark contrast to that paper's position on other conflicts between local activists and the system. Indeed, by 1971 the black papers in Milwaukee were filled with cynical denouncements of what they termed "government efforts to placate blacks." Only with respect to Head Start did the editors side with the system rather than members of their own community.

By not supporting the PAC's effort to gain real control of the Head Start program, Milwaukee's black newspapers endorsed the Head Start shift away from community action in their city. The papers' focus on the program's benefit for children and their disregard for the importance of parent participation in the program reinforced, albeit unknowingly, the Office of Child Development's position on Head Start. Just as Edward Zigler, the director of OCD, disparaged the tendency of local activists to get in the way of the good work of Head Start, the

Milwaukee Courier and *Star* rebuked local mothers for endangering the program's progress. The press in Milwaukee's black community looked on approvingly as Head Start abandoned its community action roots.

Nationally, various Head Start observers have noted that the shift of Head Start to OCD coincided with a de-emphasis on community action and a re-emphasis on parent education as the primary goal of parent involvement in the program. The emphasis on educating, rather than empowering, parents seems to have extended beyond Head Start. In 1971 child development experts across the country hailed the potential in parent education as a strategy for helping children, and Zigler was the movement's most influential supporter.[115] Of course, as indicated previously, there always had been support for parent education among Head Start staff members, even under OEO. At OCD, however, parent education became the primary focus of adult participation.[116] This perspective—that parent involvement should clearly benefit children—was in keeping with Zigler's personal conviction that Head Start was, first and foremost, about children.[117]

Zigler's leadership marked a return to the ideas of the original planning committee. By 1970, however, the assumptions underlying this perspective belonged to conservatives, not liberals.[118] Liberal critics had recognized that this focus was deficit-based and assumed that poor parents could not or did not know how to care for their children. Senator Walter Mondale challenged the assumptions underlying OCD's focus in 1971 hearings, noting, "I think all of these programs suffer from, at least in my opinion, an erroneous but traditional assumption that parents and particularly the poor parents don't know anything. In fact, it has been my impression that they not only know more about their children but are more deeply committed to their development than any outsider could possibly be."[119]

Other developments, including the black power movement, provided an additional critique of this view. Still, as demonstrated in Milwaukee, local leaders did not view all government intervention with the same level of suspicion.

Despite new criticisms of the deficit model, many policy makers continued to describe a culture of poverty where, due to the lack of good male role models, "boys drifted into gangs where they learned the 'extraordinarily violent' style of lower-class life."[120] One of the important themes emerging in discussions of poor children in the early 1970s related to crime. Perhaps in response to the urban riots of the late 1960s, social welfare literature began to emphasize helping children so that they would not turn to violence. A 1971 publication by the

Head Start Bureau for child care workers emphasized the importance of providing "mothering" to children from disadvantaged backgrounds. Assuming that poor children did not receive appropriate nurturing in their homes, the authors warned that without intervention, poor children would "begin to hate school and teachers, the law and police."[121] Publications such as this one suggested that Head Start not only could break the cycle of poverty but also could reduce crime. By 1972 Head Start officials seemed convinced that poor children needed outside intervention to save them from the crime and poverty exemplified by their mothers.

SUCCESS AT WHAT COST?

There are several factors that help to explain Head Start's shift away from community action. First, the program was back in the hands of the original planners and people like them; HEW, which included the Office of Education, was full of health and educational experts. The community action perspective, which had helped shape Head Start under OEO, was absent in HEW. Additionally, particularly due to the Westinghouse study, Head Start officials believed the future of the program was at stake.[122] To maintain support for the program they needed to make the program as appealing as possible, which meant a re-emphasis on children rather than community action. The OCD staff, under Zigler's leadership, took advantage of the same social biases toward innocent children that Shriver had capitalized on when he conceived Head Start. While Shriver and his colleagues in OEO had hoped those biases would facilitate community action, Zigler used them to protect Head Start as a noncontroversial early childhood education program.

The OCD staff rescued Head Start from its critics by disassociating the program from community action. Indeed, there is some evidence that this process of disassociation became a cornerstone of Head Start's administration well into the 1980s.[123] This effort to depoliticize Head Start might have been more difficult—or at least more public—had OEO officials explicitly acknowledged and encouraged the program's activists—Head Start mothers. As it was, however, no one seemed to notice the systematic silencing of these women.

Assessing Head Start's shift away from community action requires consideration of both what did happen and what might have happened. Under OCD, Head Start survived its critics and became institutionalized. By the mid-1990s it became clear that the program could survive even the stigmas associated with its origins in the War on Poverty. Millions of children in thousands of communities continue to benefit from Zigler's political maneuvering in the early 1970s insofar as a range of services—from preschool education to medical exams—continue to be available through the program.

By maintaining a focus on preschool children, however, the program does not address larger community-based issues. Head Start has launched no attacks on the daily dangers urban children face in their neighborhoods or the underfunded public schools that often await Head Start graduates. These issues likely would have been addressed by a community action-oriented Head Start, although it is not clear that such a program would have been successful. After two decades of attacks from the right, the typical community action agency today is struggling to survive; most spend more time providing services than acting as a catalyst for institutional change. Indeed, some observers even question whether institutional change was ever the real goal of these agencies.[124] It is difficult, then, to assert that a community-action-style Head Start would have succeeded in changing local institutions as effectively as the preschool-style Head Start succeeded in serving children in the last two decades. Such a program might have raised awareness about certain issues and even made progress in particular areas, but at the same time it would have had to contend with deep budget cuts and hostile members of Congress.

The final alternative, of course, would have been for Head Start leaders to have sought to maintain the balance between a focus on community and one on children. While this is generally what occurred inside OEO between 1965 and 1969, it is unlikely that the uneasy alliance could have held indefinitely. After all, the interests of children and the interests of communities are not the same; any program with limited resources must, eventually, prioritize one objective over another. Polly Greenberg argues that Shriver was de-emphasizing community action as a goal for Head Start before the transition to ODC and OEO's action with respect to the Child Development Group of Mississippi certainly supports this assertion.[125] Sooner or later it is likely that ODC would have had to make a choice between community action and early childhood education—between communities and children.

Given these alternatives, OCD's choice to focus on children rather than communities seems rather practical. Given these choices, even the most activist of Head Start mothers might have decided that an effective program for their children was better than the alternatives. After all, the resulting program has delivered medical, educational, and social services to millions of children. However, it is unfortunate that the choice was largely made by experts in Washington, D.C., without input from the mothers who were effectively using Head Start to challenge local institutions and, more important, without recognition of what was happening at the local level and what this decision would cost in terms of lost activism. Those in charge—in Milwaukee as well as Washington—remained oblivious to the contributions of Head Start mothers. Whereas other War on Poverty activists were silenced amidst much politicization, these women were hushed in much the way one might quiet an overexcited child.

In the end this is the greatest loss associated with the transition away from community action. The women who formed the activist backbone of the program were set aside and ignored. With the exception of Polly Greenberg's history of CDGM, we do not acknowledge their accomplishments and we do not grieve their silencing. Schools and clinics in hundreds of places are different, in part because Head Start mothers were committed to making them different. While CDGM might be the best example of a Head Start program that did community action effectively, many other programs also accomplished important community action objectives. The mothers who led these fights deserve the same attention and accolades as the other activists of their generation. To ignore their role in Head Start's history is to perpetuate a gender myth that was already outdated in 1965.

NOTES

1. Leon H. Keyserling, *Progress or Poverty: The U.S. at the Crossroads* (Washington: Conference on Economic Progress, 1964) and James N. Morgan, Martin H. David, Wilbur J. Cohen, and Harvey E. Brazer, *Income and Welfare in the United States* (New York: McGraw-Hill, 1962) quoted in James T. Patterson, *America's Struggle against Poverty 1900–1985* (Cambridge, MA: Harvard University Press, 1986), 112–13.

2. Michael Katz, *The Undeserving Poor: From the War on Poverty to the War on Welfare* (New York: Pantheon Books, 1989), 80. As was the case with civil rights legislation, John Kennedy sought antipoverty legislation earlier, as part of his New Frontier program, but the efforts stalled in Congress. Following Kennedy's assassination, Johnson pushed his version of the programs through under the War on Poverty and, later, Great Society frameworks.

3. Robert F. Kennedy, quoted in Patterson, *America's Struggle against Poverty*, 138.

4. Edward Zigler and Karen Anderson, "An Idea Whose Time Had Come: The Intellectual and Political Climate for Head Start," in *Project Head Start: A Legacy of the War on Poverty*, ed. Edward Zigler and Jeanette Valentine (New York: The Free Press, 1979), 5; Labor Secretary W. Willard Wirtz, 1964 National Urban League Conference Press Release, August 2–6, 1964. Milwaukee Urban League Papers, State Historical Society of Wisconsin.

5. Labor Secretary W. Willard Wirtz.

6. Zigler and Anderson, in *Project Head Start*, 6–7.

7. Edward Zigler and Susan Muenchow, *Head Start: The Inside Story of America's Most Successful Educational Experiment* (New York: Basic Books, 1992), 4–6.

8. Katz, *The Undeserving Poor*, 21.

9. Patterson, *America's Struggle against Poverty*, 146.

10. Jeanette Valentine, narrative of interview with Sargent Shriver, "Head Start, a Retrospective View: The Founders," in *Project Head Start*, 52.

11. Katz, *The Undeserving Poor*, 23.

12. Patterson, *America's Struggle against Poverty*, 110.

13. Shriver was not the first American social reformer to look to children as a means to an end. Shriver's strategy echoed that of settlement house workers who set up free kindergartens in urban communities during the Progressive Era. The settlement workers used kindergartens as a way to draw parents into the settlement house. "As a wedge into the homes and an avenue to parents' hearts, the kindergarten is indispensable," noted one settlement worker. Elizabeth Dale Ross, *The Kindergarten Crusade: The Establishment of Preschool Education in the United States* (Athens, OH: Ohio University Press, 1976), 46. Like Shriver, these reformers sought broad institutional changes but began by promoting relatively benign services for children as a means to build support for other efforts. In both instances the reformers assumed that helping children was equivalent to helping parents and helping communities; that is, they assumed the interests of children would not conflict with larger community interests. As this chapter demonstrates, Shriver's strategy ultimately backfired; other historians document a similar ending to Progressive Era efforts. Linda Gordon provides the best discussion of the pitfalls of child saving in Linda Gordon, "Putting Children First: Women, Maternalism, and Welfare in the Twentieth Century," University of Wisconsin-Madison, Institute for Research on Poverty, Discussion Papers, DP#991–93, (1993). For more information on the kindergarten effort see Barbara Beatty, *Preschool Education in America: The Culture of Young Children from the Colonial Era to the Present* (New Haven: Yale University Press, 1995). The women behind the kindergarten movement are part of a larger group of reformers that historians label

"maternalists" in recognition of their efforts on behalf of children, and the historical scholarship on maternalists has exploded in recent years. See, for example, Linda Gordon, *Pitied but Not Entitled: Single Mothers and the History of Welfare* (New York: The Free Press, 1994); Robyn Muncy, *Creating a Female Dominion in American Reform, 1890–1935* (New York: Oxford University Press, 1991); and Molly Ladd-Taylor, *Mother-Work: Women, Child Welfare, and the State, 1890–1930* (Urbana: University of Illinois Press, 1994). The parallels between Head Start and these earlier efforts are important.

14. According to Polly Greenberg, Shriver's initial focus was on child health and nutrition; she writes that OEO staff members added education and community action to the mix. The membership of the original planning committee supports her assertion. The thirteen-member committee included several medical experts and child psychologists but only two experts in early childhood education, neither of whom represented the leading professional organizations in early childhood education. Polly Greenberg, *The Devil Has Slippery Shoes: A Biased Biography of the Child Development Group of Mississippi (CDGM) A Story of Maximum Feasible Poor Parent Participation* (NY: Macmillan, 1969/Washington, D.C.: Youth Policy Institute, 1990), 181.

15. The document is referred to as "Report prepared for the Office of Economic Opportunity by a panel of authorities on child development" in some of the literature. Sugarman gives the January date in his account in "Head Start, a Retrospective View: The Founders," in *Project Head Start*, 115.

16. Office of Economic Opportunity, "Improving the Opportunities and Achievements of the Children of the Poor," A report prepared for the Office of Economic Opportunity by a panel of authorities on child development (Washington, D.C.: Office of Economic Opportunity, 1965), 1–2.

17. Improving the Opportunities and Achievements of the Children of the Poor, 4.

18. Ibid., 5.

19. Office of Economic Opportunity, *The Quiet Revolution: Second Annual Report of the Office of Economic Opportunity* (Washington, D.C.: Government Printing Office, 1967), 4, 15.

20. Valentine and Stark, in *Project Head Start*, 303.

21. Ibid., 291–313.

22. See, for example, Frances Fox Piven and Howard A. Cloward, *Regulating the Poor: The Functions of Public Welfare* (New York: Pantheon Books, 1971), and Samuel F. Yette, *The Choice: The Issue of Black Survival in America* (New York: G. P. Putnam's Sons, 1971). Polly Greenberg makes a similar argument in *The Devil Has Slippery Shoes*, 311.

23. Lady Bird Johnson, "Head Start, a Retrospective View: The Founders," in *Project Head Start*, 44.

24. Office of Economic Opportunity, "The First Step . . . on a Long Journey," Congressional Presentation, April 1965, Volume 2 (Washington, D.C.: Government Printing Office, 1965), L-1.

25. Office of Economic Opportunity, *A Nation Aroused: First Annual Report* (Washington, D.C.: Government Printing Office, 1966), 31.

26. Sargent Shriver, from interview with Valentine, "Head Start, a Retrospective View: The Founders," in *Project Head Start*, 54–55.

27. Ibid., 56.

28. House of Representatives, Committee on Education and Labor, *Elementary and Secondary Education Amendments of 1967*, 90th Congress, 1st Session, Part 2, 956, 1040; U.S. Congress, Senate, Subcommittee on Employment, Manpower, and Poverty of the Committee on Labor and Public Welfare, *Examination of the War on Poverty*, 90th Congress, 1st Session, Part 11, 10, 11 May 1967, 3556; U.S. Congress, Senate, Subcommittee on Employment, Manpower, and Poverty of the Committee on Labor and Public Welfare, *Examination of the War on Poverty*, 90th Congress, 1st Session, Part 6, 8, 9 May 1967, 1983.

29. House of Representatives, Committee on Education and Labor, *Elementary and Secondary Education Amendments of 1967*, 90th Congress, 1st Session, Part 2, 1234.

30. These witnesses did not complain about inappropriate decision making by Head Start parents, but rather by CAP personnel. They may have realized that complaining about CAP staff would generate more sympathy than complaints about parents, of course, but it is also possible that few of these superintendents worked in programs with significant parent involvement in decision making. In 1967, parents were involved in the hiring of teachers at less than one-third of Head Start programs nationally. See Department of Health, Education and Welfare, Office of Child Development, Bureau of Head Start and Early Childhood, *Project Head Start 1968: The Development of a Program* (Washington, D.C.: Government Printing Office, 1970), 21.

31. U.S. Congress, Senate, Subcommittee on Employment, Manpower, and Poverty of the Committee on Labor and Public Welfare, *Examination of the War on Poverty*, 90th Congress, 1st Session, Part 9, 22, 23, 26, 27, 28 June 1967, 2833–2848.

32. U.S. Congress, Senate, Subcommittee on Employment, Manpower, and Poverty of the Committee on Labor and Public Welfare, *Examination of the War on Poverty*, 90th Congress, 1st Session, Part 9, 22, 23, 26, 27, 28 June 1967, 2833.

33. See, for example, OEO annual reports *As the Seed Is Sown: 4th Annual Report of the Office of Economic Opportunity* and *A Nation Aroused: 1st Annual Report of the Office of Economic Opportunity.*

34. House of Representatives, Committee on Education and Labor, *Elementary and Secondary Education Amendments of 1967*, 90th Congress, 1st Session, Part 2, 1041, 1045, 1125, 1126, 1603. This sense that school systems were not willing to work on behalf of the poor had precedent at the federal level; New Deal reformers had worked around educational bureaucrats rather than with them in the 1930s, guided by a belief that these individuals supported the status quo. David Tyack, Robert Lowe, and Elisabeth Hansot argue, in *Public Schools in Hard Times: The Great Depression and Recent Years*, that Franklin D. Roosevelt and his advisors were disdainful of the nation's educators' satisfaction with the status quo and consequently that in setting up New Deal programs, they primarily bypassed the school system. It's conceivable that F. D. R.'s attitude influenced legislators such as Lyndon Johnson (who was a freshman congressman during F. D. R.'s tenure in the White House) and Carl Perkins, who, in 1967, was the House chair of the Committee on Education and Labor, as well as other leading Democrats. David Tyack, Robert Lowe, and Elisabeth Hansot, *Public Schools in Hard Times: The Great Depression and Recent Years* (Cambridge: Harvard University Press, 1984) 107, 109.

35. Office of Economic Opportunity, *A Nation Aroused: First Annual Report*, 65–66.

36. U.S. Congress, Senate, Subcommittee on Employment, Manpower, and Poverty of the Committee on Labor and Public Welfare, *Examination of the War on Poverty*, 90th Congress, 1st Session, Part 11, 10, 11 May 1967, 3484.

37. U.S. Congress, Senate, Subcommittee on Employment, Manpower, and Poverty of the Committee on Labor and Public Welfare, *Examination of the War on Poverty*, 90th Congress, 1st Session, Part 6, 8 and 9 May 1967, 1991.

38. U.S. Congress, Senate, Subcommittee on Employment, Manpower, and Poverty of the Committee on Labor and Public Welfare, *Examination of the War on Poverty*, 90th Congress, 1st Session, Part 11, 10, 11 May 1967, 3484.

39. House of Representatives, Committee on Education and Labor, *Economic Opportunity Act Amendments of 1967*, 90th Congress, 1st Session, Part 2, 1080.

40. House of Representatives, Committee on Education and Labor, *Elementary and Secondary Education Amendments of 1967*, 90th Congress, 1st Session, Part 2, 1042–43.

41. U.S. Congress, Senate, Subcommittee on Employment, Manpower, and Poverty of the Committee on Labor and Public Welfare, *Examination of the War on Poverty*, 90th Congress, 1st Session, Part 9, 22, 23, 26, 27, 28 June 1967, 2834.

42. For a history of federal aid to education and the issues surrounding aid to parochial schools, see Julie Roy Jeffrey, *Education for the Children of the Poor: A Study of the Origins and Implementation of the Elementary and Secondary Education Act of 1965* (Columbus: Ohio State University Press, 1978).

43. David B. Tyack, *The One Best System: A History of American Urban Education* (Cambridge: Harvard University Press, 1974), 131.

44. "Head Start Information Sheets," 1966, Barbee Papers, Box 78, Folder 2, State Historical Society of Wisconsin. The 1966 data from the public schools indicates that of the children attending school-sponsored Head Start programs, 68 percent were African-American, 23 percent were white and 9 percent were Hispanic.

45. "Religious Calendars Out at Head Start," *The Milwaukee Journal*, July 23, 1966; Kenneth Bedford, "Head Start Underway," *The Milwaukee Star*, July 3, 1965, 1; "Protest Possible on Head Start," *The Milwaukee Journal*, September 1, 1966; "Bussing Integrates Head Start Classes," *The Milwaukee Journal*, January 22, 1968.

46. "Head Start Methods Suggested for Schools," *The Milwaukee Journal*, November 19, 1966; "Spurned Grant Irks Head Start Citizens," *The Milwaukee Journal*, October 4, 1967.

47. Head Start Policy Advisory Committee letter to Mr. Gerald Farley, Director of Federal Projects, Milwaukee Board of School Directors, June 30, 1967, Barbee Papers, Box 78, Folder 3.

48. "Little Leaguers," *The Milwaukee Journal*, no date, Barbee Papers, Box 78, Folder 4.

49. "Minutes of the Meeting of the Committee on Appointment and Instruction," November 28, 1967, 11, Barbee Papers, Box 78, Folder 3.

50. "Minutes of the Meeting of the Committee on Appointment and Instruction," February 27, 1968, 55, Barbee Papers, Box 78, Folder 3; Milwaukee Head Start Policy Advisory Committee letter to the Milwaukee Board of School Directors, September 28, 1967, Barbee Papers, Box 78, Folder 3; "Minutes of the Meeting of the Committee on Appointment and Instruction," November 28, 1967, 7–8, Barbee Papers, Box 78, Folder 3.

51. "Minutes of the Meeting of the Committee on Appointment and Instruction," February 27, 1968, 55, Barbee Papers, Box 78, Folder 3, December 5, 1967; "All Day Kindergarten Classes in 13 Inner City Schools," *The Milwaukee Courier*, March 20, 1971, Section 2, 2; "Black Controlled School Plans Fall Opening," *The Milwaukee Courier*, April 26, 1969, 1.

52. U.S. Congress, House of Representatives, Committee on Education and Labor, *Elementary and Secondary Education Amendments of 1967*, 90th

Congress, 1st Session, Part 2, 9, 10, 12, 14, 15, 16, 17, 18, 20 March 1967, 979.

53. Office of Economic Opportunity, Community Action Program, *How to Apply for Head Start Child Development Programs* (Washington, D.C.: Government Printing Office, 1966) and Valentine and Stark, "The Social Context of Parent Involvement in Head Start," in *Project Head Start*, 304.

54. According to the 1980 publication *A Handbook for Involving Parents in Head Start*, decisionmaking appeared first on the list because "it was anticipated this would be the most difficult to implement." Department of Health, Education, and Welfare, Administration for Children, Youth and Families, Head Start Bureau, *A Handbook for Involving Parents in Head Start* (Washington, D.C.: Government Printing Office, 1980), 3.

55. See for example: Zigler, *Head Start*, 111; Richard E. Orton, "Head Start, a Retrospective View: The Founders," in *Project Head Start*, 132; and Robert E. Cooke's testimony at *Economic Opportunity Act Amendments of 1969*, 91st Congress, 1st Session, Part 2, 1146.

56. Office of Economic Opportunity, *The Quiet Revolution: Second Annual Report of the Office of Economic Opportunity*, 31.

57. Office of Economic Opportunity, Project Head Start, *Parent Involvement: A Workbook of Training Tips for Head Start Staff* (Washington, D.C.: Government Printing Office, 1969).

58. Office of Economic Opportunity, Project Head Start, *Psychologist for the Child Development Center* (Washington, D.C.: Government Printing Office, 1969), 14–18.

59. Womens historian Sara Evans notes that "by 1970 'women's lib' was on everyones lips. Between January and March substantial stories on the women's liberation movement appeared in virtually every major journal and broadcast network." Sara M. Evans, *Born for Liberty: A History of Women in America* (New York: The Free Press, 1989), 287.

60. Senate, Subcommittee on Employment, Manpower, and Poverty of the Committee on Labor and Public Welfare, *Head Start Child Development Act*, 91st Congress, 2nd Session, Part 2, 10 February 1970, 354.

61. Office of Economic Opportunity, *Women in the War on Poverty*, Conference Proceedings, May 8, 1967 (Washington, D.C.: Government Printing Office, 1967), 5. During the conference one OEO official asserted that "the feminine influence upon the national character of this country has been a dominant factor in the conception of the War on Poverty and it should be, I think, a driving force behind its application," 52.

62. Office of Economic Opportunity, *Women in the War on Poverty*, 50–51.

63. Ibid., 25.

64. Several conference attendees did criticize OEO, however, for emphasizing "safe" programs such as Head Start rather than the women's Job Corps program, which was acknowledged to be more susceptible to criticism since its enrollees were more likely than four-year-old Head Start children to get into trouble with men or alcohol. OEO officials deflected this criticism by noting that the emphasis on Head Start over other programs was a local decision, adding, "But to some extent, of course, the Congress does establish it, the Congress did fall in love with Head Start." The official went on to express a wish that Congress would fall in love with all OEO programs, not acknowledging that Shriver had realized Head Start would garner a support that the other programs was unlikely to get. This omission was in keeping with the mood of the conference; OEO gathered key women in 1967 to praise them for their efforts and to encourage them to continue supporting OEO programs. They did not intend the conference to politicize gender. As a result, the gender assumptions about Head Start and their subsequent influence on parent participation policy remained inarticulated. Office of Economic Opportunity, *Women in the War on Poverty*, 22.

65. Penelope K. Trickett, "Career Development in Head Start," in *Project Head Start*, 320–22.

66. Still, it should be clear that Head Start never rejected the two-parent family. One list of activities for fathers included the item: "Get it across to the father no matter what his income or education, his staying with his family makes him a big success." Office of Economic Opportunity, Community Action Program, Project Head Start, *Criteria for Evaluating a Head Start Parent Participation Program* (Washington, D.C.: Government Printing Office, 1968), 9.

67. Patrick Moynihan, "The Negro Family: The Case for National Action," in Katz, *The Undeserving Poor*, 24–27. Moynihan's paper suggested that strong black women were, at least in part, to blame for the emasculation of black men. While various groups ultimately denounced Moynihan's position, the paper had credibility within the administration, at least initially. The first public references to Moynihan's paper came, after all, in President Johnson's speech at Howard University during the summer of 1965.

68. Senate, Joint Hearings before the Subcommittee on Employment, Manpower, and Poverty and the Subcommittee on Children and Youth of the Committee on Labor and Public Welfare, *Comprehensive Child Development Act of 1971*, 92nd Congress, 1st Session, Part 2, 526–27.

69. Senate, Subcommittee on Employment, Manpower, and Poverty of the Committee on Labor and Public Welfare, *Head Start Child Development Act*, 91st Congress, 1st Session, Part 1, 26 May 1971, 161.

70. Department of Heath, Education and Welfare, Office of Child Development, *A National Survey of the Impacts of Head Start Centers on Community Institutions*, Prepared by Kirschner Associates, Inc., May 1970 (Washington, D.C.: Government Printing Office, 1970), 82–108.

71. Based on my own research as well as gleanings from Head Start hearings held across the country, I am confident that gender was a key variable both in African American and in white settings. I suspect, however, that the pattern varied in Hispanic communities; the evidence from hearings and various Head Start publications suggests that Hispanic men may well have been active participants in the Head Start programs in their communities. Obviously, this is an issue that merits more attention. Similarly in need of more research is the impact of Head Start among Native Americans, especially those still living on reservations. Various references in the existing histories of Native American education suggest that OEO and Head Start were catalysts for community-controlled schools. See, for example, Estelle Fuchs and Robert J. Havighurst, *To Live on This Earth: American Indian Education* (New York: Doubleday and Company, 1972), 16, and Margaret Szasz, *Education and the American Indian: The Road to Self-Determination, 1928–1973* (Albuquerque: University of New Mexico Press, 1974), 152, 225.

72. "Head Start Director Demanded," *The Milwaukee Journal*, May 18, 1969; "SDC Votes Head Start Fund Block," *The Milwaukee Sentinel*, June 13, 1969; "SDC Votes to Block Head Start Funds," *The Milwaukee Journal*, June 13, 1969; "Francis Starms Is Head Start Supervisor," *The Greater Milwaukee Star*, July 5, 1969, 2. For a more detailed account of this struggle, see Kathryn Kuntz, "Aiming for the Children: A History of Head Start, 1965–1972." Madison, unpublished thesis, 1995.

73. Beyond suggesting that the women were overzealous, the article implied that they were misguided and naive about the real state of affairs at their local school. Walter Jones, "Straight Facts," *The Milwaukee Star*, February 4, 1967, 1.

74. "Kamera Karavan, picture page: Mini Skirts and Things," *The Milwaukee Star*, May 25, 1968, 19. Some of the evidence suggests that activities by parents of older children was taken more seriously by the black newspapers than activities of parents with young children, particularly when the children—teenagers, really—participated along with their parents. The actions of parents at the city's junior highs and high schools, for example, made the front pages of the *Star* and *Courier* regularly. See, for example, "Parents Demand Changes," *The Milwaukee Star*, December 23, 1967, 1. Interestingly, accounts of activism at the junior high and high school level rarely referred to mothers; instead, the papers reported on "parent" participation.

75. Greenberg, *The Devil Has Slippery Shoes*, especially 369–436.

76. Zigler and Muenchow, *Head Start: The Inside Story of America's Most Successful Educational Experiment*, 79, 90–91.

77. Richard Nixon, *The Memoirs of Richard Nixon* (New York: Simon and Schuster, 1978), 424–25.

78. House of Representatives, Ad Hoc Hearing Task Force on Poverty of the Committee on Education and Labor, *Economic Opportunity Act Amendments of 1969*, 91st Congress, 1st Session, Part 2, 1040. Officials also interpreted the 1969 report by the comptroller general, which praised OEO's efforts at innovation but criticized the agency for lack of administrative procedures, to support the delegation of OEO programs to other departments of the cabinet. Comptroller General of the United States, *Review of Economic Opportunity Programs: Report to the Congress of the United States* (Washington, D.C.: Government Printing Office, 1969).

79. Some of these letters appear in the appendix to the testimony. House of Representatives, Ad Hoc Hearing Task Force on Poverty of the Committee on Education and Labor, *Economic Opportunity Act Amendments of 1969*, 91st Congress, 1st Session, Part 5. Appendix. A 1968 rumor that Congresswoman Edith Green was going to propose an impromptu amendment to move Head Start to the Office of Education so jammed the telephone lines to the House of Representatives that they were "almost inoperative," prompting Congresswoman Green to publicly deny that she intended to make such an amendment; this suggests that the 1969 move would have elicited many more letters and phone calls than are included in the hearing testimony. Orton, "Head Start, a Retrospective View: The Founders," in *Project Head Start: A Legacy of the War on Poverty*, 130.

80. House of Representatives, Ad Hoc Hearing Task Force on Poverty of the Committee on Education and Labor, *Economic Opportunity Act Amendments of 1969*, 91st Congress, 1st Session, Part 1, 108.

81. Department of Health, Education, and Welfare, *Parents as Partners*, Task Force on Parent Participation, A Report to the Secretary of the Department of Health, Education, and Welfare, August 1968 (Washington, D.C.: Government Printing Office, 1968).

82. House of Representatives, Ad Hoc Hearing Task Force on Poverty of the Committee on Education and Labor, *Economic Opportunity Act Amendments of 1969*, 91st Congress, 1st Session, Part 1, 318.

83. In 1967, in part as a result of the Green Amendment to the OEA, local community action programs, previously called "CAPs," were renamed Community Action Agencies or CAAs. House of Representatives, Ad Hoc Hearing Task Force on Poverty of the Committee on Education and Labor, *Economic Opportunity Act Amendments of 1969*, 91st Congress, 1st Session, Part 2, 1146.

84. Senate, Subcommittee on Employment, Manpower, and Poverty of the Committee on Labor and Public Welfare, *Head Start Child Development Act,* 91st Congress, 1st Session, Part 1, 4, 5, 6, August 1969, 160.

85. House of Representatives, Ad Hoc Hearing Task Force on Poverty of the Committee on Education and Labor, *Economic Opportunity Act Amendments of 1969,* 91st Congress, 1st Session, Part 2, 1089.

86. The leak was acknowledged in *The New York Times* article, "Education—Dispute over Value of Head Start," which appeared on Sunday, April 20, 1969. House of Representatives, Ad Hoc Hearing Task Force on Poverty of the Committee on Education and Labor, *Economic Opportunity Act Amendments of 1969,* 91st Congress, 1st Session, Part 2, 1064. Orton discusses the leak and Head Start's plans to release the study along with an explanation in Orton, "Head Start, a Retrospective View: The Founders," in *Project Head Start: A Legacy of the War on Poverty,* 133.

87. Although a thorough discussion of the limitations of the Westinghouse study is beyond the scope of this chapter, it should be noted that most of the original planning committee opposed the design of the study, which did not differentiate between children in the 1965 summer Head Start and children in the full-year program in 1965 and 1966. Planning committee members also opposed the study's emphasis on IQ, arguing that Head Start was far more than a preschool education program. Conspiracy theories regarding the Westinghouse study abound. In addition to alleging that Nixon deliberately leaked the study to hurt Head Start's reputation, Cooke suggested in one hearing that the community action staff members in OEO had supported the study because they knew it would reflect badly on Head Start. House of Representatives, Ad Hoc Hearing Task Force on Poverty of the Committee on Education and Labor, *Economic Opportunity Act Amendments of 1969,* 91st Congress, 1st Session, Part 2, 1146.

88. The *Star* argued both points in an editorial. "Discrediting Head Start," *The Greater Milwaukee Star,* May 31, 1969, 4.

89. Mendelsohn quoted a passage from William Glasser's *Schools without Failure,* which noted that, under the present conditions, to say that Head Start prepared children for public schools was like saying that a vacation on the Riviera prepared soldiers for combat. House of Representatives, Ad Hoc Hearing Task Force on Poverty of the Committee on Education and Labor, *Economic Opportunity Act Amendments of 1969,* 91st Congress, 1st Session, Part 1, 34.

90. House of Representatives, Ad Hoc Hearing Task Force on Poverty of the Committee on Education and Labor, *Economic Opportunity Act Amendments of 1969,* 91st Congress, 1st Session, Part 1, 35; Senate, Subcommittee on

Employment, Manpower, and Poverty of the Committee on Labor and Public Welfare, *Head Start Child Development Act*, 91st Congress, 1st Session, Part 1, 22.

91. House of Representatives, Ad Hoc Hearing Task Force on Poverty of the Committee on Education and Labor, *Economic Opportunity Act Amendments of 1969*, 91st Congress, 1st Session, Part 2, 1068.

92. House of Representatives, Ad Hoc Hearing Task Force on Poverty of the Committee on Education and Labor, *Economic Opportunity Act Amendments of 1969*, 91st Congress, 1st Session, Part 2, 1044, 1072.

93. House of Representatives, Ad Hoc Hearing Task Force on Poverty of the Committee on Education and Labor, *Economic Opportunity Act Amendments of 1969*, 91st Congress, 1st Session, Part 2, 1078. Governors clearly pressured Congress during these hearings to give them a larger role in OEO; in addition to a statement supported by all of the governors, thirty-five governors wrote letters to the House committee requesting changes in the administration of OEA.

94. Julius B. Richmond, "Head Start, a Retrospective View: The Founders," in *Project Head Start*, 126.

95. Jule M. Sugarman, "Head Start, a Retrospective View: The Founders," in *Project Head Start*, 118.

96. House of Representatives, Committee on Education and Labor, *Economic Opportunity Act Amendments of 1971*, 92nd Congress, 1st Session, Part 1, 402; and Julius B. Richmond, Deborah J. Stipek, and Edward Zigler, "A Decade of Head Start," in *Project Head Start*, 149.

97. Milwaukee was one of the cities included in the study. Although all anecdotes in the report are anonymous, newspaper accounts verify that aides became a frequent sight in Milwaukee classrooms by the early 1970s, even becoming an issue in the union bargaining. See, for example, "Teacher Aides Help at Keefe Avenue," *The Greater Milwaukee Star*, February 20, 1971, Section 2, 5; "Volunteers Serve Milwaukee Schools," *The Greater Milwaukee Star*, March 6, 1971, 5. On union bargaining, "Schools Must Not Close," *The Greater Milwaukee Star*, December 19, 1970, 1.

98. Department of Heath, Education, and Welfare, Office of Child Development, *A National Survey of the Impacts of Head Start Centers on Community Institutions*, Prepared by Kirschner Associates, Inc., May 1970 (Washington, D.C.: Government Printing Office, 1970), 258–59.

99. The HEW resistance may have been, at least in part, a reaction against that program's earlier growth since Zigler had been one of the original planning committee members who had worried that Head Start's quality suffered when it expanded so rapidly.

100. House of Representatives, Committee on Education and Labor, *Economic Opportunity Act Amendments of 1971*, 92nd Congress, 1st Session, Part 1, 407. The OCD resisted additional funding under both the Head Start Child Development Act of 1969 and the Comprehensive Child Development Act of 1971.

101. House of Representatives, Committee on Education and Labor, *Economic Opportunity Act Amendments of 1971*, 92nd Congress, 1st Session, Part 1, 420.

102. Department of Health, Education and Welfare, Office of Child Development, *A Manual of Policies and Instructions, September 1967* (Washington, D.C.: Government Printing Office, 1969), title page.

103. The school-based Head Starts in Kansas City and Omaha withdrew from the program in reaction to the 70.2 policy statement, refusing to permit parents a role in personnel decisions. OCD threatened other districts with defunding to gain their compliance to the rule. Zigler and Muenchow, *Head Start*, 112.

104. Although there is no evidence that OCD supported any form of community action, it is conceivable that OCD did not intend to eliminate institutional change but assumed that this would happen, as the Kirschner report had suggested, more effectively through example than through activism.

105. Zigler and Muenchow, *Head Start*, 111.

106. Polly Greenberg's account of CDGM reminds us that power on paper does not always translate into actual power. One needs to look carefully at what actually happened at the local level before concluding that parents really had power after 70.2.

107. Michael Gotthainer, Letter to Harriet McCraney and "Proposed Reorganization of Full Year Head Start Program," McCraney's files. Social Development Commission, Milwaukee, Wisconsin.

108. "Mis-Use of Federal Funds by Mrs. McCraney," attachment to Mrs. Beverly Hightower letter to Friend of Head Start Children, August 1, 1971, Maier Papers, Box 91, Folder 20. State Historical Society of Wisconsin.

109. In recognition of the existing tensions federal officials put special conditions on the refunding grant which required the CAA (the Social Development Commission or SDC) to establish new procedures for parent participation; they also required SDC to submit an "annual report on parent activities to the regional office." "Office of Child Development, Head Start Program, Special Conditions," in 1972–73 Head Start refunding materials, McCraney's files.

110. "Head Start's McCraney Charged," *The Greater Milwaukee Star*, June 19, 1971, 1.

111. "McCraney Issue Splits Headstart," *The Greater Milwaukee Star*, June 26, 1971, 1.

112. "Head Start Refunding Remains Doubtful," *The Milwaukee Courier*, October 23, 1971, Section 1, 3.

113. "Head Start Parents Bypassed," *The Milwaukee Journal*, November 10, 1971. The *Journal's* defense of Head Start parents is best understood as part of their long-standing critique of SDC administrators.

114. "Head Startled," *The Milwaukee Courier*, November 6, 1971, 4.

115. Senate, Joint Hearings before the Subcommittee on Employment, Manpower, and Poverty and the Subcommittee on Children and Youth of the Committee on Labor and Public Welfare, *Comprehensive Child Development Act of 1971*, 92nd Congress, 1st Session, Part 3, 918.

116. Zigler's concerns on this point extended beyond parents to the classroom aides. An advocate of credentialed staff in Head Start centers, Zigler supported the development of a certification program for Head Start staff members. By the 1980s Head Start mandated the certification, no longer asserting—as Marian Edelman had in the 1960s—that Head Start programs worked whenever they included local adults who cared about the children of their community. Zigler and Muenchow, *Head Start*, 159–63.

117. This is the theme of Zigler and Muenchow's *Head Start*. Testifying in 1971, Zigler noted that the final payoff from Head Start would be evident in twenty years—through examination of the welfare rolls to determine if, indeed, Head Start children avoided poverty as adults. He did not suggest that Congress should measure the level of institutional change that had occurred. House of Representatives, Committee on Education and Labor, *Economic Opportunity Act Amendments of 1971*, 92nd Congress, 1st Session, Part 1, 421.

118. Katz, *The Undeserving Poor*, 16–17.

119. Senate, Joint Hearings before the Subcommittee on Employment, Manpower, and Poverty and the Subcommittee on Children and Youth of the Committee on Labor and Public Welfare, *Comprehensive Child Development Act of 1971*, 92nd Congress, 1st Session, Part 3, 870.

120. Katz, *The Undeserving Poor*, 32.

121. Department of Heath, Education and Welfare, Office of Child Development, Bureau of Child Development Services, *More Than a Teacher*, by Lois B. Murphy, Ph.D., and Ethel M. Leeper, Bureau of Head Start and Early Childhood Caring for Children Series, Number 2 (Washington, D.C.: Government Printing Office, 1970), 5.

122. Orton, "Head Start, a Retrospective View: The Founders," in *Project Head Start*, 133; Zigler and Muenchow, *Head Start*, 60–73.

123. Interview with Don Sykes, September 15, 1993. Sykes was the executive director of Milwaukee's CAA.

124. See, for example, Frances Fox Piven and Richard A. Cloward, *Regulating the Poor: The Functions of Public Welfare* (New York: Vintage Books, 1993).

125. Greenberg, *The Devil Has Slippery Shoes*, 779–81.

2

The Origins of Head Start and the Two Versions of Parent Involvement: How Much Parent Participation in Early Childhood Programs and Services for Poor Children?

Polly Greenberg

Your answer to the question posed in the title will depend upon your reason for supporting such programs. Your answer will depend upon the priority concerns undergirding your work relating to programs or services for children from low-income families. Your answer will depend upon your bigger than do-good goal. We do not all have the *same* reasons, priority concerns, and goals. *Why* are we providing early childhood programs and services—Head Start and others—for (some of) the children of low-income families?[1]

Everyone involved in Head Start and "Head Start–like" preschool programs for low-income children from 1964 until the present has wanted to give poor kids a chance to not fail in school, but *not* everyone has been thinking about the dynamics and parameters of poverty.

HOW MUCH POVERTY DO YOU WANT TO ELIMINATE?
HOW MUCH DO YOU WANT TO "ELIMINATE" POVERTY?

Though we rarely discuss it, we do not all agree regarding the degree to which we want to reduce poverty in America. No one wants poverty,

49

but only a small group of people seek to reduce it *significantly*. That is what the 1960s War on Poverty was about; it was *not* about a model preschool program to promote narrowly defined "cognitive development"! We wanted to close in on "forced choice" poverty from all sides and to cut it off at the roots. There are still poverty warriors around, us old-timers and a new crop of them, although times are quieter now, so they do not hit the streets shouting or head South as we did. To reduce poverty *significantly*, the political equation has to change, and one way to contribute to changing it is to maximize the participation of poor parents and poor communities in authentic decision making on issues that are meaningful to *them*—not decision making about who will bake what for the fundraiser. Through the processes of analyzing the issues, studying and clarifying the options, hiring, evaluating, and firing in early childhood programs and services for their own children, disenfranchised, often disenchanted people learn and develop a good deal—sometimes gaining the same power of knowledge that the professionals charged with "caring for them" have.

Therein lies a problem: *Truly* sharing power with parents is too terribly scary for almost everybody who at present *has* any power over children. It feels safer to

- *teach* parents (parenting skills, how to do what the health professional says to do, how to help in minor ways in—and in behalf of—the classroom, ways to help children learn in the home),

- *brief* parents (so they give teachers less trouble about the philosophy, curriculum, and methods selected by educators and perhaps even vigorously support it all),

- *permit* parents to become involved in all sorts of *peripheral* activities and decision making,

rather than to *really* be "partners with parents"—a widely used euphemism for coercing parents (in a socially acceptable way, of course) to cooperate with educators. The vast difference between *parents as participants on the perimeter*, and *parents as partners at the core* has been apparent in Head Start since its inception.

Head Start guidelines for parent rights and responsibilities were created years after the creation of Head Start by the insightful, delightful, determined social worker Bessie Draper (a Head Start staffer starting in the program's earliest months, a nonexpert in parent empowerment who became a super expert). Following these guidelines requires remarkably in-depth involvement compared to the tokenism reluctantly tolerated by the average health, social services, or public school program. And some Head Start programs implement the guidelines thoroughly. They are a joy to behold!

However, in contrast to the attention to Head Start's education component, there has been much less attention to parents: money for training, supervisory staff, and monitoring and evaluation in terms of *parents as equals in decision making* has been inadequate, defunding due to noncompliance with regard to *parents as decision makers* has been rare, and researchers' attention to parents as *real* partners to study has been almost nonexistent. This is because, except for the nine-month period between Head Start's conception (October, 1964) and first center openings (June 1965), few people at the national leadership level were interested in anything more than training parents to parent better and to help staff more. These are not trivial goals, but neither are they true parent involvement in operating children's programs. (Even *during* the pre-opening months, the group of fourteen expert advisors that helped staff plan Head Start—the Planning Committee—included only four people who talked about parents sharing control in local Head Start programs.)

The monsters in the dark under America's bed are classism and masculinism. In recent years, it has become "okay" to talk about racism, ageism, disabilities, homosexuality—but classism and masculinism are still too taboo to mention. In this chapter, I mention both briefly, because both tie into our topic.

WHERE DID THE WAR ON POVERTY BEGIN?
WHO WANTED TO FIGHT POVERTY?

The War on Poverty was the result of several political and social forces reaching a confluence and pouring forward with the roaring power of water and boulders bursting a dam, combined with creative responses from strong leaders in the White House, all three branches of the federal government, and on Capitol Hill. Those who were not concerned with the problems of poverty could not stop the overwhelming accumulation of volatile issues and emotions leading to the creation and passage of the Economic Opportunity Act of 1964, although they could and did start to attack even before it was passed. And they continue to this day to undermine substantial efforts to reduce increasing poverty. In September 1996, Census Bureau data showed that without government programs, 57.6 million people would have been poor the year before, but when government benefits are counted, 3.3 million people still live in poverty in what is by far the wealthiest country in the world.

Perhaps the most important force pushing national leaders toward mounting a war on poverty was the rising unrest of African American leaders. Black leaders everywhere, as well as their white allies, were insisting upon equal opportunity for their people in all aspects of life in this democracy.[2] And, when the cultural afterdust of World War II had settled, many average middle-class citizens and members of the country's leadership groups began to realize how good they had it. Many ordinary people, no longer feeling stressed by hard times or the fearful shadows they cast, felt, instead, prosperous, generous, and a touch guilty—"There but for the grace of God . . ." There was an increasing awareness in the air of the poverty in our backyards, and of racism. Both struck comfortable people as simply out of sync with the ideals of our country. The early 1960s were years of national affluence, of optimism among liberals that problems standing as barriers between many poor white and minority Americans and the American dream—the promises implicit in American ideals—were soluble, and of growing political power among black people, who were beginning to vote in large numbers.

President John F. Kennedy created the President's Committee on Juvenile Delinquency and named Attorney General Robert F. Kennedy its chairman. With the help of two distinguished sociologists, Lloyd Ohlin and Richard Cloward, Robert Kennedy, in charge of crime fighting for our country, came to understand apathy, juvenile delinquency, crime, and many other ramifications of poverty as *lack of opportunity*. Robert Kennedy grew increasingly convinced that innumerable poor people, particularly young people, particularly young minority people, become disillusioned, resign themselves to small futures, and drop out (of school, of the struggle to "succeed"), or turn their energy, leadership skill, and entrepreneurism (sometimes brave, sometimes clever) to underworld endeavors because, due to the inferior educations they have received, the biases they confront in our society and the lack of contacts and networks that are their lot, few are likely to make it regardless of what they do.

The President's Committee on Juvenile Delinquency (PCJD) was housed across the hall from the attorney general's office in the U.S. Justice Department. It was the bright, dedicated, multitalented PCJD team members who discovered, through their work in ghetto neighborhoods from coast to coast, through the guidance of their ever curious Executive Director Dave Hackett, and through consultation with a number of poor people in many cities, that if human services and other self-improvement efforts are to be effective, poor people must be encouraged to *participate* to the maximum feasible extent in designing and directing them. Like everyone else, poor people want to feel a meaningful degree of "ownership" of circumstances and institutions (such as schools, human services, and jobs) affecting them. If essentially disempowered people are merely "recipients" of programs and services, many feel alienated from them and oppressed by them. PCJD devoted itself to the dissemination of this principle.

Because it had little money of its own, the President's Committee on Juvenile Delinquency's carefully thought-out strategy was to work through progressive people in as many federal agencies as possible to build maximum feasible participation of the poor into all pertinent programs. In the early 1960s, I was a staff person at the Department of Education (then the U.S. Office of Education). I worked for Francis A. J. (Fritz) Ianni in the Developmental Activities program of the Cooperative Research Bureau. (Since, Fritz Ianni, an anthropologist, has been at Columbia Teachers College.) This program gave "by invitation only" grants to "underdeveloped areas of education" (inner cities, rural areas, southern "Negro" colleges, and early childhood education, especially for low-income minority children). President Kennedy had selected Francis Keppel, on leave as dean of the Harvard School of Education, to be U.S. commissioner of education. Commissioner Keppel was very cooperative with the President's Committee on Juvenile Delinquency. I was one of his "progressive people," although a junior staff member. Therefore, I was one of the few USOE staffers who worked with several PCJD staff members—primarily junior staff members—with "Bobby's guerillas," as the group was affectionately called.

A NEW FEDERAL AGENCY IS CREATED TO FIGHT POVERTY
THROUGH BOTH INDIVIDUAL AND INSTITUTIONAL CHANGE:
THE OFFICE OF ECONOMIC OPPORTUNITY (OEO)

In response to the swelling national feeling that "something must be done," president Kennedy's economic advisors and the president himself were looking at their options for preparing an all-out assault on the factors contributing to racial and economic inequality in the United States.

During the spring of 1964, shortly after President Kennedy was assassinated, the War on Poverty (originally suggested by his economic advisors) was being planned by representatives of each federal agency and a select group of outside consultants named by the agency heads.

The confederation was called the "President's Task Force against Poverty." It functioned under the direction of R. Sargent Shriver, appointed poverty tsar by newly installed President Lyndon B. Johnson. All involved were convinced that serving poor people, with a focus on helping them get out of poverty, was not a priority at any relevant existing federal agency—the Department of Health, Education, and Welfare or the Department of Labor, for example. Like any organization, the task force had a staff. I was assigned by Fritz Ianni to serve as the staff support person for Wade Robinson, a consultant from Harvard University's School of Education, who soon became the acting director of Job Corps.

A new agency, whose primary purpose was to help people deal with the multiple problems of poverty on a person-by-person basis and to create change in the institutions that served the middle-class better than the poor, was believed to be needed. The Task Force against Poverty was charged with designing a new federal agency (the Office of Economic Opportunity—OEO) and the programs that the legislation mandated, such as the Community Action Program and Job Corps. When the appropriation for the new federal Office of Economic Opportunity came, we became the OEO staff and moved to our own building, the one in which Head Start was created soon after.[3]

It is important to note that the philosophy of how best to enable people to exit perpetual poverty included new opportunities for individuals, as well as efforts to create institutional change. The law and OEO's programs endorsed more services *and* more activism—the two were not pitted against one another in an "either or" manner. This is important to understand when we think about how much parent involvement Head Start should have.

But we "rapid reformists" were neither naive enough nor nuts enough to imagine that entrenched bureaucracies with single subject agendas were suddenly going to change all on their own. Especially after we had watched PCJD's frustrating efforts to get each agency to integrate maximum feasible participation of the poor into all of their programs. The pace of positive change would be speeded up by a little goading from the dedicated staff, informed consumers, and an aggressive fan club of a fresh agency, free from past baggage and foot-dragging "dead wood." The creation of OEO was intended, also, to be an end run—by champions of serious social change, the rapid reformists—around sluggish, some would say snobbish, agencies.

OEO's conceptualizers intended to bring together all that was known about poverty from all relevant disciplines and professions and to attack at a number of strategic points in the circle to weaken it, so that people who were wounded and caught in its sticky web could work their way out. It was expected that the new federal agency's programs would provide the urgently needed self-improvement services that existing agencies and institutions neglected to offer to everyone eligible for them, or neglected to offer in ways that worked. For instance, the public schools were permitting (as they do today) many academically disadvantaged students to get as far as high school without the literacy and other "school skills" needed to hang in there. The dropout rate was (as it is today) alarming. Job Corps, Upward Bound, and the Work-Study Program were all designed by OEO to serve as alternative secondary school systems for those whom the "regular" high schools failed to educate.[4] Some students would fail, but most would succeed—and would soon be positive role models for *their* children, which would provide an escape route from poverty for these members of the next generation.

It also was expected that the approach of programs funded by a new federal agency would be to develop knowledgeable "equal opportunity advocates" for poor people to become healthy, well-educated, and job-ready. OEO's programs were to provide

- "training" (through guided success experiences) in constructive community activism for low-income people already functioning as leaders in their neighborhoods, and

- "training" (through eye-opening exposure) for masses of newly involved middle-class volunteers and professionals to increase their awareness of, and sensitivity to, the interlocking, seemingly insoluble problems of living in poverty, generation after generation.

We believed that naturally gifted leaders, like naturally gifted parents and naturally talented teachers, could learn to be better leaders. We believed that there were many good folks out there in middle-income America, often parents themselves, who had never come face-to-face with nor come to care about the overwhelming complexities an average poor family confronts if its members try to change socioeconomic classes. We thought many might join in a war against poverty, each in his or her own way. (I still believe both of these things.)

As Sargent Shriver, OEO's executive director, said, "There was a fantastic lack of fundamental knowledge about poor people, who they were, where their problems were" on the part of the general public, many human service professionals, and leaders at all levels. (Even today, in casual conversations "on the street" and in my profession, I find a great deal of rhetorical abuse and fact-free, myth-filled chit-chat everywhere.) VISTA (Volunteers in Service to America), which was being organized at the same time as all the other OEO programs, was intended to address this lack of knowledge. It was hoped that these young VISTA volunteers would grow up and become active in their communities in programs serving poor people. Again, it was assumed that, as the parents most of them would become, they would transmit their values and views to their children.

HEAD START: A SIMPLE AND SENSIBLE IDEA, AN IMPULSE FROM THE
HEART, AND A PERFECT POLITICAL MOVE

Head Start was entirely Sargent Shriver's idea.[5] It was not mandated in the Economic Opportunity Act. During the eight months that he had been poverty tsar, R. Sargent Shriver had become more and more convinced that the War on Poverty should provide something substantial for young children. He had been very involved with programs for low-income children and youth for years, most recently in the work of the Kennedy Foundation, of which his wife, Eunice, was executive director. He was captivated by findings that much "mental retardation" in children could be caused by the lack of a safe, stimulating, and healthy environment.

In his characteristic cyclonic manner, Shriver had started testing his emerging thoughts on any and all people he respected (and thought of at the moment). Major among the people Sargent Shriver consulted was Dr. Robert Cooke, his family's physician, chairman of pediatrics and pediatrician-in-chief of the Johns Hopkins Hospital and chairman of the Kennedy Foundation's Scientific Advisory Committee. Shriver has said, "Then I learned there are 'experts' in child development, and I started talking to some of them."[6] Sargent Shriver invited Bob Cooke—not, as many mistakenly believe, Edward Zigler, an important and forceful member of the Planning Committee—to chair a committee to plan the project later named "Head Start." Several months later Shriver invited Julius B. Richmond, M.D., to head the nationwide Head Start program. Dr. Richmond is, and was in 1965, a wise and high status physician, who had been a leading advocate for health care, social services, and early childhood education for poor children during his entire professional career. As director of the nation's about-to-begin Head Start program, Dr. Richmond was able to get the conservative American Medical Association and the American Academy of Pediatrics, whose members usually treat middle-class children, to cooperate with Head Start.

Shriver talked with many distinguished authorities, among them Urie Brofenbrener and Edward Zigler.[7] All urged a small pilot program, perhaps a group of "field trials." None mentioned that parents be pivotal in putting together, staffing, and running the programs for their children, although "community control" of schools, "new careers for the poor," and the "modeling theory of socialization" (which says that children feel they can influence their future lives when they have parents who feel able to shape *their* own lives and environment) were all well-known and obviously relevant concepts and practices.

When, at an October 1964 meeting, Shriver tossed to his senior staff his bombshell of an idea for a massive health, nutrition, and summer immunizations program for children on the brink of entering kindergarten or first grade the following fall (1965), a program including some nursery school and kindergarten-type activities and lots of field trips to ease children's transition from low-income homes to middle-class classrooms, Shriver's top staffers exploded in an enthusiastic response. Everyone, Sargent Shriver most of all, was worried about what the brand new poverty program would have to show for itself by summer. While the cynical media, always sniffing for the scent of scandal or imperfection, nipped painfully at our hurrying heels and barked harshly at our every effort, we were hastily translating a congressional mandate into many large-scale working programs all across the nation. But minority teenage dropouts (Job Corps) are not popular, and neither are (legitimately) disgruntled low-income activists (the Community Action Program). Everyone was thrilled with Shriver's brilliant idea, and instantly, imaginatively elaborated on it. Young children! Surely they are the *victims* of poverty, not the perpetrators of it! Surely young children were the deserving poor!

Said OEO senior staff member Lew Eigen, "Head Start was a temporizing measure to 'run cover' for the *real* poverty program, the one that was being mounted to break the cycle of poverty, the Community Action Program, while it converted theorizing and demonstrations into a nationwide program" (1990).

And Sargent Shriver said,

It must always be remembered that there was widespread opposition to OEO as soon as the legislation passed. Within ninety days after OEO's start, the House of Representatives authorized a special Investigations Committee to determine what OEO was doing wrong! This happened even before OEO had had time to do much, if anything at all. Local opposition also appeared. Faced with local and

congressional hostility, I felt that National Emphasis programs, one
of them being Head Start, could ameliorate some of this hostility to
OEO's CAP efforts by establishing certain national programs that
many communities would consider desirable. In other words, the
hostility to Community Action could be ameliorated by the community itself, if it was the conduit for certain desirable programs like
Head Start, legal aid, or health programs. Otherwise, the Community
Action Program would be looked upon exclusively as an effort to
empower the poor politically and economically. We knew that en-
dowing a particular group in a community with money and political
power would generate hostility toward that effort from others in that
community. If local CAPs were seen as nothing more than . . .
revolutionary centers financed by Washington to upset local government and social structure (which is what some people thought they
were), the opposition they would meet would negate all their positive qualities. We also supported the administration of National
Emphasis programs by local CAPs because these agencies were in
touch with the poor and could inform us of their reactions to these
programs. Through CAP agencies we felt we could establish very
good "consumer panels," so to speak (Shriver 1979, 59–60).

In retrospect, we realized that as fast as Head Start staff in the
Community Action Program gave parents guidelines as to the multiple and important roles they were encouraged to play, local governments and school boards set limits on parent participation. Some
communities went so far as to refuse to *have* Head Start for the children if parents were going to participate. Yes, Head Start had appeal
to leaders in localities from coast to coast, but not enough to offset
these same leaders' horror at the prospect of relinquishing in the least
degree their paternalistic management of services for the poor, and at
the destabilizing effect it would inevitably have on their political control. Nothing, not even as appealing and worthwhile a program as
Head Start, was able to save the enormous potential of the much
feared Community Action Program. It still exists and does good things
in a number of places, but was castrated in the earliest years of the
Poverty Program.

HEAD START AND COMMUNITY ACTION—HEAD START'S ORIGINATORS WERE NOT ALL TALKING ABOUT THE SAME THING

Community Action Program staff were talking about activating "indigenous" leaders living in inner-city neighborhoods, in rural areas, in

"pockets of poverty." This was CAP's priority concern. They were talking about empowering Head Start parents to go after the agencies that were not serving their children adequately and pressure them to do so.

This was in sharp contrast to what Sargent Shriver and Head Start's (temporary) Planning Committee were talking about. Sargent Shriver was talking about activating the well-meaning middle class. He was urging *everyone* to do something about "the poverty in our own backyards."[8]

Shriver had been president of Chicago's Board of Education for five years. "I had seen how the cards are stacked against kids in the slums in a huge number of ways. There are just so many ways in which they don't have a chance: no books, no parental guidance, nobody in the family who reads, nobody who ever went to school, not to mention malnutrition, bad classrooms, dilapidated housing, narcotics" (Shriver 1979, 51).

Sargent Shriver had invented and run the world's best known volunteerism program, Peace Corps. He believed that millions of ordinary middle-class people throughout America are full of good will and, given both a mechanism and an invitation, would participate—in every community—in programs for young children from poor families. And Sargent Shriver was talking about a huge program to reach as many poor children as possible as quickly as possible.

Sargent Shriver said

> I said to Dr. Cooke at the committee meeting, "Well, let's set aside, say $10 million for this program." But then the applications began pouring in. I invited Dr. Julius Richmond to Washington to run Head Start. He organized it, and I detailed one of our Washington bureaucrats—a very good one, Jule Sugarman—to work with him. Every two or three weeks, it seemed to me, they'd come back and say, "Look, Sarge, this thing is just exploding, and we certainly can't begin to finance it with $10 million or $20 million or even $30 million." By the time July came around, I had committed almost $70 million to the program! (Shriver 1979, 56)

Both the idea of involving "the maximum feasible" number of middle-class people and the idea of an instant, immense program, were dramatically different from what the Planning Committee was talking about. Dick Boone, director of the office of Economic Opportunity's division of Policy and Development, was the person responsible for writing the "maximum feasible participation of the poor" requirement into the Economic Opportunity Act of 1964 earlier in the year. As Head Start was being conceptualized within the Community Action Program by Sargent Shriver and his poverty warriors, Boone and other Community Action Program leaders at OEO headquarters in Washington were talking about action in *poor* communities.

The newly appointed very interdisciplinary Planning Committee was talking about activating the expert academic community and everyday professionals—health, mental health, and so on—the focus was on providing services; the Planning Committee also envisioned crafting a *small model program* and creating a setting in which to research how children from poor homes learn best. With regard to parents and community, the Planning Committee was talking about involving parents so as to train them in parenting skills, nutrition, and so on.

When Planning Committee members, fourteen people representing many appropriate disciplines, spoke or wrote of parent involvement in Head Start, which not all of them did, most of them expressed this viewpoint and mentioned nothing whatsoever about helping parents become advocates for their children in their communities. This included the three early childhood educators—James L. Hymes, Jr., John Neimeyer, and Keith Osborn—and the three developmental psychologists. As committee member and educator George Brain summed it up: "It was assumed that parents could learn from participation in the program" (Brain, 1979, 75). They carried their concerns to Sargent Shriver, but were overruled. How ridiculously traditional and safe this seemed to most of us at War on Poverty headquarters in Washington; to us this sounded like a hell of a way to wage a war! Mamie Clark, Edward Crump, Jacqueline Wexler, and Mitchell Ginsburg were disturbed and angry about the lack of emphasis on citizen participation and community activism on which the War on Poverty was being built.

Most of the members of the Planning Committee argued, some strongly, against a nationwide program. For example, physician Myron E. Wegman said, "I would be happier if the concept of nationwide coverage were abandoned. Whatever money could be obtained should be concentrated in selective projects located in various regions and subregions of the country" (Wegman, 1979, 111).

Staff members would laugh, making mocking comments such as, "Probably a couple more pilot projects for 90 or 100 preschoolers will solve America's massive poverty problem." OEO staff did not feel it was operating in the same universe as *any* of the special interest advisory groups for *any* of the programs. They seemed to have their own agendas—research instead of mass action.

To the few ivory tower developmental psychologists involved in early plans for Head Start, the prospect of "experimenting" with children was exotic and exciting—it was a chance to prove *untrue* the theory of "the immutable and irreversible genetic transmission from generation to generation of irresponsibility, criminality, joblessness, mental disability, and poverty" (Cooke 1979, xxiii), a theory believed until then by prominent, much-cited leaders in their academic discipline, such as J. McVicker Hunt. Psychologists had researched their middle-class "lab rat" children down to the last finding and were exhilarated by the idea of a new "laboratory" (as some literally called it) of children from low-income families about whom to study, publish, and present. This is not to say that the academics did not want to help poor children do better in school and in life. I am simply pointing out professional priorities. University professors' brownie points do not come from the number of people they have helped out of poverty, but rather from research projects, books published by prestigious university presses, articles in scholarly journals, presentations at major academic conferences, and mentoring outstanding graduate students.

Jule Sugarman, a gifted public administrator recently brought to OEO by Dick Boone (who had worked with him before and greatly admired his creative abilities) was talking about all of the above—involving parents and community, mobilizing volunteers, working with the professional community, and learning about early childhood education. Jule had been a key consultant to CAP for some time—in fact, he had *designed* its administration. Jule Sugarman was the de facto director of Head Start (although his title was associate director), from "before the beginning" until he left OEO because Dr. Richmond was dean of the Upstate Medical Center at Syracuse, and was not able to leave. (He commuted several days a week to Washington.)

Like Shriver, Boone, and most of the original War on Poverty staff, Jule was not overly enamored with experts. As we were creating and launching Head Start, he often said, "There are instinctive understandings and skills in working with children that are widely distributed in America. Given the resources, people can help children in effective ways, and they will invest a lot of themselves in doing so. They may even turn out to "know" through experience and intuition a lot more than the experts" (Sugarman 1979, 119).

Jule Sugarman was also talking about how to create an administrative operation almost overnight (staff, phones, desks, application
forms, and so on) that could launch a national program in many thousands of communities simultaneously and in only a few months. Also,
he was able to

- reach the poorest 300 counties and crevices of poverty in the United
  States. (Sugarman's concern was that big, affluent cities, with the sophistication and staff to do it, usually respond to requests for proposals or applications for funding when the federal government or states
  send out guidelines for new programs but the little places never even
  hear of the programs.)

- arrange for *advances* of money to be sent to poor people, so they could
  get Head Start going. (The government normally pays you months *after*
  you have handed in your receipts; in this case, thousands of Head Starts
  sprang up overnight and served 500,000 children in its first summer.)

- operate a massive technical assistance and training program. (500 professionals, most of them early childhood educators, traveled to tiny
  towns they had never heard of, to help people launch a kindergarten-
  type program.)

Head Start emerged and succeeded by capitalizing on everyone
involved: Were it not for the extremely knowledgeable, magnificently
well-organized low-income Head Start "family," who will not give up
the "world" about which it feels so passionately, Head Start would
have been slaughtered long ago. If clumps of determined parents in
small model projects were all there were, no matter how hard they
had campaigned, Head Start would by now be long dead.

Were it not for the masses of middle-class professionals and other
citizens of all sorts who have had firsthand experience with the human wonders Head Start routinely has wrought, and who understand
the value that care and education have for *poor* children just as for
their *own* children, Head Start would not have the political power it
has always enjoyed—power that has allowed it to take root and refuse
to be killed.[9]

And were it not for the elite academics who have advocated for
Head Start since its inception, its value and virtues would not be
heard. This is because, alas, due to the classism, masculinism, and
adulation of pseudoscience in this country, nothing is believed by law-
makers and other decision-makers unless it is backed by the research—

however flawed, tiny, and off-target the studies may be—of high ranking, usually male, academics (or sometimes their female disciples).

It has been this incredible mix that has enabled Head Start to survive its powerful enemies, in fact to *expand*, both in numbers of children served and in new projects developed.

WOMEN'S ROLE IN HEAD START DESIGN

Working with poor people and their children in an effort to understand and alleviate the sometimes inundating problems in their environment (forget the genetics!) was not exactly a new notion. Through our country's employment sector, labor unions, private philanthropists, religious institutions, voluntary sector, local and state actions, direct and indirect federal activities; through its public health, public education, public library, public housing, and social service systems (including help with housing costs); through programs such as social security, Medicaid, food stamps, and school lunch; through its academics and intelligentsia, and of course through the profession of early childhood education itself, which had a long history of involvement both in social reform and in parent involvement, America had already made one hundred years' worth of one variety or another of mini "antipoverty" efforts before the War on Poverty (1965)—including the development of theories and strategies devoted to the idea of reducing poverty.

Probably the many men involved in the original planning of Head Start were so exhilarated by the heady thrill of inclusion in such an exciting and important project that they neglected to notice the relevant pioneering work in early education, social work, child health, and parent education that women had been thoughtfully engaged in— and teaching and writing about—for several generations. Women had developed kindergarten, day care, and nursery education, including specialized training institutes, as well as co-operative nursery schools, organized and operated by parents—in other words, mothers.

Even federal participation in day care and nursery school was not new. We had federally funded day care from 1933 to 1947, first under the Federal Emergency Relief Administration, followed by the Works Projects Administration (WPA), and then the Lanham Community Facilities Act. Like Head Start, the WPA limited enrollment to children from low-income families. Head Start allows a certain percent of its enrollees to be middle-class children. The WPA nurseries had some middle-class children too, because, in the midst of the Depression, their parents *were* low-income. Like Head Start, the WPA nurseries emphasized jobs for those who needed them, as well as appropriate education for young children. Like Head Start, this was a nationwide program. The WPA spent $6 million on nursery schools in forty-seven states and Puerto Rico. The Lanham Act spent $51 million on more than three thousand day care centers. Although it never has been acknowledged by the men who originated Head Start, women were prominent and dominant in the history of early childhood education for poor children, as they were in early childhood education in general.

It would seem strange, were we not now so knowledgable about masculinism in our culture, that although the wives and mothers of some of these men were kindergarten and nursery teachers, and although most of the men's children had attended kindergarten and nursery school as a matter of course, the several dozen men at the head of Head Start never appeared to realize that there was an early childhood profession, with leaders, usually female, of its own. Some of those men, especially the CAP staff, Jule Sugarman, and Sargent Shriver, seemed unable to distinguish nursery education (now known as preschool) from public elementary education, with which they had many big and legitimate bones to pick. No OEO senior staff member involved in the origins of Head Start was female. Three of the fourteen outside expert consultants called the "Planning Committee" were female—one seldom spoke at meetings and has never written about Head Start; the other two, who had strong views, were overruled on key points. Even the three aforenamed excellent early childhood experts on the Planning Committee were male, although early childhood education has been and is an overwhelmingly female field.

Early in the design and launching of Head Start, some women, including upper-class nonprofessional wives who had exemplary records in volunteerism, were invited to join the cause. For example, Sherri Henry, wife of the Federal Communications Commissioner, and Lindy Boggs, wife of a well-known congressman, led a group of other congressional wives in Jule Sugarman's effort to get Head Start into the country's three hundred poorest counties. Mickey Bazalon, Rosamund Kohlberg, and Harriet Yarmolinsky were three other prominent men's wives who came aboard. They, too, were exceptionally able, but were not professional women. They, and later other women, were hired as midlevel staff.

Other women, most of them also socially or academically affiliated with major men involved in Head Start's initial planning, and who were professionals, were invited to help as temporary "pieceworkers" or part-time consultants—all working from home or in the field, not in the Washington headquarters. How Head Start's original decision-making staff included women was typical of how women were chosen and utilized in the 1960s, when government typists still used carbon paper.

OVER A CENTURY, WE HAVE LEARNED SOME TRUTHS ABOUT POVERTY

It is true that compared to most other countries in the world, America is a land of opportunity. Large numbers of men and women and their descendants have benefited from these opportunities, and others do so every day. That is why we have such a huge (albeit newly shrinking) middle class. A small number of people work their way into satisfying blue-collar jobs and into the "middle class" (whatever that is)—or go straight into the white-collar middle class—or even, in unusual but not unique cases, achieve distinction. Probably they are children born a bit brighter and sturdier than others, probably children lucky enough to be born to loving and encouraging mothers, who do well in school and develop constructive interests, therefore associate with peers of similar situations (and are surrounded by positive peer pressure), perhaps children fortunate enough to have a middle-class relative or unusual teacher who inspires, assists, even *insists*.

African Americans have fared less well in the socioeconomic improvement arena than have white people who chose to come to these shores. Then, too, many of the latter were able to blend in better—to be invisible—they were not black. And in America, racism is true. Many white people say they do not see it, but virtually all black people say they do.

But of course the economy has to cooperate; there have to be jobs. Whether or not there is high unemployment or a possibility of "full employment" is influenced by investor pressure for profit, a world situation that allows jobs to be moved wherever wages are lowest, the decisions of private companies, consumers, the Federal Reserve's policies, new technologies (like computer-driven technologies, which have replaced millions of workers with machines), changing tastes, domestic or international competition, new global markets, inflation, credit, price controls or lack of them, managers' competence or lack of it, workers skills and motivation—quite a few factors beyond the curriculum in the preschool.

There are not enough middle-class level jobs for everyone. Ours is a pyramid-shaped capitalist, classist culture in which some corporate executives are allowed to "earn" 350 times as much as the person who works for minimum wage in the same corporation, and where there are not enough jobs at the top no matter how brilliant and hardworking people may be. There was an automobile ad on TV in which a classy-looking older man asks why "you" work so hard, rise so early, sacrifice so much, play the game so skillfully. He asks, "Is it worth it?" The answer implied in the visuals is yes, it's worth it, look at me drive off in my snappy black Infiniti ($29,900). Are we supposed to believe that all those people unable to purchase this luxury car sleep late, sacrifice nothing, and do not "play the game" that being successfully employed demands? This TV ad plays upon the widely accepted myth that if people are poor, they are lazy.

Often forgotten by those leaders who lambaste the poor (and with them the kinder, gentler segments of society, which make these attempts to ease poor people's ills) is the fact that with or without programs and services "targeted" at them, a great many people born into poverty take one step at a time, taking advantage of the inferior opportunities available to them (bad schools, bad health care, and so on) and the extra little opportunities they accidentally come upon (a good teacher in one grade or subject, awareness of an accessible job). Some of them leave the poverty of unemployment only to join the swelling ranks of "working poor."

When current critics utter great, condemning generalizations about programs that do not work, they neglect to mention that a plethora of programs and services have helped innumerable people pull themselves from the pool of poverty, some within two years, more within five; they overlook the fact that it takes a while to learn English or get a high school or college education or job training.

Another truth: If fathers are allowed not to share care or pay court-ordered child support, as has been the case for decades, many mothers and children will be poor. Until recently, child support expectations and enforcement have been "a guy thing." This has been another example of institutional masculinism.

That schools are extraordinarily unequal in a nation that brags about equal opportunity for all is true. I often hear decent people say that if children of low-income families were not lazy, all they have to do to succeed in life is do well in school. I do not think these "commentators" have spent much time in typical inner-city schools.

In the nice (usually a euphemism for white) neighborhoods, we see beautiful homes and elegant shops, marvelous parks, and wonderful public schools. Minutes away is the inner city. The school—windows imprisoned behind metal grates—squats in a square of bleak, bare cement. There is no grass and no play equipment. Inside sit children, almost all black and Latino, many with rotting teeth, untreated health conditions of many types, and hungry. The worst teachers teach here (with an occasional remarkable exception of course, but one who is, statistically speaking, likely to burn out soon). The worst teachers are here because parents in the best neighborhoods demand the best and oust the others—who cannot actually be fired, but *can* be transferred to a filthy school in a trash-filled neighborhood, an "urban" (typically a synonym for unconscionable) school. Often, a fifth of each class in this sort of school does not even get as far as high school. Many children are not taught to read, especially those with (frequently undiagnosed) learning disabilities (Kozol, 1992).

It is true that poor communities across this country (and the world) share a cluster of characteristics in addition to lack of money. One of these is feelings of helplessness and fatalism: "I'm not able to do anything about this, so I'll accept it. This is the way our world is, it will be this way for my child too, there's no use fighting it."[10] This accommodation to life as it is (for everyone in these communities) is psychologically sound. Struggling to achieve unreachable aspirations leads to mental breakdown or rage. Accepting that which cannot be changed is considered a sign of mental health. The trouble is that sometimes people misjudge, erroneously perceiving that which *can* be changed, at least for a few individuals, as something that *cannot*.

PARENT EMPOWERMENT: AN ANTIDOTE TO FATALISM AND "APATHY"

In 1965 (and now) many parents were unanimous, adamant, and articulate about the extraordinary stresses and exhaustingly depressing forces associated with living in poverty (or as the parents of children with severe disability or chronic illness). With a consistency that should convince and appall even the skeptics among us, a high percentage of these parents describe being humiliated by hostile and judgmental teachers, principals, case workers, health and mental health professionals, and others who consider the parents inadequate and who tell them what they "should" do, despite almost absolute lack of familiarity with the incredible obstacles lying between the parents and the services, sources of support, or simple justice that they seek. These parents say (phrased one way or another) that these stresses are "disempowering" (Greenberg 1969/1990). Other people who have worked with or studied the same populations have found the same thing (Pizzo, 1983, 1987, 1990, 1993; Turnbull and Turnbull, 1978, 1985).

According to parent empowerment specialist Peggy Pizzo (1993, 9),

> *Power* means the capacity to influence both one's own destiny and the behavior of others. This capacity is developed through the acquisition and use of resources (e.g., money, knowledge, skills, legal and other authority, personal confidence, optimism, time). Disempowerment is the loss, denial, or chronic inaccessibility of the resources associated with power. Thus *parent* empowerment is the acquisition (or re-acquisition) and use of the resources that parents need to nurture and protect children, including adequate income, goods, and services (e.g., housing, medical care); a supportive network of other adults; time; legal authority; and personal skills and attributes (e.g., a deep understanding of one's children's unique strengths and needs, a sense of mastery over one's life).

We have known for many decades that most middle-class white teachers—with spectacular exceptions—are not very successful at teaching low-income minority preschool and primary children. The school failure statistics testify to our failure as a society and as educators. We also know, and have known for many decades, that parents' influence on their young children's self-esteem, mental health, motivations, aspirations, and self-imposed limitations is usually much more profound and permanent than is the influence of schools and other social institutions or individuals. Although in borderline cases where there are enough positive factors to build upon, all or any of the latter may push the child over the hump into "success," a basic fact of child development is that the feelings and beliefs of families—particularly parents—are basic.

Because a child's parents and peers are a greater influence on her than are "programs," a year, or two, or four in duration, the problem is not primarily tinkering with program quality within classroom walls (although all programs can get better, and most need to.) Focusing on the family is the wisest way to go.

If our goal is to create brighter futures for poor children, we need to "intervene" simultaneously with high-quality health, education, and other services to children, and in the *parents'* lives, by providing whatever is necessary to enable parents (or those serving in their places) to learn and earn their way out of poverty and take charge of improving their children's lives and future chances. Children probably will be impressed and motivated by their parents' efforts.

In the 1960s, CAP staff knew (as do "rapid reformists" wherever they are, and as do *all* poor people of normal intelligence, *all* African Americans, and so on), that significant social change in behalf of the underclass does not originate from, and is not facilitated by, most of the middle class—by conservatives knowledgeable about poverty or by liberal politicians, professionals, and academic gurus. They may invent theories. They may create policies. They may authorize laws and appropriate money. They may give grants, establish little model programs, and publish sleek reports about them. But few are willing to rock the boat too much. The populace will not let them; they cannot.

Significant social change—without which poverty will be reduced only in small, safe, institutional inching forward, on a one-by-one snail's pace basis—comes from masses of frustrated poor people, emboldened, organized, and guided by a well-informed, charismatic, and trusted leader (usually a former poor person), who articulates people's cumulative feelings that "we work hard, we're burdened with problems, our path is rife with roadblocks and blocked by deadends, and we deserve better"—and who, with support from rapid reformists and activist liberals, helps people focus on immediate practical goals. As they achieve their goals, often small goals at first, people develop a sense of their potential political power. "The powers that be" realize this too and begin to pay more attention to the projects being urgently advocated by low-income community people. The book I wrote back in 1969 describes an extraordinary example of this, the often cited, seldom described Child Development Group of Mississippi (Greenberg 1969/1990), as does the PBS video "Given a Chance" (1995).

More than thirty years of evidence from the nationwide Head Start program enables us to predict that "the establishment" will proudly permit a small, (safe) percentage of the people snared in the cycle of poverty to climb out of it, if they so choose.

Financial instability, insecurity, and powerlessness, combined with overwhelming busy-ness, tend to limit and distract us, to inhibit our compassionate, generous, and moral impulses. Although the extreme Right runs a noisy campaign against minorities, immigrants, gays, teenage mothers, poor people, and liberals, on the whole, it is probably not a matter of a less moral altruistic citizenry—a citizenry more racist, selfish, callous, and cruel—than we had in the sixties so much as a matter of lack of energy to be aware and a focus on the family instead of on our families and our larger society. In the sixties, there was excitement in the air. We thought we could successfully substantially reduce poverty. I wonder if that confidence and that high can be generated again.

NOTES

1. Even with all the thirty-something years of fanfare and flap about Head Start, there have been spaces for only 25 percent of the eligible children, and most of those enrolled have been offered only one year of half-day Head Start.

2. For a wonderfully researched and written background on the American race situation during and somewhat prior to this period, read Taylor Branch, *Parting the Waters: America in the King Years, 1954–63.* (New York, Simon and Schuster, 1988).

3. By that time, I was working for Jule Sugarman on starting Head Start. The Head Start Planning Committee was put together in large part by Dick Boone and Jule Sugarman, the person who almost single-handedly administered Head Start into instant nationwide existence. (Dr. Richmond had not yet been named to run it.)

4. Of course these programs "work" for many people, and in many ways. By 1996, Job Corps alone had served 1.8 million young people. Moreover, many people have learned through their experiences as Job Corps *teachers* how to teach this population more effectively and have taken their new skills into the public schools. There are many individual teachers and entire schools that are an exception to the rule that America scandalously neglects the education of its low-income children and youth.

Similarly, it was Sargent Shriver's intention—and is the reality—that many elementary teachers have become more sensitive to child development and to the needs and strengths of low-income families' children because of having worked in Head Start at some point.

5. For more about Head Start's origins from an OEO staffer's viewpoint, see Greenberg (1990) and Gillette (1997). Gillette, head of the Lyndon Baines Johnson Library's Oral History Project, interviewed all of Head Start's and OEO's key originators.

6. All quotes in this chapter that are dated 1979 and given page numbers are from Edward Zigler and Jeanette Valentine, ed., *Project Head Start: A Legacy of the War on Poverty* (New York: Free Press, 1979).

7. In August, 1969, four and a half years after Head Start was conceptualized, Ed Zigler moved to Washington from New Haven, where he had been on the faculty of Yale University for many years, where he served as the head of Head Start for three years.

8. Sergeant Shriver was also talking about attempting to make poor kids smarter so they would succeed in school, an idea he got listening to the mental retardation experts at his foundation. The Planning Committee was not opposed, but did not emphasize "I.Q. raising."

9. Thirteen million three to five year olds are enrolled in preschools, and 71 percent of them come from upper income families. We know the value of preschool and happy childhoods, for our children and, therefore, for all children.

10. At the time that Sargent Shriver, Jule Sugarman, and the Community Action Program were conceptualizing and actualizing Head Start, everyone was talking about anthropologist Oscar Lewis's book, which emphasized this point. I had learned many of these truths from my mother and earlier work by the time we were starting Head Start, and learned most of the others during my two years living in Mississippi, working with the CDGM (Child Development Group of Mississippi) (June, 1965/June, 1967). CDGM was run by 945 extremely poor African Americans serving on small community committees that hired the 2,272 parent employees who held all of the jobs in all of the Head Start centers serving 13,000 children in most Mississippi counties. CDGM received $12 million during the first summer of Head Start and many millions more in subsequent grants.

REFERENCES

Brain, G. (1979). Head Start, a retrospective view: The early planners. In Zigler, E. and Valentine, J. (Eds.), *Project Head Start: A legacy of the war on poverty*. New York: Free Press.

Cooke, R. 1979. Introduction. In Zigler, E., and Valentine, J. (Eds.), *Project Head Start: A legacy of the war on poverty*. New York: Free Press.

Eigen, L. 1990. Interview with author.

Gillette, M. L. 1996. The community action program, and an early success: Project Head Start. In *Launching the War on Poverty: An Oral History*. New York: Twayne/Simon and Schuster Macmillan.

Given a chance. 1995. Produced by Dante J. James for Blackside as part of the PBS series *America's War on Poverty*. Video Cassette.

Greenberg, P. 1990. Head Start—part of a multi-pronged anti-poverty effort for children and their families . . . before the beginning: A participant's view. *Young Children* Vol. 45, No. 6 41–52.

Greenberg, P. 1969/1990. *The devil has slippery shoes: A biased biography of the Child Development Group of Mississippi—A story of maximum feasible participation of poor parents*. Washington, D.C.: Youth Policy Institute.

Kozol, J. 1991. *Savage inequalities: Children in America's schools.* NY: Crown.

Pizzo, P. 1983. *Parent to parent: Working together for ourselves and our children.* Boston: Beacon.

Pizzo, P. 1987. Parent to parent support groups: Advocates for social change. In Kaman, L., Powell, D., Weissbourd, B., and Zigler, E. (Eds.), *America's family support programs.* New Haven, CT: Yale University Press.

Pizzo, P. 1990. Parent advocacy: A resource for early intervention. In Meisels, S., and Shonkoff, J. (Eds.), *Handbook of early childhood intervention.* New York: Cambridge University Press.

Pizzo, P. D. 1993. Parent empowerment and child care regulation. *Young Children,* Vol. 48, No. 6, 9–12.

Shriver, S. 1979. Head Start, a retrospective view: The founders. In Zigler, E., and Valentine, J. (Eds.), *Project Head Start: A legacy of the war on poverty.* New York: Free Press.

Sugarman, J. 1979. Head Start, a retrospective view: The early administrators. In Zigler, E. and Valentine, J. (Eds.), *Project Head Start: A legacy of the war on poverty.* New York: Free Press.

Turnbull, A. P., and Turnbull, H. R. (Eds.). 1978. *Parents speak out: Growing with a handicapped child.* Columbus, OH: Merrill.

Turnbull, A. P., and Turnbull, H. R. (Eds.). 1985. *Parents speak out: Then and now.* Columbus, OH: Merrill.

Wegman, M. 1979. Head Start, a retrospective view: The early planners. In Zigler, E., and Valentine, J. (Eds.), *Project Head Start: A legacy of the war on poverty.* New York: Free Press.

3

Beyond Busywork:
Crafting a Powerful Role for Low-Income
Mothers in Schools or Sustaining Inequalities?

Linda Spatig, Laurel Parrott, Amy Dillon, and
Kate Conrad

INTRODUCTION

Theresa Harmon's[1] involvement with her children's schooling did not begin until the youngest of her three children entered kindergarten. At that time Theresa accepted a personal invitation from a family service/parent specialist to visit the school's newly developed parent resource room. Three years later, she was working as a paid parent assistant in that same resource room, taking a leading role in the school's parent involvement efforts. This chapter tells the story of Theresa and eighteen other low-income mothers who participated in the parent involvement program of a Head Start to Public School Transition Demonstration Project in five elementary schools in West Virginia.

Theresa's previous lack of involvement in schooling is not surprising in light of recent parent involvement scholarship.[2] Low-income

Research for this chapter was funded by a grant from the Head Start Bureau of the Administration on Children, Youth, and Families. We are deeply grateful to the mothers profiled in this chapter. Their willingness to spend time with us and trust us enough to speak openly about their lives means a great deal to us, both personally and professionally. Also, we are grateful to the Transition staff members who so willingly allowed us to be a part of their daily work experiences.

73

parents have been, and continue to be, less involved than middle- and upper income parents (Epstein, 1995; Fruchter, Galletta, and White, 1993; Lareau, 1987; Simoni and Adelman, 1993). In addition, we know that lower income children have fewer successful school experiences in general (e.g., lower achievement, poorer attendance, greater drop-out rates) than middle- and upper income children. But many scholars of parent involvement argue that student achievement outcomes are positively affected by increased parent involvement. Walberg's (1984) meta-analysis, for example, suggested that parent involvement in school was even more predictive of children's academic success than socio-economic status. In response to this kind of information, many indi-viduals and groups, including some state departments of education, concluded that lower income children could do better in school if their parents were more involved. Consequently, there has been fairly broad support for parent involvement programs that specifically target low-income parents.

Much of the parent involvement literature represents a traditional functionalist conceptual framework (Sun, Hobbs, and Elder, 1994). That is, the focus is on how societal institutions, for example the family and the school, function interdependently for the good of the child, and ultimately, the society. Joyce Epstein's (1995) discussion of six types of parent involvement exemplifies work within this framework. She ex-plains how the school, the family, and the community provide "over-lapping spheres of influence" in which young people learn and develop. She argues that "good" parent involvement programs recognize the overlapping spheres of influence on student development and make an effort to bring those spheres closer together.

Within a functionalist framework then, the task of Head Start programs such as the Transition Demonstration Project is to provide poor children with the kind of support (including parent involvement in schooling) that will enable them to take advantage of opportunities provided within the current, basically fair, social system. In other words, Head Start need not fundamentally challenge the societal status quo. Rather, it should be about the business of helping poor children and families function more successfully within it.

Conflict theory provides a different conceptual approach, chal-lenging the functionalist assumption of a basically fair, meritocratic social system. Indeed, conflict theory begins with a recognition of built-in social system inequalities, such as those related to social class, gen-der, and race. From this perspective, it is the inherently unfair system itself that must be exposed and challenged.

Drawing on conflict theory, Lareau (1987) examined the issue of parent involvement in relation to Bourdieu's (1977) idea of cultural capital. Lareau's comparative ethnography of parent involvement in lower and upper income schools reveals that higher social class provides parents with more resources (greater cultural capital) to become involved in schooling. If upper income parents activate their resources (invest their capital), there is often an educational pay-off for their children. In other words, Lareau is arguing that lower levels of low-income parent involvement are not a result of low-income parents valuing education less than high-income familes; nor is the lack of involvement a result of institutional discrimination in the form of teachers expecting and asking for less or different kinds of involvement from low-income families. Rather, the different levels and kinds of involvement are a result of social class inequalities.

> Social class offered parents, and ultimately children, an advantage in discovering and complying with [school] standards. It facilitated—or impeded—parents' educational involvement in terms of the amount of work they did with children at home, the kind of work they did at home, and the interpretation they made of why they attended school events. Most importantly, social class position largely excluded working-class parents from taking a leadership role in education and gave upper-middle class parents the opportunity to take such a role (if they wanted to). . . . Social class gave children a home advantage. (Lareau 1987, 176)

Along the same lines, in this chapter we depart from a functionalist approach and examine parent involvement in light of prevailing gender and class inequalities. Examining the Head Start Transition Demonstration Project in relation to societal inequalities is essential. After all, Head Start is a major social reform effort designed to break the cycle of poverty in the United States. As such, it is reasonable to expect it to challenge, rather than support, the inequitable system that continues to spawn such poverty. There is no question that Head Start has succeeded in assisting some children and their families to live more comfortably; and the value of this, particularly to the individuals who have benefitted, should not be underestimated. However, to the extent that Head Start also has played a role in sustaining an inherently unequal social system, with the wealth and comfort of the elite dependent upon the impoverishment of low-income workers and those who are unemployed, it certainly has not broken the cycle of poverty in this country.

Drawing on observation and interview data collected over a three-and-one-half-year period, we discuss the nature of low-income mothers' experiences with their children's schooling and with the Head Start Transition Demonstration Project (TDP) in West Virginia. Our discussion focuses on the extent to which school and project experiences benefitted them and their children personally as well as the extent to which the experiences strengthened or challenged broader social inequalities.

Laurel, Amy, and Kate are ethnographers, employed by the Transition Demonstration Project, upon whose observational and interview data this chapter is based. Linda is a university-based researcher (coordinating the qualitative evaluation of the Transition Project) who provided guidance and support to the data gathering, and who took the lead on coding, analyzing, and writing. Each ethnographer focused on one or more of five project schools and developed relationships of various strengths and duration with participants and stakeholders, including the nineteen women whose experiences are discussed here.

After a brief introduction to the Transition Project, especially its parent involvement component, this chapter focuses on the nineteen mothers, beginning with an examination of their past and present lives as Appalachian women. Then we discuss the mothers' experiences as school and project volunteers, addressing personal and societal implications of their experiences.

THE HEAD START PUBLIC SCHOOL TRANSITION DEMONSTRATION PROJECT AS CONTEXT

The Head Start Public School Transition Demonstration Project (TDP) is a federally funded social reform effort designed to provide low-income children and their families with continuous Head Start–like services through the early elementary years. This includes comprehensive health and social services, parent involvement activities, and the provision of developmentally oriented schooling experiences. The goal is for low-income children (e.g., those who were previously in Head Start) to maintain gains, academic and otherwise, that they made in the Head Start program. The West Virginia project is part of a national research study of approximately thirty local Transition Projects. As in all Head Start programs, one of the major components of the Transition Projects is facilitation of parent involvement in children's education.

The general purpose of the parent involvement component of the West Virginia TDP is to "support and enhance the role of parents as the major influence in a child's development and education" (Grant proposal, 1991). In fact, a fundamental tenet of the West Virginia TDP was the belief that the best way to have an impact on children's lives is to help the adults who are important in their lives. Project founders expected this approach to "provide continuity and increase children's chances of success in school." The proposal goes on to say that parents know their own children better than teachers do, want good things for their children, and need support and nurturing in order to develop confidence in themselves as parents. The following three goals represent the original vision of the West Virginia TDP parent involvement component:

1. providing opportunities for parents to extend their knowledge and understanding of the educational and developmental needs of young children;

2. involving parents in curriculum development as well as school- and project-related decision making and;

3. familiarizing parents with the Transition Project and including them in the evaluation of it.

Transition Project staff members at the West Virginia site included six family service/parent specialists responsible for addressing social service needs of Transition families (similar to the role of a social worker) as well as coordinating parent involvement efforts. One family service/parent specialist was assigned to each of four small schools, and two were assigned to the larger school. One nurse, one social services/parent involvement coordinator, one project director, one executive director, and one consultant served all five schools. About a year and a half into the project, five parent volunteers were hired to work as part-time parent assistants, one in each school. To some extent, all staff members worked toward meeting the project's parent involvement goals. However, most of the frontline, day-to-day work was accomplished by family service/parent specialists and parent assistants assigned to particular schools.

TDP schools were located in poor communities in two adjacent counties. Two schools were in rural, mountainous areas, and three were in a small city. The most rural school had 275 children and was wedged between a small river and railroad tracks which run about thirty feet from the school. The playground was a partially paved area with no equipment other than two broken basketball goals, neither of which had nets. In contrast, the largest school, with 579 students, was located in a city. The school was relatively new, featuring a well-stocked library (one of the few elementary school libraries in the county) as well as several well-equipped playgrounds. In four schools, between 70 and 80 percent of the students received free or reduced-cost lunch. In the other school, one of those in the small city, approximately 50 percent qualified for these subsidies.

In each school, the family service/parent specialist(s) worked with available parents to set up a parent resource room that served a variety of functions. The rooms were organized as lending libraries where parents could borrow books and educational games to use with their children. Books about child development and educational activities also were available for adults. The rooms were to be places where parents could feel at home in the schools, where they could meet and talk informally and attend meetings and workshops. The rooms also provided a place for parents to perform school volunteer work and for TDP staff to meet with parents to plan activities.

Some parent involvement activities, such as a parent discussion group and meetings about attention deficit disorder, directly related to the project's goal to educate parents about child development and schooling matters. Others were less directly related. For example, parents participated in social get-togethers, such as bowling parties, shopping trips and cosmetic make-overs. Also, they attended workshops on topics of personal interest such as women's health and credit counseling. In addition to participating in planned activities, parents spent countless hours providing assistance to teachers and schools. Many of the parents served on the TDP Governing Board. The parent involvement experiences will be described more fully in a later section of the chapter.

Whereas the Transition Project attracted both low- and middle-income parents (including a few fathers) and individuals' involvement ranged from sporadic to nearly full-time, this chapter tells the stories of nineteen low-income mothers who were regularly involved for some time. They volunteered in the school or attended activities on a daily, weekly, or monthly basis over a period of at least a few months.

THE MOTHERS AS APPALACHIAN WOMEN

To understand the relationship between these mothers' experiences with school involvement and the reproduction or transformation of social inequalities, we need to contextualize their circumstances as women in Appalachia. Appalachia is a region that stretches along a mountain range from western New York to northern Georgia, including parts of twelve states (New York, Pennsylvania, Maryland, Ohio, Kentucky, Virginia, Tennessee, North Carolina, South Carolina, Georgia, Mississippi, Alabama) and all of the state of West Virginia. It is an area where extreme human poverty is juxtaposed with rich natural resources and inequalities are blatant. The majority of the residents are poor, but a relatively small number of people—many of whom are not residents—benefit from the wealth generated from the extraction of natural resources (Gaventa 1982).

With the exception of one African American, the nineteen mothers we studied are white and range in age from twenty-three to thirty-eight. They lived on annual family incomes ranging from $3,754 to $19,000. Five of the women were employed, two as part-time employees of the project itself. Sixteen women were married or living with male partners; three were separated or divorced. All but two women had family incomes at or below the federal poverty guidelines.[3] The two women with family incomes over the poverty guidelines had husbands who work in construction. Whereas their family income disqualified them from most public assistance, children from both families were participants in Save the Children, whose income guidelines were slightly higher.

For the most part, the women grew up in small towns and rural communities in the region. Many of them did not finish high school, and they described their parents as having little formal education and being uninvolved in their children's schooling. For example, Theresa Harmon, who stopped attending school after ninth grade in order to take care of her sick father, explained that neither of her parents attended school beyond eighth grade. In this sense, she is typical of many Appalachian women who are undereducated and un- or underemployed. In this section of the chapter, we weave together the stories of these nineteen women with information about the Appalachian region generally.

Families of Origin

These women were raised by parents who, for the most part, had little formal education and were sporadically employed in low-paying, low-status jobs. As children in poor families, they learned to do with little, or to do without, in terms of material goods. For Brenda Morris and her brothers and sisters growing up on a small farm, money was scarce. Her father worked at a factory job, while her mother stayed home to raise the kids. "With five kids and just one working, money was tight." She remembered getting one pair of shoes and one toy each year. "When we were growing up, I think we got our last toy when we were ten or twelve years old. Each year [each of us] could choose one toy from the JC Penney's catalog." Although material comforts were sparse, Brenda recalled a happy, busy childhood: "[Once a year] Daddy would sell a hog and we'd go get our school clothes. It sounds terrible now, but it really wasn't. . . . I was happy, so I guess that's the main thing. . . . We weren't like kids nowadays, sitting in front of the boob tube all the time. . . . We were always busy, but [we] played, too."

In some ways, Brenda's fond childhood memories differ from those of the other women, many of whom described their early years in terms of emotional insecurity and anxiety that often go hand in hand with poverty. The families in which many of these women grew up were often unsteady, characterized by crises and upheavals such as parental separation, abandonment, job insecurity or unemployment, and struggles with alcoholism and other illnesses. For example, at age six Rhonda Dixon was temporarily abandoned by her parents. "When they got divorced . . . my mother left, and me and my three sisters were all in different homes for years. . . . We were all split up separate. . . . For about six years I didn't see my mother. My father, I never heard from him. . . ." She recalled her unhappiness with her "foster" family and discussed it in relation to her early school experiences.

> I didn't like them. . . . I tried to run away. . . . [Were you part of their family?] No. I just felt like I was there to have a house to live in. . . . If I needed help with something I just did it myself or I wouldn't get it done. . . . They never helped me with nothing that I can remember. . . . I failed first grade from all these problems. . . . I would always keep to myself. I never talked to anyone. I never participated in class. I sat in class one day and cried and peed on myself.

Rhonda, who lived with her mother again after a six-year separation, also failed fifth grade and dropped out of school after completing the ninth grade. She was pregnant with her first child when she left school. It was thirteen years before she regained contact with her father, an alcoholic living out of state.

Penny Wheeler's parents also split up when she was a child. Although she was not physically abandoned as a result, she describes her parents as having taken no interest in their kids. Her mom worked as a custodian in the elementary school Penny attended; however, she "never did anything to reinforce school. Homework didn't matter. Being involved with the kids didn't matter."

Along the same lines, Sharon Ramsey said that her parents "didn't care—neither one of them. They were alcoholics." Neither of her parents helped her with schoolwork or got involved in the school in any way. She recalled how the school bus driver used to drop her off at a bar because that's where her parents were. Sharon dropped out of school in the eleventh grade.

The experiences of these women are typical of women in the region. Hannah (1995) reports high rates of poverty among West Virginia families, with 16 percent of all West Virginia families living in poverty as of 1989. However, the situation for women and children in that state is worse than this percentage suggests. In West Virginia, as in the United States overall, more women than men live in poverty. In 1989, the West Virginia rates were 21 percent for females compared to 18 percent for males. Sadly, the highest poverty rates are among children. Sixty percent of West Virginia children living with a single mother lived in poverty in 1989, compared with 36 percent living with a single father. According to the 1995 *Kids Count Data Book*, 28 percent of all children in West Virginia were living in poverty.

Not surprisingly, Hannah also reports that West Virginia families headed by nonhigh school graduates were more than twice as likely to live in poverty as those headed by high school graduates. Most of the mothers we studied grew up, and continue to live, in families such as these. According to the statistics Hannah compiled, as of 1990, 34 percent of West Virginia women over age twenty-five had not graduated from high school. The West Virginia Department of Education reports that about 17 percent of female dropouts in West Virginia cited marriage, pregnancy, or both as their reason(s) for dropping out of school. In 1990, 18 percent of all babies born in West Virginia had mothers under the age of twenty (Hannah, 1995).

Current Life Circumstances

It is common for individuals, especially those of modest financial circumstances, to express a desire for their children to "do better than I did" in terms of educational attainment and occupational success. It is not clear that the current life circumstances of the women we studied represent an improvement over those in their families of origin. General information concerning the education and employment status of these women is not the same as getting a glimpse of their everyday lives and experiences. Getting such a glimpse is important in terms of contextualizing the parent involvement experiences of these women. Such contextualization is critical to understanding the parent involvement experiences in terms of their meaning and implications for the women and their children, as well as for the schools and society.

In this section of the chapter, we focus on three mothers, each chosen to illustrate particular circumstances and issues that emerged as significant in this group of women. Brenda is a high school graduate employed full-time in a factory; the other two, Theresa and Tanya, dropped out of school in the tenth grade. Tanya was unemployed, and Theresa went from unemployment to working two, sometimes three, part-time jobs during the course of this study.

Brenda Morris

Brenda Morris is the thirty-eight-year-old mother of two children, a daughter (Chrissy) in second grade and a son (Joseph) in seventh. During the time of this study she was divorced from Frank, who paid no child support and was unemployed and living "on the street and at the mission." Prior to that, Frank had held a twelve-dollar-an-hour job. According to Brenda, he did not assist her financially while he was employed and said he would quit his job if he had to pay child support. Moreover, Frank has had virtually no contact with the children since the divorce five years ago. Their separation and divorce were precipitated by Frank's involvement with another woman and their physical assault on Brenda. In an interview, Brenda recalled what happened five years ago when she moved out of the house: "Frank and his girlfriend come to the house, opened the door, tore my phone out of the wall and he sat on me while she kicked the s-h-i-t out of me; beat the tar out of me—in front of the kids."

Brenda has worked as a seamstress at a local clothing factory for eighteen years. She "hates" her "dead-end" job at the factory where "they have no feelings for you whatsoever. None." Her job, sewing the notched part of the waistband of slacks, was piecework: "You have to put out so many pairs of pants a day to make so much money." If she completed a thousand pairs of pants a day, she made ten dollars an hour. She occasionally accomplished this, but it was difficult because of the carpal tunnel syndrome in both her arms—a condition afflicting many of the women who work at the factory. She worked half-time for months after having surgery for this condition, which comes from making the same movements over and over again. Her half-time daily quota was 550 pairs of pants. "Sometimes I can; sometimes I can't. It depends on how bad my hands are hurting. Because the more I do, the more my hands hurt."

Her daughter, Chrissy, has had extensive health problems, including four bouts with pneumonia. She was hospitalized at age three for pneumonia, asthma, and bronchitis. When she came home from the hospital Brenda had to purchase a breathing machine and give her breathing treatments four times a day. Brenda was off work an additional three weeks after Chrissy was discharged from the hospital. As a result, the factory issued her a warning for absenteeism, saying her daughter's hospitalization was "no excuse."

Brenda began volunteering at her daughter's school for the first time this year. It was a way to get out of the house and avoid boredom and depression while recuperating from the carpal tunnel surgery. "That's when I started volunteering here, because I was bored sitting at home. It was either sit home and watch soap operas, or sit home and eat. I couldn't sew. I couldn't do any of my crafts, so I was bored." Brenda became a reliable volunteer, spending most of her volunteer time copying, laminating, making booklets, and doing other clerical work for teachers.

Tanya Walker

Tanya is the twenty-five-year-old mother of Sarah, a first grader. She divorced Sarah's father ("because he let his thirteen year old hit me") when Sarah was three years old. At the time of this writing she was receiving three hundred dollars a month for child support. She lived in a small one-bedroom apartment with her daughter and her male partner Jeff, who worked full-time in shipping and receiving. Sarah had the bedroom, and Tanya and Jeff slept on the couch.

Tanya dropped out of school in tenth grade and has tried unsuccessfully to get her GED several times: "I loved school. . . . I done good all the way up until I . . . hit eighth grade. I failed eighth grade, as a matter of fact, because I didn't like it. . . . I thought I would do better if I went [to a different school] but I didn't. I quit in tenth grade." Tanya was unhappy with her relationship with Jeff who has physically abused her (most recently giving her a black eye and bruised chest) and tried to control her.

> I love him to death, but I'm tired of being bossed around. I'm not allowed to do anything. He's one of those jealous types. I'm not supposed to talk to nobody. He gets mad when I volunteer up here. . . . In the evenings, it's bad. . . . When he comes home he's like—he wants me right there with him, and it's hard to be with [Sarah] with him hollering at me every five minutes. . . . When he's home he don't want me doing nothing. I can't leave. I'm not allowed to go nowhere. Like if he's home, . . . I can't even go in the kitchen to do dishes.

Because Tanya was unemployed and received only the monthly child support payments, she was dependent on Jeff for financial support. "He gets paid every week, and I don't see hardly none of it. He gets mad if I want to go spend some of it. I did get me a new purse last night. . . . He's controlling. . . . It's hard. He drinks. He drinks every evening." Tanya volunteered at school (mostly laminating, cutting, copying, "just whatever I can do to help the teachers") in order to get away from the apartment during the day. She explained that the reason she came to school most every day was to

> [be] around people. . . . Because you know, I'm home all by myself, and then I come up here, and I mainly come up here to help out and have somebody to talk to. It gets lonely. . . . I'd go insane sitting at my house all the time. . . . I don't get around. I keep my car every once in a while to go to the grocery store or something. . . . It takes me two hours at the grocery store. . . . It's peaceful. . . . I do it just to get away. . . . But I don't get out very much. . . . He don't want me to go anywhere.

More than anything, Tanya wanted to get a GED so she could obtain a good job and reduce her dependency on others.

> I want a job. I don't have the education to do it. I worked for four months before I turned eighteen. I bagged groceries. I loved it. I was bringing in my own money. I didn't have to depend on my mom and her boyfriend for nothing. I would give them gas money to take me for my GED. I bought my own clothes and stuff. I've never really been on my own, because I went from my mom and got married and got out of that situation, and then I met Jeff. . . . It's hard. . . . I would like to learn some independence, because I depend on everybody else.

Theresa Harmon

Theresa Harmon is the thirty-seven-year-old mother of three children—Steven, age seventeen, Nathan, age ten, and Angela, age eight. Recently she married Nathan and Angela's father, Tony, with whom she had been living for thirteen years. Tony works at a car wash when weather permits. When this project began three years ago, Theresa was unemployed and receiving public assistance in the form of food stamps and a welfare check; she, Tony, and their two children were living in a public housing facility near the elementary school the younger two children attend. In order to enable Theresa and the children to receive a more substantial welfare check, Tony also maintained a small apartment as his official residence. Theresa often voiced concerns about living in the housing project. When she moved there she specifically requested an apartment on the outside of the complex, closest to the street, hoping this location would enable her children to escape some of the negative activities of the inner complex. She often did not permit her children to play outside and expressed feelings of shame about living there. As it turns out, the Transition Demonstration Project played a major role in facilitating her move away from the housing facility.

Theresa became actively involved in the parent resource room in September 1992, when a family service/parent specialist invited her to volunteer at the school. Eventually, Theresa became a paid parent assistant in the project, a role that involved working part-time (fifteen hours per week at $4.25 per hour at the beginning), basically keeping the parent resource room organized and functioning. She enjoyed working in the parent resource room and getting paid for it, but the paycheck created unexpected problems. As a result of her part-time employment with the project, her rent in the public housing complex increased from fifteen dollars to sixty-two dollars a month. In addition, her food stamp allocation was reduced by thirty dollars and her welfare check was reduced by ninety-eight dollars. Theresa worked with individuals at the Welfare Department to address her financial concerns. One case worker commented that it did not pay for her to get a job, saying she could do just as well on full welfare. At one point, Theresa commented that she "couldn't win for losing" and wondered if the job was worth the trouble. After a great deal of deliberation, she decided to continue in the parent assistant position, primarily because she enjoyed the work experience and "loved" the school.

In September 1994, when Theresa was rehired as a parent assistant at the same school, her hours were increased to thirty per week and her pay was increased to $5.00 an hour. This enabled her to move from the housing project into a rented house at the foot of the hill below the school. However, the increase in hours and pay also resulted in Theresa losing all public assistance. In order to pay her bills, it was necessary for her to take another part-time job, working the night shift (typically 11:00 P.M.—7:00 A.M.) as a nursing assistant for an agency that contracted with hospitals, convalescent centers, and the like. This job paid $5.75 an hour, with no benefits. Working both jobs, Theresa was barely able to fulfill her financial obligations. For some time she took on a third part-time job, independently contracting to sit with an elderly, bedridden neighbor on Sundays.

In addition to feeling the strain of a tenuous financial situation in terms of making ends meet from week to week, Theresa's jobs took an enormous toll on her physically and emotionally. Some weeks she worked as much as 94 hours in a six-day period. When she was offered overtime in her night job, she felt compelled to accept the work. The following entries written in her journal illustrate how difficult the experience was.

Well, it's September 23rd and I'm at my 11–7 job. I really hate having to get the kids up out of bed just to bring me to work. Nathan has already said he wants me to quit. I guess he just doesn't understand that I have no choice. I miss being at home at night . . . I want to go to sleep in my bed at home. It's hard sitting up all night. . . . It's 2:30 A.M. and Mrs. Carson just had a breathing spell. I have to stay beside her while she is like this. . . . September 26th—Well, I had an awful day. I don't think it could have been any worse than it was. I left here [night job] at 7 A.M. I went home. I decided to go to work at school at 10 A.M. instead of 8 A.M. because I was tired and sleepy so I slept from 8:30 til 9:30. One hour. Got up, went to work. Worked for the teachers copying, laminating, cutting out, [and] cleaned out the storage closet and shelves in [the parent resource room]. Got off work at 3 P.M., went home and found out that I didn't win the $20 that I thought I did. . . . That was OK. I still had $12 left after I spent $8 at the store out of the $20 from working. . . . [Later that evening] Tony started accusing me of stupid things as he usually does. I just can't believe how he acts sometimes. I bust my butt for my family and no one cares. I get no respect at all for working two jobs, cleaning the house, washing dishes, doing laundry, watching the kids, paying bills, cooking [and] getting *NO REST* at all. And no one cares about me. I wonder sometimes why God hasn't taken my life before now. Why don't I ever get anything in return for what I'm doing for my husband and my kids? All I've ever wanted to do is make a home for them, but it seems like I can't do nothing right. . . . If they only knew how much I care for them. I miss them when I'm down here watching Mrs. Carson. . . . I do it for them, . . . but I guess it's not enough. It's just not enough.

Whereas the details of the women's experiences differ, these three women (as well as others in the group we studied) had several things in common with each other, as well as with other low-income women. They received little or no support from, and in some cases were abused by, their male partners; they were financially dependent upon public assistance, male partners, and/or low-status, low-paying jobs; and they experienced emotional and social isolation. Additionally, all of these women were regularly involved in their children's schools at least in part because of the Transition Demonstration Project.

THE WOMEN AS INVOLVED PARENTS

In this section of the chapter, we describe the kinds of parent involvement activities the Transition Project provided as well as the nature of the mothers' experiences with and perceptions of the activities. For purposes of this discussion, we have separated the activities into the following five categories:

1. Social get-togethers;

2. Activities to encourage parent's personal development;

3. Assistance for teachers and schools;

4. Activities concerning parenting to enhance children's development and learning; and

5. Membership on the Transition Project Governing Board.

First, activities in each category are described and discussed in terms of benefits for the mothers as well as in terms of their consistency with TDP goals for parent involvement. For example, we discuss how some activities, while personally meaningful and valuable to the mothers (and their children) we studied, probably did little to enhance the mothers' knowledge of educational and developmental issues or to assist them in playing meaningful decision-making roles in their children's schooling. Then we examine the parent involvement experiences in terms of educational pay-offs for the children of these women, exploring the possibility that children did not benefit academically as a result of their mothers' involvement with the Transition Project and the schools. Finally, we return to the question of social reproduction, arguing that the parent involvement experiences may have served to strengthen, rather than to challenge, current gender and class inequalities.

Social Get-Togethers

During the initial phase of the project, a major focus was on doing whatever was necessary to get parents into the schools. Early on, staff members discovered that one way to attract parents to the school was to provide social get-togethers of various kinds. Craft activities, a major Appalachian tradition, were a favorite of many mothers, some of whom appreciated them as vehicles for getting parents involved in the schools: "There was a couple of parents . . . in the [craft] workshop that had no involvement in this school until the workshop started. . . . I think . . . doing this workshop is really going to get more parents involved. . . . After they start getting involved with the workshops, then they will . . . get more involved in school" (Parent interview).

Many craft workshops were offered in the five project schools, especially during the first two years of the project. Typically, these consisted of three to ten mothers and a couple of project staff members getting together to make items such as trinket boxes, Halloween decorations, paper twist baskets, scented hot pads, fall wreaths, cloth dolls, boo-boo bunnies, potato sack dolls, wallpaper fans, and Christmas ornaments, sweatshirts, and angels. Whereas the stated objective (e.g., on flyers advertising the events) of each workshop focused on producing a particular type of craft item, the workshops served another purpose as well; they provided opportunities for social interaction. A Valentine's craft workshop, for example, was an occasion for the six mothers who attended to make lace hearts, have refreshments, and engage in conversation. Carol Russell, a mother of two who was previously hospitalized as a result of physical abuse by her first husband, led the workshop.

> When people came in, they found a seat around the table. . . . Several people admired the heart that Carol had done up earlier. . . . Carol explained that she had free-handed the rose and then filled it in with colorful fabric glue. . . . There were a lot of different conversations

> going on in the room. . . . Mostly it was individual conversations between two or maybe three people. . . . Much of the conversation . . . had to do with the hearts themselves—helping each other choose which lace and ribbons looked good together, deciding where to place flowers and beads, and asking how well the glue worked. (Fieldnotes)

Conversations at craft workshops usually were not related to parenting, child development, or schooling issues. The craft workshops, as well as other social get-togethers discussed below, were mainly vehicles for recruiting new parents as well as providing comfortable and enjoyable activities for regular parent volunteers.

In addition to craft workshops, TDP arranged other types of social get-togethers for parents. These included a tea and fashion show, cosmetic make-over sessions, mall shopping, bowling, cake decorating, and gift wrapping classes. Such activities provided opportunities for the mothers who attended to enjoy themselves and to meet and interact socially with other mothers and with TDP staff members. As with the craft activities, a primary goal was to recruit parents to the schools. As one staff member put it, "If going to the flea market is the only way to get parents in, then it's good."

The Transition Project also arranged social get-togethers for parents and children together. Examples of these activities included bowling, skating, swimming, and trips, for example, to an Ice Capades performance and to a children's museum. These events provided opportunities, and sometimes encouragement, for parents to playfully interact with their children, as illustrated by fieldnotes of a skating party: "I counted about fifteen kids skating. . . . There were two adults skating. . . . Most parents were sitting around the side watching their kids skate. . . . More parents went and got skates after [a project family service parent specialist] and I were skating around. They held hands with their kids and smiled and laughed. The parents and kids were having fun together" (Fieldnotes).

The social get-togethers were occasions for relaxation and enjoyment for TDP staff, parents, and sometimes children. Moreover, they proved to be successful methods of recruiting at least a small group of regular parent volunteers in most schools and in familiarizing these volunteers with the Transition Demonstration Project. However, the social get-togethers probably did not accomplish much in terms of TDP's goals of extending parents' knowledge and understanding of the educational and developmental needs of young children and involving parents in curriculum development and school decision making. Recently, project administrators made an attempt to reduce the number of social get-togethers, such as craft activities, by stipulating that only parent activities with an educational component may be supported by TDP funds.

Activities for Personal Development

In addition to social get-togethers, the Transition Project arranged numerous activities which offered parents opportunities for expanding their knowledge and skills in a variety of ways. Most activities were single sessions on a particular topic in which parents, primarily those who were regular volunteers, had expressed an interest. Many of the sessions, which addressed issues such as women's health, assertiveness training, and credit counseling, consisted of a speaker presenting information and then answering parents' questions. At a credit counseling workshop, for example, a speaker from the local credit counseling office presented information about the importance of spending wisely, developing a budget that factors in all family member expenses, getting out of debt, and handling problems with a credit bureau.

Similarly, two of the low-income mothers we studied attended an assertiveness training workshop, where a member of the local mental health community talked about three elements needed for assertiveness: good self-esteem, good communication skills, and conflict resolution skills. She equated assertiveness with expressing one's wants, needs, and opinions, saying, "You need to know your values and rights, and you need to be persistent." The women who attended were particularly interested in discussing parenting issues, such as saying no to young children, and relationship issues, such as arguments with husbands and male friends. Unfortunately, the presenter directed most of her remarks to other issues, such as dealing with bosses (four of the five women attending the workshop were not employed) and how teenagers can be assertive even in the face of strong peer pressure. Nevertheless, Theresa Harmon said she benefitted from the workshop: "I learned a lot. I've learned to say no to a lot of things. . . . I need to say no once in a while, and a lot of other girls [do too]. . . . If it wouldn't have been for the project they wouldn't have gotten that. That's something Transition offered these parents."

Some of the personal development activities were ongoing classes. For example, CPR classes, which were held in all five schools, consisted of three half-day sessions. Parents who attended all three sessions and passed an examination were certified in CPR. Along the same lines, TDP organized, or helped to organize, ongoing GED classes in two schools and a series of computer classes in three schools.

Activities in the personal development category certainly could be construed as positive experiences for the women we studied, offering them opportunities to gain knowledge and/or skills that may be useful in securing paid employment at a later time and that may enable them to have fuller and more healthy, satisfying lives. In the sense that many of the sessions were initiated at the suggestion of one or more of the mothers themselves, they also were consistent with TDP's goal of involving parents in project-related decision making. However, as in the case of the social get-togethers discussed above, it would be difficult to argue that the personal development activities were helpful in meeting TDP's goal of extending parents' knowledge and understanding of the educational and developmental needs of young children.

However, the social get-togethers and personal development activities *were* consistent with the Transition Project's desire to nurture and support parents. In a staff-meeting discussion of the value of these kinds of parent activities, a staff member articulated a position defending the value of providing support, both educational and personal, to parents. In her view, a person who feels good about him- or herself will be a better parent. Whereas the personal development activities were not directly related to knowledge and skills concerning child development and schooling, participation in them may have had an indirect beneficial influence on these mothers' parenting.

Assistance for Teachers and Schools

Social get-togethers and personal development activities, discussed above, occurred with some regularity—approximately one or two a month in each project school. At the same time, a cadre of "regulars" began to gather in the five schools on a regular, often daily, basis. For the most part, these women, including many of the nineteen low-income mothers we studied, as well as others, spent their time in the parent resource rooms. They worked with family service/parent specialists to organize resource-room lending materials and plan for parent and parent-child activities such as those discussed above. Often at the suggestion or encouragement of project staff, the women also spent their time working for the teachers and the schools. In some cases, TDP coordinated the parent assistance with other parent groups, such as PTA. In other cases, TDP was solely responsible for organizing the teacher and school assistance activities.

The regular volunteers provided a great deal of assistance to the schools. They helped with tasks, such as schoolwide vision screening, weight and height checks, and fluoride rinses. They assisted with clerical work, such as recording school attendance data and maintaining records for schoolwide programs such as Read with Me, where children submit the number of pages or minutes they read at home each day or week. They were the organizers and workers at school book fairs, and they were the Friday popcorn poppers. They wrote, typed, copied, and distributed school newsletters and yearbooks. They renovated and redecorated school bathrooms, lounges, and parent rooms. They raised money, in some cases large sums of money, for schools to use for expenditures, such as playground equipment and fieldtrips.

A particularly noteworthy fundraising effort was made by a group of parents whose goal was to build a playground for one of the rural schools. The effort began with a few middle-income parents trying to interest school and community people in developing the playground. These parents approached the school's family service/parent specialist and received a favorable response. Parents in the group, which eventually included two of the rural low-income mothers we studied, spent countless hours and days primarily focused on raising money. Beginning with a hot dog sale that raised almost $500, the group (operating in one of the most impoverished communities in the area) went on to raise over $100,000 over the next two years. The list of their fundraising activities is enormous, including, for example, organizing raffles, making and selling crafts, collecting pennies in classrooms, and selling tickets to events such as spaghetti dinners and skating parties. In addition, they successfully solicited funds from the local school district as well as grant money to support their project.

Whereas the women we studied spent countless hours working on schoolwide projects such as those discussed above, they spent as much or more time working directly for teachers. Some of this work involved assisting teachers by working in the classrooms with children (e.g., reading aloud to the class or tutoring an individual child). However, most of the work was of a clerical nature, involving tremendous amounts of photocopying, cutting, stapling, gluing, laminating, and the like. At some schools, the volunteers were almost overwhelmed with teacher requests for this kind of assistance. For example, Penny Wheeler, a parent assistant, was once "bogged down" to the point of crying, saying, "If I'm spending all my time doing this [paperwork for teachers], I'm not spending enough time recruiting more parents." Not only the paid parent assistants experienced this strain. Carol Russell, a parent at the same school, stayed up an entire night cutting out shapes that second grade teachers wanted to use in preparation for an upcoming achievement test.

Volunteers at other schools also were swamped with teacher requests for clerical assistance. For example, Theresa Harmon (the mother working two, sometimes three, part-time jobs) talked about teachers at her school who sometimes expected too much of the mothers who volunteer:

> They take advantage of us being here and doing the materials they want done—lamination, copying, etc. . . . And I know they need the materials in their room, . . . but I just think they sometimes take advantage of it because they don't just bring in one or two items. They bring a whole stack in. We have to laminate it and cut it out. . . . You can't imagine some of the things we've had up here. We've worked from the time we came in of the morning to the time we went home. . . . The other day I had a stack, you couldn't imagine the stack I had to copy. I had to sit in a chair because my back was hurting. . . . I mean, it was like five or six [reading] books each grade.

As mentioned above, some volunteers assisted teachers in their classrooms on occasion, but this was not the norm for the women in our study. In some cases, this was because the mothers felt uncomfortable assisting in the classroom. More often, it was a result of teachers' preferences. For example, a teacher explained to us that she was uncomfortable having people in her room and that she was not good at delegating responsibility. The mothers were aware that some teachers did not want parents in their rooms, and they believed it was the teachers' prerogative to determine whether and how a parent might assist. In discussing the kinds of things parent volunteers did in her school, for example, Theresa explained, "Well, some read aloud. With some of the teachers we're allowed to do that. It's just according to the teachers—what teachers want done—[whether the] teachers want parents in their class. A lot of them might not want parents in their class, to interrupt and stuff like that. . . . That's their privilege not to want it. That's fine with us if they don't want it."

Obviously, the mothers provided much-needed and valuable support services for teachers and schools, and in some cases, the broader school community. One teacher commented that she was able to arrive at school half an hour later thanks to having the assistance of the volunteers at her school. But how did this kind of school involvement benefit the mothers and their children? As some mothers commented above, these activities—often carried out in the parent resource room in the company of other mothers—were preferable to being bored and lonely at home. In that sense, they were similar to the social get-togethers and personal development activities in providing a respite for women seeking opportunities for enjoyable and meaningful social interaction. Also, providing these services for schools and teachers may have been personally satisfying to these women because they felt a sense of accomplishment in being able to make a contribution to their children's schools. But we are still left with the question—To what extent were the support services, primarily in the form of clerical work for teachers, consistent with the project's goals of enhancing parents' knowledge and understanding of educational and developmental needs of young children and involving parents in curriculum development and decision making?

Parenting and Education

Periodically, a parent, staff member, or teacher questioned the infrequency of TDP-sponsored parent activities directly related to children's success in schools. For example, in a staff-meeting discussion of the parent involvement component of the project, a family service/parent specialist pointed out the discrepancy between a major project goal—in her words, "to improve the kids' ability in school," and the nature of the project's work with parents. She argued for trying to involve parents in activities more directly related to what their children were doing in school. In this section of the chapter we discuss TDP-provided opportunities for parents to become more knowledgeable about formal schooling and about parenting issues relevant to the academic success of their children. It is important to note that these kinds of parent activities rarely occurred in the Transition Project. Over a three-and-a-half-year period, there were approximately thirty such activities, an average of five or six in each school—or one to two activities per year in each school.

We will address parenting and education activities in two categories, one dealing specifically with education or school issues and the other with parenting issues in general. The first group includes parent meetings with the consultant, held approximately once or twice (over the first three and one-half years of the project) in most of the schools; Read Aloud workshops, conducted once in three schools; workshops about new grading cards for primary students, conducted in two schools; presentations about attention deficit hyperactivity disorder (ADHD), in two schools; a workshop on parent-teacher conferences in one school; and a session on inclusion (including special education students in the regular classroom) in one school. These sessions, similar to workshops and activities in the personal development category above, typically consisted of a speaker presenting information and answering questions. Speakers were sometimes staff members, sometimes teachers, and sometimes outside experts. For example, an individual active in community literacy efforts conducted the Read Aloud workshops. In these two-hour sessions, she talked with parents about the value of encouraging children to develop a love of reading. Also, she led the parents through a volunteer training process, the goal of which was to certify adults to read aloud to children in classrooms. The training included pointers on selecting books to read aloud, holding books in a way that allows children to see pictures, and reading slowly with expression. In addition to following a written training manual, parents watched brief videos about the Read Aloud program and a live demonstration by the workshop leader.

Four of the involved low-income mothers we studied participated in Read Aloud training. For at least one of them, Charlene Preston, the training did not have a strong or lasting impact. Charlene, who has not been mentioned previously, grew up in a family with thirteen children. Her parents completed third grade, and Charlene herself stopped attending school after eighth grade. She is the mother of two children who attend the most rural of the five schools. When we mentioned the Read Aloud workshop to her, about a year after it took place, she had a hard time recalling it. After some prompting, she remembered attending the session and explained that she volunteers in one classroom fairly regularly, but does not read aloud to the whole group because she is too uncomfortable.

The workshop concerning the new grading cards was a briefer and less structured session conducted by a project teacher who talked with a group of seven parents, including three of the low-income mothers profiled here, about the new reporting process. She explained the differences between the old grading system of A, B, C, D, and F and the new one with marks such as P1 (progressing well without a lot of teacher instruction) and R (needs reteaching). She described the new system as a form of "authentic assessment," incorporating checklists and portfolios, that can give parents more specific information (than the traditional grading system) about their child's strengths and weaknesses.

Several mothers asked specific questions about their child's report card marks. Brenda, the piecework seamstress introduced earlier, said her daughter had two R's, in reading and in speech, and that attempts to work with her at home had not been satisfactory: "If I push her at home to work on something, she balls up and won't do it." Brenda wondered aloud whether she should try to locate a tutor for her child. The teacher advised against pressuring children, recommending instead more playful, spontaneous learning activities such as reading road signs and menus when the family is out and about. Also, she explained that R means reteach and that the responsibility for the reteaching is on the teacher, not the parent.

The sessions on ADHD were more formal, structured presentations provided by a local pediatrician. Three of the low-income mothers attended one of the presentations. The doctor cautioned parents about the dangers (specifically, adverse side effects) of using medications to control the behavior of young children and recommended that parents and teachers use behavior management strategies such as "time out" in addition to, or instead of, relying on drugs. Jackie Taylor, both of whose sons were taking Ritalin, found the session informative and wished more parents had attended. However, she was not dissuaded from preferring medication to control her sons' behavior, even when a new clinic physician began to question the boys' need for Ritalin. When the new physician took both boys off medication and assessed their responses, Jackie thought this was a mistake and told us that she believed the boys still needed Ritalin, that "they were driving their teachers crazy."

Activities related to parenting generally, but not specifically focused on schooling issues, included a parent discussion group, ongoing at one school for seven weeks; workshops on nutritional snacks, conducted at three schools; and workshops about childhood diseases, conducted at three schools. Quite a few of the ninteen low-income mothers were involved in one or more of these sessions, all of which were organized and facilitated by TDP staff members.

The parent discussion group, for example, was initiated by a family service/parent specialist at one school in the first year of the project. It originally was organized as two eight-week series of meetings, one during the day, and one during evening hours. When no one attended the evening sessions for two consecutive weeks, they were canceled. Attendance at the morning sessions, which ran for seven weeks, ranged from one to six parents. The family service/parent specialist who served as discussion group leader stressed the importance of parents building warm, trusting relationships with their children, saying "rules without relationships lead to rebellion." He also emphasized listening to children as a step to better communication with them. Whereas the family service/parent specialist used his leadership role to express certain views about parenting, he also encouraged the mothers to take an active role in the group by expressing their own views and concerns. He believed it was important not to "superimpose" what he wanted on the parents. In addition to inviting their responses to issues he introduced at the meetings, he sought the mothers' views concerning topics for discussion at future meetings by leaving a form in the parent resource room asking parents to suggest topics for discussion.

The mothers talked about how much harder it is to raise children in today's world, the difficulty of balancing their time between work and home, and the problems of single parenting. They also expressed concerns about the influence of television and peers on their children, describing their children as more materialistic in their values as a result of these influences. In addition, parents repeatedly expressed a desire for specific techniques to use in disciplining their children. Parents brought real problems to the discussion and asked for real help.

Although overall attendance was inconsistent and many parents only attended one session, the discussion group meetings had a powerful effect on one of the low-income mothers with whom we worked. Evelyn Gordon, a divorced mother of three, was working night shift as a nurse assistant. Evelyn had little contact with the school before the family service/parent specialist initiated home visits, but she responded to a personal invitation to the first discussion group meeting. She attended most of the group meetings, missing only when she or one of her children was sick, and talked about problems she was having with her children. She listened to other parents talk about their children and occasionally offered advice. In an interview after the meetings were in progress, Evelyn talked about the value of knowing other parents are having the same troubles she has: "I was under the impression there's something wrong with my whole family. There's something wrong with me, something wrong with my kids. Why are we like this? You know, I'm thinking, are my kids the only kids that just absolutely don't want to listen?" Asked about other benefits of the discussions, she commented on the importance of getting to know other adults with whom she could talk. "I just think it's good to get together with other people. I mean, I never see anybody, other than when I go to work. I don't call anybody on the phone. I don't really have anybody. . . . The only close friend I have doesn't have a phone."

The parent discussion group prompted Evelyn to get more involved in the school. By the time the series of meetings came to an
end, she had begun volunteering several days a week in a kindergarten class prior to going to her full-time job. At the time of this writing,
Evelyn volunteers at school even more regularly. She has taken responsibility for a major school task—all record-keeping and paperwork associated with the Read with Me program.

Unlike the social get-togethers, personal development activities,
and school assistance discussed in previous sections, activities pertaining to parenting and education, such as the progress report workshop
and the parent discussion group, represent more direct attempts to
enhance family-school connections in order to benefit children educationally. In addition to providing opportunities for the women to come
together socially, these activities invited them to think, talk, and ask
questions about issues directly related to their parenting, to their child's
experiences in school, and to connections between the two. Unfortunately, these kinds of activities occurred infrequently. Many of the
women in our study participated in only one or two such activities
over a three-and-one-half-year period. In contrast, many were engaged
in activities such as social get-togethers, fundraising, and teacher assistance on a nearly daily basis for several years.

Governing Board Participation

A large number of the mothers we studied (eleven out of nineteen)
were members of the Transition Project Governing Board, a group
including parents, staff members, and members of the local community. In addition to the women we have described previously, Governing Board members included Judy Mitchell, a high school graduate
who lives in a rural area and has one of the lowest incomes in our
study, and Loretta Sayre, who completed ninth grade and is the mother
of four, living in a rural area.

The Governing Board is the Transition Project's version of the
Head Start Policy Council. These bodies are designed to involve parents in program governance. However, our low-income mothers' role
in Governing Board decision making was primarily superficial, not
unlike the ceremonial power exercised by the Head Start mothers
Ellsworth and Ames (1996) studied.

Proceedings of a meeting held in the spring of 1995 illustrate the
peripheral role parents played in the Governing Board. First, the executive director of the Transition Project announced the single agenda

item for the meeting: approval of the grant refunding proposal, a request for monies to continue the project over the next school year. Then the Governing Board chairperson, the dean of the College of Education at a local university, asked for a motion to approve the grant resubmission. The executive director pointed to various papers on the front table and announced that program components for children, parent involvement, social services, and health services had not changed from last year. Then she distributed copies of the proposed budget for the following year, which she spent about twenty minutes reading orally.

Following the budget review, the executive director instructed board members to break into smaller groups by schools. Each school group was asked to examine a list of objectives and/or plans for the upcoming school year. These lists, which had been prepared by each family service/parent specialist for his or her school, were then distributed to the small groups.

In one school group, the family service/parent specialist told the three parents that she would read through and explain her objectives. The first objective was worded like this: "Facilitate improvement of parent awareness and competencies in personal effectiveness and home/community support and development." This was explained in terms of parents planning, approving, and implementing programs. One parent responded by mentioning an outdoor classroom being built as part of the school beautification program. The second objective was: "Remediate inappropriate parenting practices and facilitate appropriate practices in target parents." Strategies for meeting this objective included home visits and referrals of dysfunctional families for in-home parenting assistance. The group did not have time to discuss the other objectives because the executive director asked everyone to return to the large group. Small groups had met for about fifteen minutes.

When the entire group was seated again, the chairperson took a vote on the resubmission, and then the meeting was adjourned. The executive director asked that one parent from each school remain to sign a paper that was to be submitted with the grant proposal. Clearly, parents' decision-making power in this meeting was minimal. They were told about, but never actually shown, a resubmission proposal that had already been completed by TDP staff members. They were shown a proposed budget that also had been completed previously. They were given what could only be called a token opportunity for input into parent involvement plans for their specific schools. Then they were asked to vote and sign their names. This experience did not provide real leadership opportunities to parents nor did it provide opportunities for participating parents to play a meaningful role in TDP decision making and evaluation.

Summary of Parent Involvement Experiences

As the descriptions of the five categories of parent involvement illustrate, the Transition Project successfully initiated and maintained the school involvement of a small number of low-income mothers, many of whom were in the schools quite frequently. In some schools it was common to see two or three of these women, in addition to the paid parent assistants, for several hours nearly every day. Major factors in this success were the provision of a physical space for parents in the schools (parent resource rooms), the use of informal social get-togethers to attract mothers who may not have been inclined to spend time in the schools otherwise, and the hiring of parent assistants whose major responsibility was the coordination of parent involvement. As discussed above, the mothers as well as the teachers and schools benefitted from this involvement.

For the mothers we studied, volunteering experiences with the project and the schools were personally enriching. Theresa described the increase in her self-esteem as a result of becoming involved with the Transition Project and the school: "It's built my self-esteem up.... I feel better about myself. Working in a school and becoming friends with people that I guess you wouldn't think you would be friends with. Like going to a Governing Board meeting and sitting beside the superintendent.... Then you feel, well you are worth something. And I didn't used to feel like that."

However, we are concerned about the benefits for children. Whereas they may have enjoyed seeing their mothers in the schools and may have felt more comfortable and secure in their classrooms and schools, we are not convinced the children benefitted *educationally* as a result of their mothers' involvement with the Transition Project and with the school. Like Howley, Howley, and Pendarvis (1995), we believe that "nurturing of the intellect" is an important, perhaps the most important, mission of the schools. And the vast majority of parent involvement scholars seem to support, either implicitly or explicitly, parent involvement as a vehicle for enhancing children's learning opportunities. Clearly, most Transition Project activities were aimed at attracting parents to schools and attempting to make them feel comfortable there.

Only a few, however, the rare parenting and education activities, attempted to directly address child development and schooling issues. Although we do not have extensive information concerning the schooling experiences of each child, we have enough information to be concerned about their academic progress.

The majority of these mothers had children who were experiencing difficulties in school as evidenced by one or more of the following: scores below grade level on standardized achievement tests, low marks on report cards, in-school behavior problems, teacher recommendations for special education testing, and placement in Chapter 1 reading and math classes. In addition, several mothers had children who were diagnosed as having attention deficit disorder (ADD) or attention deficit hyperactivity disorder (ADHD), and at least three had children who were retained in the primary grades since the project began. Theresa Harmon, the parent assistant working two or three jobs, made a direct connection between the Transition Project and her daughter's retention.

> [The project] has kept me informed in how my children are progressing. . . . This project let me know that my child did not need to go on to first grade. She needed to be held back because she didn't know her ABC's. She didn't know her numbers. . . . If I hadn't been involved in this project, if I had been sitting at home, I would have never knew that. I would have probably been like maybe some of the other parents that say, "She needs to go on to first grade. She doesn't need to be held back." . . . Because I was here [volunteering in the school] I saw that she was having problems.

As a result of being in the school on a regular basis, Theresa was less inclined to question the recommendation to retain her daughter in kindergarten. In light of recent scholarship suggesting that grade retention may be detrimental to children educationally (for example, see Karweit's 1991 meta-analysis of grade retention research), this may not have been beneficial to her child.

We are not suggesting that the Transition Project or the school involvement experiences caused or increased children's difficulties in school. We are interested in understanding the extent to which the project or the involvement experiences offered these mothers and their children any advantages or assistance in terms of dealing with such problems. Unfortunately, even mothers who worked in schools on a daily basis, seeing and speaking with teachers frequently, were not collaborating with teachers and administrators concerning the academic experiences of their children. For example, a teacher removed the daughter of Penny Wheeler (parent assistant who worked almost full-time at the school) from an after-school remedial class. Penny related her unsuccessful attempt to discuss the problem with the teacher, saying the teacher "just blew up" at her, "yelling" about how her daughter had lied about the incident. This same teacher had a large sign, posted on an easel outside her doorway, asking parents not to disturb her class. Penny decided that her daughter would not go back to the tutoring sessions, saying she would "let it slide this time." She likened the experience to unpleasant interactions with her husband: "If I wanted to be yelled at like that, I can go home." She talked about how her husband blows up and she has learned to just wait it out because pursuing it often makes things worse.

Similarly, Carol Russell's daily volunteering did not result in open communication with her daughters' teachers. Because the child was struggling with reading, Jennifer's third-grade teacher referred her for testing, the results of which indicated that Jennifer had a learning disability. Carol was concerned because this conflicted with information she had received from Jennifer's teacher the year before. At that time, Carol inquired about Jennifer's school performance, and the child's second-grade teacher reported on several occasions that Jennifer was "just fine," that she was "on level." Now this third-grade child is going to remedial reading and only reading on a first-grade level. Carol's younger daughter, Allison, has the same second-grade teacher Jennifer had last year. When Carol recently asked to schedule a conference about Allison, the teacher responded, "Didn't you see her report card? She's doing fine." This response made Carol so angry she couldn't speak, "because I was afraid of what I would say." As far as we know, Carol has not followed up on this.

Sometimes what does not happen is as significant as what does. Principals and teachers at several TDP schools were concerned about children's performance on the California Test of Basic Skills (CTBS), a state-mandated achievement test. In one school, the principal, several teachers, and several TDP staff members met to discuss the unusually low scores of second graders. No parents were invited to participate in this meeting, the purpose of which was to explore the nature of the problem as well as various possible solutions to it. It is important to note that this occurred at a school that prides itself on having strong parent involvement. Even before the inception of the Transition Project, the school had a parent room, an active PTA, and a Parent Involvement Council. Whereas parents were invited, even actively recruited to the school, their involvement was limited in a way that may prohibit, or at least discourage, participation in academic issues.

These kinds of events, and nonevents, suggest that the school involvement of these mothers may not have enhanced the school learning experiences of their children. Recent parent involvement scholarship concerning the relationship between parent involvement and academic achievement may shed some light on this. While some authors suggest that any kind of parent presence in schools, even attendance at sports and drama programs, has a positive effect on student achievement (Black 1993), an increasing body of literature argues that to be effective in this way, parent involvement must be directly focused on children's learning. "In fact, parent involvement that is related to the educational values of the school community and which facilitates children's learning should be the primary, if not the only, job of the parent organization in the school" (Redding 1991, 7). Redding goes on to suggest a parent involvement model that prioritizes different kinds of involvement, with parents' involvement with their own children at the top of the ranking. Lower priorities include involvement with other parents, with other children who need attention, and with the activities of the school. In Redding's view, truly meaningful parent involvement engages parents with their children in activities "that really matter to the children's academic development."

Consistent with this line of reasoning, Hoover-Dempsey and Sandler (1995) developed a model explaining *how* parent involvement benefits children's learning. The model specifies "three primary mechanisms of parental influence on children's educational outcomes: modeling, reinforcement and direct instruction." Hoover-Dempsey and Sandler concluded that children's school learning will be enhanced if their parents are involved in their education in "ways that create or reinforce direct experiences of educational success, offer vicarious experiences of educational success, offer verbal persuasion intended to develop attitudes, behaviors, and efforts consistent with school success, and create emotional arousal that underscores the personal importance of doing well in school" (329).

Along the same lines, teachers contend that student achievement will not improve until "parents are not only involved in the school, but in the school work of their own children" (Johnson 1990). This may be as simple as talking with children and providing consistent support for homework. Clark (1983) found that poor, African American students who were high achievers had families in which homework was perceived as a normal, expected activity to be accomplished and in which there was frequent parent-child dialogue about education and school issues. Also, Coleman (1991) called on school administrators to involve parents with their own children, particularly in the area of homework.

THE PARENT INVOLVEMENT EXPERIENCES AS REPRODUCTIVE OR TRANSFORMATIVE

As stated earlier, one of our intentions in this chapter is to explore connections between the experiences of these involved low-income mothers and power relations more broadly. In other words, in what ways and to what extent have the mothers' experiences with project and school involvement provided a challenge to gender- and class-based inequities? In what ways and to what extent are their experiences simply an extension or new manifestation of their less privileged position as low-income women?

We believe the mothers' experiences have been strengthening and gratifying personally, offering substantial opportunities for individual development in some cases. However, the experiences, for the most part, were socially reproductive in nature. That is, the parent-involvement activities, while personally meaningful to the mothers and their children and beneficial to teachers and schools, did not provide a challenge to existing social-class and gender inequalities.

These women came into the project and the schools disadvantaged by their gender and class. They and their children were part of the large and growing number of women and children struggling with poverty in West Virginia and in the United States. Like many low-income women, they tended to defer to teachers and school personnel, trusting in their professional expertise (Lareau 1987). Becoming actively involved in the Head Start to Public School Transition Demonstration Project and in their children's schools has not changed that. The experiences have not increased the women's consciousness and understanding of power inequalities, nor have the experiences encouraged them to resist, confront, or critique elements of their children's schooling. Rather, they have been asked to support and help. In effect, they have come in, at a relatively low level, to do clerical work and fundraising necessary to maintain, support, and strengthen the school organization and ultimately the society as they currently exist.

Some have pointed out that school personnel make the mistake of looking down on parents—particularly low-income parents, seeing them as clients in need of services rather than as valuable resources (e.g., Ellsworth and Ames, 1996; Johnson, 1990). Henry (1996) found that parent education often consisted of zealous and disrespectful attempts to "fix" working-class parents.

Further, Ellsworth and Ames (1996) suggest that Head Start itself has adopted a model of parent involvement that, perhaps unintentionally, helps perpetuate "deficit-based assumptions about low-income mothers." Bruner (1996) concurs, arguing that Head Start, originally designed to overcome "cultural deprivation" by promoting middle-class child-rearing practices, ended up blaming the victim. "It blames the victim's mother, or at least her 'culture.' . . . Compassionate though it undoubtedly was, Head Start did not escape the kind of implicit condescension that goes with reform movements. . . . [Head Start] was a massive step forward in addressing a problem that had been ignored before. . . . Nevertheless, it was condescending. It failed to face the underlying issue of discrimination squarely" (73–74).

Transition Project staff members certainly attempted to engage parents using the kind of respectful, bottom-up approach these scholars advocate. On many occasions, staff members defended craft workshops and other activities on the basis of giving the parents what they wanted. There was a genuine desire not to impose ideas, programs, or services on parents, who often stated strong preferences for social get-togethers rather than for activities focusing on schooling issues. Also, there is ample evidence that TDP staff members and teachers saw these mothers as having something to offer, as valuable resources. However, they were seen primarily as valuable teacher and school support staff rather than as resources for enhancing their children's learning.

It seems to us there has to be some middle ground between imposing a top-down, condescending parent involvement program and taking a relatively laissez faire approach based on the spontaneously expressed interests and needs of participants—in this case, mothers and teachers. In the case of the West Virginia TDP, this latter approach (which we came to see as a sort of well-intentioned benign neglect on the part of TDP staff) resulted in an emphasis on social get-togethers, personal development activities, and support services for teachers and schools. It seems to us that both alternatives—the condescending imposition and the laissez faire approach—may serve to perpetuate the status quo; one just does it with the greater enthusiasm and cooperation of the parents.

The low-income mothers we came to know may have been willingly and happily, though unconsciously, participating in perpetuating their disadvantaged position. Their school-involvement experiences did not challenge prevailing power hierarchies in schooling and in society. These heirarchies are supported, and perpetuated, by the idea that low-income women can and should be involved in their children's schooling; but in doing so they must stay in their place—doing behind-the-scenes support work, not participating in decision-making concerning the main function of schooling—the education of children.

Thus, we believe the school-involvement experiences were reproductive of gender and social class inequalities. The nature of the mothers' experiences were consistent with the less privileged position of low-income women. Further, the experiences may not have provided educational benefits to their own children. It may seem that mothers who worked directly with teachers were provided opportunities for the kinds of advantage-producing involvement of the upper income mothers in Lareau's study. However, low-income Transition Project mothers for the most part were engaged in activities that provided them few opportunities to obtain information and use it for the benefit of their own children. Lareau's upper income mothers volunteered in their own children's classrooms in order to monitor their schooling experiences; they believed that volunteering at school gave them information that helped them work more effectively with their children and with teachers in order to improve their children's educational achievement. In many cases, they were particularly involved with low-achieving children who needed a great deal of extra assistance in order to avoid retention or special education placements. Conversely, the low-income mothers we studied worked mostly in or for classrooms other than the ones in which their own children were placed. The nature of their work (laminating, duplicating, cutting out, stapling) served more to increase the teachers' resources, by giving them much-needed clerical assistance, than to increase these mothers' capabilities for attaining academic benefits for their children.

On a more hopeful note, we believe the Transition Project, which is scheduled to continue for another year past this writing, has laid the groundwork for a kind of parent involvement that could be beneficial to children's learning and have socially transformative potential. While we do not advocate the condescending "deficit-based" view of low-income parents Ellsworth and Ames (1996) critique, we agree with Coleman (1991) that it is a "serious error" to assume that parents know how to reinforce school's educational endeavors. "The principal point is that parents are unskilled in helping their children to succeed in school. Even well-educated parents often lack the knowledge of what practices in the home will most help their children to succeed in school. The school . . . can help parents help their children" (5).

The way this help is provided is extremely important. Henry (1996) pointed out that school reform programs, operating within taken-for-granted, hierarchical school bureaucracies and societal power relations, often unintentionally maintain the status quo. We agree with her that intervention programs should provide a challenge to these inequalities by operating in a more egalitarian fashion that "begin[s] and end[s] with care and respect." Nevertheless, program implementers must provide some guidance, especially in terms of maintaining a focus on the goal of enhancing children's learning. Inviting parents to become active in school volunteering, making them comfortable in the school, and then giving them pleasant and helpful (to teachers and schools) things to do is not enough. Telling them that research shows that children whose parents are involved in their schooling do better in school is not enough either. The mere physical presence of parents in schools does not automatically produce educational benefits for students.

All parents have a right to be informed about the specific kinds of learning expectations schools have for their children. They have a right to take an active role in their children's learning experiences at home and at school, including participating in decision making about achievement and retentions. This kind of information and activity is particularly important for low-income parents who traditionally have been alienated from schools.

The Transition Project has taken steps in the right direction by providing parenting and education activities discussed above. More of these kinds of activities, focusing directly on children's learning, are needed. The afterschool parent-child tutoring sessions recently instituted by the family service/parent specialist at one school is a good example. Also, the project could attempt to bring teachers and parents together more often. The teacher-parent discussion of new report cards was an example of this. However, these activities should provide parents opportunities for participation that go beyond receiving information from professional educators. Including parents in meetings, such as the one concerning low test scores, and including teachers in parent meetings, such as those with the project consultant, would strengthen family-school connections focusing on children's learning. The fact that TDP virtually always arranged separate meetings and activities for parents and teachers did not go unnoticed, and it conveyed a message that the two groups were separate in their interests and goals pertaining to the education of children. Practices such as these tend to maintain distance between families and schools, thus limiting opportunities for them to work together for the benefit of children.

We believe the West Virginia Transition Demonstration Project's parent involvement program has a great deal of merit, but that it should not merely reinforce traditional parent-school relationships, nor should it perpetuate the subordination of low-income women. The low-income mothers we studied were living in harsh conditions, with few social and financial resources upon which to draw. Nevertheless, they gave generously of their time and energy to the schools, and they cared deeply about their children. These women deserve meaningful opportunities for participation in their children's education. They also deserve to know how the societal deck is stacked against them and that they have the right to make individual and collective efforts to challenge such inequalities, in schooling and elsewhere.

NOTES

1. We used pseudonyms throughout the chapter in order to protect the privacy of the participants.

2. See Henry (1996) for an extensive, historically located review of parent involvement literature.

3. The figures we used were based on a memorandum from the Governor's Cabinet on Children and Families in the Office of Economic Opportunity in Charleston, West Virginia. According to the memorandum, updated federal poverty income guidelines were published in the Federal Register, February 9, 1995. They stipulated an annual income of $7,470 for a family of one. With each additional family member, $2,560 is added, so that an income for a family of four, for example, would be $15,150.

REFERENCES

Black, S. (1993). The parent factor. *The Executive Educator.* April, 29–31.

Bourdieu, P. (1977). Cultural reproduction and social reproduction. In A. H. Halsey and Karabel (Eds.), *Power and ideology in education.* New York: Oxford University Press.

Bruner, J. (1996). *The culture of education.* Cambridge, Massachusetts: Harvard University Press.

Clark, R. (1983). *Family life and school achievement: Why poor black children succeed or fail.* Chicago: University of Chicago Press.

Coleman, J. (1991). A federal report on parental involvement in education. *Education Digest,* Vol. 57, No. 3, 3–5.

Ellsworth, J., and Ames, L. (1996). Power and ceremony: Low-income mothers as policy makers in Head Start. *Educational Foundations,* Vol. 9, No. 4, 5–23.

Epstein, J. (1995). School/family/community/partnerships. *Phi Delta Kappan,* Vol. 76, No. 9, 701–712.

Fruchter, N., Galletta, A., and White, J. (1993). New directions in parent involvement. *Equity and Choice,* Vol. 9 No. 3, 33–43.

Gaventa, J. (1982). *Power and powerlessness: Quiescence and rebellion in an Appalachian valley.* Chicago: University of Illinois Press.

Griffith, A. (1995). Coordinating family and school: Mothering for schooling. *Education Policy Analysis Archives,* Vol. 3, No. 1.

Hannah, K. (1995). *West Virginia women in perspective 1980–1995.* Charleston: West Virginia Women's Commission.

Hashima, P., and Amato, P. (1994). Poverty, social support and parental behavior. *Child Development,* Vol. 65, 394–403.

Henry, M. (1996). *Parent-school collaboration: Feminist organizational structures and school leadership.* Albany: State University of New York Press.

Hoover-Dempsey, K., and Sandler, H. (1995). Parent involvement in children's education: Why does it make a difference? *Teacher's College Record* Vol. 97, No. 2.

Howley, C., Howley, A., and Pendarvis, E. (1995). *Out of our minds: Antiintellectualism and talent development in American schooling.* New York: Teachers College Press.

Johnson, S. (1990). Building bridges between home and school. In *Teachers at work.* New York: Basic Books, Inc.

Karweit, N. (1991). Repeating a grade: Time to grow or denial of opportunity? Report No. 16. Center for Research on Effective Schooling for Disadvantaged Students. Baltimore, MD.

Kids Count Data Book (1995). West Virginia Task Force on Children, Youth and Families, Charleston, West Virginia.

Lareau, A. (1987). *Home advantage: Social class and parental intervention in elementary education.* New York: Falmer Press.

Mills, K. (1993). Edward Zigler: Head Start's architect reflects on building achievements. California: *L.A. Times*, April 4.

Redding, S. (1991). Creating a school community through parent involvement. *Education Digest*, Vol. 57, No. 3, 6–9.

Simoni, J., and Adelman, H. (1993). School-based mutual support groups for low-income parents. *The Urban Review*, Vol. 25, No. 4.

Sun, Y., Hobbs, D., and Elder, W. (1994). Parent involvement: A contrast between rural and other communities. Paper presented at the Rural Sociological Society, Portland, OR.

Walberg, H. (1984). Families as partners in educational productivity. *Phi Delta Kappan*, 397–400.

4

Parent Involvement in a Rural Head Start and the Reproduction of Class

Roslyn Arlin Mickelson
and Mary Trotter Klenz

INTRODUCTION

The massive school reforms that are sweeping the nation share a number of themes. Two of the least controversial ones are that increased early childhood education and greater parent involvement in schools will ultimately lead to improved school outcomes, especially for poor children. Head Start has incorporated parent involvement into its operations from its inception. The Head Start emphasis on parent involvement derives from a number of assumptions, including the belief that greater parent participation in children's schooling will enhance poor children's social and cognitive skills, as well as improve their attitudes toward education. In addition, parent involvement in Head Start is envisioned as a vehicle that can empower poor parents to transform their own and their children's lives.

Drawing upon a case study of parent involvement of mostly African Americans in a Head Start program located in the rural South (Klenz 1993), we critically examine claims for the efficacy of parent

An earlier version of this chapter was presented at the annual meeting of the American Educational Research Association, Atlanta, Georgia, April 1993. The authors wish to thank Judy Aulette, Lynda Ames, Jeanne Ellsworth, Joyce Epstein, and Sally Lubeck for helpful comments on earlier drafts, and Susan Masse for her technical assistance.

involvement as a tool of parent empowerment and transformation. In this chapter we show how parent involvement in Head Start is more form than substance and thus does not empower parents to change their own or their children's lives. The chapter demonstrates how the poor rural southern community's racial and class boundaries—expressed in the restricted linguistic codes and traditional paternalistic authority relations among parents, administrators, and staff—shape and restrict parent involvement. Consequently, rather than transforming and empowering parents, involvement in Sandy Hills Head Start program was likely to reproduce the unequal social relations of domination and control grounded in class, race, and gender divisions of the region. The insular and stifling localism of this poor, rural, and largely minority community's lived culture contributed to these processes. The participation of the children and adults in Sandy Hills Head Start largely prepared them for the same, not transformed, lives.

BACKGROUND

Popular cultural accounts of diverse school outcomes focus on variations in family structure and "values." The presumed connections among family structure, values, and school outcomes, especially among low-income groups have crystallized into renewed attention on parent involvement in schools. Reformers, educators, and politicians noting greater parent involvement in education among middle-class parents and higher achievement among middle-class students (Baker and Stevenson 1986; Epstein 1995, 1990; Lareau 1989; Stevenson and Baker 1987) have prescribed greater involvement for poor, and particularly minority, parents as one key factor (among many) for improving their children's school outcomes.

With some important and thoughtful exceptions, much of current scholarly research and most popular culture literature on parent involvement in education presents explicitly or implicitly the traditional two-parent family, father-as-primary-breadwinner model as the standard. The contemporary rhetoric about students at risk and their less than adequate families derives from this view. Conservatives view single-parent households, career-oriented mothers, out-of-wedlock births, substance abuse, teenage pregnancy, school dropout rates, and an absence of "family values" that embrace education and hard work as the ultimate causes of the class and racial gaps in school outcomes (Bennett 1992; Loury 1985). From this individualistic perspective, weak or absent parent involvement in children's education is another symptom of the lack of family values and a crucial contributing factor to unsatisfactory educational outcomes. Larger structural forces in the political economy and the internal dynamics of educational institutions are largely ignored or considered to be secondary factors when compared to the individual and familial causes of school failures.

Other social analysts who advocate greater parent involvement do so from a more liberal deficit model of poor families which relies on a social systems approach. Expectations are that parent involvement, especially at the preschool level, will create an improved social climate within schools (Comer 1988, 1993, 1995), improve reading and language skills of both parents and children, enhance academic and parenting skills of parents (Comer 1988, 1993, 1995; Powell 1990) and change parents' and children's views of schools. (Comer 1988, 1993, 1995; Zigler 1992; and Zigler and Valentine 1979). Furthermore, greater parent involvement in school is expected to effect positive changes in pupils' cognitive development and performance, social attitudes and life chances (Comer 1993; Epstein 1995; Schweinhart et al. 1993). A number of advocates also anticipate that poor parents will themselves become transformed by their involvement. Adults' own education will be expanded, self-esteem and parenting will improve, and their participation will engender a sense of social and political efficacy that will transform them (Comer 1993; Ellsworth and Ames 1995; White 1991). According to this more radical paradigm, parents ultimately will transform the social institutions they enter once they leave Head Start and, say, become community activists. The Head Start model is grounded in all of these paradigms of parent involvement.

Yet little empirical research has examined systematically the long- or short-term effects of parent participation in Head Start, especially the claims that such activities empower parents to transform their own and their children's lives for the better (c.f., Washington 1995 for an exception). In light of the current interest at the national and state levels in the issues of preschool education and parent involvement, this chapter offers a timely exploration of the ways parent involvement in a rural southern Head Start program, rather than equipping the parents and children to transform their lives, unfolds in rather conservative ways. Far from empowering and educating parents, the actual processes at work may contribute to the reproduction of the class, race, and cultural domination that already characterizes their lives.

THEORIES OF SOCIAL AND CULTURAL REPRODUCTION
AND TRANSFORMATION

The role of educational institutions in the reproduction of culture and social class has been the source of a great deal of scholarly research and debate in the last twenty years. Notable early theorists who posited that schools contribute more to the reproduction than to the transformation of culture and class are Samuel Bowles and Herbert Gintis who argued (1976) that schools operate in ways that replicate, transmit, and thus reproduce, the unequal social relations of the workplace through class-specific educational practices and differentiated curricula. In the last twenty years, the theoretical and empirical research of a number of scholars has critiqued and refined this initial conceptualization of the correspondence among social class, schools, and social reproduction. The research of Jean Anyon (1980), Sally Lubeck (1985), Annette Lareau (1989), Darla Miller and Mark Ginsburg (1989), Jay McLeod (1987), Roslyn Mickelson (1980, 1987), and Paul Willis (1977) have traced the dynamic interconnections among students' lived culture, their social class, the social relations of the workplace and the social relations of various school settings.

While theories of reproduction in education have been criticized on a number of grounds, extended, and elaborated (Carnoy and Levin 1985; Giroux 1983; Morrow and Torres 1995, 1994), they nonetheless offer a starting point for understanding the particular contours and consequences of parent involvement in the rural Head Start program under investigation. Particularly useful elaborations are the concepts of cultural capital (Bourdieu 1990; Bourdieu and Passeron 1977; Bourdieu and Wacquant 1992) and restricted linguistic codes (Bernstein 1975, 1990). In any society, schools are essentially middle-class institutions whose knowledge base and linguistic forms privilege those of the dominant class and racial group. Mastery of verbal skills in the language of the school is related to development of cognitive skills (Heath 1983). Students from poor and working-class families are disadvantaged relative to their middle-class peers because their everyday language, according to Bernstein (1990), is different from the middle-class language of the school. All children learn ordinary conversation, or what Bernstein terms "restricted codes." This form of language is grammatically simple and context dependent. Middle-class children learn, in addition, a formal or elaborated code, which is also the complex language of instruction, textbooks, and the formal curricula. Students who use elaborated codes possess more of the cognitive and linguistic tools necessary for formal school success. According to Heath and Bernstein, the relationship between the language of the home and the language of the school is a critical factor in class differences in school outcomes. Similarly, the culture of the school, especially its official knowledge, privileges the cultural capital of middle-class children.

For poor children, then, the disjuncture between their cultural capital and linguistic codes is central to the educational problems they encounter. In fact, the use of restricted codes among poor parents also influences parent-school interactions. Julia Wrigley's (1995) study of class differences and in-home child care demonstrates how crucial cultural capital and linguistic codes are to early childhood socialization. Head Start was conceptualized as a programmatic intervention to bridge this disjuncture.

PROJECT HEAD START AND PARENT INVOLVEMENT

The belief that involvement of poor parents in the governance process of their children's preschool can enable them to effect personal, educational, and social change contributed to Congress's affirmation of the parent governance focus of Project Head Start (White 1991; P.L. 90-222, Sec.222(a)(1)(b); Head Start Bureau, 1967). The statutory mandate for parent involvement reflects the widely held belief in education's efficacy in personal and social change. If one assumes, as do most people, that the poor are deficient and need to be "fixed," then the solution is to design certain kinds of preschool opportunities for them that are different from those offered for middle-class children. But if one believes that poor people need avenues through which to gain power and control, one creates vehicles such as Head Start Policy Councils and other opportunities for empowerment. Parent involvement, then, stands out as a potentially progressive component of the Head Start program because it is conceived as a mechanism that can alter the processes and outcomes of disempowerment typically associated with the interaction between schools and poor parents. In essence, parent involvement in Head Start was conceived by its advocates to be part of the process of empowering poor, disenfranchised parents to transform their own and their children's lives, and, ultimately, their communities.

Document 70.2

Head Start's Document 70.2 mandates policies and procedures that engage parents in the Head Start program through participation in a

Policy Council, as employees, and as participants in center meetings. The Policy Council is the governing body of Head Start, and 50 percent of its membership is supposed to be comprised of parents. Representatives of the local community are also members of the Policy Council and act as a link to the community by providing mentoring and network resources to parents. Document 70.2 specifies that the Policy Council has the power and authority to approve budgets, hire and fire staff, develop programs, policies, and grievance procedures, approve the employment appointment of the grantee agency, and distribute funds.

Monthly center meetings are another official avenue for parent involvement. Parent involvement at the center level is defined officially in terms of staff support, attendance at center meetings, and employment as teachers or aides. In theory, then, parents are empowered through participation in local center meetings and membership on the larger Policy Council which serves all the centers affiliated with Sandy Hills Head Start.

Yet, it was here in the Policy Council and the center meetings that the parents' potential power was undermined and opportunities for social transformation and empowerment were lost. In the program under study, parent involvement took a very different form than that envisaged by Head Start's creators. Sandy Hills Head Start's organizational structure operated within traditional southern race, class, and gender hierarchies that are marked by the social relations of domination typical of traditional, insular, rural southern communities (Goldfield 1990). Moreover, the cultural capital of the participants, especially their restricted linguistic codes, limited their ability to transcend the program's organizational constraints and the local class, race, and gender hierarchies that contextualized their social interactions.Together, these micro and macro processes blunted meaningful parent innovation and participation, especially interactions that could truly empower Head Start parents and their children and ultimately transform their communities.

Context and Methods

Site

The site of this case study is Sandy Hills Head Start, one of five programs administered by Sandy Hills Community Action in a poor rural section of a southern state. A community action program is an umbrella agency that coordinates a number of social service agencies in a given jurisdiction. As figure 4.1 illustrates, the Sandy Hills Community Action program includes Head Start, Job Training Partnership Program (JTPA), the weatherization program, and a program that assists homeless families. In an article in the local newspaper, Sandy Hills Community Action's executive director described Sandy Hills Head Start as "one-half" of the Community Action program and "the other half is all the other programs." At the time of this research (1991–1992), Sandy Hills Head Start had eight centers located in public schools and community centers in three contiguous counties—Bradley, Addison, and Carter (pseudonyms). One of these counties was the site of a 1992 fatal fire in which twenty-eight people died while locked inside a chicken processing plant. A number of the children, teachers, and parents involved in Sandy Hills Head Start were related to the victims of the fire.

The racial demographics of the population of the three-county area are not mirrored in the students who attend Sandy Hills Head Start centers. Although African Americans are no more than 32 percent of the population in any of the counties, about 80 percent of the students are black. Eighteen percent are white, and 2 percent are Asian American. This means the students are drawn disproportionately from the African American population. At the time this study was conducted (1991–1992), few if any Latino families lived in the area. Since this time, a notable number of Latinos have located near the major employers, the chicken processing plants and textile mills.

One way to appreciate the insularity of the rural, southern counties is to envision the fictional town of Mayberry twenty-five years after Sheriff Andy Taylor has retired and his son Opie has moved to Sunbelt City, the metropolitan area thirty miles west, which offers better jobs and the amenities of modern, urban life. In the Sandy Hills three-county area, family farms and small businesses have succumbed to the pressures of agribusiness and Wal-Mart. Many families have followed the example of the young Taylor, and moved to the city. Large numbers of those who remain are poor and relatively uneducated. Although the area is within a thirty-minute drive from the outskirts of a banking and finance center of almost 1 million people, the three-county area is much closer in tone and pace to provincial Mayberry than to modern Sunbelt City. The exception to this pattern is the western edge of Addison County which abuts Metro County. In recent years it has experienced high growth rates where its new suburban neighborhoods have absorbed the residential overflow from its urban neighbor. This means the county's population has become

MICKELSON AND KLENZ

TABLE 4.1
Selected Statewide and County-Specific Demographic Indicators, 1990

	Southern State	Metro County	Carter County	Bradley County	Addison County
1992 Population					
Total	7,064,470	561,223	24,009	45,041	94,352
% White	75.8	71	51.5	86.2	83.6
% Nonwhite	24.2	29	24.2	31.8	16.4
Black	20.5				
Asian	<1				
Amer. Ind.	2				
Latino	<1				
1995 Infant Mortality Rate per 1000 Births					
Total	15.1	14.1	19.1	16.4	11.7
White	10.8	10.5	17.2	10.2	7.9
Nonwhite	24.6	20.0	20.6	25.3	24.9
1992 Percent Rural	49.7	9.9	84.5	55.6	64.4
1994 Percent Households Receiving Food Stamps	—	8.2	18.6	14.2	7.2
1992 Median Family Income	$31,548	$40,904	$25,838	$26,747	$35,527
1992 Percent Families with Children Under Five Years of Age Living Below Poverty Line	17.2	15.0	23.8	24.5	11.7
1992 Percent High School Grad or More	70.0	81.6	60.8	60.4	69.0
1992 Percent B.A. or More	17.4	28.3	7.3	7.9	13.2

Sources: U.S. Census 1992
    North Carolina Vital Statistics 1995, 1994

heterogeneous; the western portion is made up of well-educated, middle-class suburbanites, while the rest of the population is relatively poor, undereducated, and has more minority families. The official demographics, then, are misleading because they represent county averages.

Textile mills and poultry processing plants are the major employers in all three counties. According to the last census, the official unemployment rate in the area averaged 7 percent but ranged as high as 12 percent. In the nearest metropolitan area, Sunbelt City, the unemployment rate hovered under 3 percent. Within the three-county area there are 267 Protestant churches, two Catholic churches, four community colleges, and one four-year church-affiliated college with close ties to a well-known conservative southern senator.

The gender, class, and racial stratification of a traditional southern society is reflected in Sandy Hills Community Action's own organizational structure. Most positions of power and authority are in the hands of middle-class whites. Consistent with the traditional public role of middle-class southern women working in helping professions, the administrators of Sandy Hills Head Start were almost all women. Figure 4.1 presents the organizational chart of the agency. Both the regional administrator and the local administrator are middle-class white women. The fourteen teachers and co-teachers are working-class and working-poor black and white women. The center custodian was a black man, and the after-school program coordinator was a black woman. Some of the younger Sandy Hills Head Start teachers were graduates of this Head Start program, and none had formal education beyond high school. The vast majority of the fourteen teachers or co-teachers had not received specific training in early childhood education, and those who had, had attended a brief on-site noncredit course sponsored by a local college.

None of the teachers, volunteers, or administrative staff was formally educated in any institution beyond the three-county area. Most of the administrative staff attended or graduated from the local community college or the nearby private Christian college. This college cost five times as much as the nearest branch of the University of North Carolina, only a fifteen-minute drive west of the private college. This is significant because students who attend this college are less likely to be exposed to perspectives that broaden or even challenge their own. Together these factors contributed to the insular, traditional southern, working-class cultural capital, which was the currency of Sandy Hills Head Start teachers, administrators, parents, and students.

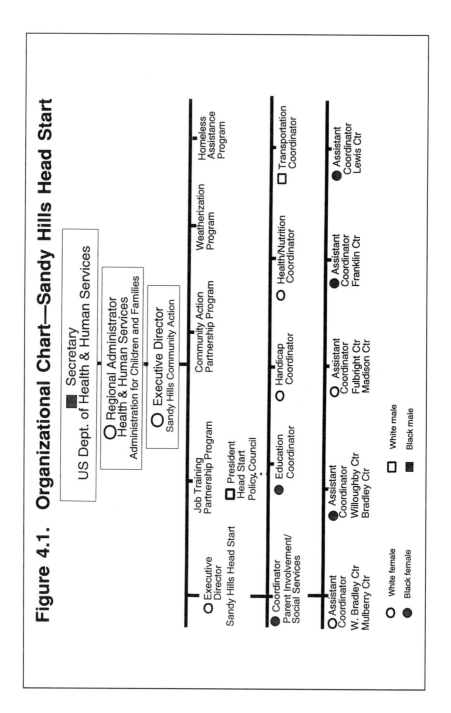

Figure 4.1.   Organizational Chart—Sandy Hills Head Start

Four of the eight Sandy Hills Head Start centers were single class-rooms located in local public school buildings, and the other four are located in local community centers. The community centers are older buildings with multiple classrooms, gymnasiums, parent meeting rooms, and food service facilities. Enrollment ranged from twenty in a center with a single classroom to as many as one hundred in a center with five classrooms. During the period of study, attendance at parent center meetings ranged from 10 to 25 percent of the parents of each preschool's students. The preschool children, brothers, sisters, moth-ers, fathers, grandmothers, and aunts attended the meetings at vari-ous times throughout the period of the research.

Data

Data collected by the second author over a nine-month period from October 1991 to June 1992 included field notes and field journals; indepth interviews; and documents (see Klenz 1993 for details). She attended parent meetings, an annual state convention, and special events involving parents and staff where she took field notes and tape recorded meetings and interviews. She also acted as a volunteer in classrooms at three separate centers. Program administrators, staff, teachers, and parents were interviewed both individually and in group roundtable discussion. Questions were open-ended. A total of ten in-terviews averaging approximately one and one-half hours were tape recorded and later transcribed. Documents relating to the history of Project Head Start, and policies and procedures of parent involvement at both the national and local program level were analyzed both for content and for language. Both researchers visited the sites several times after the formal period of observation during which time they informally interviewed staff and teachers. More than two hundred hours of on-site observations and participation were conducted for this study.

Analysis

Conventional methods of qualitative data analysis were employed in this research. Formal documents were analyzed for their content and language and then contrasted with the dynamics and outcomes of interactions among parents, staff, and community representatives. Transcribed interviews and field notes were similarly examined. Docu-ments, formal and informal interviews, field notes and journal entries from the second author's participant observations were triangulated to reach and verify findings.

Several themes emerged from the analysis of the data. The first suggests that parent involvement in Sandy Hills Head Start takes on the required form, but has little substance. Staff control the meetings' agenda, dialogue, expenditures, hirings, and the content of the program. Although parents serve on the Policy Council and attend center meetings, their initiatives are blunted or undermined, their ideas dismissed, and their questions ignored or answered incompletely. Consequently, parents are marginalized, not empowered. Second, the insular rural southern working-class cultural context in which Sandy Hills Head Start operated, in conjunction with participants' restricted sociolinguistic code, worked together as microprocesses of cultural and social reproduction. Third, given this marginalization, parent involvement became a very conservative force in the lives of the adults and children. Instead of transforming their lives, parents' involvement with Sandy Hills Head Start was more likely to reproduce the lived culture and social relations of racial, class, and gender domination which characterize them now. In the sections that follow, we describe how parent involvement in Sandy Hills Head Start acts as an essentially conservative force, unlikely to transform participants' lives.

Interaction at Policy Council meetings and center meetings was almost entirely controlled by staff. While the meetings followed the "correct" format for a formal policy-making body (e.g., Robert's Rules of Order), Policy Council agendas were controlled by staff, not parents. Attempts by parents at meaningful dialogue and decision making were undercut. Staff framed issues and questions as narrow choices without alternative solutions. At both Policy Council and center meetings significant policy decisions, such as the location of a new center, the content of the curriculum, or the amount of the budget for teachers and training were never discussed. Instead, discussions of insignificant expenditures or the form of Robert's Rules of Order were covered in great detail. Reports given by parent representatives were reduced to two or three sentences about fund raising. Discussions of substantive issues and the exchange of information relevant to the education of the children, the broader context of the program, and operational decisions were not part of the agenda. Meeting agendas, the way in which the meetings were controlled by administrators, the manner by which parents' questions were evaded, and the way in which parents' attempts at genuine innovation and participation were undermined revealed the lack of meaningful involvement.

Parent Involvement at Policy Council Meetings

Policy Council meetings were scheduled on the first Monday of each month beginning at 6:30 P.M. A light supper was served at each meeting. Staff arrived a few minutes before and set up the buffet-style meal, typically cold cuts, bread, potato chips, soft drinks, and cookies. Council members would arrive between 6:45 and 7:15 P.M. The meeting began when a quorum was present and adjourned about 8:45 P.M.

Agendas were made by the director (staff), not the Council president (a parent). Typically, meetings were structured around the director's reports of routine program procedures. For example, seventy-seven of seventy-nine minutes of discussion at the April 1992 Policy Council meeting were devoted to the director's monthly report of daily operating procedures. Two minutes of the seventy-nine-minute meeting were devoted to parents' reports of their center activities. The particular two-minute sequence below is significant because it represents the typical level of parent interaction at such meetings during the one portion of each meeting that was officially set aside for parent interaction. After finishing her report, the director turned over the floor to the Council president:

President: All right. We'll now have our center reports. And the first one is Willoughby. Miss Virginia Stowe [isn't here]. We'll go on to Western Bradley.
Parent 2: Nothin' happen'n.
President: You mean you all didn't have a meetin'?
Parent 2: Yes, but I wasn't there, so. I was sick.
President: OK. Ah. Mulberry rep is not here. Hollywood Godson. So I'll read Bradley. OK, our meetin' was held April 5th and we, ah, discussed a fund raiser comin' up April tenth. It will be a donut sale. And we also discussed a cookout for parents and children. And then, ah, [we] sent out information.
President: Us. Fulbright Center.
Parent 5: Fulbright. Fulbright doesn't have a report this time.
President: Madison?
Community Representative 1: Nobody from Madison.
President: Ah. Franklin Street.

Parent 7: Us. We talkin' about, us, rafflin' off ticket and sell for a dolla. One of the parents goin' to make a Easter basket. And we tryin' to raise the money to get a TV and a VCR . . . That's about it.
President: Lewis Street?
Parent 8: No report.

A motion was made to adjourn. The entire meeting, and this exchange in particular, illustrates the absence of genuine involvement in the governance of Head Start during the critical Policy Council meetings, which were designed to be the core of parent participation.

A number of other interactions at Policy Council meetings illuminate similar dynamics among parents and staff. Staff vigorously sought the presence of parents at the Policy Council meetings. "PLEASE MAKE EVERY EFFORT TO ATTEND! WE CANNOT CONDUCT BUSINESS WITHOUT YOU!!!" appeared at the bottom of each agenda mailed home during 1991 and 1992. This statement has the appearance of a friendly reminder and a heartfelt plea. In fact, it is the law: business cannot be conducted without a quorum of policy members. But as we have shown, the presence of parents at meetings did not ensure their genuine participation. Policy Council meetings were characterized by controlled agendas. Parent participation was confined to approving predetermined staff initiatives already put into practice or the perfunctory reporting of center meetings. Moreover, attempts by some parents to enter into the genuine processes of the meetings were undercut by staff. The following interchange between the parents and the director illustrates this dynamic.

Parent: [to director] I, um don't know how to word this but, ah, . . . parents got together and we would like for it, you know, for the graduation to be brought up, you know, . . . about the graduation for Head Start children.
Director: Let me tell you where we come from in Head Start. It's not just me, but when we do things for children we need to look at what is the best thing that we can do, whether it's in our classroom, whether we doin' activities for children and a long time ago [we decided] graduation is really done for the adults. That little children. There's a lot better use that can be made of little children's time other than rehearsing for a graduation. It's not that I want to forbid you [parents] from having a graduation but. . . .
Parent: In other words, you're sayin' no to the graduation but you will say yes if all the parents got together and gave the kids a party?

Director: Oh yes, I think that that would be wonderful idea to do something like that.

At this point, other parents protested the decision and cited other Head Start programs that they knew had graduations. Finally, the parent involvement coordinator intervened and supported the director's decision. In this instance, parents ultimately deferred to the authority of the director who evoked her professional expertise and experience in order to maintain dominance and control. The director's response implied that graduations sacrificed children's valuable time on the shallow altar of parent pride. A request for a traditional ceremony signifying the rite of passage, in some respects, was turned into an issue of poor parenting.[1]

Monitoring Employment. During the nine-month period during which this observational research was conducted, specific information given to parents regarding hiring procedures and reasons for termination of staff was vague or nonexistent, although Document 70.2 requires parent oversight of personnel matters. Employment opportunities, job descriptions, and hiring policies and procedures were not discussed at the Policy Council meetings. Personnel needs were not usually brought to the attention of the Policy Council until the interview process had been completed and a candidate selected. The names of those who conducted the interviews and selected the candidate were rarely discussed. Reasons for staff terminations were unclear. Confidentiality was usually cited as a reason for the staff's hesitation to discuss the specifics of employee termination. During the entire period of observation, members of the Policy Council had no real input in any personnel matters other than to rubber stamp actions already decided by the administrative staff.

On one occasion the executive director told the Council that she had hired a staff member without its approval, stating she knew she was "out of compliance," but acknowledged that she did not know what else to do about it. One of the community representatives assured the director that she had acted in a "timely manner" and suggested to the other policy members that the director be commended. There was no further comment about the hiring, the person selected, or a discussion of alternative strategies should this situation arise again in the future. The following excerpts from the minutes of another Policy Council meeting illustrate the extent of the Council's typical involvement in the hiring process. Nine new employees were presented to the Council for approval when, in fact, all personnel were already working in their new jobs.

[the director presents a list of the following new staff members for council's approval:]

    teacher Addison County
    assistance coordinator Addison County
    custodian Sandy Hills Head Start
    family service worker
    teacher Franklin Street
    coteacher/bus driver Addison County
    from coteacher/bus driver to teacher Addison County

The floor was opened for questions. None were asked and a motion was entertained to approve the new employees.

Financial Oversight. In spite of a substantial budget and Document 70.2's specific charge that parents oversee it, financial information such as the allocation of funds or the monitoring of costs and expenditures of program operations were absent from discourse during the nine-month period of observation. For example, a major expenditure—over $600,000 on annual salaries—was never discussed. At one meeting the executive director presented a proposal to the Policy Council in which she detailed budget items ranging from $162 to $23,000. She explained one of the expense items by describing the services received and the way that the charges for the service were computed.

Director: The . . . charges for the administration, they do the accounting. They are legally and physically [sic] responsible for the financial end of the program as well as the overall responsibility.

The Policy Council then had the opportunity to ask questions following the budget presentation.

Director: Now, that's a lot for you to take in at one time but do you have any questions about, about the information?
Community Representative 1: I think you pretty much covered it.
Director: Thank you.
Community Representative 1: I make a motion that the report, the final report be accepted.
Community Representative 2: I second it.

The motion carried. This specific interchange was significant because it was representative of the typical discourse regarding fiscal oversight that occurred throughout the period of research. It illustrates parents' focus on the formal process, not the substantive aspects of genuine oversight. Further, it shows the paternalism of the director who, drawing upon her "official knowledge," suggested that parents may not be able to understand budgetary complexities, but are, of course, free to ask any questions. Not surprisingly, none did.

Governance. At the December meeting of the Policy Council the president, who was the only white male on the Council, solicited volunteers to serve on a By-Laws Committee. Four black female parents volunteered. The program director had requested that the by-laws be revised and that the parent involvement coordinator act as the committee advisor. Functions of the By-Laws Committee were not discussed at the meeting, and copies of the current by-laws were not available for the committee. However, the Policy Council president advised the committee that "we would like to be ready for the January [Policy Council] meeting."

At the January meeting the By-Laws Committee recommended changes in three articles of the Sandy Hills Head Start Policy Council By-Laws. Two of the proposed changes represented an effort to enhance the nature and content of the participation of the Policy Council in Head Start governance. The third concerned the role of parents in the hiring process. First, the committee proposed that Policy Council representatives, rather than the sponsoring agency [Sandy Hills Community Action], select the members from the local community that would serve on the Policy Council and suggested the formation of an "ad hoc committee" of representatives. A parent representative reported to the Policy Council on the By-Laws Committee proposal for an ad hoc committee.

Parent 1: OK, um, there was two [proposed changes] that we had left . . . open for discussion. That III-7, that was talkin' 'bout the ad hoc, right? Don't nobody have that old [current] by-laws. OK, if not I'll let you know that this is about Article III, number 7. OK. 7-B. OK, I'm going to read it as it was, and then I'll read it the corrected. Lemme rephrase that. We didn't correct it, but what we did was we decided on how we would go about, you know, voting for the ad hoc member. . . . We decided that ad hoc representatives should be picked by secret ballot from the Policy Council and the person be a member. We feel like the person should be a member who was supportive 'n knowledgeable of the council activities and was an active member. In other words, we want someone that we feel like will be an asset to us, you know, from the Policy Council, to sit in. We feel like with everybody's involvement, then, you know, then it will be a matter of choice 'cuz everybody's not goin' to feel like this particular person is qualified, so the secret ballot we can come up with more.

Director: Question! Um, what about Policy Council representatives, because one of the things you may have someone with the way the Policy Council is set up and [the] three year limitation on the number of years that you can serve, and you may have someone that rotated off of the Policy Council several years ago that served on the ... [inaudible] that they could serve as a voting member on the council but may not belong to this group because their term expired sometime before this group came into [being]. Have you thought about how you might go about opening it up for those kinds of representatives?

Parent 1: No we didn't, but ... um, I guess that would be up to, uh, I guess the coordinator to maybe get us information on that person, um, to let us have some idea what type of person he or she may have been at, you know, during their serving on the Policy Council.

This exchange illustrates the confusing, repetitive nature and implied content of the language used by staff and parents. In her report to the council, Parent 1 discussed the committee's recommendation for an ad hoc committee, how that committee would be selected, and the qualifications of prospective members. But the By-Laws Committee recommended the formation of a committee of local citizens with no prior affiliation with Sandy Hills Head Start. Members should be experienced in the processes of governance and would advise and support the involvement of parents on the Sandy Hills Head Start Policy Council. They would, in effect, be an independent resource for the parents who would exercise the authority delegated to parents by Document 70.2. The committee recognized that some members of the Council may be reluctant to openly vote against some of those nominated to the ad hoc committee and therefore, recommended a secret ballot.

The director's intervention is in the form of a question that points out insignificant procedural difficulties but overlooks the larger idea of an advisory body as an independent resource for parents. In more explicit language, the director objects to former members of the Policy Council being excluded from serving on the advisory committee. That objection became the barrier to an open discussion. Warnings to parents, "this suggestion needs a lot of thought" and "you need to think about that [the correct wording]," are condescending, paternalistic maneuvers. They are coded phrases that imply that the parents had not given the issue much thought. By phrasing her objections to an independent advisory body in the context of an innocuous concern for excluding past Policy Council members, the director undercut parents' efforts to open up Sandy Hills Head Start to new people and ideas. This would mean that parents remain more dependent upon her and other staff. Parents struggled for greater power, but in the end they were out maneuvered by staff. Parents acquiesced to the director's efforts when they deferred to the coordinator for more information and then tabled the motion for future action. In effect, then, the director and parent involvement coordinator blunted the efforts of parent representatives to open up the Policy Council to greater democratic participation among more parents.

Another change that the committee proposed dealt with the role of the parents and staff in the hiring process. Parents recommended a change that limited their power, and the director then moved them even further along the path of limiting parental power. The discussion and resolution of the proposal unfolded over a period of three months. The process of interviewing and hiring of staff was an ongoing issue for the program director. Both Document 70.2 and the by-laws directed that parents be involved in the process, but their involvement was complicated by the practice of conducting interviews at the administrative offices located a considerable distance from many of the centers. The distance from the residences of many of the parents and the absence of public transportation made it difficult for many parents to get there. The executive director explained, "It's the way it has to be done." During the period of research, no one ever questioned why it had to be done that way.

Under the then-current by-laws, the Personnel Committee could also appoint a center representative to "take full responsibility" for the hiring process. The Review Committee recommended that the by-laws be revised to delete the phrase *take full responsibility* and that the future personnel committees include the director, the staff coordinator, and one parent representative from the Policy Council. This would shift responsibility away from parents, and the director asked for a clarification of the proposed change.

Director: Let me ask one question. What if, you're saying, that the representative from each center would be on the review committee for the application. And then would sit in on interviews. Um.

When I have positions, I interviewed two days last week because we've got positions that NEED to be FILLED, and so when you talk about MAY and SHALL you need to look carefully at your wording on that so that you're giving everybody the same opportunity to be involved in hiring and you're not going to short-change the program by delaying hiring. . . . simply because we can't get a representative in to sit in on the interview, um [emphasis in the original].

The change that the By-Laws Committee ultimately recommended reduced the power of parents on the Policy Council even further. Rather than having the full responsibility as the by-laws originally stated, or sharing it as the Review Committee proposed, the final proposal gave parents *the option* to sit in on the hiring process. The director cited long distances (that parents must travel) and the inability of parents to alter their work schedules (to the interview schedule) as reasons to support the proposed change. The director emphasized that by wording the revisions in this way "the program would not be shortchanged." Without seeming to reject their initiative, she nonetheless blunted it. The direct consequences of the change in the by-laws limited the opportunity of parents to participate in the hiring process of the staff; it diminished the power of the policy council as a collective body and of the representatives as individual members. Yet these changes were not part of any discussion at the policy council meeting. The net result of the change was that parents on the policy council, with the aid of the director, participated in the reduction of their own power.

Parent Involvement at Center Meetings

Center meetings are monthly forums open to all parents where all matters pertaining to a particular center are discussed. At Sandy Hills Head Start, topics such as early childhood education, child development, or programmatic oversight were never discussed during the period under investigation. Meetings at the five sites that the researcher observed were characterized by themes of fund raising or educational programs instructing parents in matters of hygiene and nutrition conducted by local area social service representatives. Any indirect or direct connections among these themes and Head Start were rarely made explicit to parents.

Occasionally, parents attempted to shape the direction of the program by making constructive, educationally germane, and developmentally appropriate suggestions for utilizing money they raised. The following scenarios are illustrative of the power relations among parents and administrators and how the latter undermined effective parent involvement.

Assistant Parent Involvement Coordinator: The only thing we have to discuss tonight other than Mary Kay [cosmetics] was about the money and how to spend it, you know. Josie [parent] is over here tryin' to count up all the money and still have a little bit of it out. Ah, I believe the candy bill was—I can't really remember the exact number, but I think it was about 430 or 450 [dollars] . . . should have close to $200 profit, clear.

Parent 1: Right.

Assistant Parent Involvement Coordinator: Western Bradley, I have an account that has stayed open for two years for Western Bradley that we can take the money and deposit it in the checking account 'til ya'll decide what you want to do with it. Or, if you want to, ah, talk about it tonight and discuss what you want to buy for the classroom. Or what you want to let the teachers buy, um. Sue [teacher] had asked me if you all were just going to give it to them to let them buy something for the classroom. They have a workday this Friday that they can use to go buy stuff. And use it as a shopping day, but that's entirely up to ya'll, whatever you decide, if you just want to put it in the bank and let it stay there for a while until you decide. Or whatever you'd like to do. It's up to ya'll. The four of ya'll are the only ones that are here tonight.

Parent 2: We 'bout the only ones here every night. N, no I can't do that . . . it's up to whatever, I mean."

Assistant Parent Involvement Coordinator: So you've only got three months if you want to buy something for your classroom now.

One father then suggested that the teachers purchase blocks and a fish tank, and the others concurred. The next month, the teacher reported that she had purchased games and arts and crafts materials at a local discount store and had not spent all of the money. The items, still in their cellophane wrappers, were displayed for the parents to see.

Another activity at one of the center groups departed significantly from this norm in the sense that it represented an initiative by parents to fulfill a need that they themselves deemed important to their children. However, the executive director interceded in this process, and the wishes of the parents were subordinated to the more immediate needs of the program as defined by the director. The following interaction is indicative of the way genuine parent initiatives and power were undermined or undercut by the Head Start administration and staff, thus reducing parent involvement to what appears to be form without much substance.

Early in 1992 the parents at Fulbright Center expressed a concern about the playground equipment at the center that their children attended. The equipment was too big for preschoolers, and parents decided to raise money to purchase equipment more appropriate for small children. Plans for fund raising began in November and continued throughout the year. The parents held two activities to raise money and accumulated $1,400 for equipment. In March the director attended the Fulbright Center parents' meeting to speak to the parents.

Director: I've been hearing a lot about the parent group here at the Fulbright Center and . . . that you do fund raising. And she [center coordinator] told me what you were planning to do with the fund raising money, . . . [that it may] go toward playground equipment. So we have the money for a new playground at the Louisville Center. There was money appropriated for a playground there, but we have a playground there, and what we proposed to do, because that money is earmarked for playground equipment and, you know, . . . when you put down what you're going to use the money for they want you to use it for that. So we propose that we put the playground, uh, on this facility out here. And that we can encourage you, because I didn't put any money in the budget for blinds, or anything—see how bad the windows look over here, and one of the new regulations that has come out [has to do] with sanitation, uh regulations, and the lady comes around and she checks our facilities to see if we meet day care licensing, licensing standards on sanitation regulations for day care licensing. They have a light meter, and when they come in they check and, because some of our shades are so bad they won't stay up or they won't stay down unless they're tied. And it makes the room darker, and she . . . could have counted off all these points, but she felt like we . . . so I'd like to propose to you that, if we [put] the playground out here that you sure would make the facility look *sooo* much nicer on the inside if you would put your money towards blinds on the windows.
PARENTS: [parents responded by clapping].

Director: I, I want to commend you, because this is really been a working group of parents down here, and I just really want to commend you for the work that you do for your involvement, because parent involvement is what makes a difference in Head Start . . . so you just keep up the good work.

The blinds were purchased shortly thereafter with money that had been raised by the parents for the playground. Fifteen months later, long after the families who had worked to get it were out of the program, the playground equipment was installed at this center. The parent involvement coordinator could not explain the reason for the delay.

This incident, perhaps more than others, epitomizes what we term "parent involvement in form but not in substance." It also demonstrates the ways that the staff undercut genuine parent initiatives. By framing the request for blinds as meeting the needs of the program and praising parents when they acquiesced to her request to use their playground money for blinds, the director turned parent involvement on its head, marginalizing parents.

Conferences

Official Head Start conferences were special events, and attendance was an honor coveted by parents. The annual state convention could have been an opportunity to share ideas, broaden the knowledge base of parents, network, and learn about the latest in child development and early childhood education. Instead, the oppressive aspects and paternalistic social relations characteristic of the local rural, southern culture and of the Sandy Hills Head Start organization were replayed and amplified at the convention. In addition, the substantive content of conferences offered little to broaden the knowledge base of parents. Instead, sessions drew from popular culture and traditional knowledge grounded in the southern, rural, lived culture of parents. The absence of alternative perspectives, then, failed to enhance parents' knowledge and contributed to social and cultural reproduction instead of transformation.

The program's executive director received several formal invitations for lunch and the official opening of the annual State Head Start Association convention, and she was entrusted with distributing the invitations to parents. A memo sent to the parents planning to attend the convention framed attendance as a privilege ("CONGRATULATIONS on being selected to attend"). Reminders dealing with behavior were interwoven throughout the memo. Phrases such as "Please be on time," "Appropriate dress and conduct are expected," "Missing items . . . will be reported . . . That would be very embarrassing" conveyed the director's expectations of the behavior of parent and staff while they were at the conference.

The main session for administrators was a workshop about funding, personnel, and the future. The Head Start regional director was the featured speaker at a workshop titled "Dialogue with Head Start Directors and Executive Directors." The session's content focused on management and bureaucratic issues, and goals were linked to the theme The Year 2000. Directors were reminded that "the federal government is no higher than you." Delegates were told to deal with their own adversarial relationships and improve communication with the regional office and local agencies. The analogy to "big business" was interwoven throughout the session. Head Start programs were compared to "corporations with directors as CEO's." Directors were warned of the possibility of "hostile takeovers of unhealthy companies," limited funding, and the monitoring of "at-risk programs." Staff turnover was viewed as an inevitable "brain drain" caused by "the law of the jungle" and beyond resolution ("can't help that"). Problems were framed as threats without solutions. The group of executive and program directors responded to the address of the regional director with two questions and one hour and forty-five minutes of seemingly attentive listening.

This workshop for directors is consistent with the new "business management" style of social services administration noted by Ellsworth and Ames (1995). This growing emphasis on accountability and productivity in social services tends to pressure directors to become more goal oriented and provides a rationale for circumventing time-consuming parent involvement, for example, when hiring people to fill open positions. This external organizational imperative, then, contributes to the disempowerment of parents.

In contrast to the themes of management issues, parents' workshops were devoted to individuals in need of reform. Eight of ten parent involvement/social services workshops tied program development to issues of child abuse, family violence, the development of parenting skills, social service burnout and case management. A three-hour workshop called "The Year 2000—Parent Involvement" engaged parents in activities that defined children and families as sources of current social problems and developed strategies for parents to deal with these problems. The presenter, a black female and former Head

Start parent, linked both her business and her personal success to her involvement with Head Start. Larger societal problems such as increased poverty, racism, violence, and unemployment were defined in terms of individual behaviors such as drug abuse, child abuse, and illiteracy. Typical solutions were framed as suggestions to parents to "give 100 percent," monitor television, increase discipline, manage their money, work hard, and compete for jobs at fast food restaurants.

A local conference sponsored by Head Start parents continued the themes of the annual state convention. In the spring of 1992, the parent involvement coordinator planned a joint conference with parents and a group of African American students from a local college. The theme of the conference was Saving the Black Male: An Endangered Species. Workshops titled "Overrepresentation of Minority Males in Jails," "Underemployment of Minorities," and "Miseducation of Black Youth" were scheduled in the morning and repeated in the afternoon. Panel members and workshop facilitators were African American males and females from the community. The program listed their occupations as law enforcement officers, ministers, retired educators, Head Start parents and staff, and students from the local college. Despite what the provocative workshop titles suggested, the definition of the problems and the solutions offered focused on personal traits, individual shortcomings, and behavior of participants. Again, the way each of these social problems as discussed implied that their causes and their solutions lay in the choices available and under the control of individuals; structural forces were ignored.

At both the state Head Start convention and the local conference, there was an absence of any discussion or analysis of the larger social structural forces which affected the "problems" under discussion: the restructured U.S. political economy and its effects on the rural South, the growing emiseration of the poor, racism, class privileges, sexism, or why there was a paucity of decent jobs (c.f., Tomaskovic-Devey 1991) in the rural three-county area served by Sandy Hills Head Start. The absence of any social critique or analysis was as striking as the ocean of individualistic, self-help rhetoric that washed over the conference attendees.

Parent Employees of Head Start

Work experience is a form of involvement critical both to parent empowerment and to transformation. Employment in Head Start is one form of parent involvement specified in Document 70.2. The founders of Head Start and its current administrators view this form of involvement as an opportunity for parents to build a foundation for their future employment elsewhere while they earn money and serve as role models for their children. This component of Head Start is designed as a key point of involvement and empowerment. But like so many of the other aspects of Sandy Hills Head Start, the way that parent employment unfolded often contradicted and undermined the spirit and letter of the policy.

As anticipated by policy makers, a number of parents aspired to positions within the Sandy Hills Head Start program. At one Policy Council meeting a parent asked the director how parents could get information about employment.

PARENT 1: [Parents] are interested in the types of work . . . [so] they have the opportunity.

Director: It's set up for parents to be paid as substitutes, but they have to have a certain number of hours, volunteer hours. They also have to have some training, because, you know, if you get volunteer hours but you don't have the training to back that up. You know, that you have to look closely at that too. And then if they're going to be serving as paid substitutes they also have to have a recommendation from the education coordinator if they're going to be substitute teachers.

PARENT 1: But most of the parents do know that. They know about the volunteer hours, and there's a possibility that they might have a chance to work in Head Start, but they don't know about the training. How—how do you get it out to the parents, about the training?

Director: Well, generally, if there's training it's going to be offered, you know. We try to send notices out. Ah. So parents, if they are specifically interested in training, working with early childhood, they will ask, you know, and Head Start has always [paid] tuition for parents.

This segment of mottled, coded dialogue is significant for several reasons. It represents an effort by one of the parents to obtain information for herself and other parents about training and job opportunities and the manner in which they can gain access to that information. That it also is an attempt by the director to convey specific information illustrates how the participants' restricted sociolinguistic code and cultural capital shaped the questions, the answers, the content of the information exchanged, and the outcome of the inquiry—parents failed to receive the information they requested about employment.

What is not exchanged is significant, too. Parent 1 did not directly ask for and the director did not give information concerning the types and availability of training and employment, various sources of information within Head Start and the larger community, and the earning potential of jobs within Head Start and the field of early childhood development. The director did not indicate the number of positions available, at which centers there were openings, where one could apply for training, how to get further information, or when the routine notifications about training and employment alluded to in her answer would be sent out next. Because the insular, rural, southern cultural capital of parents incorporated few, if any, alternative channels for receiving job information, parents were dependent upon the director. They relied upon her. This is characteristic of the paternalistic social relations that mark the race and class divisions of this poor, rural community. To request the director to clarify her answer or to provide greater details would require more middle-class cultural capital and command of a more direct, explicit language—linguistic codes and cultural capital different from that of the parents. As an opportunity for employment, Sandy Hills Head Start remained as shrouded in mystery to parents in the three-county area as jobs on Wall Street.

DISCUSSION AND CONCLUSION

In the following discussion, we attempt to make sense of the findings reported in the preceding paragraphs. We focus upon the social relations among parents and staff, restricted linguistic codes of the participants, and the cultural capital of the school and the community in order to examine the processes of social and cultural reproduction we found in this preschool. Basil Bernstein's concepts of restricted codes and Pierre Bourdieu's notion of cultural capital link the cultural content of interactions involving language, the social relations of domination, and the organizational culture of Sandy Hills Head Start.

We begin with the last example of parents' attempts to gain information about employment. The exchange about employment opportunities between Parent 1 and the director epitomizes what Bernstein labeled "restricted sociolinguistic codes." It illustrates how restricted codes, characteristic of working-class families, imply rather than explicitly state meaning and are clear only if the listeners share a common history or relationship (Bernstein 1975; Sadovnik 1991). Like so many of the dialogues presented in this chapter, the exchange about job openings is repetitive in nature, context dependent, and does not take into consideration alternatives outside of the immediate environment. Both parties are dependent upon each other's understanding of the meanings implied in their questions and answers. In this instance, the discussion is context dependent; that is, the meaning of the text and the intent of the exchange is dependent upon a mutual understanding that Head Start offers training and opportunities for jobs, that Parent 1 and other parents of Sandy Hills Head Start are interested in training and jobs and that Sandy Hills Head Start has programs that offer training and opportunities for employment. Parent 1, unfamiliar with policies and procedures, is dependent upon the director's understanding of her implied questions. The scope of the questions and answers is particularistic in that they are relevant only to immediate circumstances, the here and now.[2]

In other examples we have provided, parents both acquiesced to staff, and at the same time they actively sought their direction in the governance process of the program. Staff challenged parents when the latter attempted to enter into the dialogue at Policy Council meetings, and parents deferred to the staff's expertise and power. Staff assumed that the content of materials distributed at Policy Council meetings was beyond the understanding and outside the interests of the parents. Resistance to parent involvement took the form of staff's attempts to control the Policy Council meetings and to undercut parents' initiatives for greater involvement. Although parents repeatedly attempted to gain greater power over the operation of Sandy Hills Head Start, their efforts were overwhelmed. All actors engaged in patterns of interaction shaped by their shared understanding of traditional southern, rural, working-class culture, with its racial, class, and gender hierarchies and deference to authority. Because parents' own cultural resources did not include alternative strategies for how to challenge the director and her associates, and because parents believed their own substantive knowledge about budgets, employment practices, and child development was inferior to the director's, they deferred to her. This continuous flow of obstacles to parents participating as actual decision makers contributed to the replication of hierarchical social relationships and reinforced the cultural and social status quo. Parent involvement in Sandy Hills Head Start was largely reduced to form without substance.

Jeanne Ellsworth and Lynda Ames (1995) chronicled the way the power of low-income women in a rural New York Head Start became largely ceremonial. They posit that this Head Start had adopted a version of parent involvement that essentially co-opts community action principles. Virtually all issues brought before the New York Head Start Policy Council were merely issues to be voted upon and approved. The women they observed had little opportunity to substantially shape the program and were largely silenced by staff whenever they challenged any aspect of the operation. Because of the asymmetry of knowledge and power (elements of cultural capital), conversations between staff and parents were enormously disempowering. The similarities between the dynamics there and those in Sandy Hills are striking.

Given the insularity of the organizational and cultural environment of Sandy Hills Head Start and the paucity of jobs available to parents, adults were unlikely to acquire job skills they could transfer later. And, sadly, the social relations of authority within the organization, in interaction with parents' restricted codes and cultural capital, blocked them from truly participating in the governance of Head Start in empowering ways that could transform their lives. Moreover, the dynamics we describe are deceptively conservative because they are understood by most participants—staff, parents, and teachers—as truly empowering parents through experience, employment, and adult education, even though very little of this actually goes on for most parents. For example, among those who do gain a job, employment at Head Start has the likely effect of locking Head Start families into their current class position for the foreseeable future. By working in Head Start where the average annual pay is very low, parents remove themselves from the job market. Work and the volunteering that must precede it, then, preclude parents from seeking more education, training, and other, better paying jobs. The job experiences they gain, furthermore, are not easily transferable to other occupations. Finally, because virtually all the employees in the Head Start program come from the same insular, rural, southern culture, parents have limited exposure to middle-class cultural capital or elaborated linguistic codes, which could better equip them should they try to move beyond their community of origin.

The findings we report here should not be taken as an argument against parent involvement in Head Start. Genuine parent involvement must be supported, nurtured, and sustained for all the reasons that progressive advocates have articulated. All parents, especially less educated ones, must be further educated in order to be more effective partners in their children's education. At Sandy Hills Head Start parents were not formally educated or trained for their work. Volunteer experience alone is an inadequate foundation for successful involvement in schools. Parents need to receive education in a formal curriculum relevant to child development. Our research suggests that administrators require further training as well. They must be made aware of the unintended consequences of their paternalistic behavior and taught how to foster and nurture genuine parent involvement, even if it is inconvenient, time-consuming, inefficient, and diminishes staff's autonomy and power.

Finally, this chapter should not be read as an argument that if only Sandy Hills Head Start operated differently (that is, parent involvement were truly substantive, and parents were educated, trained, and empowered by their participation), the lives of children and parents would be transformed. The poverty and powerlessness of their lives ultimately are rooted in the political economy of the rural South and in its traditional class, gender, and racial hierarchies, not in the operations of Sandy Hills Head Start.

NOTES

1. In his stunning, but disturbing treatise *Savage Inequalities,* Jonathan Kozol (1991) discusses the symbolic importance of children's graduation rites to poor parents. For many, these ceremonies are the first in their families.

2. The following conversation starkly illustrates how the use of restricted sociolinguistic codes is characteristic of the Head Start participants. Volunteer Alice, a recent Ph.D. in English, and Louise, the Head Start parent coordinator, a local resident who has a B.A. from a nearby conservative Christian college, discuss the latter's educational plans:

"I'm bound and determined to get my Ph.D." exclaimed Louise upon learning that Alice recently received her doctoral degree.
"I have a copy of my dissertation. Would you like to read it?" asked Alice.
"Well, tell me about it. I hate to read and write," replied Louise.

REFERENCES

Anyon, J. (1980). "Social Class and the Hidden Curriculum of Work." Journal of Education. 162: 93–107.

Baker, D. P., and Stevenson, D. L. (1986). Mothers' strategies for children's school achievement: Managing the transition to high school. *Sociology of Education,* Vol. 59. 156–66.

Bennett, W. J. (1992). *The devaluing of America: The fight for our culture and our children.* New York: Simon and Schuster.

Bernstein, B. (1975). *Class, codes, and control,* Vols. 1–3. London: Routledge & Kegan Paul.

Bernstein, B. (1990). *The structure of pedagogic discourse.* New York: Routledge.

Bourdieu, P. (1990). *The logic of practice.* Richard Nice (Tr.) Stanford: Stanford University Press.

Bourdieu, P., and Passeron, J. C. (1977). *Reproduction in education, society, and culture.* Beverly Hills: Sage.

Bourdieu, P., and Wacquant, L. (1992). *An invitation to reflexive sociology.* Chicago: University of Chicago Press.

Bowles, S., and Gintis, H. (1976). *Schooling in capitalist America: Educational reform and the contradictions of economic life.* New York: Basic Books.

Carnoy, M., and Levin, H. (1985). *Schooling and work in the democratic state.* Stanford: Stanford University Press.

Comer, J. P. (1988). Educating poor minority children. *Scientific American,* Vol. 295, 42–48.

Comer, J. P. (1993). A brief history and summary of the School Development Program. Paper presented at the American Educational Research Association, Atlanta, GA.

Comer, J. P. (1995). *School power: Implications of Intervention Project.* NY: Free Press.

Ellsworth, J., and Ames, L. (1995). Power and ceremony: Low-income mothers as policy makers in head start. *Educational Foundations* (Fall): 5–23.

Epstein, J. L. (1990). School and family connections: Theory, research, and implications for integrating sociology of education and family. In Unger, D., and Sussman, M. (Eds.), *Families in community settings: Interdisciplinary perspectives,* New York: Haworth Press.

Epstein, J. L. (1995). School/family/community partnerships: Caring for the children we share. *Phi Delta Kappan,* Vol. 76, 701–712.

Giroux, H. (1983). *Theory and resistance in education.* New Hadley, MA: Bergin and Garvey.

Goldfield, D. R. (1990). *Black, white, and southern: Race relations and southern culture 1940 to the present.* Baton Rouge: Louisiana State University Press.

Head Start. (1967). *Head Start Policy Manual. Instruction 1–30. Section B-2.* Washington, D.C.: U.S. Government Printing Office.

Heath, S. (1983). *Ways with words: Language, life and work in communities and classrooms.* New York: Cambridge University Press.

Klenz, M. (1993). Parent involvement in Head Start and the reproduction of social class. Unpublished master's thesis, Department of Sociology, University of North Carolina, Charlotte.

Kozol, J. (1991). *Savage inequalities: Children in America's schools.* New York: Crown.

Lareau, Annette (1989). *Home advantage: Social class and parental intervention in elementary education.* London: Falmer Press.

Loury, G. C. (1985). The moral quandary of the black community. *The Public Interest,* Vol. 9, 9–22.

Lubeck, S. (1985). *Sandbox society, early education in black and white America: A comparative ethnography.* London: Falmer Press.

McLeod, J. (1987). *Ain't no makin' it.* Boulder, CO: Westview.

Mickelson, R. (1980). The secondary school's role in social stratification: A comparison of Beverly Hills High School and Morningside High School. *Journal of Education,* Vol. 162, 83–112.

Mickelson, R. (1987). The case of the missing brackets: Teachers and social reproduction. *Journal of Education,* Vol. 169, 52–53.

Miller, D. F., and Ginsburg, M. B. (1989). Social reproduction and resistance in four infant/toddler daycare settings: An ethnographic study of social relations and sociolinguistic codes. *Journal of Education,* Vol. 171, 31–50.

Morrow, R., and Torres, C. A. (1994). Education and the reproduction of class, gender, and race: Responding to the postmodern challenge. *Educational Theory,* Vol. 44, 43–61.

Morrow, R., and Torres, C. A. (1995). Social theory and education: A critique of theories of social and cultural reproduction. Albany: State University of New York Press.

North Carolina Department of Human Resources. (1995). *Statistical Journal* (July–December). Raleigh, NC: Division of Child Development.

North Carolina State Center for Health and Environmental Statistics. (1994). *North Carolina Vital Statistics.* Volume 1. Raleigh, NC.

Powell, D. R. (1990) Home visiting in the early years: Policy and program design decisions. *Young Children* (September): 65–73.

Public Law 90–222. December 23, 1967. Part B. Section 222, (a) (1), (B).

Sadovnik, A. (1991). Basil Bernstein's theory of pedagogic practice: A structuralist approach. *Sociology of Education,* Vol. 64, 48–63.

Schweinhart, L. J., Barnes, H. B., Weikart, D. P., Barnett, W. S., and Epstein, A. S. (1993). *Significant benefits: The High/Scope Perry Preschool students through age 27. Monograph 10.* Ypsilanti, MI: High/Scope Educational Research Foundation.

Stevenson, D. L., and Baker, D. P. (1987). The family-school relation and the child's school performance. *Child Development,* Vol. 58, 1348–1357.

Tomaskovic-Devey, D. (1991). *Sundown on the sunbelt? Growth without development in the rural South.* Report to the Ford Foundation. Department of Sociology, North Carolina State University, Raleigh.

United States Department of Commerce. (1992). U.S. Census Summary Tape File 3A, CD ROM, North Carolina U.S. Bureau of the Census. Washington, D.C.: Government Printing Office.

Washington, V. (1995). *Project Head Start: Models and strategies for the twentieth century.* New York: Garland.

White, L. (1991). Grant proposal narrative submitted to the National Science Foundation. Los Angeles: UCLA School of Law.

Willis, P. (1977). *Learning to labor.* New York: Columbia University Press.

Wrigley, J. (1995). *Other people's children.* New York: Basic Books.

Zigler, E. (1992). Strength in unity: Consolidating federal education programs for young children. Conference Paper, University of North Carolina, Chapel Hill, April 3.

Zigler, E., and Valentine, J. (1979). *Project Head Start: A legacy of the War on Poverty.* New York: Free Press.

5

Head Start Bilingual and Multicultural Program Services

Patricia A. Hamilton
Katherine Hayes
and Henry M. Doan

INTRODUCTION

This descriptive study examines how Head Start programs use bilingual and multicultural practices to serve children from diverse linguistic and cultural backgrounds.* It defines multicultural services from the Head Start population's point of view, a population that includes administrators, teachers and other staff, parents, and community members. The chapter will illustrate the range of diversity within Head Start and its delivery of multicultural services. It will demonstrate the ideological and structural constraints to implementing a multicultural program that, in keeping with the commitment of Head Start, "serves the needs of the various cultural and linguistic subgroups in a culturally sensitive manner in order to maximize the effectiveness of the Head Start experience."[1]

Although Head Start multicultural services were designed to cover all four component areas (health, education, social services, and parent involvement) of the program, the bulk of research and publication regarding multiculturalism is found within the field of education.

*This study was commissioned by the Administration on Children, Youth, and Families (ACYF) of the U.S. Department of Health and Human Services (1993–1996).

Research regarding the educational and social experiences of immigrant children and their families has resulted in widely diverse definitions of multiculturalism. Some scholars lament the fact that multicultural education lacks expression as a single viewpoint, "There is no intellectually coherent construct, systematic in its practices and consistent in its policies."[2] The original mission of multicultural education as conceptualized in the 1960s was, however, to create "new collective identities that emphasize strength and pride" as part of a larger social movement "directed toward equalizing power and legal status among racial and gender groups."[3] This definition was accepted as the guiding principle for the study. The civil rights movement articulated a vision of equality and rights among racial groups, and that vision resulted in the attempt to make social institutions more accessible to people of color. Since 1965, when the War on Poverty was declared, Head Start has served over 13,000,000 children and their families. It currently serves more than 750,000 children each year, excluding those in the expansion program for children from birth through three years of age.[4] The program serves growing numbers of bilingual (or multilingual), multicultural populations and, in keeping with its vision, includes requirements for serving multicultural children and families in its *Head Start Performance Standards* (1975), which is currently under major revision. Additionally, in 1991 the Administration on Children, Youth, and Families (ACYF) issued *Multicultural Guidelines* to further direct Head Start on the needs of the growing bilingual, multicultural population. Following are ten multicultural principles that support these guidelines:

1. Every individual is rooted in a culture.

2. The cultural groups represented in the communities and families of each Head Start program are the primary source of culturally relevant programming.

3. Culturally relevant and diverse programming requires learning information about the culture of different groups and discarding stereotypes.

4. Addressing cultural relevance in making curriculum choices is a necessary, developmentally appropriate practice.

5. Every individual has the right to maintain his or her identity while acquiring the skills required to function in our diverse society.

6. Effective programs for children with limited English speaking ability require continued development of the primary language while the acquisition of English is facilitated.

7. Culturally relevant programming requires staff who reflect the community and families served.

8. Multicultural programming for children enables children to develop an awareness of, respect for, and appreciation of individual cultural differences. It is beneficial to all children.

9. Culturally relevant and diverse programming examines and challenges institutional and personal biases.

10. Culturally relevant and diverse programming and practices are incorporated in all components and services.[5]

A substantial body of literature reinforces the appropriateness of these multicultural guidelines as a Head Start emphasis. Especially in reference to principle 6, research has shown that children benefit by being taught in their home language and by having role models with whom they can identify.[6] The use of first language instruction for language minority children is generally held by educators to be the most effective form of education for cognitive development and academic progress. It fosters self-respect.[7] Head Start has attempted to respond to the needs of its diverse population by encouraging the use of the child's home language as well as English in the program. A number of studies, related to the use of language as a social tool, point out the importance of the difference between home and school language use by children. Research has suggested that in Head Start classrooms with bilingual (Spanish/English) teachers, interactions with students are similar to those of mother and child within the home.[8]

Other findings also suggest that the influence of English among bilingual children in the United States is powerful. In one study, preschoolers were found to interact with peers and siblings in English, although their interactions with parents occurred in Spanish.[9] Wong-Fillmore notes that the preponderance of English-language interactions in preschool or day care programs may result in a change in parent-child discourse patterns and a breakdown of parental authority.[10] Implicit in the findings is the notion that young children should be instructed in their home languages and that their culture should be affirmed in order to achieve optimal academic and personal success. The Head Start multicultural principles directly support such concerns.

The next section presents the methodology used in the study to research multicultural services among Head Start programs around the country. It is followed by a section that explores the demographics and diversity found within Head Start families and presents data on who is being served by Head Start. The chapter then offers a description of the multicultural nature of Head Start services. An overview is presented on the administrative structure of Head Start, staffing patterns, and the strategies used by different programs to meet the needs of their rapidly changing client base. The chapter ends with a discussion on the problems in providing Head Start multicultural services and possible solutions.

METHODOLOGY

The primary purpose of the study was to provide information to help inform policy and programming decisions, thereby improving the overall quality and effectiveness of Head Start service delivery options. More specifically, the objectives of the study were to

- obtain a profile of currently eligible families and children as well as document past and future trends;

- describe the number and distribution of children and families of bilingual and multicultural backgrounds currently served by Head Start;

- determine the characteristics of current efforts undertaken by Head Start grantees throughout the United States to assist diverse Head Start families; and

- explore features of current programs as they relate to the development of social competencies of children in bilingual and multicultural environments.

To fulfill these objectives, the study systematically collected information not only on the nature and range of services provided to children and families from diverse cultural and linguistic backgrounds but also on the number and distribution of Head Start eligible children and families based on income and minority group membership. Three interrelated data collection and analysis activities were conducted.

- Census and PIR Data. Census and Head Start Program Information Report (PIR) data were analyzed and compared to determine the characteristics of the Head Start-eligible population and the served population. Data from the PIR also were used as the source for the Head Start program population, to whom a longer version of the survey (described below) was sent.

- Survey Data. The team conducted a national survey of all Head Start grantees and delegates to describe the population served and to determine the range of services available to bilingual and multicultural children and families. The data sources included two surveys. Survey 1 was sent to 1,906 grantees and delegates, and survey 2, a longer version, was sent to the remaining 100 grantees. Survey 1 requested information on the language and ethnicity of children and staff as well as brief descriptions of waiting lists, materials, and innovative components. Survey 2 elicited more in-depth information on all program components for specific cultural and language groups. Extensive contact by mail and telephone was conducted to ensure a high response rate (the rate was 72 percent for survey 1 and 61 percent for survey 2). As completed questionnaires arrived, staff followed a strict protocol to ensure that returned questionnaires were recorded and entered into a Microsoft Access database.

- Site Visit Data. Field workers made in-depth visits to thirty programs to gather qualitative data on services designed to meet the needs of diverse cultural and ethnic groups. Interviews, focus groups, and classroom observations were used to collect this information. The site visits allowed for an even greater in-depth understanding of the challenges and solutions to serving bilingual/multicultural populations. While the surveys provided broad, general information on Head Start programs, the site visits offered additional insights into the actual implementation of the multicultural practices. Site visit interviews with Head Start staff, focus groups with parents, and classroom observations yielded program descriptions, comparisons, and perceptions and added greatly to an understanding of multicultural issues facing Head Start. The survey findings as well as suggestions from the National Advisory Panel, Head Start Bureau program staff, and Regional Office staff were used to stratify and select the sites according to geography, population served, and innovative multicultural services.

Each data set collected from the above sources was analyzed and integrated to produce the findings of this study.

THE CHANGING FACE OF HEAD START

Demographics and Diversity

Minority groups are growing faster than the white majority. According to the 1990 census, the combined growth (15,549,000) from 1980 to

1990 for four minority groups—black, Hispanic, Asian, and other—was more than one-third greater than that of the majority white non-Hispanic population. This was the case even though the minority groups together had a population less than 31 percent of the majority. Hispanics alone accounted for nearly 50 percent of the increase among minority groups.

Higher fertility rates are an important contributing factor to the increased growth rate among minority populations. All minority fertility rates, with the exception of those for Asian/Pacific Islanders, outpace non-Hispanic whites. Native Americans and Alaska natives have the highest fertility rates, followed by Hispanics, then African Americans (census 1990). The high fertility rate among these groups has a direct impact on educational programming because there will be many more multicultural children entering school and in need of preschool programs to assist them.

The percentage of blacks, Hispanics, and native Americans living in poverty is about three times that of non-Hispanic whites. Asian Americans are also more likely than non-Hispanic whites to live in families with incomes below the poverty line established by the Office of Management and Budget ($14,350 for a family of four in 1993).[11] Hence, most children eligible for Head Start, as well as most children enrolled in Head Start, represent minority groups. Using the 1990 census, it was projected that 55 percent of the children eligible for Head Start in that year were American Indian, Asian American, African-American, or Hispanic American; this percentage has increased considerably since that year. Similarly, the 1992 through 1993 PIR data show that 65 percent of the children enrolled in Head Start represent minority groups.

Head Start enrolls higher proportions of eligible minority children than white children. Of those qualifying for the projection in 1992, two of every three American Indian youngsters were enrolled; as were 59 percent of black children, 45 percent of Hispanic children, and 43 percent of Asian youngsters. Only 34 percent of eligible white children were enrolled in Head Start in 1992 (table 5.1).

The trends become clearer when federal regional and state data are examined (table 5.2). In regions II, IV, VI, and particularly IX, there were more eligible minority children than there were eligible white youngsters. Black children were a majority of eligible children in region IV. Region IX showed 76 percent minority children and the greatest diversity. Of the 217,060 children estimated to be eligible for Head Start in region IX, 4 percent were American Indian, 9 percent were

TABLE 5.1
Enrollment by Ethnicity

Ethnicity	Eligible Children[1]	Children in Head Start[2]	Proportion of Eligible Children in Head Start
American Indian	40,800	26,632	0.65
Asian or Pacific Islander	37,270	16,026	0.43
Black (Not Hispanic)	432,080	253,658	0.59
Hispanic	309,290	138,223	0.45
White (Not Hispanic)	680,480	231,811	0.34
Total	1,499,920	666,350	0.44

1. Children below the poverty line, 3 or 4 years old, estimated from 1990 census.
2. Children served by Head Start, from 1992–93 PIR. This may include <3 and >4 year olds.

Asian, 12 percent were black, 24 percent were white, and a majority 51 percent were Hispanic. In contrast, in region VII, three of every four eligible children were white.

With respect to the state level analysis, three findings are noteworthy. First, percentage enrollment of eligible children in Head Start varied enormously. Five states (Florida, Louisiana, Nevada, Texas, Utah) enrolled 35 percent or less of eligible children. In contrast, five states (Alaska, Maine, Mississippi, North Dakota, South Dakota) and the District of Columbia enrolled over 67 percent of eligible children. This enormous diversity held among the minority poor. Three states (Nevada, Tennessee, Texas) enrolled less than 40 percent of the eligible minority children, but twelve states (Alaska, Delaware, Idaho, Iowa, Minnesota, Mississippi, Montana, Nebraska, North Dakota, Ohio, South Dakota, Washington) enrolled over four out of every five eligible minority children. Second, Head Start enrolled a higher percentage of eligible minority children than of their white counterparts. Only in Tennessee was the proportion of eligible white youngsters enrolled (40 percent) higher than the corresponding minority percentage (37 percent). In many states, the proportion of eligible minority children enrolled was twice that for white youngsters. The extreme case is South Carolina, which enrolled 51 percent of eligible minority children but only 9 percent of the white youngsters who qualified.

TABLE 5.2
Regional Composition by Ethnicity of Children Eligible for Head Start

Region	% White	% Asian	% Black	% Hispanic	% American Indian	Total
I	59	3	13	23	2	49,440
II	41	2	26	29	1	125,750
III	60	1	33	5	0	119,080
IV	40	1	54	5	1	306,390
V	62	2	28	7	2	256,470
VI	30	1	29	36	4	258,970
VII	75	1	18	4	2	64,640
VIII	63	1	3	20	12	48,890
IX	24	9	12	51	4	217,060
X	66	4	5	15	10	53,230

Source: 1990 Census, PUMS.
Region I—Connecticut, Maine, Massachusetts, New Hampshire, Rhode Island, Vermont.
Region II—New Jersey, New York, Puerto Rico, Virgin Islands. **Region III**—Delaware, Washington DC, Maryland, Pennsylvania, Virginia, West Virginia. **Region IV**—Alabama, Florida, Kentucky, Mississippi, North Carolina, South Carolina, Tennessee. **Region V**—Illinois, Indiana, Michigan, Minnesota, Ohio, Wisconsin. **Region VI**—Arkansas, Louisiana, New Mexico, Oklahoma, Texas. **Region VII**—Iowa, Kansas, Missouri, Nebraska. **Region VIII**—Colorado, Montana, North Dakota, Utah, Wyoming, South Dakota. **Region IX**—Arizona, California, Hawaii, Nevada, Pacific Insular Areas. **Region X**—Alaska, Idaho, Oregon, Washington.

Finally, among minority groups, enrollment was highest proportionally among African Americans and native Americans. A small number of states enrolled a higher percentage of Hispanic children than black children, but these states had relatively small numbers of Hispanics. In all of the states with the largest Hispanic populations (Arizona, California, Colorado, Florida, Illinois, New Jersey, New York), the percentage of African American children enrolled was higher than the percentage of Hispanic youngsters in Head Start.

Languages of Eligible and Enrolled Head Start Children

As with the analysis by racial and ethnic group, using the 1990 census, the number of eligible children from the nation, regions, and states was estimated and compared with actual enrollment figures from the 1992 through 1993 PIR.

Table 5.3 profiles the languages spoken at home by Head Start–eligible children and those actually enrolled. Twenty percent of eligible youngsters and 17 percent of children in the program did not speak English at home. Head Start enrolled a higher percentage of eligible English-speaking and Chinese-speaking children, both 46 percent, than those speaking other languages. The program enrolled 39 percent of the youngsters who speak Spanish.

In six of the ten Head Start regions, the vast majority of *eligible* children and their parents spoke English. In three other regions ap-

TABLE 5.3
Enrollment by Eligibility, by Home Language

Language	Eligible Children[1]	Children in Head Start[2]	Proportion of Eligible Children in Head Start
English	1,193,620	550,716	0.46
Spanish	240,773	94,150	0.39
Cambodian	5,351	1,145	0.21
Chinese	5,370	2,465	0.46
French/Haitian	8,328	2,430	0.29
Hmong	5,830	2,403	0.41
Japanese	612	79	0.13
Korean	2,526	295	0.12
Vietnamese	6,955	2,683	0.39
Other	30,555	9,649	0.32
Total	1,499,920	666,015	0.44

1. Children below the poverty line, 3 or 4 years old, estimated from 1990 census.
2. Children served by Head Start, from 1992–93 PIR. This may include <3 and >4 year olds.

proximately one-quarter of the eligible children spoke Spanish. California stood out from the rest of the nation in the breadth and depth of its linguistic diversity: half the children eligible for Head Start did not speak English; over 10 percent spoke a language other than Spanish or English.

These concentrations of language groups varied by state. More than 40 percent of children *enrolled* in California Head Start programs spoke a language other than English, as did over 30 percent in Arizona, Texas, and Washington (figure 5.1). Clearly, the greatest majority of non-English languages were in the West, Southwest, Florida, and New York. Spanish was spoken by numerous children in several of the states; in the state of Washington, Asian languages predominated.

Children enrolled in Head Start programs in California, Washington, and New York spoke at least ten languages other than English (figure 5.2).

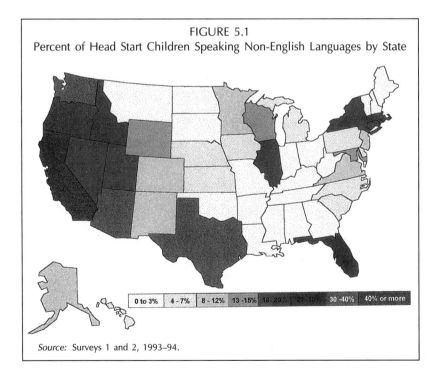

FIGURE 5.1
Percent of Head Start Children Speaking Non-English Languages by State

0 to 3%   4 - 7%   8 - 12%   13 -15%   16 - 20%   21 - 30%   30 - 40%   40% or more

Source: Surveys 1 and 2, 1993–94.

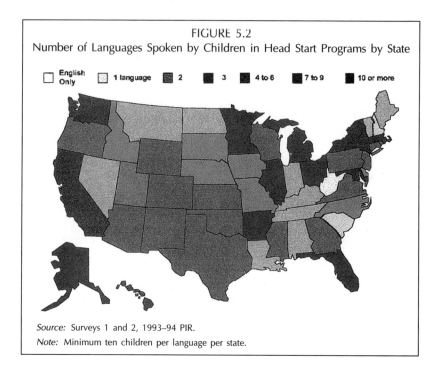

FIGURE 5.2
Number of Languages Spoken by Children in Head Start Programs by State

☐ English Only   ☐ 1 language   ☐ 2   ■ 3   ■ 4 to 6   ■ 7 to 9   ■ 10 or more

Source: Surveys 1 and 2, 1993–94 PIR.
Note: Minimum ten children per language per state.

MULTICULTURAL APPROACHES

Staff Language and Ethnicity

According to the national survey, staff language was by far the most frequently mentioned challenge in programs serving families whose home language was not English. Programs had great difficulty, confirmed during the site visits, in finding trained personnel with both the appropriate cultural background and the necessary language skills. Not surprisingly, such individuals were not always available. The magnitude of the problem becomes more clear when one considers the survey finding that only 26 percent of the universe of 2,006 programs had children from only one language group. Thirty percent have two languages, and 8 percent, had four. Several programs have more than ten languages represented in their centers. As will be demonstrated later in the chapter, with more than 140 languages spoken by Head Start families, it is little wonder that many programs are at a loss as to how to offer services in the home language of the family.

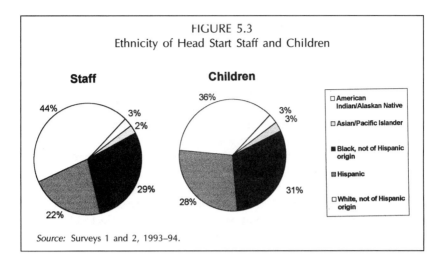

FIGURE 5.3
Ethnicity of Head Start Staff and Children

Staff

44%
3%
2%
29%
22%

Children

36%
3%
3%
28%
31%

- ☐ American Indian/Alaskan Native
- ☐ Asian/Pacific Islander
- ■ Black, not of Hispanic origin
- ▨ Hispanic
- ☐ White, not of Hispanic origin

Source: Surveys 1 and 2, 1993–94.

The survey also revealed that only when thirty non-English-speaking children enrolled in a program spoke the same language was it very likely (an 80 perent chance) that a staff member could speak that language. Spanish-speaking children had more staff who spoke their language than did children from other language groups. When there were both children and staff who spoke Spanish in a program, there was usually one Spanish-speaking staff member for every seven children. In contrast, in programs with both staff and children speaking Hmong, the ratio was 16:1. Staff generally reflected the ethnicity of the children and families they served (figure 5.3).

The match between Head Start staff and families is important in providing multicultural services. The problem of finding bilingual staff is not easily resolved, however. On close examination of the site visit data, it was discovered that ethnic representation frequently was absent in the upper part of the Head Start hierarchy. Only about half of the sites visited were run by administrators whose language and culture reflected that of the families they served. Administrators were mostly white or Hispanic. Nor did coordinator-level positions reflect the ethnic composition of the children at many of the centers. In contrast, on the lower rungs of the Head Start ladder, staff such as service assistants and aides represented the ethnic background of the children to a far greater extent than did more senior staff. This observation is not surprising, as minorities are often poor, and poor people frequently do not have the credentials to obtain higher paid and higher status positions. The fact that the ethnicity and language of the children and families were underrepresented in the program concerned most sites, as in the case of the following: "This site has made an effort to meet the needs of the communities served through designing and implementing several programs. Programs have been developed in direct response to the fact that certain ethnic groups in the community were either not being represented at all in the Head Start classrooms, or they were severely underrepresented."

Despite the lack of ethnic representation, field workers found that administrators fully believed in the use of materials and methods that reflect and are sensitive to the ethnic/racial and cultural heritage of children enrolled in Head Start. According to one staff member, "If you recognize their culture, that recognition will be reflected in everything you teach the children. Beginning with this solid foundation makes learning easier for that child." Those staff believed that respecting cultural differences was the bridge toward harmony in an increasingly violent and racially tense society.

Ethnicity and Language in the Classroom

Children and parents spoke a wide assortment of languages in the classrooms. Although teachers usually spoke with the children only in English or to a lesser degree in Spanish, we observed children speaking Spanish, Chinese (Mandarin and Cantonese), Vietnamese, Hmong, Cambodian, and Creole among themselves or with adults who shared their languages. Usually, the bilingual teaching assistant played an integral role in classroom communication. She or he talked to the non-English-speaking monolingual children and translated for the teacher, the children, and the parents. Bilingual children also became their teachers' intermediaries, translating commands, activities, and other concepts to their monolingual peers. Furthermore, bilingual children acted as liaisons between non-English-speaking monolingual and other bilingual children. Although the children entered the classrooms at different stages of English fluency, most children (both monolingual and bilingual) spoke some English upon graduating from the Head Start program. Many teachers marveled at the pace at which children acquired English in their classrooms.

In many Head Start classrooms that lacked bilingual staff to communicate with non-English-speaking monolingual children, the teaching staff attempted to communicate with children by memorizing certain phrases. The teachers used command phrases such as "Sit here,"

"Listen to me," and "Stop doing that" in the children's home language. Even when teachers did not speak the home language of the children, they often used the child's home language for commands, which may have given a negative connotation to the use of the home language. When more complicated messages needed to be communicated, the monolingual teachers relied on the bilingual children to translate, a phenomenon commonly observed in multilingual classrooms. In one classroom where there was no match at all between the teaching staff and children, the teacher reported that the class had adopted sign language as its universal means of communication.

Parents representing the Head Start communities' cultures and languages were observed in the classroom in about only half of the cases. Non-English-speaking parents were generally most comfortable working with children from their own language groups. Sometimes parents who came to the classrooms did not talk with children who did not speak their language. When they could not communicate with the children, they may have felt a loss of control (or face).

The range of ethnic and linguistic differences found among the families at many Head Start sites constituted one of the major barriers to providing multicultural services in accord with the ten multicultural principles. To address those barriers a variety of programs were developed. The next section provides an overview of the multicultural programs we observed.

Multicultural Approaches in the Classroom

As observed during in-depth site visits, multicultural lessons were introduced effectively in Head Start classrooms using a variety of approaches, including a "multicultural day," a "multicultural week," a "tourist approach," and an "all-inclusive approach." The latter which focused on all cultures reflected by children in the classroom and others that were not; it "incorporated multiculturalism into everything." Other classrooms preferred a bicultural mode, integrating the culture of children with that of the mainstream society. Whatever the approach, by presenting a variety of foods, stories, songs, manipulative toys, and traditions, the staff made the children aware of the beauty and value of diversity. Approaches emphasized not only cultural representation in materials but also the incorporation of traditional and nontraditional aspects of a culture. For example, a teacher was observed having children compare skin colors and explaining the differences and similarities in people regardless of the color of their skin.

An example follows:

The teacher opened the Large Group lesson by saying: "I have some dolls from around the world. They are like us, but they are also different. Let's look and talk about them." She held a Hawaiian girl and asked: "What can you tell me about this girl?" The children volunteered answers by raising their hands. They answered that the girl was brown and had long hair. The teacher asked in English, "Is this the kind of outfit that you wear?" The children answered, "No." Teacher: "Do you know where she comes from?" Children: "No." The teacher said, "She is from Hawaii. Can you say that?—Repeat, Hawaii." The children repeated in chorus: "Hawaii." In addition, on that day, the children sang songs in different languages, tried culturally specific dishes, and engaged in learning activities about other cultures.

Another approach called for an entire "multicultural week," in which lesson plans focused on multicultural activities exposing children to foods, songs, and customs of other cultures. The teachers highlighted traditional activities of different cultural groups and tried to involve the children in the activities. For example, one day the children danced a Chinese dance and another day they did the zapateado from Mexico. Many times, parents or guests from the community celebrated with the children by making presentations, doing puppet shows, or demonstrating dances.

The "tourist approach" to multiculturalism consisted of presenting aspects of a certain culture without making that culture a part of the daily activities in the classroom. For example, many classes had decorations, posters, materials, and books from other cultures on display to introduce and familiarize children to various aspects of these cultures. Their classroom activities, however, were all mainstream. One site used "Asian baskets" containing items from various Asian cultures. The "Asian basket" circulated around the different centers, and teachers would use it to talk about Asian cultures.

The celebration of holidays was a controversial topic at several Head Start sites. Those in support of celebrating holidays believed that different cultures could be included in the classroom through the celebration of cultural holidays. Those who opposed such festivities felt that those celebrations could not and did not accurately and properly represent the cultures. These two conflicting views seemed to shape the "holiday policy" of many Head Start programs.

Programs that celebrated the holidays tended to concentrate on one specific culture during the holiday season but virtually ignored that culture the rest of the year. For example, during Chinese New Year, teachers exposed the children to Chinese culture, but made minimal reference to it at other times. In "holiday-celebrating" classrooms, parents brought traditional items to reflect the specific holiday and/ or cooked traditional dishes for the children. One site reported that during Chinese New Year, the children learned about the dragon dance, the fireworks, the kind of food Chinese people eat, and the meaning of the New Year. That program stressed the celebration of cultural holidays as an integral part of being multicultural.

The "no-holiday" sites refrained from celebrating the commercial or religious holidays and replaced them with seasonal activities to teach common underlying concepts believed to be age-appropriate, open-ended, and relevant. Proponents stated that this approach did not discriminate against any culture or religion because it did not select which cultural holidays to celebrate. For example, instead of having Christmas, they celebrated the Winter Festival, attaching no association to Christianity. Although some programs believed that their particular holiday policy was the best approach to multiculturalism, this policy occasionally sparked criticism from parents and staff who wanted to celebrate certain holidays.

Multicultural Materials

According to the survey responses from Head Start staff and the information collected during site visits, almost all programs had books, dolls, and music representing different ethnic groups. Traditional multicultural activities and dress were represented in more than half of the classrooms visited, but materials depicting differently capable children were found in less than one-third of the classrooms. English and Spanish books were in relative abundance, as were books about African Americans and Asian cultures. Posters showed traditional and nontraditional family units to roughly the same degree. Audio visual materials were somewhat less available. One of the strongest findings from the site visits is that, while multicultural materials may have been available in the classrooms, teachers did not often use them in their daily activities.

Teachers said that they struggled to find multicultural materials best suited to the children they served, but it was found that when the materials were available, the teachers often did not know what to do with them. It was observed that although many teachers participated in multicultural classes, they could not translate the multicultural content into productive and beneficial teaching.

The following excerpts were taken from the field workers' classroom observation notes to provide a picture of the kind of materials seen in the Head Start classrooms. The first example illustrates a classroom with multicultural materials:

> In the pretend area, there's a rug on the floor, four dolls (one black male doll, one Asian female, one black female, and a white female). . . . Throughout the area are a number of multiethnic foods and materials. . . . In the computer area there is a low table with two CD-ROM computers. The computers "speak" in English, Spanish, and Vietnamese. . . . There are shelves with small plastic items and an abacus, a puzzle of a Chinese dragon. . . . The posters depict men from different ethnic traditions. The calendar of the week is written in English, Spanish, and Vietnamese.

The following example was taken from a classroom without multicultural materials:

> The pretend area contains a small table and chairs, a play washing machine and dryer, a microwave, sinks and stove. . . . There is a mirror for the children to use, dishes, purses, and shoes. . . . The posters in or near this area included: Nursery rhyme posters of "Mary Had a Little Lamb," "Jack and Jill," and "Humpty Dumpty." . . . The manipulative area has a puzzle of a city street drawn in "cartoon" form. . . . The science area contains a book on trains, one on planes, and one on boats (this seemed to be a theme they are working on, since they also have a train station).

Head start teachers were generally observed to be dedicated educators well versed in child development practices and early childhood education. They were less well versed in multicultural awareness or knowledge, although they seemed genuinely interested in learning as much as they could. They tended to focus more on multicultural materials than they did on interactions, attitudes, biases, or behavior. Most were monolingual English speakers who interacted with the children almost exclusively in English.

Multicultural Health Services

Some sites had no problems obtaining community health providers and health services for non-English-speaking children and families, while others experienced difficulty in obtaining low-cost services and identifying health providers who spoke the families home languages. The Head Start healthcare coordinators complained about not having informational material translated into several languages and said that they could not always appropriately inform parents about doctor visits or direct them to appropriate medical services. Administrators complained that it was very difficult to obtain translators because of the high cost and paperwork required.

Health care coordinators were often faced with situations calling for cross-cultural sensitivity and understanding and many felt unqualified to address those situations. Health staff wanted training about culture-specific beliefs about medical treatment, health care practices, and discipline, as well as training about cross-cultural communication. They needed materials specific to the different groups they served. For example, the growth charts used by health coordinators used to determine healthy physical development are normed to U.S. population groups and do not provide the necessary indices for Asian immigrants, who tend to be smaller in stature. Head Start health coordinators struggled to find qualified bilingual personnel to conduct screenings and to provide parents with guidance regarding the healthcare of their children.

Multiculturalism in the Social Services

Head Start personnel often viewed social services as the best vehicle through which to provide multicultural services. In their roles as caseworkers or social services aides, staff conducted needs assessments and health/medical follow-ups and provided translations for the families. Social services staff also conducted recruitment efforts for the Head Start program, since they were most connected with the community. They visited many of the parents and went door-to-door to distribute flyers, many of which were translated into several languages. They assisted parents with basic needs, such as obtaining jobs, training, housing, food and clothing, especially for Head Start families who were recent immigrants and did not know where to find these resources. Thus, these staff members knew the families well and had access to them. The social service component had the reputation of being closest to the families and, as such, was in the best position to deliver services in culturally appropriate ways.

Case loads, however, are often too large. Repeatedly, during the site visits, social service staff reported that they were months behind in their case work, understaffed, and overworked. Several sites also complained of the difficulty in finding services for undocumented families. This problem was shared by the health care staff as sites (located in states denying services to nondocumented families) were forced to pay doctors and dentists from their Head Start budgets.

Recruiting Multicultural Children

To enroll children in Head Start, the majority of the programs in the survey relied primarily on recruitment by word of mouth. Others thought that having recruitment materials available in the family's own language was most important aspect of recruitment, while some found home visits to be most crucial. If not the most important aspect of recruitment, many staff believed that advertising on the radio and television and in the newspaper and having a presence at community functions were necessary to reach all members of the community.

Many sites reported recruitment problems due to language differences. Low native-language literacy was also frequently cited, as was the parents' unfamiliarity with the program and the staff's corresponding lack of cultural knowledge about the families. Public perceptions of Head Start may have some impact on recruitment problems. Around the country, the following remarks by Head Start staff were made:

- Head Start is perceived as a "day care program, so parents don't come."

- Head Start is "a stigmatized program because it is designed for underprivileged kids."

- "Too many people are ignorant about us and what we do." and

- Parents "think Head Start is a welfare program and therefore lacking in quality."

These remarks gathered during the site visits indicate that Head Start outreach should extend beyond the community it traditionally has served to a larger constituency that is more representative of the eligible population, both minority and white.

Multicultural Parents

Although most staff described parent involvement as being very good, there were always some staff and parents at each site who emphasized the lack of parent involvement. The Head Start coordinators tried to include parents in training activities related to health, nutrition, financial matters, and the procedures used by the Head Start program, but problems related to translation, transportation, and child care affected the level of participation.

Many bilingual and multicultural parents who did not volunteer in the classroom on a regular basis nevertheless provided important cultural resources to the Head Start programs. They made presentations, cooked ethnic dishes, translated for monolingual non-English-speaking children and parents, and provided input on policy. Unfortunately, parents who did not have English language skills often did not access the decision making power afforded by participation in the program and on councils. Sites, meanwhile, relied heavily on parents and contracted outside agencies to assist with verbal and written translations.

According to the findings from the survey and the site visits, another reason why Head Start parents may not be more involved in their children's Head Start experiences has to do with their low self-esteem and feelings of inadequacy. It was reported that many immigrant females were depressed. Often they were separated from their extended families and had no social supports in a strange (sometimes hostile) land. One of the strongest strategies by which to encourage parent involvement was the use of former parents as staff or volunteer outreach workers. Many Head Start staff also mentioned the importance of building trust between parents and staff. Head Start personnel may require extra training to become especially sensitive to the needs of parents who are untrusting, depressed, and/or afraid.

Parents benefited from the multicultural services provided by Head Start by enrolling in classes and workshops on English as a second language (ESL), literacy, parenting, cooking, self-esteem, child development, child/spousal abuse, general equivalency diploma (GED), and Child Development Associate (CDA) programs. The survey results indicated that parenting-skills classes were viewed as most important. Furthermore, parents received assistance with basic needs (housing, food, and clothing), family health care, and social support. Although not all parents took advantage of such services because of the lack of transportation, child care, motivation, or translation services, staff were eager to offer these services. Head Start programs across the country seemed to make a sincere effort to improve the economic, intellectual, and emotional status of enrolled families even though many programs lacked the experienced bilingual staff to do so as effectively as they would like.

This research indicates that despite the wonderful experiences described by many Head Start parents, the parents least served are those from cultural groups least known by programs. It is apparent that the language match between parents and staff is crucial for facilitating parental involvement. The most successful sites provided translators at parent meetings and during activities. Parents came to more events when flyers announcing an activity were sent in the home language.

Targeting workshops or training to a specific culture group created a high level of parental involvement among parents from that group. Reflecting parents' home cultures in activities encouraged them to participate because they felt welcome, knowledgeable, and confident. When parents were invited to activities involving their children, they were more apt to attend.

SUMMARY AND SUGGESTIONS FOR FUTURE RESEARCH

This study has depicted the range and extent of diversity that exists within Head Start, both in the cultures represented by the programs and in the approaches used by programs to serve people in those cultures. The study raises as many questions as it answers. The emphasis of reports of this kind naturally falls on areas for improvement. The tendency is to note where there is confusion over goals, contradiction in practices, controversy, and a large number of eligible children who are not enrolled. This descriptive study has reported Head Start's challenges in these areas. Nonetheless, these limitations do not lessen the significance of one critically significant finding: across the country Head Start programs are approaching the challenge of serving children from diverse backgrounds in an enthusiastic and positive manner.

The following are issues that could benefit from further investigation and that have implications for practice, policy, and future research:

- Head Start needs to clarify support and expectations of grantees regarding multicultural and bilingual programming.

- Head Start needs to consider ways to include multicultural and bilingual practices as part of the grantee monitoring process.

- Head Start needs to train grantees to better implement the multicultural principles.

- Research is needed to explain the underenrollment of white children in Head Start programs.

- Research is needed to identify the type of training and the conditions that will help make staff more sensitive to the needs of culturally diverse children and families.

- Research is needed to identify methods for describing and disseminating multicultural and bilingual materials.

- Research is needed to assess the effectiveness of multicultural and bilingual practices.

Most differences and disagreements about culturally diverse Head Start programs are about the means to best serve the multicultural and bilingual population, not about the importance of bilingual and multicultural program services. Head Start administrators know the importance of addressing the needs of the entire family, and not just the individual child. And administrators recognize that Head Start programs must tailor their services so that they work well with all ethnic, racial, and language groups.

NOTES

1. Administration on Children, Youth and Families, "Descriptive Study of Head Start Bilingual and Multicultural Services," Statement of Work, 1993.

2. John Nixon, *A Teacher's Guide to Multicultural Education* (New York: Basil Blackwell Ltd., 1985), 17.

3. C. E. Sleeter, *Multicultural Education as Social Activism.* (Albany: State University of New York Press, 1986), 12.

4. U.S. Department of Health and Human Services, *Create a 21st Head Start, Final Report of the Advisory Committee on Head Start Quality and Expansion.* (Washington, D.C.: Government Printing Office, 1993).

5. U.S. Department of Health and Human Services, "Multicultural Principles." Log No ACYF-IM-91-03 March 1991.

6. James Cummins, *Empowering Minority Students* (Sacramento: California Association for Bilingual Education, 1989).

7. Kenji Hakuta, and C. E. Snow, "The Role of Research in Policy Decisions about Bilingual Education," *NABE News* 9 #3 (Spring 1986): 1, 12–21.

8. E. Garcia, *Early Childhood Bilingualism*. (Albuquerque: University of New Mexico Press, 1983).

9. Ibid.

10. L. Wong-Fillmore, "When Learning a Second Language Means Losing the First," *Early Childhood Research Quarterly* (1991): 6, 323–46.

11. U.S. Department of Health and Human Services, *Create a 21st Head Start*.

6

High/Scope in Head Start Programs Serving Southeast Asian Immigrant and Refugee Children and Their Families: Lessons from an Ethnographic Study

Eden Inoway-Ronnie

This chapter explores issues of cultural diversity within Head Start classrooms, focusing particularly on Head Start programs serving Southeast Asian immigrants and refugees. I weave together a discussion of culturally diverse Head Start classrooms with concerns about the High/Scope curriculum approach, based upon a two-year ethnographic study. Arising out of these analyses are broader questions about Head Start's and all schools' diversity policies and notions of parent participation.

From 1975 through 1988, over 1,208,000 refugees from around the world resettled in the United States (Trueba, Jacobs, and Kirton 1990, 19). With increasing immigration from Southeast Asia, Latin America, and other parts of the world, as well as other demographic changes, Head Start programs, like most schools and other institutions, are increasingly racially and ethnically diverse. In urban and even rural settings, students from different cultural backgrounds are educated in classrooms together. As one example of the diversity in Head Start, an estimated 20 percent of children currently enrolled in Head Start programs across the country live in homes where the primary language spoken is not English (Powell 1995).[1] Logic suggests that many of these families are relatively recent immigrants, migrants, and refugees.

Research among immigrant groups demonstrates that the values and beliefs often held by members of these groups are sometimes quite different from those values and beliefs held by nonimmigrants (Gibson 1988; Goldstein 1985; Olneck 1995; Smith-Hefner 1993; Trueba, Jacobs, and Kirton 1990). The basis of these different values and beliefs may be practices in their native countries or cultures of origin. But the differences also may be connected to their status as immigrants, coming into a new culture with particular economic and other life circumstances that have shaped their outlook, beliefs, and values (Ogbu 1987). Prior education and socioeconomic status also shape how immigrants' culture "looks" in contrast to dominant norms and values. Regardless of the origins of these differences, the fact remains that these differences in beliefs and values do exist. Consequently, educational programs such as Head Start are faced with the responsibility to respond to these differences as they seek to accomplish their multiple goals.

As evidence of its commitment to serving these diverse populations, Head Start issued the "Anti-Bias Committee Philosophy Statement and Principles for Head Start."[2] Included in the document are the following principles that are intended to help guide local agencies in establishing antibias programming and responding to diversity within their programs.

1. Effective Head Start programming requires understanding, respect, and responsiveness to the cultures of all people but particularly to those of enrolled children and families.

2. Children must be given skills to deal with bias. . . .

3. Appropriate multicultural programming is imperative in order to fully achieve Head Start goals. . . .

4. These principles go beyond what takes place in a Head Start classroom. They apply to *all component services* (emphasis in original).

The existence of this philosophy statement and related principles implies clearly that knowledge and understanding of other cultures is necessary.

One way in which we might expect Head Start to respond to the cultural diversity within the population it serves is through its parent involvement components. Head Start has a longstanding history as a program committed to parent participation. From the start, the program planners articulated the importance of lower income parents having some control over institutions that served them (Ellsworth and Ames 1995; Zigler and Muenchow 1992). Parents may become involved on a number of levels within the organization, including in curriculum development.

HIGH/SCOPE

Head Start guidelines do not specify the particular curriculum approach that should be used in individual classrooms. According to one of the program's founders, "From the beginning, local programs have been allowed a great deal of flexibility in planning educational curricula that meets the needs of their own children and communities. Since the Improvement and Innovation effort began in 1973, Head Start programs have been encouraged to become even more flexible in programming" (Richmond, Stipek, and Zigler 1979, 138).[3] One educational approach used in many Head Start programs across the country is the High/Scope curriculum. According to one study, approximately 25 percent of Head Start programs use the High/Scope approach in some form or another (Epstein 1993), but current figures may be much higher, as High/Scope has grown in recognition.[4]

High/Scope is an early childhood curriculum approach developed through the Perry Preschool Project in Ypsilanti, Michigan (Schweinhart, Barnes, and Weikart 1993; Zigler and Styfco 1994). It is based on Piagetian theory, intended to be "an educational approach that supported the development of young children's cognitive and social skills through individualized teaching and learning" (Schweinhart, Barnes, and Weikart, 1993, 33). High/Scope stresses active learning, where children learn through exploration (Hechinger 1986). The approach calls for teachers to "deliberately and systematically help children predict, observe, describe, explain, manipulate, hypothesize, and find alternatives" (Weikart 1986, 87). At its best, the approach is a very time-consuming and intensive endeavor for teachers, because the approach relies on teachers and other adults helping guide children and teach them as they engage in activities of their own choosing.

According to High/Scope, in order to maximize opportunities for students to develop, one-on-one interaction between a child and an adult is desirable. Thus, parents are encouraged to interact with their preschool children in the home in ways that model the approach used in the classroom. Parents are taught how to ask questions that will build upon their child's knowledge, encouraging their child to explore and manipulate objects around them as a part of their learning process. Understandably, the impact of High/Scope depends on the quality of training teachers receive, how they in turn implement it in their individual classrooms (Zigler and Styfco 1994), and the extent to which parents also follow the approach in their interactions with their children at home.

High/Scope is considered by many to be a very effective curriculum approach, and research from the Perry Preschool project has been very encouraging (see Berrueta-Clement et al. 1984; Schweinhart, Barnes, and Weikart 1993; Schweinhart and Weikart 1993). Bredekamp (1996, 340), in a summary of research on early childhood education, notes that "access to diverse materials and a systematic approach to planning, implementing, and reviewing experiences (the High/Scope "plan, do, review" cycle) were related to children's development." While there is evidence that different early education curriculum models are equally effective in achieving positive results in the area of intellectual and scholastic performance (to the extent that they can be measured accurately), some research suggests that High/Scope can have important social consequences that may not be as strong as those resulting from other early childhood curriculum models (Weikart 1987). Writes Weikart (1987, 187), "Although *good* early childhood programs are an effective way to improve the life chances of disadvantaged children, *formal academic* programs as represented by teacher-directed learning models may be inadequate to the task, because they fail to have the desired social behavior consequences."

Several questions emerge from this intersection of immigrant and refugee students in Head Start, Head Start's commitment to parent involvement, and High/Scope. First, how well does the High/Scope curriculum fit into multicultural Head Start classrooms? What do immigrant and refugee parents, many of whom may have values and beliefs that are different from mainstream, middle-class beliefs and values, think about High/Scope? Second, Head Start has some very specific ideas about multiculturalism and dealing with diversity. Is the High/Scope approach consistent with these other Head Start policies? Finally, the Head Start program has some very specific ideas about parent participation. The program is designed to encourage parent involvement and parent participation in decision making. Is the use of a prescribed program such as High/Scope consistent with the parent involvement goals?

I explored these specific questions as a part of a two-year ethnographic study of teachers in two ethnically and racially diverse Head Start classrooms located in a medium-sized midwestern city. The city, like many in the upper Midwest, experienced a relatively small but significant in-migration of lower income Southeast Asians from countries such as Cambodia, Laos, Thailand, and Vietnam. The Asian ethnic group with the largest number of children in the Head Start agency studied was the Hmong, an ethnic group with roots in mainland China and more recently in Laos, many of whom came to the United States as refugees after assisting the U.S. military during the Vietnam War.

Both Head Start programs I studied are walk-in programs, which are "a community based model located in housing developments that have a high population of eligible families. Parents walk their children to class four days per week. Home visits with the teacher occur once a month" (*Evergreen Head Start Parent Handbook*, 5). Both programs served very diverse communities, with children from at least four ethnic groups in both classrooms.

Data were gathered primarily through a combination of observations and formal and informal interviews, as well as through document analysis. Observational data collection took place in the primary site from September 1993 through June 1994, and from early September 1994 through June 1995. During the 1993 through 1994 school year, observations were made at the primary site usually four days per week. Observational data collection at the secondary research site started in the fall of 1994 and continued on a one-day-per-week basis through the spring of 1995. In addition to classroom observations, informal interviews and observations were made throughout the two years at staff trainings, parent meetings, team meetings at the two sites, and home visits and included initial orientation meetings for parents and children.

Several formal, open-ended interviews with the two Head Start teachers were conducted over the period of the study. Open-ended interviews with the teaching assistants also were conducted, and numerous informal interviews with these and other staff members, such as nutrition service providers, family outreach workers, and program managers, provided data for this study. The majority of interviews with parents at the primary site took place during the summer after the 1993 through 1994 school year.[5] Several more interviews of parents at the primary site, including several parents who were new to the program during the second year of the study, were conducted in spring and summer 1995. Informal interviews were conducted with a few parents at the secondary research site.

The primary research site, a program called the Green Court Head Start program, was located in a community center in the middle of a low-income apartment complex.[6] During the time of my research, there were Hmong, African and African American, Mexican American, Chinese from Vietnam and China, Cambodian, Laotian, and white families living there. Some families had been in the community for at least two generations, while others were new residents who had moved there from larger metropolitan cities or from abroad. A number of the Southeast Asian families had been in this apartment complex for approximately ten years.

The community center in which the classroom was located was used for a number of programs throughout the day and into the evening hours. Girl Scout troop meetings, a tutoring program for students after school, and sewing and cooking classes for adults and young people were held in the community center. Head Start also offered English as a second language (ESL) classes for parents and relatives of Head Start children at the center several days each week in collaboration with the local literacy council.

The classroom itself was located on the first floor of the building and had windows that looked out toward one section of apartments, with a small bricked patio where children could play. There was also a larger play area with swings, slides, and other climbing equipment close by. The classroom was both carpeted in some areas and tiled in others, with housekeeping, blocks, art, "quiet," and "manipulatives" areas. Posted around the classroom were suggested guidelines for adult volunteers on ways to interact with the children, both in English and in Hmong.

The Green Court Head Start class met from 9:00 A.M. to 1:00 P.M., Tuesday through Friday. Mondays were days during which the staff had their team meetings, had all-staff training sessions, planned for the week, and sometimes made home visits with families.

During the 1993 through 1994 school year, there were eleven Hmong, three Chinese, one African, one Mexican American and three African American children in the program. This count includes one child who left the program midyear and the child who took his place. During the 1994 through 1995 school year, there were twelve Hmong, one Cambodian, two Chinese, two Mexican American, and three African American children in the program. Thus, while Southeast Asian children were in the majority, the students in the classes were very racially and ethnically heterogeneous. The children varied in their ability to understand and speak English. While some were fluent, including the African and African American children and several of the Southeast Asian children, other children knew much less English, and some of the three-year-olds understood and spoke very little.

Given the diversity within the classroom, it should be no surprise that the parents of the students were a diverse group as well. While some of the Hmong parents were in their forties, other Hmong parents were much younger. Some parents spoke English fluently, while others spoke very little. Education levels varied as well. Some parents had had very little formal schooling and were illiterate in their native languages, while other parents had attended schools entirely in the United States and now were pursuing college degrees. There were several Hmong families who had had anywhere from four to six or seven children (within the same family) in this Head Start program over the last eight or ten years.

The teacher, Laura, was a married, white female with two young children. She had been with Head Start programs in several areas for twelve years. She came from a large family of working-middle-class background. Her training as a Head Start teacher involved one year of postsecondary education at a technical college for her associate's degree in early childhood education.

The teaching assistant in the Green Court Head Start program, Bee, was a Hmong male who was born in Laos and went to public high school in the United States. He was in his midthirties, married to a Hmong woman who was studying for a professional degree, and they had three young children. He had taken early childhood education courses at the local technical college, but indicated that he never intended to pursue a career in early childhood education. Rather, he took the job because the program needed a bilingual teaching assistant, and at the time, he was looking for employment.

Both the teacher and the teaching assistant at this program went on home visits. Bee, the teaching assistant, primarily visited the Hmong families, while Laura completed home visits with the non-Hmong families. When the balance between Hmong and non-Hmong families was not quite even, Laura did home visits with Hmong families who were fairly fluent in English. In addition to Laura and Bee, this program had a nutrition services provider who not only prepared the meals for this Head Start class, but also was involved in leading small group activities which conveniently occurred between meal preparation periods. The family outreach worker, who worked with the Head Start teacher and assistant to provide assistance to Head Start families, visited the classroom occasionally, regularly attending parent meetings and team meetings on Mondays. This classroom also had a number of college student volunteers throughout the school year.

SUNNY VIEW

The secondary research site, Sunny View Head Start program, also was a walk-in Head Start program located in a different neighborhood in Evergreen. This program was an afternoon program, starting at 12:30 P.M. and running until 4:00 P.M., Tuesday through Friday. The Sunny View classroom was located on the upper level of a newly constructed community center in the middle of a low-income apartment complex. Similar to the Green Court program, the community center provided a number of programs for families who live there, including computer, ESL, and GED classes.

During my observations over the 1994 through 1995 school year, the enrollment in this class changed quite a bit. At the start of the year, the class had nine African American, three Hmong, three Cambodian, one Laotian, one Mexican American, and two white children. During the year, several of the African American children and the Mexican American child left the program because their families moved out of the apartment complex, and the three-year-old siblings of two children in the class (one Cambodian and one Hmong) joined the program, in addition to another new Hmong child.

Children and parents in this program varied in their fluency with English. There were several Southeast Asian children in the program who understood and spoke limited English, while others, particularly those who had been in the program for two years, were quite fluent in English. Similarly, the Southeast Asian parents varied in their ability to speak and understand English. Several grandparents played a significant role in the care of their grandchildren, and their ability to speak English was quite limited.

This Head Start classroom also was the site of a new "wraparound" childcare program. Several Head Start children with working parents, along with a number of other children, were enrolled in the childcare program, arriving in the morning for childcare and often staying after the Head Start class was officially over until family members picked them up. Additionally, several elementary-aged children attended the childcare as well, arriving after their school was dismissed. The total enrollment in the childcare program varied from week to week, with anywhere from four to ten or so additional children in the classroom during the Head Start class.

The classroom itself was quite large, with several movable dividers to separate different areas. There was a tiled area near the kitchen with both adult and preschool-aged children's tables and chairs. There were several carpeted areas that were used for circle time, reading, and housekeeping areas. The flexibility to change the arrangement of the room was particularly important for this program because it offered the Head Start and child care programs the opportunity to create separate spaces for different activities, such as nap time for the childcare group while Head Start students were engaged in other activities.

The teacher, Denise, was a white, single mother in her early thirties who had been with the Head Start program for approximately five years. She grew up on a farm in the Midwest, and she held a bachelor's degree from a large public university. Her undergraduate training was not in early childhood education, although she had taken early childhood education courses and read quite broadly in the education literature. She was an enthusiastic teacher who constantly challenged the children in her class to solve problems independently. She brought from her own home all sorts of manipulatives for the students to work with, ranging from an apple press to make apple sauce to a shoebox full of old keys.

The teaching assistant, Edna, was an energetic, white female from a working-class background who also grew up in the Midwest. She graduated from high school and held a number of different jobs before working for Head Start. She had taken several early childhood classes at the local technical college and had worked as a nutrition services provider as well as a teaching assistant over the dozen or so years she had been with Head Start. She also worked part time at a fast food restaurant and helped care for her grandchild on a regular basis.

Both Denise and Edna went on home visits with the families in this program. Edna generally visited the Southeast Asian families, while Denise visited the non-Asian families. The program also had a nutrition services provider who was the mother of one of the students in the class and who prepared and served meals. A family outreach worker who was also assigned to the program (along with several other centers) made infrequent visits to the classroom while the students were present, but attended staff meetings and parent meetings. Additionally, one and sometimes two other adults hired as childcare providers were present during parts of the day, depending on the number of children enrolled in the childcare program.

This detailed description of Sunny View, and the previous description of Green Court, is intended to give the reader a better sense of the daily rhythm and the wonderful diversity within these Head Start classrooms. I provide these descriptions with the hope that the following discussions of High/Scope, multiculturalism, and parent participation will be enhanced by the reader's deeper understanding of the social contexts in which these questions are raised.

How Well Does High/Scope Fit into Multicultural Classrooms?

I begin by describing the perspectives of the Southeast Asian parents I interviewed with regard to High/Scope. Then I describe the teachers' perspectives, showing how they responded to parents' expressed concerns. Parents' and teachers' different cultural backgrounds, skill levels, information, and purposes all shaped their attitudes and beliefs regarding the High/Scope curriculum approach in important but divergent ways.

PARENTS' PERSPECTIVE

My research revealed that many Southeast Asian parents in the two programs objected to Head Start's use of the High/Scope curriculum approach in their children's classrooms with its emphasis on social skills and what many parents considered "free play." These parents, through various means, including written comments, verbal comments in parent meetings, informal conversations, and informal, open-ended interviews, indicated their preference for more explicit instruction on traditional skills *in English,* such as knowing colors, letters, and shapes and being able to write one's name.

One Hmong mother told me, when asked in an interview if there were aspects of what took place in her child's Head Start classroom that she would do differently: "Maybe [there is] too much play time, playing. They eat at nine, right? So one hundred and forty-five minutes [of play/work time]. Maybe do more reading, reading activities." When this mother visited the classroom, I observed her on several occasions reading books in English to her son and other children. This mother also expressed some concern that her son did not know his numbers but then said that she believed he would learn them eventually. Another Hmong mother, a young woman in her early twenties who was educated primarily in the United States, told me in response to a question about what she would change about the Head Start program if she could, "Try to teach kids how to write ABCs."

These were not unusual concerns expressed by parents interviewed. A Hmong couple said in an interview that they wished that the children were taught their colors and numbers more explicitly in Head Start. They wanted the educational approach to be, in their words, "more structured." They said they wished the teacher would "get to the point, not just [let the kids] play with things."

This Hmong couple wanted their daughter to become fluent in English as soon as possible so that she would not be placed in ESL classes in elementary school, fearing that she would "never have a chance to get out of ESL." These parents spoke from experience, having had several of their other children in the Head Start class in previous years who were now in elementary and secondary schools. They knew that students from grades one through three were in the same ESL class together, and their concern was that in ESL, teachers, "don't teach specific to child[ren]'s needs."

The acquisition of English was a crucial issue in these parents' minds. Many of the parents I interviewed, who are not native speakers of English, expressed concerns that their children master the English language so as to maximize their chances of gaining a good education in order to find gainful employment. Wong Fillmore (1991) found similar concerns among the Asian parents she studied. Many of the parents I interviewed believed that children who were placed in ESL upon entering public schools received an inferior education. For this reason, most of them wanted their children to master English as early as possible. Studies of Hmong high school students by Goldstein (1985) and Rhoades (1991) suggest that these parents' concerns were not unwarranted.

These Southeast Asian immigrant and refugee parents also were very concerned about the acquisition of particular skills and knowledge. For example, at the end of my second year of research, Laura and I talked about summaries of children's progress that she would write for Head Start files. With parent permission, the progress report also would be forwarded to the elementary school if the child was to start kindergarten the following year. Laura mentioned that parents were given an opportunity to write responses to what she had written about their children. The responses could either provide additional information that the parent wanted the kindergarten teacher to know, or perhaps even dispute what the teacher had written, although this never occurred in the two programs I studied. I asked how often parents wrote additional comments, and she said that it happened occasionally.

Laura told me of a Laotian father who wrote that he wanted his child to "expand his ability to read and write, recognize letters [in English]." She said that the father was happy with the fact that his son's ability to speak English had developed during his year with Head Start, but that he wanted much more of the same. He wanted teachers to know that this was a priority for him as a parent.

Bee, the Hmong teaching assistant in the Green Court classroom, confirmed that the parents he worked with (virtually all Hmong parents) wanted the program to focus on academic skills and teach the children English. In an interview, he described what he knew about other parents' wishes:

E: Is it most important for the Hmong parents that their kids learn English or that they learn social skills? Or something else . . . ?
B: Learn English.
E: It seems like Laura's priority is social skills. . . . Is there any conflict?
B: Yeah. When Laura looks at it, both true, important. But when I talk with parents, they want kids to learn ABCs, write his or her name.

Bee also said later in the interview that sometimes parents write in on their Parent Observation forms[7] that they want the teacher to teach counting and ABCs. He confirmed what other parents had told me about their own wishes. When I asked him at the end of the interview what he himself would change about Head Start if he could, he indicated that he would make sure that the staff read more stories to the children and "teach them how to write more—alphabet, letters, numbers. Play less."[8]

As an example of why he was concerned about this issue, he described a situation in which a Hmong boy went through two years of Head Start and at the end was not even able to write his name. Bee said to me, "When I went to Neng's house, I asked him to write name. And he couldn't do even 'N.' " In this case, Bee and I both knew that

Neng's parents spoke little English and that his parents would be virtually unable to help him learn to write his name, let alone other words, in English. Bee said he believed the public school teachers would ask "Why can't [Neng] write his name?" He concluded this story by saying, "In Head Start, [we] play a lot."

From the Sunny View classroom we find similar evidence that some Southeast Asian parents also sought more direct instruction for their children. One Cambodian mother in particular was quite explicit about her desire to see her son learn specific skills. Consider the following interaction I observed in the fall in the Sunny View classroom:

> Kurt's mom and Denise are talking near the door. I see Kurt's mom handing Denise some sort of paper and saying something to Denise about how "I've done my part; now you do yours. Teach him his colors." She is laughing as she says this, and Denise laughs too, saying, "OK. You held up your end of the bargain." I talked with Denise about it later, and she told me that Kurt's mom expressed concern about him not knowing his colors and implored Denise to make sure that he learned them. Somehow, they made a deal whereby if the mother made and took him to some dental or doctor's appointment that he needed to be up to date, Denise would see to it that he was taught his colors. Denise tells me, "We do whatever it takes to get them to get those kids to their appointments."

This mother perceived that her son was not learning his colors in Head Start, and she wanted to be sure that he knew them before going on to kindergarten. She was more straightforward than most parents regarding what she expected the teachers to teach her son. However, her message was consistent with that of other Southeast Asian parents. Similar to them, she wanted to ensure that her child learned certain skills in English. Because she had observed that the skills were not directly taught, she negotiated with the teachers to teach her son by agreeing and following through with something that the teachers wanted her to do in exchange for their promise to do with her child what she wanted them to do.

The level of concern and pressure did vary somewhat among parents. For example, Bee indicated to me that while most parents have similar goals for their children that involve making sure that their children leave Head Start with the ability to write their names, know their colors, shapes, and the alphabet, some parents do not care about these skills. In another example of differences between parents, one parent indicated that she thought that some of the Southeast Asian parents had even higher expectations than she had. These parents, some of whom may have had very little schooling, relied on the teachers to teach more than social skills. The parents worried that because the classrooms did not emphasize the acquisition of these skills, their children might slip through the cracks and that ultimately the children might fall further and further behind in elementary school.

TEACHERS' PERSPECTIVES

In contrast to how many of the Southeast Asian parents felt about High/Scope, the teachers I studied felt that High/Scope was a very defensible program. Laura, the teacher at Green Court, explained that High/Scope helps students to explore, be creative, and build self-esteem. She believed these to be valuable skills and traits. She said: "It's really social. It really helps them feel good about themselves, but it also helps them solve problems. The children set goals. We talk about their plans and ask them how they worked. People in life have to make decisions, and that's what we're teaching them." Laura indicated that High/Scope emphasizes process over product, building on children's interests rather than working from a set schedule of activities. She believed that this difference was important. When explaining High/Scope to some university students who were observing her Head Start class as part of an assignment, she said: "With High/Scope, we want, overall, for the kids to have high self-esteem and feel good about themselves. . . . We want to see the kids develop life skills—sharing, getting along, problem solving. . . . We don't sit down and make sure they learn their ABCs. We build on what their interests are. We talk about colors, but we wouldn't sit down and just paint with blue all week."

Laura's experience with the High/Scope approach as a teacher in the Green Court program over several years had been quite positive. She not only had received praise from the Head Start agency for her success with her classes year after year, but the kindergarten teachers who have her students after they leave her classroom also praised her for her work. In a meeting I observed between Laura and the kindergarten teachers at the school where her students would attend after Head Start, Laura told the teachers that she used High/Scope and that the development of social skills was part of her emphasis. She received very positive feedback from the teachers in this meeting in response to her brief description of what she tries to do in the classroom with High/Scope, with one of them telling her that she should "keep doing what [she's] doing," and confirming that they believed in the importance of entering kindergarten with social skills above academic skills and knowledge.

Laura was aware of some parents' concerns that their children were not receiving direct instruction. Several years prior, at a parent meeting she missed, several Hmong parents expressed to the Hmong teaching assistant that they were concerned about the lack of focus on traditional academic skills in her classroom. They held the perception that the children were simply allowed to play for extended periods of time. Laura analyzed their assessment of the situation herself by saying:

> I think some parents were really concerned that their child was going to go to kindergarten and not know their ABCs or not know enough English. You know, "We want them to learn English, and here you are just playing all day, and we want them to study." That's another thing that I heard when I confronted them. And I also explained how they're picking up English during work time. They're talking to the other children. They're hearing English. And I think parents have realized that they are getting a lot of the things that they wanted.

Laura said that she had been disappointed that they had not felt comfortable coming to her with their concerns, and that she attempted, in the next parent meeting, to explain the logic of the High/Scope approach. She showed parents how children learned numbers, colors, sequencing, and other skills in a less formal manner through what is called the "play" or "work" time. Her efforts to explain High/Scope included drawing up a chart to show parents what skills their children were learning.

Laura believed, consistent with the High/Scope philosophy, that children learned words and developed language skills through the use of an approach called "self-talk." This involves an adult speaking out loud as she or he engages in activities throughout the day. At snack time, Laura knew that adults engaged in self-talk by saying phrases such as, "Now I'm using my spoon to scoop the strawberries out of the bowl." She also spoke about the importance of labeling objects for children as they played or worked as a behavior that helped students learn words in English.

At Green Court, children also traced their symbols on a piece of paper, and those who had the desire and skill copied or wrote their names on their "plans" before handing the sheet of paper to an adult so that the adult could write down where the child intended to work.

Some children, generally the older children, copied their names on their plans, and over the course of my observations, I saw children learn to write their names by the end of their second year in Head Start.

Laura also emphasized to parents the important role that the High/Scope approach can play in developing social skills, telling them that the kindergarten teachers view social skills as one of the most important skills their children will bring with them from Head Start to kindergarten.[9] She also believed that some parents, after having several children in Head Start who are now in the elementary school or beyond, understood that the school their children would attend next did want them to come with social skills, and that they did develop social skills through the High/Scope approach.

Similar to Laura, Denise at Sunny View believed in the value of High/Scope and was a strong advocate for it, particularly with respect to how it helped children develop social skills, something she felt strongly about: "My primary goal as a Head Start teacher is socialization—is really getting the kids to get along with each other and learn how to solve problems both with material and with other kids. All the academic stuff will come later if they know how to interact." Denise further believed that preschool should be a positive, fun experience, and she found the High/Scope approach with its emphasis on learning based on children's individual interests to be an excellent way to make learning fun for children. Denise described how she believed their positive experiences in Head Start would carry over to later learning experiences:

> And four-year-olds shouldn't figure out that school is awful when they're four years old. It should be fun and interesting, doing what they want to do.... Finding out that flour and salt feel and taste different even though they're the same colors. And that when you mix water with them and heat it up it makes play dough. I mean, fun stuff.... Some day when they're in chemistry and they're talking about that, you know, if you get that real basic stuff, that it was fun to do, they'll have fun doing it [later on].

Denise, similar to Laura, acknowledged that some parents did not wholeheartedly embrace the High/Scope approach. In her words, some parents simply did not "get" the underlying logic of High/Scope. She told me in one interview that sometimes she does have parents ask her when she intends to teach children their ABCs. She said that her immediate response was to say, "When they're ready to recognize letters, etcetera, and have an interest in them." Her response reflected her belief in developmentally appropriate practice, where children show an interest in activities when they are developmentally ready and where teachers then build on that interest.

Denise's more general response to all parents, some of whom expressed concern about the High/Scope approach, was to engage parents, at a parent meeting near the start of the year, in an activity that would show them the difference between traditional teaching methods that focused explicitly on learning academic skills and her use of the High/Scope curriculum that taught these skills through High/Scope's "plan, do, review" structure. She explained to me in an interview that what she did to explain the logic of High/Scope was to show a drawing of an apple to the parents and ask them to write down as many characteristics of the apple that they could, based upon the picture. Next, she showed parents a plastic apple and asked them to write down all of the characteristics of the apple that they could think of. Finally, she brought out real apples, handed each parent an apple and a knife, and encouraged them to manipulate the apple, cut it open, eat it, and so on, and then make a list of the characteristics of the apple they worked with. Then she told parents to compare their lists, crossing off all the items that appeared on both lists. Presumably, the list from the real apple exploration was much lengthier than the list created from the drawing or the plastic apple. Finally, she told them that they had a choice. She told them that they could have her teach their children using the drawing or an apple or a plastic apple, or they could have her teach using real apples, where children learned through hands-on experiences.

Through this hands-on demonstration, Denise was convinced that parents better understood the logic of the High/Scope approach and that they became supportive of the approach. While I was not present when she did this demonstration at the parent meeting, Denise informed me that after the presentation, several parents who she knew had wanted their children to learn academic skills through direct instruction understood that the children would learn through experientially grounded activities by using her approach.

In further detailing her explanation of High/Scope to parents, she stressed that the introduction, using the apple example, gave parents the sense that she knew what she was talking about as a teacher—that there was a theory behind the appearance of "free play" in her classroom. She said that she thinks the approach also gives parents an opportunity to get to know her better, and that it increases the chances that parents will feel comfortable approaching her later and saying, "I think my child is ready to read. How can you help? I think I've set a goal that's too high. But I want this. How can we get him there?"

Denise's belief in the value of this approach stemmed not simply from a blind allegiance to High/Scope. Rather, she claimed that she used an experience-based approach where she challenged children to problem solve and develop a sense of curiosity even before she knew of the High/Scope curriculum. She said, "I really think that the most important thing for kids to learn is to think. They'll learn the other stuff if they know how to think. If they can't learn to think, they're sunk."

These teachers supported the use of the High/Scope approach because they believed it provided an ideal balance between structure and freedom. Furthermore, they believed that it accomplished more than the goals most parents set for their children because it helps develop social as well as academic skills. Given the attempts made by both Denise and Laura to explain the benefits of the High/Scope approach to parents, why did many parents continue to express concerns about High/Scope?

There appear to be several interrelated factors contributing to this disjuncture in views. This was not a simple situation where parents could not understand the concepts imbedded in the High/Scope curriculum. One reason why these Southeast Asian parents appeared to resist the High/Scope approach was because it conflicted with deeply held cultural beliefs and practices. As I shall describe in greater detail in the section on High/Scope and Head Start's policies toward diversity, American society condones individual motivation and personal autonomy and High/Scope is consistent with these behaviors. However, these notions may be contrary to the traditional culture of the Hmong and other cultural groups (Goldstein 1985). This suggests that if behaviors and attitudes regarding independence and autonomy were not valued by members of a cultural minority community such as the Hmong, it is reasonable to assume that these parents would not readily embrace a curriculum approach that promoted such behaviors and attitudes.

A second possible explanation for this conflict is that many immigrant and refugee parents were concerned because the High/Scope approach relies upon children learning language by listening to adults and other children who can model speech and language, yet many of them were not fluent enough in English to interact with their children in English in this manner. In short, parents may have wished for more direct instruction in the classroom because they were unable to provide it themselves in the home.

Parents who observed their children in Head Start classrooms presumably could see that during mealtimes teachers asked students questions and talked about the foods they were eating, noting different colors and shapes. Parents were able to see that children could learn vocabulary and sentence construction using the High/Scope approach throughout the day. During work time, teachers and others ask children questions that will help them develop their ability to reason, as well as teach them concepts such as 'bigger than' and 'smaller than.'

On home visits, teachers and teaching assistants modeled these speech techniques with parents, showing them how they could help their children learn these concepts and words in their everyday interaction with their children. Children were encouraged to "read" stories from books they were familiar with, or work on special projects that the staff brought, such as cutting and gluing projects, where children could learn to count and learn their colors and shapes. These activities demonstrated by the teacher or assistant in the home were meant to model interaction between children and parents, such as asking probing questions and asking known-answer questions, that would extend children's knowledge.

But the problem for many parents was that their knowledge of English was so limited that their ability to engage in these activities in the home was severely compromised. And the parents themselves recognized this barrier. Many refugee and immigrant parents with limited English were not able to model correct speech and language with their children at home. To my knowledge, none of the parents had been told explicitly that they could engage in these activities in their native language. Furthermore, even if they *had* been, this would not have responded to the parents' concern that their children be exposed to formal instruction *in English* in order to master the language as quickly and thoroughly as possible.

If High/Scope were followed in the highest quality manner, the evidence of High/Scope's success tends to suggests that even immigrant and refugee students who come speaking little or no English would have the exposure necessary for them to acquire the knowledge and skills in English that their parents wanted them to learn. Unfortunately, my observations of the classrooms suggested that with a ratio of nineteen or twenty students to two and sometimes three trained adults, rarely did students have sustained interaction that would allow for the kind of high acquisition of skills and knowledge that was found in the results from the Perry Preschool studies and other studies of High/Scope. In other words, while in principle the High/Scope curriculum works, in practice with children and families who speak limited or virtually no English, High/Scope simply did not appear to be the ideal method of preparing children for the English-speaking world of the public schools.

Thus, at Green Court and Sunny View, for many parents High/Scope may have sounded very good in theory. But in practice, parents came to conclude that it simply left too much to chance. "Work" time, parents knew from their own observations, often did not entail a great deal of adult-to-child interaction. This meant that children were not consistently and regularly challenged to develop their problem solving skills and other higher order thinking skills, let alone have significant interaction with adults so as to develop the vocabulary and language skills in English that parents viewed as crucial. Despite what was said about the value of "self-talk," parents observed that this activity did not consistently take place in the classrooms.

This point is not intended as a criticism of the two teachers I observed, for they were good, highly qualified, and committed teachers. As I have described elsewhere (Inoway-Ronnie 1996) there were a number of interrelated factors that constrained how and what these teachers were able to do in their classrooms on a daily basis. These factors include, among others, time and resource limitations and limited access to interpreters and other social service providers.

A third explanation for why parents and teachers did not agree on the merits of High/Scope is that the parents wanted the Head Start program to give their children a familiarity with the forms and patterns of schooling that they believed their children needed to succeed in school, and they were concerned that High/Scope did not provide this. Mehan (1991) uses the term *culture of the classroom* to refer to these tacit aspects of schooling, such as appropriate ways of interacting with the teacher to show knowledge and obtain assistance:

> In general terms, the communicative aspect of competence . . . in the classroom involves knowing that certain ways of talking and acting are appropriate on some occasions and not others; knowing with whom, when, and where to speak. Although it is incumbent upon students to display what they know during lessons, they must also know *how* to display what they know. They must bring their action into synchrony with people who are already talking. To do so, class-

room rules for taking turns, producing ordered utterances, making coherent topical ties, and participating in ritualized openings and closings must be negotiated (Mehan 1979, 169; see also 1991).

Perhaps it is to this classroom culture and corresponding classroom discourse that parents wanted Head Start teachers to socialize their children because they themselves were unfamiliar with its rules and nuances. Not only were most of the older parents unfamiliar with the culture of the classroom in *American* schools, but also a few may have been unfamiliar with school culture in general because they themselves had never attended school. Similar findings are noted in research by Trueba, Jacobs, and Kirton (1990) and Goldstein (1985).[10] These parents relied upon Head Start to teach their children how to behave in school in ways that would help them become successful students. They may have perceived that High/Scope classrooms were unlike elementary school and high school classrooms, and they wanted their children to become as familiar as possible with these settings as soon as possible.

Lisa Delpit (1988, 28) writes about this tension, saying:

> Many liberal educators hold the primary goal for education is for children to become autonomous, to develop fully who they are in the classroom setting without having arbitrary, outside standards forced upon them. This is a very reasonable goal for people whose children are already participants in the culture of power and who have already internalized its codes. . . . But parents who don't function within that culture often want something else. . . . [Parents] want to ensure that the school provides their children with discourse patterns, interactional styles, and spoken and written language codes that will allow them success in the larger society."

Any or all of these three factors may explain why parents who speak limited English do not react more positively to the use of High/Scope in their children's classrooms. Their concerns about the amount and quality of time spent learning the English language, coupled with their hope that children would leave Head Start with a familiarity with the forms and patterns of interaction that take place in school lead to a rejection of High/Scope as the best curriculum choice for their children. Unfortunately, as I have suggested, parents' concerns were not really "heard." In the final section of this chapter I address the possible ramifications beyond Head Start itself of parents' perceptions that their concerns were not given true consideration.

TO WHAT DEGREE IS HIGH/SCOPE COMPATIBLE WITH
HEAD START'S POLICIES TOWARD DIVERSITY?

Apart from parent concerns, there is the separate issue of High/Scope in the context of Head Start's policies about diversity. As described in the Introduction, Head Start programs follow the "Anti-Bias Committee Philosophy Statement and Principles for Head Start." The statement calls for the "understanding, respect and responsiveness to the cultures of all people" and states that Head Start must teach children how to deal with bias. It says, "As we celebrate diversity, Head Start children will grow more competent and be able to accept the commonalities and differences in people." But is the High/Scope approach compatible with the program's policies toward diversity?

According to a handbook distributed to parents, the following definitions of anti-bias curriculum and multicultural principles are listed under classroom programs:

> Anti-Bias Curriculum: What children learn in the preschool years greatly influences whether they will grow up to value, accept and comfortably interact with diverse people or whether they will succumb to the biases that result in, or help to justify, unfair treatment of an individual because of his/her identity. Between the ages of two (2) and five (5), children become aware of gender, race, ethnicity and disabilities. Building positive self-identity and skills for appropriate social interaction are two major goals of this curriculum.

> Multicultural Principles: Multicultural Principles guide programming to require understanding, respect and responsiveness to the culture of all people (*Evergreen Head Start Parent Handbook* 1994, 6).

While the Head Start policies contain multicultural principles, it can be argued that in practice, Head Start programs tend to focus on issues of ethnicity—that is, they work to remove discriminatory practices and eliminate stereotypes, and they promote the notion of equality among different ethnic groups. There is nothing inherently wrong with these goals. But what they fail to take account of is the ways in which cultural differences perhaps warrant deeper consideration in curriculum development.

In examining the goals of the High/Scope approach, it is arguable that they reflect mainstream, middle- to upper-middle-class American ideas regarding the importance of individualism, initiative, and autonomy (see Bowles and Gintis 1976; Anyon 1981). High/Scope has children making plans, setting goals, completing tasks, and showing initiative and creativity. These skills, abilities, and traits are considered valuable in the professional middle- and upper-class communities. However, not all cultural groups share these values (Tobin, Wu, and Davidson 1989). And generally only members of the middle and upper class are afforded opportunities to use these skills and abilities. By promoting High/Scope, the Head Start program in fact may be violating its own commitment to affirm the diversity of those whom it serves by failing to acknowledge, for example, the legitimacy of more group-centered orientations and the value of conformity versus creativity and initiative.

Goldstein (1985) suggests that the notion of each individual having his or her own independent identity is a cultural construct. Different cultural communities may place a different value on this particular trait and on other traits and skills. Goldstein (1985, 206–7), for example, found that teachers who worked with Hmong high school students, "did not realize that competition and individualized motivations were culturally foreign to Hmong conceptions of appropriate interpersonal relations, and that they were consequently difficult learning strategies for Hmong to grasp."

Goldstein's (1985) findings suggest the possibility that the teachers I observed did not recognize that part of what many of the Hmong parents may have been objecting to, even if they themselves did not articulate the concept in this manner, was that the High/Scope approach focused on developing an individualistic orientation that conflicted with values and norms within their cultural community. In other words, parents were aware of the clash between the dominant American norms of independence and personal autonomy and their own cultural norms, which tended to place greater emphasis on group identity. They observed their older children rejecting the notion of collective responsibility and instead engaging in more individualistically oriented behaviors. These parents responded by resisting the teaching method, in this case the High/Scope approach, that undermined their cultural beliefs.

But other cultural differences may have played a role as well. Lau and Longmire (1994) describe a Cambodian language program for first grade children in which the teacher maintained and reinforced status differences between himself as the teacher and his students, in keeping with dominant traditions in Cambodian culture. They point out that distinctions made between the status positions of different people in Cambodian society are further reinforced by the Cambodian language, in which different words are used in phrases to acknowledge differential status. Lau and Longmire report that this type of reinforcement of status differences in the Cambodian language program contrast with the more mainstream American norm of playing down status differences. Smith-Hefner (1990, 256) similarly emphasizes the importance of hierarchy as an "integral and natural part of [the Cambodian] social order" in her study of Boston-area Khmer. There are parallels to Hmong culture as well, where Hmong adult males traditionally have higher status and authority in Hmong communities than women and children (Chan 1994).

The importance in certain Asian cultures of recognizing and maintaining a formal hierarchical structure of social relationships, according to Ima and Rumbaut (1995, 194) can be traced back to the influence of Confucian traditions from China, which is "based on vertically organized, hierarchical, patrilineal, highly disciplined extended-family systems that instill deeply felt norms of filial piety and ancestor worship." Southeast Asian parents in the Head Start programs, in reacting negatively to the High/Scope approach, may have felt that the attempts to equalize status among teacher, teaching assistant, and students, and even between teacher and parents violated their deeply ingrained values regarding the importance of acknowledging status differences and honoring such differences.

At Green Court, Laura knew that many of the Southeast Asian parents held a great deal of respect for teachers. She said, "Teachers are really high up in their culture." Yet in the same breath, she went on to say, "What we try to do is to get the focus back on parents." Laura did not see any tension between Head Start's attempt to place more responsibility for learning in the hands of parents and parents' deeply held beliefs about the important status and role of teachers as conveyors of knowledge.

One could argue that the teachers' efforts to promote parents' status as equal to teachers' status contradicts Head Start's position as an agency committed to affirming differences and respecting diversity. For what the policies essentially did was to ignore parents' deeply held beliefs. Teachers tended to assume that these parents would acculturate to the dominant norm which declares as desirable efforts to minimize status differences between adults and between adults and children. Most parents I observed and interviewed did not make explicit their objection to teachers' efforts to minimize status differences, perhaps in part because these aspects of culture are so tacit that they themselves were unaware of this cultural difference. Others appeared more aware of the cultural difference, but they were unable to change classroom practices in ways that made interaction between students and teachers more compatible with their cultural norms.

The issue raised above regarding High/Scope and Head Start's policies toward diversity are closely related to a third question: Is the use of a prescribed program such as High/Scope consistent with Head Start's stated goals of encouraging parent involvement and parent participation in decision making?

Ellsworth and Ames (1995) identify three aspects of Head Start's parent involvement component (see also Valentine and Stark 1979 and Zigler and Muenchow 1992). The first aspect of parent involvement is Head Start's commitment to hire and train parents of Head Start children for positions within the Head Start organization in order to provide employment opportunities for parents. The second aspect is the Head Start program's goal of educating parents, where parents are offered "both didactic and informal experiences aimed at making them 'better' mothers—that is, training and modeling in middle-class and schooling-oriented habits of child-rearing, theoretically so that their children will be better equipped for educational, social, and economic success" (9). And the third aspect is parent involvement in program policy making, which stems from Head Start's origins as a community action program, where the goal was to obtain the "maximum feasible participation" of lower income parents. In order to demonstrate how this aspect is defined, Ellsworth and Ames (1995) cite section 70.2 of Head Start's performance standards, which describe the program's intention to maintain the community action component of the program:

> If Head Start children are to reach their fullest potential there must be an opportunity for Head Start parents to influence the character of programs affecting the development of their children. The organizational structure of every Head Start program must provide this opportunity by increasing the effectiveness of parent participation in the planning and implementation of programs on the local level, in order that parents may also become more effective in bringing about positive change in the lives of their children. . . . Successful parental involvement enters into every part of Head Start, influences other antipoverty programs, helps bring about changes in institutions in the community and works toward altering the social conditions that have formed the systems that surround the economically disadvantaged

child and his family. Project Head Start must continue to discover new ways for parents to become deeply involved in decision-making about the program and in the development of activities that they deem helpful and important in meeting their particular needs and conditions. (*Head Start Policy Manual* (1970), Instruction 1–31, section B2, "The Parents." ACYF Transmittal Notice 70.2)

Clearly, the program's policies call for parent participation in a range of areas, in theory giving parents a great deal of power to influence what takes place at a number of organizational levels. Unfortunately, like other inquiries into actual practice, my research demonstrates that parents in Head Start wield very little power and influence.

While in written policy parents are said to have an important role in the education of their children in Head Start, what I found in my research with regard to High/Scope was that parents' objections and expressions of concern were not given a great deal of credence. Both Laura and Denise were aware that some parents had expressed concern about the High/Scope approach, knowing that parents were asking for more direct instruction for their children in learning letters, numbers, colors, and how to write their names. The teachers believed that through the High/Scope method the children eventually would learn the skills that their parents wanted. In the teachers' opinions, the disagreement between parents and teachers was more a disagreement about the means used to reach a similar end.

Both Laura and Denise had reason to believe that their students were mastering important skills using the High/Scope method in their respective Head Start classrooms. Not only had they received positive feedback from the kindergarten teachers, but both were recognized as outstanding teachers and won praise from their supervisors, other administrators, and colleagues. Additionally, both teachers perceived that their students were developing social and "critical thinking" skills that were just as important as the academic skills for success in kindergarten and beyond. Teachers also expressed concern that if they did not follow the High/Scope approach, they would be "written up" by their program managers and might face discipline and possibly the loss of their jobs for noncompliance because the Head Start program they worked for had adopted the High/Scope approach.

My findings suggest that parents in the program who expressed concern and objections to the use of the High/Scope approach may become skeptical about their role as participants in the Head Start program. In other words, many of these parents may come to view their inability to effect change in the classroom curriculum and activities as a sign that their desires were inappropriate.

I am concerned that one of the messages parents in these program are left with is that their participation and input into Head Start policies and procedures are limited. From this, they also may infer that their participation and input into the public schools their children attend after Head Start also is unwanted. In this regard, I believe it is very important to recognize the relative status of the parents of many of these children in relation to parents who may be fluent in English and may have attended public schools in the United States their entire lives. These immigrant and refugee parents often appeared quite intimidated by the Head Start organization, being unfamiliar with educational institutions. Many of them deferred to the teacher as the ultimate authority. Yet others did voice concern. And their concerns were essentially not acknowledged.

CONCLUSION

In this chapter I have described how many Southeast Asian Head Start parents in two Head Start classrooms expressed dissatisfaction with the High/Scope approach. Teachers in these two classrooms were aware that parents did not share their own belief in the value of the High/Scope approach, making attempts to show parents how High/Scope taught their children not only the same skills parents wanted taught, but went beyond those skills to develop social skills and "critical thinking" skills that would benefit them in years to come. Yet parents appeared unconvinced. I suggest three possible interrelated explanations. One possibility for why their concerns persisted is that the parents felt that High/Scope promoted values and orientations that conflicted with their cultural beliefs. Another possibility is that parents knew they were not able to contribute to the full effect of High/Scope because they were unable to model speech and language for their children in their homes in English, and they could see that in practice the children did not have a large amount of interaction with English-speaking adults and peers in the classrooms. Finally, these parents, as immigrants and refugees, most of them with limited English language skills, relied upon the teachers to teach their children the culture of the schools. They felt that the High/Scope approach simply failed to provide the necessary exposure to procedures and practices in traditionally structured school settings.

This research also addressed the question of Head Start's antibias and diversity policies, suggesting that these policies tended to focus on issues of ethnicity rather than to address some of the needs of immigrant and refugee families, such as reliance on teachers to help immigrant and refugee children learn English so that they were not behind their native-English-speaking peers when they entered public school. The use of High/Scope appeared to contradict Head Start's commitment to diversity by ignoring the possibility that parents' objections to High/Scope reflected cultural differences.

With regard to parent participation in Head Start, this research demonstrates with the High/Scope example that even when parents expressed concerns about High/Scope, their concerns were not given much consideration. Claims of true parent involvement and "parents as partners" must be called into question, and consideration also must be given to the impact this pattern of behavior may have on parents' willingness and desire to become involved in the education of their children at the elementary and secondary school levels.

Throughout this research project, what I found the most disturbing was the lack of acknowledgment that teaching young children *is* a value-laden process (Powell 1994) and that by selecting the High/Scope approach, Head Start promoted certain values. While there are important underlying reasons for the differences in the parents' and teachers' perspectives, what I advocate as a first step is much more explicit dialogue regarding what and how children are taught (Delpit 1988, 1995).

Children in Head Start are being socialized primarily into dominant norms of behavior, including the dominant social norm in this country to uphold the rights of individuals and promote individual achievement. This research reveals differences between dominant American cultural beliefs of independence, and autonomy and notions of what should constitute early childhood education experiences and those held by many Southeast Asian immigrant and refugee parents. Head Start programs that articulate antibias policies and promote the notion of parents as partners must deal with these differences in values and beliefs. To the extent that Head Start defines its primary mission as one of helping prepare students for success in a society that may not recognize certain cultural norms and values as legitimate, perhaps policy makers ought to make this fact more clear.

Certainly one way of dealing with them might be to acknowledge the priority given to mainstream norms. A more careful negotiation might take the direction Lisa Delpit (1988, 1995) suggests, whereby students and parents are taught explicitly that there are two (or more) different ways of speaking about, approaching, and dealing with these issues, and that both can be simultaneously affirmed as appropriate for different situations. This would acknowledge parents' beliefs and recognize theirs as legitimate concerns while at the same time move forward with Head Start's agenda to prepare the students for success in kindergarten and beyond.

NOTES

1. Greg Powell, Director of Research and Evaluation at the National Head Start Association in Alexandria, Virginia, indicated in a phone conversation (September 1995) that exact figures on the number of refugees and immigrants in Head Start programs across the country are not available, in part because of concern regarding the use of such data by the Immigration and Naturalization Service.

2. This document was distributed by the Evergreen Head Start Agency to new staff along with their *New Staff Orientation* handbook. The document is undated. It is my understanding that this document was drafted by the National Head Start Anti-Bias Committee to be used by agencies around the country.

3. See also Miller (1979).

4. Even though the estimated number of programs that have officially adopted the High/Scope approach is not large, the general theme of child-centered activities based on a developmental model in which independence, initiative, and creativity are rewarded is common among many early childhood programs.

5. When necessary, a translator was used for interviews with parents and other family members. Previous research with Southeast Asian immigrants suggests the importance of sensitivity to gender roles and clan membership (Rhoades 1991; Goldstein 1985), and every effort was made to use translators who were familiar with the families. Sometimes the translator for the interview was another family member. Unfortunately, several Hmong and African American families declined to be interviewed or were unavailable for interviews we scheduled.

6. All names and locations are pseudonyms, used in order to protect the privacy of those involved.

7. These are forms parents are invited to fill out near the beginning of the year when they first come to observe their child in the classroom.

8. There is evidence that these Southeast Asian parents are not alone in expressing concern about approaches such as High/Scope. Joffe (1977) found in her study of African American and Caucasian parents with children in child care settings that African American parents expected the early childhood education programs to use more direct teaching methods. Lubeck (1985) indicates that the African American teachers in the Head Start program she studied made a similar assessment of the expectations of parents in the program (and the expectations of the elementary school teachers who would work with the students next), using a very explicit and didactic teaching approach with the African American children despite formal Head Start policies that advocated an approach similar to High/Scope.

9. High/Scope does not explicitly emphasize socialization. However, the Head Start teachers I studied placed a great deal of emphasis on the development of social skills, and they viewed the High/Scope curriculum as playing an important part in children's social development. As noted previously, Wiekart (1987) emphasizes that High/Scope can have important social behavior consequences.

10. Goldstein (1985, 91) reports that Hmong attendance in schools in Laos was quite low. Sixty-eight percent of Hmong in Laos attended no school whatsoever, while 11.9 percent attended school for one to three years; 13.1 percent attended school for four to six years; and only 7 percent attended school for seven or more years.

REFERENCES

Anyon, J. (1981). Social class and school knowledge. *Curriculum Inquiry*, Vol. 11, No. 1, 3–42.

Berrueta-Clement, J. R., Schweinhart, L., Barnett, W., Epstein, A., and Weikart, D. (1984). *Changed lives: The effects of the Perry Preschool Program on youths through age 19*. Ypsilanti, MI: High/Scope Educational Research Foundation.

Bowles, S., and Gintis, H. (1976). *Schooling in capitalist America*. New York: Basic Books.

Bredekamp, S. (1996). Early childhood education. In Sikula, John (Ed.), *Handbook of Research on Teacher Education*. (Second Edition). New York: Macmillan.

Chan, S. (1994). Hmong life stories. In Ng, F., Yung, J., Fugita, S. S., and Kim, E. H. (Eds.), *New visions in Asian American studies: Diversity, community, power*. Pullman, WA: Washington State University Press.

Delpit, L. (1988). The silenced dialogue: Power and pedagogy in educating other people's children. *Harvard Educational Review*, Vol. 58, No. 3, 280–298.

Ellsworth, J., and Ames, L. (1995). Power and ceremony: Low-income mothers as policy makers in Head Start. *Educational Foundations* (Fall):5–23.

Epstein, A. S. (1993). Training for quality: Improving early childhood programs through systematic in-service training. *Monographs of the High/Scope Educational Research Foundation.* No. 9. Ypsilanti, MI: High/Scope Press.

Evergreen Head Start parent handbook. (1994). (14th Edition), August.

Gibson, M. A. (1988). *Accommodation without assimilation: Sikh immigrants in an American high school.* Ithaca, N.Y.: Cornell University Press.

Goldstein, B. (1985). *Schooling for cultural transitions: Hmong girls and boys in American high schools.* Unpublished doctoral dissertation, University of Wisconsin, Madison.

Head Start Policy Manual, Instruction 1–31, Section B2, The Parents (ACYF Transmittal Notice 70.2). Washington, D.C.: U.S. Government Printing Office, 1970.

Hechinger, F. M., (Ed.) (1986). *A better start.* New York: Walker and Co.

Ima, K. and Rumbaut, R. G. (1995). Southeast Asian refugees in American schools: A comparison of fluent-English-proficient and limited-English-proficient students. In Nakanishi, Don T., and Nishida, T. Y. (Eds.). *The Asian American educational experience.* New York: Routledge. (Originally published in *Topics in Language Disorders,* Vol. 9, No. 3, 54–75, 1989).

Inoway-Ronnie, E. (1996). Teachers' constructions of cultural diversity: An ethnographic study of two multiethnic and multiracial Head Start classrooms. Unpublished Doctoral Dissertation, University of Wisconsin, Madison.

Joffe, C. E. (1977). *Friendly intruders: Childcare professionals and family life.* Berkeley: University of California Press.

Lau, E., and Longmire, B. J. (1994). Value differences as reflected in interactions in a Cambodian and an American first grade class. In Ng, F., Yung, J., Fugita, S. S., and Kim, E. H. (Eds.), *New visions in Asian American studies: Diversity, community, power.* Pullman: Washington State University Press.

Lubeck, S. (1985). *Sandbox society—Early education in black and white America.* London: Falmer.

Mehan, H. (1979). *Learning lessons.* Cambridge: Harvard University Press.

Mehan, H. (1991). *Sociological foundations supporting the study of cultural diversity.* San Diego: National Center for Research on Cultural Diversity and Second Language Learning.

Miller, L. B. (1979). Development of curriculum models in Head Start. In, Zigler, E., and Valentine, J. (Eds.), *Project Head Start: A legacy of the war on poverty*. New York: The Free Press.

Ogbu, J. (1987). Variability in minority school performance: A problem in search of an explanation. *Anthropology and Education Quarterly*, Vol. 18, No. 4, 312–334.

Olneck, M. R. (1995). Immigrants and education. In Banks, J. A. and Banks, C. A. (Eds.), *Handbook of research on multicultural education*. New York: Macmillan.

Powell, G. (1995). Phone conversation, September 1995. Powell is Director of Research and Evaluation for the National Head Start Association in Alexandria, VA.

Rhoades, K. A. (1991). Cultural borderlands and educational frontiers: Hmong students in two American high schools. Unpublished MA thesis, University of Wisconsin, Madison.

Richmond, J. B., Stipek, D. J., and Zigler, E. (1979). A decade of Head Start. In Zigler, E., and Valentine, J. (Eds.) Project Head Start: A legacy of the war on poverty. New York: Free Press.

Schweinhart, L. J., Barnes, H. V., and Weikart, D. P. (1993). *Significant benefits: The High/Scope Perry Preschool study through age 27*. Ypsilanti, MI: High/ Scope Educational Research Foundation.

Schweinhart, L. J., and Weikart, D. P. (1993). Success by empowerment: The High/Scope Perry Preschool study through age 27. *Young Children*. Vol. 49, No. 1, 54–58.

Smith-Hefner, N. J. (1990). Language and identity in the education of Boston-area Khmer. *Anthropology and Education Quarterly*, Vol. 21, No. 3, 250–268.

Smith-Hefner, N. J. (1993). Education, gender, and generational conflict among Khmer refugees. *Anthropology and Education Quarterly*, Vol. 24, No. 2, 135–158.

Tobin, J. J., Wu, D. Y. H., and Davidson, D. H. (1989). *Preschool in three cultures*. New Haven: Yale University Press.

Trueba, H. T., Jacobs, L., and Kirton, E. (1990) *Cultural conflict and adaptation: The case of Hmong children in American society*. New York: Falmer Press.

Valentine, J., and Stark, E. (1979). The social context of parent involvement in Head Start. In, Zigler, E., and Valentine, J. (Eds.), *Project Head Start*. New York: The Free Press.

Weikart, D. P. (1986). Basics for preschoolers: The High/Scope approach. In Hechinger, F. M. (Ed.), *A better start*. New York: Walker and Co.

Weikart, D. P. (1987). Curriculum quality in early education. In Kagan, S. L., and Zigler, E. (Eds.), *Early schooling: The national debate*. New Haven: Yale University Press.

Wong Fillmore, L. (1991). When learning a second language means losing the first. *Early Childhood Research Quarterly*, Vol. 6, 323–346.

Zigler, E., and Muenchow, S. (1992). *Head Start: The inside story of America's most successful educational experiment*. New York: Basic Books.

Zigler, E., and Styfco, S. J. (1994). Is the Perry Preschool better than Head Start? Yes and no. *Early Childhood Research Quarterly*, Vol. 9, 269–287.

7

Family Literacy Informing Head Start: Lessons from Hmong and Latino Families

Elizabeth P. Quintero

Many of the chapters in this book question Head Start's mixed performance regarding the original goals, visions, and promises. Yet, through my experiences working with Head Start staff and parents, I have seen some glimmers of hope. The hope has revealed itself to me through activist caring parents and strong resilient children. The contexts that stand out the most clearly to me have been in critical, family literacy projects that were serving Head Start families in conjunction with a Head Start program. The two family literacy projects I will discuss are critical family literacy projects in two different geographical locations with two different cultural groups. And as previously stated, I will give examples of things learned from these Head Start/family literacy families that I believe inform us as providers of Head Start programs.

Who am I, and why do I have something to say about rethinking Head Start? The neighborhood children on my street in Mexico labeled me "the woman who speaks strangely" when I spoke to them in my mixture of Cuban and Mexican Spanish as I strolled my baby through their street soccer game. Now, depending on where one sees me, I might be involved in different, but related, tasks. At Copeland Head Start, one might point me out as the teacher from "the U" who is holding a Hmong infant (from the family literacy class in the next room) in one arm and bending over talking to Pae, a Hmong four year old in Head Start, about the fantastic environment he has made for his collection of toy humpback whales. At the university, one might point me out as "that early childhood faculty person who cares deeply about *her issues*." My issues revolve around paying attention to parents' and children's strengths. By doing this I believe educators and leaders in all arenas can learn more about how culture, language, and varying concepts of family affect child development, community development, and ultimately our ability to live with each other with respect and peace.

By briefly going back in time, I will highlight a few instances relating to why these issues became so important to me. I grew up in Florida in the 1950s when it was okay to speak Spanish only at dance class (in Tampa) on the weekends. When I was sixteen, I worked for Project Head Start in the summer of 1966. I was an assistant for a home-based teacher who visited rural black families in central Florida. All these years later, one of my most vivid memories is of the homes where the family members of various ages gathered on their front porches telling stories and "acting them out."

Later, after graduating from college with an English degree and working as a waitress, I decided early childhood education was what I would do. Yet I had had friends in teacher education programs who told me about classes of boring and superficial memorizing of various "methods" of teaching and "recipes" for discipline. I guess as a result of the combination of life experiences and personal philosophy, I wanted to study early childhood education from an alternative perspective. I went to visit the British Infant Schools and Summerhill. Fairly soon after arriving, I learned about a training program for preschool teachers that involved much practical experience in various inner-city neighborhood preschools. I plunged in, and to my delight I was placed in a school in a Middle Eastern immigrant neighborhood.

Later, back in north Florida, I found work in a small preschool for three- and four-year-old children. After I finished my masters in education/early childhood studies, I expanded my work to kindergarten teaching. It was during this chapter of my life that I became very involved in asking the question, What's left out . . . of my personal experience, of my education, and ultimately of my teaching? This was the beginning of the conviction about which I talk now when I tell students to always ask the questions about whose stories and opinions are left out of every text book, every research study, and every news report. I was becoming a critical pedagogist and developing the perspectives and commitments that would lead me in the directions that guide my work today.

I was still learning about culture, language, teaching, and learning during the next decade when I lived in Mexico where my three sons were born. I learned that in Mexico, as in the United States, color matters. After a few years, I went to New Mexico to work on a doctorate in early childhood/bilingual education. This was when Yetta Goodman and others—during the beginnings of the whole-language movement—spoke of young children's play and communication as exemplifying the "roots of literacy." I realized that I had been studying and observing firsthand these roots of literacy in the three- and four-year-old children I had been working with for years. And, over the years in different settings, as I had observed the communication of monolingual English-speaking children, of African American children both in rural schools and in inner-city schools, of monolingual Spanish-speaking children in Mexico, of Spanish-English bilingual children in Texas and New Mexico, and of the Middle Eastern children in London, I had seen the "roots of literacy" as an integral part of what children do as they understand and take part in their world. Ironically, when families do not speak English, this "world" of language and literacy is often considered less than adequate and even deviant because it is different.

During these times of observation and reflection about these developing literacies, I had the opportunity to work in Head Start programs and other programs with many parents of young children as we collaborated about the task and pleasure of positively affecting the children's lives. Children come to early childhood programs straight from the influence and "cariño" of their parents' arms. Every parent I had met—from a diversity of circumstances, from difficulty to comfort—cared deeply about his or her child who was being entrusted to my care.

As I worked and raised my own children, I saw firsthand how conflicts about traditions and myths, and a lack of cultural sensitivities on the part of educators affect families. Shortly after moving from the Southwest to the Midwest, I was still quite consistently reminded how much color matters—sometimes for good reasons, sometimes not. Being a single mother in a small, conservative town and insisting on adherence to certain cultural, childrearing principles provided many challenges for me. Several incidents at my oldest son's middle school jolted me into realizing how insensitive educators can be. For example, I was told that my son showed disrespect by breaking eye contact and looking down when being reprimanded by some of his teachers and sometimes not answering when they knew he disagreed with them. I went briefly into the "Human Diversity 101" lecture about cultural differences in terms of eye contact and in terms of whether it is appropriate to argue outwardly with an elder. Then there was a bus incident. Making a very long and painful story short, my son was picked out by a line-up identification procedure and wrongly accused of "gang" activity. When he and I resisted, the dean of his school (herself an Asian) said that essentially, if one is not white and middle class, in Duluth, one must work harder, dress better, make better grades, and make more money to be equal. I was incredulous. I wanted to make sure that my son knew that her opinions were not acceptable ones for a responsible adult to have—according to my family's value system. So I pushed it. I asked her a few more questions about equality, respect, and dignity. At which point she said, "I know, it's not right. But that's just the way things are, and I don't think we can do anything to change it." Angrily, I asked that if any people have any hopes of affecting change, is it not the people in education.

So, in the processes of parenting, living my life, and pursuing my work, I collected observations about multilingual children's roots of literacies and the effect that their parents and early teachers could have on this development. These varied experiences made me believe that critical participatory literacy programs are worthwhile partners or integral components for a program such as Head Start. In part, this because teachers are able to see what is not now seen: parents and children can show strengths and needs that sometimes are not obvious in the regular Head Start contexts.

THE FAMILY LITERACY PROJECTS

The family literacy groups with which I have been involved are organized according to a model designed to provide participatory, critical literacy and biliteracy development opportunities for families in diverse communities. One family literacy project was for Mexican and Mexican American families in El Paso, Texas. The project provided service for families with four- and five-year-old children, most of whom were in Head Start programs during the morning. In addition, many of the teachers who were hired on a part-time contract to facilitate the family literacy classes were Head Start teachers. The other project is the Poj Niam Thiab Meyuam (mother/child school) and is ongoing in Duluth, Minnesota, for Hmong women and their infants, toddlers, and preschoolers. The preschoolers and toddlers of these participating groups are in center-based and home-based Head Start programs. The family literacy staff, teachers, and assistants are Head Start and Early Childhood Family Education staff collaborating on the literacy project.

El Paso, Texas

The project involving Mexican, Mexican American, and Chicano parents and their children, Project FIEL (Family Initiative for English Literacy), brought parents and children together once a week after school for approximately an hour of activities. The classes, which consisted of five to seven parents and their Head Start, kindergarten, and/or first-grade children, were facilitated by an instructor with the help of an assistant. In many ways, the goals of the family literacy project were striving for the same active parent involvement, holistic family health, and overall family education goals of Head Start. Project FIEL's goals were more specifically literacy oriented, but certainly encompassed all the intentions of Head Start. They were

1. to enhance literacy and biliteracy development of the parents and children through a series of participatory intergenerational activities;

2. to provide information regarding the literacy development process in children to the parents and to provide a setting for the parents to utilize the information;

3. to enhance parents' self-confidence to contribute to their children's literacy development through participatory group interaction; and

4. to empower the participants to connect the literacy activities to their own social and cultural situations, thus encouraging their use of literacy for personal, family, and community purposes.

Duluth, Minnesota

The project involving Hmong women and their infants, toddlers, and preschoolers is currently in its fourth year at Copeland Community Center, in Duluth, Minnesota. The program is a collaborative effort of Head Start staff, Early Childhood Family Education staff, Adult Basic Education/English as a Second Language staff, parents, and children. The goals of this project are reflected in the goals of Project FIEL, with two added related goals:

• a collaboration model of professional and paraprofessional staff working with Asian families in education and social services was devised to more effectively and efficiently serve the needs of the Asian families consistently from the time a child is born until the child becomes a high school student;

• a concerted effort is made to involve all members of the family.

The mothers, infants, toddlers, and young children come to the school four days a week after the children finish their regular Head Start. The mothers attend an English as a second language (ESL) literacy class, which includes a parenting component. In the same building the children attend a mixed-age group activity session modeled after Head Start curricula with an emphasis on ESL literacy in developmentally, culturally appropriate ways.

I believe that the most important function of a critical, participatory family literacy project is the service provided for the participating families. It can support the efforts and activities of existing Head Start programs. The activity of critical, participatory literacy provides to the family participants information about literacy and codes of power (Delpit 1988; Reyes, 1993) in the United States in a context where they are able to explore the relationship this information (both the literacy and the political aspects) has on their own way of life. Furthermore, this critical, participatory literacy setting also uses the background knowledge of the participants in a valued, active situation and can provide Head Start teachers and staff with concrete examples of sociocultural information and factual information that is necessary in any educational setting and information that is, to a large degree, not available in books or teacher development class content. We can learn from parents about sleeping routines and family roles as we engage in conversation about storytelling and storybook reading at bedtime. I will tell a few stories from these two family literacy projects that illustrate the transformative potential and the information potential, in albeit complex ways.

I see early childhood programs with strong ties to the families of the children as the most hopeful contexts for transformation or as Freire (1985, 106) explains, "the process by which human beings participate critically in a transforming act." Head Start is *the* model in this regard, both historically and currently. Freire (1994, 91) in his recent *Pedagogy of Hope* says, "There is no authentic utopia apart from the tension between the denunciation of a present becoming more and more intolerable, and the 'annunciation,' announcement, of a future to be created, built—politically, aesthetically, and ethically—by us women and men."

PARENTS DO TAKE TRANSFORMATIVE ACTION

We have seen the "other side" of critical literacy. In other words, the parents and children are not always directly involved in issues of "power," but as they have been respected and encouraged to read their "world" (Freire and Macedo 1987) their power of life experiences and potential in their new cultural context both encourages us and informs us as staff. While many people define "transformative action" in different ways, most would agree that a prime example is a parent doing something to make a situation better for her or his child. A few years ago the Hmong women, in one of the first family literacy classes, came to class with a critical question. The question was, "Why doesn't Lowell School [the elementary school that their older children attended] tell us about parent conferences, send us notification in our language, or provide an interpreter at meetings?" With the interpreter at the family literacy class and the literacy facilitator taking part in the discussion, the women discussed at length how angry they feel when they hear of the teachers' comments about how the Hmong parents just do not care about their children's education. The staff at the elementary school say this because the Hmong parents never come to parent conferences, PTA meetings, or other school functions. The women commented on how they had been able to be active in Head Start, in part because the staff always made the effort to provide interpreters at meetings, provide information in their language, and respectfully talk to parents about issues regarding their children. After comparing the two situations (Head Start and the elementary school), they decided to take action. They wrote the following letter:

November 3, 1993

Tus saib xyuas nyob rau hauv tsev kawm ntawv.

Dear Principal,

Peb yog cov ua niam ua txiv muaj me nyuam tuaj kawm
ntawv hauv tsev kawm ntawv Lower School. Peb xav
thov kom nej muab cov ntawv xa los tsev txhais ua
ntawv Hmoob. Thaum twg nej muaj tej yam uas tseem
ceeb nyob rau hauv tsev kawm ntawv los peb thiaj
paub tias yog ntawv tseem ceeb thiab.

Ua tsaug ntau koj muab koj lub sij haum los twm peb
tsab ntawv no.

As can be seen in this letter, English was used only for the principal's name and the name of the school (both changed here to protect privacy). To paraphrase the letter, the parents asked the principal why they were not notified of school information regarding their children in their language. They stated that they are active parents who care deeply about their children's education, but when information is illegible to them they cannot participate.

The principal responded with a letter, written in Hmong, a week later. Since the incident, interpreters have been provided at all school functions in which the parents participate, and school notices have been translated into Hmong. Participation by the Hmong parents in school activities has risen to over 90 percent.

Examples of parent advocacy growing from family literacy can be seen in the El Paso project as well. A family literacy lesson was developed on "School and You: Avenues for Advocacy," because several of the parents had inquired into or expressed discontent with specific situations they had encountered in their children's schools. The class discussion focused on the different procedures they could use within the school systems to voice their complaints and advocate for change. Some of the guiding questions of the lesson were the following: "When you have a question about what is happening in your child's class at school, when and how can you talk to the teacher?" "If you are not happy with what the teacher tells you, or if the teacher won't talk to you, what can you do then?" "What are all the avenues you can think of to be an advocate for your children?"

One parent during the class talked about her child's bilingual teacher. The teacher was treating the child in a disrespectful way that, the parent felt, was damaging the child's self-confidence and inhibiting her learning. Her child had entered kindergarten, after the generally supportive context of Head Start, but day after day as she struggled with various writing tasks, her kindergarten teacher consistently reprimanded her for poor performance and grabbed her paper, crumpled it up, and dramatically threw it in the trash in front of all the students. After discussing this situation with other parents in the family literacy class, the parent found other parents outside the class who shared similar stories. They all decided they wanted to meet at the school for a parent discussion group to brainstorm how they could deal with "children's abuse by teachers." The parents began to meet regularly, sometimes with their school administration, and they sometimes attended school board meetings to make their concerns known (Quintero and Macías, 1995).

LEARNING FROM THE FAMILIES: CHALLENGING ASSUMPTIONS

Head Start, like all educational institutions, can be dominated by dogma, myth, and general incongruities between intentions and day-to-day realities of practice.

One tenet of early education in terms of caring for infants in a safe and quality-oriented environment in the current U.S. culture involves the safety, hygiene, and comfort of providing a crib for each infant. In the description of the program for Hmong families in Duluth, Minnesota, the example was mentioned of the infants "coming to school" in a different room, albeit in the same building, from their mothers. This has allowed us to make observations regarding emotional development and social development. For example, it has been documented that the babies become emotionally calm and apparently content quicker when they are held upright or carried strapped on a staff member's back in the mother's traditional cloth baby carrier or, in some cases, sitting in an infant seat on a carpeted, safe area of the floor. The infants are accustomed to being in the upright position, in the baby carrier, for most of their waking hours. The mothers are busy and, in all cases in our group, responsible for many children in their constant care. Thus, a crib isolated in a quiet room is not a comfort for these babies. Separation fears and stages of fear of strangers seem to appear and disappear for the young children in the project in much the same sequence as for babies from Western cultures, but the presence of older (aged two through five) siblings, cousins, and relatives is a comforting social development scaffold.

Another tenet of many early childhood programs (though not all) has been promotion of separation of age groups for various reasons. Head Start is a program with national guidelines for specific age-group participation. One of the reasons is safety—especially in the case of infants being separated from toddlers, because it is believed that toddlers are clumsy and egocentric and not as cautious as necessary to coexist in the same room with babies crawling around on the floor. Many child development experts would concur regarding both the egocentric personality characteristics and the physical ineptness of the typical two year old. Consequently, when the staff at Copeland realized the infants needed the emotional support of their toddler siblings and cousins and friends, we all worried about the safety of the infants, especially the ones who were playing on the carpets either in infant seats or on a blanket with a toy or a staff member if we opened up the room to the mixed age groups. Would the toddlers and preschoolers not start running around, step on the babies, or at the very least, bump into them and startle them with their noise and raucous behavior? Several days during the first two weeks when we had a good adult/child ratio, we tried it. Over and over again we were proven wrong. The toddlers, even the ones just learning to walk on wobbly legs, were always careful of the babies and apparently cognizant of their presence.

Another assumption has been critically questioned as a result of the strong Hmong family structure and early childhood practice in terms of home-based Head Start education. One reality in many Hmong families is that parents have maintained the practice of having many children in close succession. It is not uncommon for a Hmong family to have from six to ten children with only one year or, at the most, two years in between the births. The Hmong mothers are extremely attentive and affectionate caregivers of all the children, but the newborn baby is the unquestioned focus of the mother's attention. Thus, when a new baby arrives, the previous newest born's care is transferred to older siblings or extended family members. Siblings, especially the girls, are taught to take on much of the childrearing responsibilities at a young age. This brings to mind the question for Home Based Head Start and other early childhood programs that provide in-home suggestions for parents to work with toddlers and three year olds at home. Our staff is wondering whether we should we be focusing on encouraging and supporting—with activity suggestions and other education— older siblings who really are the family members who interact most with the two and three year olds at home.

Another set of tenets in early childhood practice focus around issues of Developmentally Appropriate Practice. The National Association for the Education of Young Children (NAEYC) developed a position statement regarding appropriate learning contexts and methods for young children regarding cognitive, social, emotional, and physical development (Bredekamp 1987). While many programs, including Head Start, use the guidelines in varying ways, early childhood educators do not all agree on the emphases of the Developmentally Appropriate Practice. This is especially true regarding sociocultural development and learning for groups of children from diverse backgrounds in the United States (Bloch 1991; Swadener and Kessler 1991; Walsh 1991). For the most part, Developmentally Appropriate Practice is based upon the premises of developmental psychology and constructivism (McLaughlin 1992). Constructivism generally is considered to be the theory that humans learn through creating cognitive structures from interaction with the environment. The way early childhood educators are taught to create and enhance these "environments" for young children is through an understanding of "norms" of cognitive development, social and emotional development, and physical development. However, these "norms" were developed by well-intentioned scholars from either the same or very similar cultural groups, so that cultural values were used as static facts of nature (Lubeck 1994). As critical theorists and practitioners, it is important that we reevaluate established norms of development as are currently reflected in psychology texts and many assessment measures—especially considering children from diverse backgrounds. Head Start, while committed to Developmentally Appropriate Practice, can be an arena in which professionals challenge the dogmas of what has much more aptly become culturally, developmentally appropriate practice. It is urgent that Head Start programs stay tuned to this idea of culture being closely tied to development, because the families served are so diverse.

In this area of cognitive development, for example, Developmentally Appropriate Practice promotes nondirective, exploratory contexts for optimum development of literacy and other cognitive skills for young children. The staff involved with the literacy project in El Paso, Texas, stressed emergent literacy and developmental writing. We were careful to explain the principles behind this way of learning, while adamantly committed to respecting the parent's choice in method of interaction and teaching with her child. Diana, one of the Family Literacy participants in this project, lived with both her parents in a working-class neighborhood. She was an only child. The family spoke only Spanish at home. Diana's mother was adamant about being a direct part of her daughter's education—directly even when she was given information about the importance of her daughter's independence in learning and literacy events.

Diana was just beginning to learn English as the literacy groups started in September. She was in kindergarten. She had not been able to attend Head Start. Diana exhibited familiar patterns of behavior for a five year old at the beginning of the literacy sessions. She spoke little at first, mostly in Spanish, often answering the instructor's questions with a "yes," "no," or short phrase. When the teacher asked her a question in English, she did not seem to understand, so she looked to her mother for a translation. She also often seemed to wait for a response from her mother, even when she understood the language used. As the classes progressed, Diana began to participate more in class in terms of her oral language.

Regarding the mother/daughter interactions in the literacy class, at first, the observers perceived that Ms. García was impatient with her daughter and had a persistent tendency to dominate the interactions. For example, during a lesson on the seasons, the following interchanges took place:

Ms. G.: ¿Qué vas a pintar en este arbol de winter? (What are you going to paint on this tree in winter?)
Diana: Hojas. (Leaves.)
Ms. G.: No, no, no, ¿qué es eso? . . . toma . . . no tienes ganas o sí . . . No, Diana! . . . ¿Qué tienes? Dime, qué tienes. Espérate para que hagas bien y no cochinadas (No, no, no, what's that? Do . . . you want to or not? . . . No, Diana. . . . What's the matter with you! Wait so you'll do it right and not make a mess.)
Diana: ¿Qué parezcan leaves?.acá . . . necesita más brown. (How do leaves look? . . . Here . . . they need more brown.)

While this type of interaction went on, the teacher noted Ms. García's action and tactfully told her that Diana could write and draw on her own; she said it was not important at this point in Diana's literacy development whether her writing was misspelled, not on the line, or that the letters were not correctly shaped. She also told Ms. García that her constant corrections may make Diana dependent on her for approval of everything she does. The advice, however, had little effect on the mother. She continued to erase portions of her daughter's work that she did not think were acceptable and made her redo them. This practice certainly is the antithesis of "literacy development" and DAP guidelines. The mother was certainly not abusive, but clearly she was authoritative. Developmentally Appropriate Practice Guidelines fail to take account of cultural differences in child-rearing practices or the negotiation of the tension that results between home and school disparities. Diana respected her mother's strong personality and interaction style, yet maintained her own willful intentions when it was important to her. The teacher working with this family literacy class expressed frustration with her attempts to convince the mother to give the daughter more freedom to do activities in a developmentally appropriate way. However, the literacy staff tried to keep perspective and keep in mind the critically foremost goal of the project, which was to respect the parents as the most important teachers of their children. We began to feel confident when we explained our teaching methods to the parents as collaborators (not directors), some parents (Ms. García included) felt confident enough to disagree, do some teaching in their own way, and still keep attending classes. In spite of the frustrations, we realized that this mother must have felt some parts of the experience were useful for her daughter and herself, because she did not miss a class during her two years of attendance. All early childhood educators can learn from this family literacy staff, who respectfully present the "why" and "how" of developmental literacy activities as examples while at the same time respecting Ms. García's more traditional approach.

Regarding the cognitive issue of language development, Ms. García was realistic to insist that her daughter write well and correctly both in her mother tongue and in English. She conceivably had had experiences both in Mexican and in American society which had stressed the relationship between success and hard work to conform to form, in this case, correct English. She was determined to insure that her daughter succeed in learning English. Yet, at the same time, she and her family continued to speak only Spanish in the home. Research now shows that their speaking Spanish at home supports the children's English development at school (Cazden 1981; Cummins 1989.).

Parental authority is an important value in Latino culture. Latino parents inculcate in their children a profound respect for teachers and for school. As Reyes (1993) reports, Latinos hold high regard for teachers as authority figures. Thus it is her opinion that direct instruction or active, direct interaction from the teacher is expected. This direct interaction does not necessarily have to take away from a goal of learning to be an independent thinker on the part of the child, but the path leading to the goal is more familiar with a respected guide. "Respeto" (respect) is a central cultural value and requires deference to older and more skilled individuals who have a greater command of the skills being learned. Having said this, it must be pointed out that the directive nature of Ms. García could be because of temperament, personality, or individual family situation. Her story is not told to type-cast all Latino families. Her story simply shows the complexities involved in being sensitive to families.

Going on to another Mexican American family, that of Andre and Ms. Mora, if this parental authority is a wide-spread value, it is manifested in different forms of parent/child interactions. In the case of this family, we see a parenting style quite consistent with the practices and assumptions of family literacy. However, working with Andre and his mother caused us to challenge another myth. Some researchers (Stitcht and McDonald 1989) believe that a parent must have a formal education in order to be supportive of her children's academic development. Andre, age five, and his mother, Ms. Mora, attended Project FIEL activities in central El Paso for two semesters. Andre lived with his mother, father, ten-year-old brother, nineteen-year-old sister, and twenty-one-year-old sister. Ms. Mora had only six years of formal schooling in Mexico. Yet, her *biblioteca* (library) in her home, her literacy practices with her children, and her own habits show no lack of academic support. Furthermore, the academic success of all four children—those in elementary school and those in high school and the university—contradicts the myth that unless mothers obtain a high school diploma, the children will not succeed in school. However, Weinstein-Shr (1992) cites research that discusses the Moras' family strengths. The research indicates that when families participate in a variety of literacy activities, including home language literacy and activities in which children read to parents (Ada 1988; Tizard, Schofield, and Hewison 1982; Viola, Gray, and Murphy 1986), the literacy development of the children is enhanced.

Ms. Mora also reported that she reads aloud from the Bible daily and that her home is "una biblioteca" (a library). Both Andre and Ms. Mora talked about the two sisters who are honor students at the University of Texas at El Paso. Also, the tradition of literacy in the home and in the family seems to be taking root in Andre and his brother, who are always on the honor roll at their elementary school.

Furthermore, the family's near perfect attendance to classes assures that they were exposed to literacy information and in a setting that encouraged use of the information. Ms. Mora's comments about being an avid reader herself indicate that while she is a monolingual Spanish speaker she is quite literate in her native language. Videotaped interactions of her and her son during the FIEL classes further showed that she is indeed proficient in literacy behaviors as well. That is to say, she calmly and consistently prompted and encouraged Andre and appropriately explained things to him in Spanish. Andre often then explained to the class the issue or story in perfect English (usually his writing was in English). Thus, while Ms. Mora doesn't consider herself bilingual or biliterate, she is an effective leader of this bilingual, biliterate family team. She let Andre work independently, while never leaving him without moral support. She accepted his independent thinking and ideas, while informing him in appropriate contexts about cultural and family values. Examples from field notes and video taped class sessions show mother/son interactions that reveal her leadership on both a literacy development level and a social context level and consequently that Andre, at age five, is proficiently bi-lingual and on his way to becoming biliterate.

Likewise, the children in the Minnesota project speak in two lan-guages—Hmong and English. When their mothers join them in the room, they sing and "show off" their English with storybook reading in one breath and turn to their mothers and elaborate on the story, in Hmong in a private conversation. Pae, age four, then may turn to one of the teachers and ask a question in English. His cognitive flexibility is not slowing down at all while his two languages develop. The Hmong children in the family literacy project in Minnesota are showing com-plex cognitive processing and development in spite of language differ-ences. For example, Pae is a child who attends the Head Start classroom in the morning where the programming for a multicultural group of children consisting of American Indians, African Americans, European Americans, and Hmong children is done primarily in English. In the afternoon, Pae attends family literacy class and extends his learning from the morning. With the assistance of a Hmong speaking assistant, and mostly the conversations in Hmong with his buddies and rela-tives, he sings, draws, discusses, and writes about what he has learned about whales, dinosaurs, the moon, fish and sea life, and folktales from Africa, Thailand, Laos, and England. These examples of literacy communication in his first and second languages are closely tied to complex cognitive functioning (Quintero 1986). Cognitive connections, both in terms of factual information and socioemotional relevance to personal life, build strong critical thinkers and students who are suc-cessful in school (Cazden 1981; Cummins 1989; Freire and Macedo 1987).

MAGIC AND RISK: MORE THAN PARENT EDUCATION,
MORE THAN EARLY CHILDHOOD EDUCATION

Family literacy programs are complex by their very nature, and they differ according to participants' needs and strengths. Yet it has been my experience that these programs offer more than most parent edu-cation programs and more than many early childhood education pro-grams. Family literacy programs have had the advantage of what I consider to be a natural form of magic. Magic happens because of what families across cultures do best—care for, attend to, and love each other, regardless of conditions. The magic is produced by parent-child love, trust, and shared understandings and experiences. I have seen in family literacy programs aspects of this magic, which I hope to see influencing other learning contexts for immigrant learners and their families.

Family literacy programs also require risk taking on the part of both parents and staff. This comes in the form of collaborating in ways that often "go against the grain" (Cochran-Smith 1991) of traditional practice. For some of the parent participants, it is a risk to enter a school building in a foreign country where the expectations are unknown. Almost all parents risk disruptions in already busy and difficult family routines. In addition, for all parents—regardless of background—the risk of addressing creativity, child development, and learning needs is a struggle. To decide when to help, how to help specifically with a learning task, and when to encourage independence in their children is a challenge. Yet, by working alongside one's child, the task becomes clearer. "Today I'm learning about my children's creativity and understanding and helping them in whatever I can because I like to share the hour with my children. . . . Here I feel comfortable and confident" (Translated from Spanish, Parent from Project FIEL, El Paso, Texas).

Children have taken risks. In the excitement of working with parents and elders some children have risked using innovative literacy practices. Some family literacy projects put aside the textbooks and use elders' storytelling as authentic history lessons. Other literacy projects let go of the "American Way" in which students study the Columbus story of Europeans coming to the Americas and how the United States began with thirteen colonies and then became a republic and so on, to instead encourage children to discuss and value their cultural traditions and family routines. Some family literacy projects leave behind strict adherence to English grammatical rules and formal writing rules and encourage the use of code switching, both in oral and in written form. Celia, a kindergarten student in El Paso, Texas, chattered in writing about the Valentine activity done in her family literacy class where code switching was encouraged. *"Voy a mordir a Grandma with the love bug porque le quiero."* (I'm going to bite Grandma with the love bug because I love her.) She gets to speak from the heart, but she risks forgetting to use only English the next morning in her regular class setting, where she may be admonished for mixing Spanish and English.

And finally, we see risk on the part of teachers. Teachers in family literacy programs have had to risk working with unfamiliar age groups and often trying out newly developed lessons that have never been field tested or are antithetical to how they were taught or taught to teach. One teacher voiced in her journal the risks and rewards of teaching in a nontraditional setting with intergenerational groups:

> I have witnessed growth within myself. This growth has been af-
> fected by the children. Because of them, I've pushed myself to pro-
> vide interesting activities that are appropriate. My confidence increases
> with each opportunity. The family literacy project has provided me
> with unforgettable experiences. Working with parents has also added
> to my growth. I know with every experience comes change, and
> luckily [my changes] have been positive. With change though, I al-
> ways keep in mind to respect my students. For it is through respect
> that I will gain as well. Moreover, I accept and acknowledge them,
> because without them, growth would not result.

Head Start programs based on culturally sensitive child-centered curriculum models and authentic and meaningful parent involvement are providing positive examples of programming for Mexican and Hmong families. However, because of the changing needs of families, and because of the persistence of Western intellectual, psychological, and cultural perspectives, adaptations must continue to be made.

Family childrearing practices must be supported and built upon to enhance social, emotional, cognitive, and physical development. Schools and parents must determine together appropriate early child-hood programming that recognizes that the school's developmental milestones may be different from those of a cultural group or an in-dividual family. Head Start programs can build rapport through an informal, nonthreatening environment, an environment in which staff members help parents to feel welcomed and comfortable so that they share the important sociocultural and personal meanings in their lives. It takes risk on the part of the staff, the parents, and the children; the magic that is generated is overwhelmingly exciting.

REFERENCES

Ada, A. F. (1988). The Pajaro Valley experience: Working with Spanish-speaking parents to develop children's reading and writing skills in the home through the use of children's literature. In T. Skutnabb-Kangas and J. Cummins (Eds.), *Minority education: From shame to struggle*. Philadelphia, PA: Multilingual Matters.

Bloch, M. N. (1991). Critical science and the history of child development's influence on early education research. *Early Education and Development*, Vol. 2, No. 2, 95–108.

Bredekamp, S. (1987). *Developmentally appropriate practice in early childhood programs serving children from birth through age 8.* Washington, D.C: National Association for Education of Young Children.

Cazden, C. (1981). *Language in early childhood education.* Washington, D.C.: NAEYC.

Cummins, J. (1989). *Empowering minority students.* Sacramento, CA: CABE.

Cochran-Smith, M. (1991). Learning to teach against the grain. *Harvard Education Review,* Vol. 61, No. 3, 279–310.

Delpit, L. (1988). *The* silenced dialogue: Power and pedagogy in educating other people's children. *Harvard Educational Review,* Vol. 58, No. 3, 280–298.

Freire, P. (1985). *The politics of education.* Granby, MA: Bergin & Garvey.

Freire, P. (1994). *Pedagogy of hope.* New York: Continuum.

Freire, P. & Macedo, D. (1987). *Literacy: Reading the word and the world.* South Hadley, MA: Bergin & Garvey.

Lubeck, S. (1994). The politics of developmentally appropriate practice: Exploring issues of culture, class, and curriculum. In Mallory, B. L. and New, R. S. (Eds.), *Diversity and developmentally appropriate practices: Challenges for early childhood education.* New York: Teachers College Press.

McLaughlin, M. (1992). Appropriate for whom? A critique of the culture and class bias underlying developmentally appropriate practice in early childhood education. Paper presented at the Conference on Reconceptualizing Early Childhood Education: Research, Theory, and Practice, Chicago, IL.

Quintero, E. P. (1986). Preschool literacy: The effect of sociocultural context. ERIC # ED282181.

Quintero, E. & Macías, A. H. (1995). To participate, to speak out . . . : A story from San Elizario, Texas. In Martin, R. (Ed.), *On equal terms: Addressing issues of race, class and gender in higher education.* New York: State University of New York.

Reyes, M. de la Luz. (1993). Challenging venerable assumptions: Literacy instruction for linguistically different students, *Harvard Educational Review,* Vol. 62, No. 4, 427–446.

Sticht, T. G., and McDonald, B. A. (January 1989). *Making the nation smarter: The intergenerational transfer of cognitive ability.* Executive Summary, San Diego, CA: Applied Behavioral and Cognitive Sciences, Inc.

Swadener, E. B., and Kessler, S. (1991). Introduction to the special issue. *Early Education and Development,* Vol. 2, No. 2, 85–94.

Tizard, J., Schofield, W., and Hewison, J. (1992). Symposium: Reading collaboration between teachers and parents in assisting children's reading. *British Journal of Educational Psychology*, Vol. 52.

Viola, M., Gray, A., and Murphy, B. (1986). *Report on the Navajo parent child reading program at the Chinle Primary School*. Chinle School District, AZ.

Walsh, D. J. (1991). Extending the discourse on developmental appropriateness: A developmental Perspective. *Early Education and Development*, Vol. 2, No. 2, 109–119.

Weinstein-Shr, G. (1992). Learning lives in the post-island world. *Anthropology and Education Quarterly* Vol. 23, No. 2, 160–165.

8

Reform and Empowerment: Rural Mothers and Head Start

Lynda J. Ames and Jeanne Ellsworth

In the summer of 1965, Head Start came to upstate New York—the North Country—as it came to many communities that promising season. The new program offered hope to children and families who had so far been left out of the American Dream. In the thirty plus years since, North Country Head Start has won the respect and devotion of countless families in this rural mountain region. Children have been given, truly, a head start on their education, though that education has not necessarily brought them economic success. Further, *mothers* of children enrolled in the program themselves have been changed, they say for the better, by participating in various aspects of Head Start's parent involvement component.

Head Start was always intended as a two-generation program, providing assistance and training to parents as well as to preschoolers. In seeking to fulfill its promises to the parent generation, North Country Head Start provides many of the same involvement opportunities as the programs detailed in other chapters in this volume: center parent meetings, helping in classrooms, serving on the Policy Council, seminars in "Looking at Life," fundraisers, socials, and so forth.

This chapter is a brief synopsis and update of our book, *Women Reformed, Women Empowered: Poor Mothers and the Endangered Promise of Head Start* (Ames and Ellsworth, Temple University Press, 1996). See also "Power and Ceremony" (Ellsworth and Ames 1996).

The content of these programs, though, was developed by professional program specialists based largely on assumptions that Head Start parents are deficient in various ways. Parents, according to these assumptions, need to be trained to do what they have not done, trained to provide their children with "appropriate" environments so that the children will prosper in this land of equal opportunity. This intervention into the family lives of poor children is expected by policy makers to break the "cycle" of poverty and give those children "enriched" experiences to counteract the deficiencies of their parents' homes and child-rearing methods. Hence, North Country Head Start provides mothers opportunities such as cooking and nutrition classes and, perhaps most crucial, both formal and informal parenting training. Mothers are carefully trained at Head Start to rear their children in ways deemed suitable by professionals.

And yet some of the involvement opportunities Head Start provides are based on entirely different assumptions, assumptions left over from the more radical designers of the 1960s' War on Poverty. Poor people are not assumed deficient and in need of training. Instead, it is assumed that poor people need only be provided appropriate avenues of power so that they can make changes in their own lives as *they* see fit, and make changes in social structures as *they* see fit. Only these eventual changes in structure, designed and executed by the disadvantaged themselves, can provide genuine opportunities for the poor and their children. Thus, Head Start requires that parents be a majority on the governing body of local programs. In this way, parents can decide what early educational experiences are appropriate for their children and then see to the delivery of those programs. This radical model was best played out, perhaps, in Mississippi, as Kuntz suggests in a chapter in this volume.

North Country Head Start, then, like Head Start programs across the country, attempts two—perhaps two contradictory—changes in parents. They are to be *reformed*, to have their deficiencies corrected, and made to behave in ways more typical of middle-class communities (though they still will lack the resources of that class). However, they are to be *empowered* to make their own changes in the world, not necessarily the same changes deemed worthy by middle-class professionals. It is this seeming contradiction and its effects on mothers and on Head Start itself that is the subject of this chapter.

We will see that, in fact, programs aimed at reforming women can be seen by mothers to be empowering. That is, the programs designed to correct parent deficiencies can be, and in fact were, trans-

formed by mothers to give themselves space to breathe and work—
a genuine element of empowerment (Bunch 1981). Women also use
the more explicitly empowering programs in genuinely empowering
ways. However, we also will see that this empowering potential of
Head Start—even the empowering potential of reform—is in grave
danger.

NORTH COUNTRY HEAD START

The North Country is a land of spectacular physical beauty. The
Adirondack Mountains are home to Lake Placid, site of two winter
Olympic games. There are lakes, rivers, forests, meadows, and mountain peaks providing incomparable outdoor recreation and sight-seeing
for all seasons. Tourism is an important aspect of the North Country
economy. There are extraordinarily luxurious vacation homes right
next door to pockets of grinding poverty (Fitchen 1991). Indeed, amid
this natural splendor and social wealth, the North Country has a
poverty rate higher than the overall state average.

Winters here are long and cold. Snow and ice on irregularly maintained rural roads are a constant danger to all, but especially to those
driving old or substandard vehicles. Heating costs are high, and there
are many fires each winter caused by faulty wood- and oil-burning
heat sources, most of the fires in homes of low-income families. As one
Head Start mother puts it, "It's just that life is so much more of a
struggle when you don't have any money."

For three years, from the fall of 1992 through the summer of 1995,
we participated in the lives and struggles of North Country Head
Start and its members. We observed meetings of the Policy Council
and many other formal and informal meetings of parents. We formally
interviewed and informally chatted with many parents and staff members. We came to know how Head Start programs helped—or did not
help—poor families to cope with life. We came to know how women
could be empowered or not.

We should be clear here at the beginning that in this chapter we
talk about "mothers," not "parents." Though Head Start refers often to
"parents," the vast majority of those parents who participate are
women, and it always has been that way. Head Start itself always has
assumed that parents participating in its programs are really mothers
(Valentine and Stark 1979). Further, we have come to see that Head
Start, since it involves the education of children, provides rural, poor

women with one of the very few possibilities for socially approved community involvement. This is much less true for men.

North Country Head Start funds are channeled through and administered by the local community action program (CAP)—a now-cold leftover of the War on Poverty. These days, CAPs are not the power vehicles for the poor they were intended to be by radical poverty warriors. Rather, they are nonprofit corporations administering a variety of grants and programs for low-income residents in their counties. In the North Country, the CAP is run by an executive director who answers to a Board of Directors made up of local business people and social service professionals. There is no representation of the poor on this board and no recognition that such representation might be appropriate.

However, Head Start's 70.2 requires that a parent-dominated Policy Council oversee the Head Start program. Again, this body is the site of parent power over the program, the site of explicitly empowering parent involvement, the site where parents have *power*. However, the dual chain of responsibility and authority—the CAP and Policy Council—presents problems for the exercise of genuine parent power. The CAP sees its mission as ministering to the poor, not empowering them, and the other programs it administers have no requirement for participation by service recipients. Thus, the tendencies in Head Start programming for reforming presumedly deficient mothers are emphasized by this CAP's philosophies. The empowering potential of Head Start involvement clearly becomes deemphasized under these circumstances.

Mothers in the North Country, though, were very interested in exercising genunine power over the program as promised them by 70.2, as we will show. These mothers clearly recognized condesencion and "reforming" when it was directed against them. Their consequent fight against the CAP at first served to empower the women on the Policy Council—conflict can be invigorating, after all. However, after losing battle after battle, the women were eventually and quite deliberately drained of energy and resolve. It is this disempowering process we find so frightening for Head Start's future.

In the next section of this chapter, we will discuss the way mothers of North Country Head Start children used reforming programs to make their lives easier, perhaps to empower themselves. Then we will highlight the women's more explicit fight for power over the program.

We originally became interested in North Country Head Start by listening to stories of women who had used their Head Start experience as a launching pad for "success." We heard stories of women returning to school, getting professional training, and becoming economically stable for the first time in their lives. These were remarkable stories of women learning their own strengths and using them to achieve in a world stacked against their success.

When we began looking deeper into the programs offered, though, it was clear that most of the changes made by mothers are not dramatic or related to conventional success. Instead, mothers were learning to make "small" changes in their lives, changes that gave them a bit more control over everyday life than they had had before. We were constantly reminded by staff and by mothers that these changes were critically important to their "complicated" lives:

Louise: Well, we all lead complicated lives. I realize that. But sometimes their basic needs are not being met, and they just are struggling to meet those very basic needs. Can we pay the bills? Will the electricity go off? Will there be someone home when they get home? Will there be a fight? Will there be money? Will there be food? Will the food stamps run out? All these kinds of things.

Sometimes we have to ask questions [of the parents]. I know one of my family workers said she felt awful. She would have to ask someone, what are your goals for the next three years? You know, and that's a very logical question, but she knows that this poor woman is trying to get through the next three days. She said they would look at me and say, three years, my heavens, you know. So, that's what I really mean with complicated lives.

These "small" things were the issues most commonly described by parents.

Parenting

A recurring theme in the women's stories is that Head Start helped them learn to parent. However, this learning did not typically occur in didactic sessions, with the family worker or teacher instructing the parent in how to discipline or raise children. Instead, parents assisting in the classroom observed the way the teacher handled the group of small children, and how she meted out discipline. Mothers routinely report, for example, that relationships with children have become warmer and richer simply because they (the mothers) have been in the Head Start classroom.

Lisa: I think as parents, we don't mean sometimes to suppress them or keep them down, but it's like, oh, let me do that, you know, or let me pour that. We can come to Head Start and see how good [the kids] do and when, you know, it makes us think, you know, they can do it.

Genine: I don't know of any child that wouldn't want their mom or dad or somebody there. I walk in down there and [my daughter] is like, "Mommy!" You know, I'm there if they fall, to kiss their boo-boo or give them a hug. I don't care what child it is.

Amy: Because I was a single parent. . . . It was being more like, I don't know, friends. I hated being the bad guy because Dad was the one with the presents, and he always got to be the good guy, and so I didn't want—you can't look at it that way. I'm more like friends with them now.

Janna: And I've learned, you know, better ways to discipline [my daughter] so I don't distance her.

Hannah: That's another thing Head Start does too. They try and make you understand that you are a role model for your children, so that you need to feel good about yourself in order for your children to. If I feel so bad about myself, how can my children feel good about me if all they hear me talk about is how bad I am?

The discipline modeled by Head Start staff never includes corporal punishment, but might include techniques such as "time-out."

Lisa: And parenting has changed. You know my parents—if my kids do something, you know, all he needs is a good spanking. And now, we don't do that, you know. There's alternatives. I think a spanking is appropriate in certain instances, like if they're doing something dangerous or they're endangering somebody else or— not a real spanking, spanking but, they just, you know.

Margaret: And there was one time I told them, I just want to beat that kid until he can't move. They told me it was the wrong thing to do. Well, I knew beating a kid was wrong. And being hit quite a few times when I was a kid, I swore I'd never hurt my kids. And this is what I was trying to prevent. So, anyways, they helped me through that. Which I'm very thankful for.

Genine: And they told us about time out. So now when the girls get out of control, we just tell them, "Time out!" And they go to their room for a few minutes. It works! It's not like when we were kids. We don't spank them anymore.

Being a mother is a large part of the lives of our respondents, as it is for most mothers in the world. Poor women, especially those receiving public assistance, are often and widely vilified for their parenting skills, or lack thereof. In Head Start, mothers may learn very useful techniques for child rearing, and they may simply develop some confidence in themselves. In any case, what they learn is often a considerable boost to their lives.

Amy: Because at first I was—I mean I'm only twenty-seven, so this all started and I was like, my husband and I separated when I was 22, and I hadn't had my third baby yet when we separated. So it was like all down on me at the same time. So it gives you, you know, "I can do this." If you didn't have—like you aren't born knowing all the answers. You know, they say that a mother has an instinct. Well, I didn't have all the answers. And there's other ways to do it. I mean everyone—you take your own, you put your own touches to it, but they give you other ways to do it.

There is some evidence that noncorporal discipline is more characteristic of the middle class than of the working class (Powell 1982; Oyemade 1985). Certainly, though, corporal punishment is more likely to be seen to be inappropriate when used by poor parents. Parents under the control of Social Services are subject to regular home visits and quick reporting to the state's Child Protective Services (CPS). Parents with more resources are less prone to being scrutinized and "hotlined" for administering coporal punishment.

It is tempting to dismiss these concerns as examples of class-based cultural imperialism or of the general practice of demeaning and devaluing poor women and their customs by social service professionals (Mink 1990; Joffe 1977; Gordon 1990). And yet the stories here are changes that women are proud of having made in their lives, changes they say have made it possible for them to live more easily day-to-day. In the most extreme cases, learning "appropriate" discipline techniques

allows mothers to keep their children instead of having them removed
by social service professionals who see corporal punishment as abuse.
This *is* an empowerment, then, giving mothers a way to keep their
families together. That's what they tell us, and we ought to believe
them.

Self-Respect

Despite the also-clear message of condescension and patronization
in the various lessons taught by Head Start providers, mothers routinely accepted their parenting training. Key in this process is *respect* from the frontline staff. The mothers were clear that, otherwise,
the various programs and training would not be as positively received. They were also clear that Head Start staff treated them very
differently than did other social service providers, including public
school teachers.

Lois: They didn't make you feel like you just came in for the day. They
    really made you feel like one of the people, you know. . . . It's
    more like you're [just] a parent [in the public schools]. You stand
    over there, and you don't participate. I don't know the word to
    use. They scare me a little bit or whatever, but down at Head
    Start, you can mix right in and ask them anything you want, talk
    to them, tell them if you don't like something. [L.J.A.: And they'll
    listen?] Oh yeah. They listen. All of them do.
Dorothy: It's like a big family. That's what it makes you feel like. Like
    the teacher she says, and like [the family worker] told me, if you
    ever have a problem or something, you don't have to keep it to
    yourself. Tell somebody.
Jodi: As a matter of fact, they're very helpful. I was collecting unem-
    ployment. I lost my unemployment, and one of the teachers had
    called me to set up a parent meeting and I had told her. She like
    talked to me for like an hour about all my options and what I
    could do and what to try, so they're very helpful. I think because
    they're like us. They're not very highly paid themselves, I don't
    think.
Hannah: And I guess that's probably the biggest thing about Head
    Start is that teachers rely on parents, as well as the parents to
    teachers. And the family worker, the same way. The family worker
    relies on parents just as much as they do the family workers. . . .

They make you feel like, you know, that you're a part of them. That means you don't have to be afraid to ask questions, and that everybody's a person, and you are a person, so don't feel afraid to ask questions, or whatever.

Clara: [A Head Start staffer] was down to earth with us. I mean, she said things that we understood. She didn't say these long words that nobody understood what they were. She always talked with us in a common language that everybody knew.

Allison: Because they make you feel like more of a family probably. They involve the parent, they involve you, you know. That's all I can think of. They offered, do you need help? You know, I was going through a really bad relationship with a boyfriend, and [the teacher] was really supportive, you know. Come on in with [my son], you know, and we'll, you know, and I don't know. She just made you feel comfortable. I enjoyed going there. I enjoyed being around.

Over and over again in our conversations with mothers, the issue of self-esteem came up. Mothers felt that Head Start had given them the opportunity to develop self-respect.

Janna: It's got me motivated, which is a very hard thing to do. My self-esteem is a lot higher. Well with going on those trips [to state-wide parent conferences]. And then we had that parent recognition day. I almost started crying.

Jodi: People that are on PC, it builds up their self-esteem, I think. I had a really low one, and now I think I can do more than I thought I could before. I don't want to give up things as easy. I'm like a vacuum lately, sucking up information everywhere. I'm actually thinking about going to college.

Hannah: And everybody was so supportive that it wasn't a hard thing to do. Everybody made it very easy, you know. Oh, you can do it. And there's gonna be people here to help you and back you up. And everybody- it seems like everybody who is associated with Head Start seems to give you that uplifting feeling. Do you know what I mean?

I wouldn't be in college right now if I hadn't went through the Head Start program. I don't think, anyway. If I hadn't gone through the Head Start program, I think I still would have been intimidated by people.

Evelyn: Well, [they helped] me gain self-esteem and courage and confidence. I was able to go back to school, which certainly helped my family financially. It also helped my family in that I was able to say, number one, I had learned that it was not good to keep shifting these kids around from place to place every six months. And number two, I had gotten the courage and self-confidence to be able to say [to my husband], I am not changing school systems with these kids again. If you want to move again then go ahead, but we are staying here.

The frontline staff of the various Head Start centers simply expected mothers to be able to do things. That expectation was transmitted; the mothers did what they were expected to be able to do and began to see themselves as competent. For many of the women, this was the first time in their lives such a view had been possible.

Developing this new sense of self-confidence is a key factor in women's empowerment. Though most of the mothers in North Country Head Start never went on to challenge power structures or to change their poverty, many had come to see themselves as worthwhile people. That is empowerment.

EMPOWERMENT AND DISEMPOWERMENT

Though the "small" empowerment potentials of Head Start's reform-oriented programs are not to be dismissed, there are more significant possibilities for empowerment. Women come to North Country Head Start's Policy Council shy, timid, unused to having control over so significant a program. They learn, sometimes very quickly, how to wield that control in what they see as the best interests of their children. Yet, the deficit assumptions of Head Start and its administrators very much get in the way of the women using their new power.

Though we observed women growing stronger and developing some political consciousness during their time on the PC, in the end, we observed mostly resignation and defeat. While spouting platitudes about parent involvement and empowerment, Head Start administrators nevertheless set about methodically wresting control from parents and consolidating their own power. This behavior was much more similar to "ordinary" social service agencies and very much unlike Head Start's rhetoric and unlike the respect demonstrated by frontline staff.

First we will examine the powers of the Policy Council in more detail. Then we will tell two stories illustrative of the empowerment/ disempowerment process we watched.

The Policy Council

North Country Head Start's Policy Council is composed of parents of children currently enrolled in Head Start, two elected from each of ten classroom centers scattered around the county. There are also eight community representatives drawn from various other social service agencies in the area, from schools and colleges, from local businesses, and sometimes from among parents of formerly enrolled children. The PC elects officers (chair, vice-chair, secretary, treasurer) and sorts its members into committees (personnel, budget, by-laws, etc.). Policy work typically is done in committee, and the committees bring issues and recommendations back to the whole PC for action.

The full PC meets once a month. Meetings are conducted by officers according to Robert's Rules of Order. Staff members routinely attend the meetings, and the Head Start director is usually an active participant, providing information and making suggestions.

New PC members are elected by their centers in October, at the beginning of the school year, and given training in their new roles. A new group of parents is on the PC every year, then, though community representatives serve for three-year terms. For each meeting, the centers' social workers (called "family workers") are responsible for providing transportation—sometimes over an hour each way in good weather, much more in bad—and the program reimburses baby-sitting costs for parents. In other words, Head Start does much to encourage and facilitate parent participation in this policy-making body.

Head Start's 70.2 requires that the PC approve and/or be consulted for a variety of program decisions. It is to approve (but not initiate) all hiring and firing (including of the Head Start director), to approve the program's budget and participate in its generation, to monitor and approve substantive programming, and to approve many lesser decisions necessary to running the program.

In theory, the PC could use its authority to design a Head Start program uniquely suited to the specific community and its self-identified needs. In the early days of the War on Poverty, that is what the Child Development Group of Mississippi did before 70.2 existed (Greenberg 1990 [1969]; Kuntz this volume). This scenario would fulfill the more radical notion of empowering parents to teach their kids what the parents thought they needed to know.

However, it is also possible that this policy-making body might exercise little actual power, serving primarily to validate decisions made by professional staff. In the case of such a "rubber stamp" PC, the experience also could be seen to serve the more conservative intent of participation, training parents "how to behave as adults in the world." This latter was the characterization actually given by a trainer funded by Health and Human Services, giving a workshop to the CAP agency Board of Directors on the functioning of the PC. This training occurred in the middle of our field research, after considerable power struggles.

When we began our study, either kind of PC was possible for North Country Head Start.

Using Power, Taking Charge

When mothers are elected to the Policy Council, they are most often unsure of how to use their power. However, they are also often quick to see when their interests are being given short shrift. They are sometimes very quick to use their new power see to their own concerns.

For example, at the very first meeting of a new PC, mothers were asked to vote on a change in Head Start personnel policies. Parents were given next to no information about the old policies or even the changes. They were told that the previous year's Personnel Committee had approved the policies, though there had been no time to bring the issue before the full PC until now.

The policies themselves were, in fact, quite controversial. The CAP executive director had insisted upon making Head Start's policies the same as the other programs the CAP administered. However, Head Start staff did not like the new policies, arguing that they did not fit well with Head Start philosophy. Moreover, there was no need, except in the executive director's mind, to have uniform policies across quite different programs.

In the meeting, the executive director (who was attending as a guest) tried to convince the mothers that there was little choice in the matter for them.

ED: You don't understand. These are already in place. The [CAP] board has approved them.

The parents on the PC did not bow under to that imperative. Though new to policy-making roles, these mothers were not about to pass the new policies without very careful scrutiny. They demanded that scrutiny.

Genine: I don't think we should be asked to vote on it before we had a chance to read it.
Abbey: I'm not gonna approve it if I can't see it.

But they wanted more than just to read the policies; they wanted to hash out the implications among themselves.

Genine: I just want to clarify something. The committee that approved these was the old committee right? And they were recommending to the old group, right? Well we have a new group and a new personnel committee now. Shouldn't we get a recommendation first from that committee? Isn't that how it should work?

If the Policy Council was to be a genuine policy-making body, not just a rubber stamp and training ground, that is indeed how it should work. That's what parents then insisted upon.

Genine: I motion that we send this back to have the Personnel Committee give us recommendations.
Iris: I second.

The motion passed, and parents were able to review the new policies both in committee and in informal conversations among themselves and with frontline staff. After that review, they strongly objected to one particular clause, which allowed staffers to use sick time for family emergencies (such as a child's illness), but limited the number of available sick days usable in that way.

Obviously, this is an important issue for all parents, to be able to take care of their children in emergency situations without losing pay. Head Start parents wanted their staff members to be able to do that. They insisted upon it. In negotiations with the board's Personnel Committee, moreover, they later achieved it.

Mothers involved in making this difference felt that it was an important use of their authority.

Janna: And those personnel policies! Remember how we fought about that! We won, too. Remember that?

The mothers used power. They saw an avenue to make some changes they found useful, and they learned thereby to create other avenues for using power. This is empowerment.

Resistance and Withdrawal

Of course, not all the women's attempts to use power were successful. Sometimes roadblocks or setbacks can serve to energize women to seek new ways to exercise their power (Costello 1987). However, when those ways are also blocked or the new actions still have no impact in the end, women may well become more apathetic and powerless than they had been to begin with (Acklesberg 1988).

When we began our study, changes had begun to occur at the level of the CAP, changes that we will argue are the result of national initiatives. The changes included the new personnel policies (which were less generous than the old) and a new, more authoritarian attitude from administration toward staff. This attitude and its consequences caused several conflicts with the PC—whose attitude toward staff had not changed.

A long-time, much-loved staffer, Lila, had requested from the PC an unpaid leave to go see her children. Lila herself had been a Head Start parent back when the program was new. She had used her newfound, Head Start–inspired self-confidence to return to school. She had eventually assumed a professional-level staff position with North Country Head Start. During her long career, she had inspired many other parents to similar achievements.

PC gladly approved her leave. However, *later* the Head Start director denied Lila the time to go, directly and secretly contradicting the PC's decision. PC parents were incensed. Only because Lila requested it did they let the insult pass.

Lila later took an extended leave of absence. PC parents were convinced that Lila had been driven away by the adminstration. Lila had always been an advocate for parents and for Head Start's adherence to the letter and spirit of 70.2. She had long worked diligently for parents' genuine empowerment. For this reason, the theory went, administration had to get rid of her; she was a threat to their power. The story continued that administration had made working so uncomfortable for Lila that she was unable to report for work.

There was a similar saga about another long-time, parent-oriented staffer, Nancy. The PC had approved a raise for this dedicated teacher. However, unbeknownst to the PC, the raise had never been granted. After a year or more without her raise and under considerable pressure from administration, Nancy resigned. Her resignation was the first the PC had heard about her nonraise, and the members were angry. They refused to accept the resignation—though Nancy had already stopped working. They were intent on holding administration responsible for what they saw as an affront to PC power and to Nancy's dedication.

However, that very afternoon administration advertised to fill Nancy's position. The ceremonial, nonsubstantive quality of PC "approval" was thereby made very clear. PC had not approved the resignation (much less the hiring of a replacement), yet administration was going merrily about the business of finding a new teacher anyway. A parent on the PC said,

Hannah: What difference does it make what we do? They just do what they want anyway! Why should we bother? I'm just so frustrated.

Over the year this group was on the PC, we indeed observed the administration exercising and demanding more and more control. PC members—parents and community representatives—clearly felt deluded by administration.

Janna: (PC mother) They only tell us what they want us to know.
Jody: (PC mother) We aren't told a lot of things. They don't want us to know about a lot.
Margot: (PC community representative) It may be because I'm new, but I always get the feeling there's a hidden agenda, that I'm not being told everything.
Geri: (PC community representative) There's a lot of things I should hear about, but I don't. I hear them from the staff, not at Policy Council. That's not right.

The parents involved in Head Start are, by definition, economically disadvantaged. They are used to losing battles with employers, banks, social services, schools, and so on (Calabrese 1990; McAtee nd). At the time they begin Head Start involvement, they typically report their self-confidence to be low (Parker, Piotrkowski, and Peay 1987; Reiner, List, and LaFrenier 1983). Their confidence in themselves as capable administrators is virtually nonexistent. When their efforts to exercise their statutory control over the program are met with paternalism, with disrespect, with disdain, it seems to mothers to be just business as usual (Fruchter 1984; Rosier and Corsaro 1993).

Jody: (PC mother) I don't think we make any real difference. They don't really listen to us. They don't have to. They want to look good. But they don't care about helping low-income people get back on their feet.

Under such circumstances, women often withdraw from the illusory power and return to their immediate, validated interests in their children's well-being.

Carol: (PC mother) It's here [at the center with the kids] that I want to be. Here's where I matter.
Janna: (PC mother) I love being with the kids. PC makes me crazy.

Administration, by simply ignoring the decisions the PC made, got its way. Nancy resigned without her raise; Lila never returned from her leave. The program lost two strong advocates for parents' power. Mothers active in the two battles went on with their lives at the end of their PC year. They had, during that year, been energized to seek and use power for the good of the program. In the end, they left the experience largely dispirited and disheartened. The experience had been successfully empowering, for a time, but was ultimately dangerously disempowering.

Hannah: I know I told you that Head Start gave me self-esteem. But now I can't justify that, with what you've seen. I mean. It's so different now. They *try* to make me feel stupid. I feel so bad for all the new parents. And the kids.

STAFF RESISTANCE AND EMPOWERMENT

During this year of parent empowerment and subsequent disempowerment, the staff also experienced considerable pressure from the administration. This is clear from the tales of Lila and Nancy above. Generally, the staff felt that the way the current administration was moving was dangerous for the vitality of North Country Head Start.

In the "good old days," there was, they remembered, great energy and creative flexibility.

Louise: So we had such freedom. If we couldn't go on a field trip that was planned because of the weather or something, I could call [the previous Head Start director] the following week and say, "It's a lovely day today. Can we go to the park or something?" And he would say, "Yes." So there was a different kind of freedom.

That flexibility had stopped.

Carla: Everybody bent all the way around [before]. But all of a sudden, it was like really important to be at a certain place at a certain time. And the rules were having to be followed.

This was problematic insofar as it negatively affected the program. Staff felt they were unable to offer the quality services they were used to offering.

Doris: And Head Start staff people are not like that. We're people people. We don't work in a business world. . . . [Head Start's] been part of the North Country for all these years and we're not used to dealing with people like this. . . . We are not used to dealing with people that come from a business background or a business world who want to save money, get money. You know, you don't get money from a program that's federally funded for children.

I was afraid that [the CAP executive director] was going to take away what everybody had fought for for years. Take away the staff and the program. . . . And I'll be dipped to see him destroy it, and in my eyes, he is slowing destroying this program.

The staff unionized. They wanted more money and more job security, to be sure, and these are standard reasons for unionizing. But the staff also feared for the program, feared that the administration was destroying the ability of the program to truly help families. They hoped that the power of a union contract could stall the transfer of power from frontline staff and parents to the administration.

In practice, the power of the union *did* prevent certain staffers from being fired. Still, many dedicated, long-time staffers have left "voluntarily" because they feel they can no longer do their job the way they want to. And, the union contract has put further constraints on the flexibility the staff thinks the program needs.

The staff members, like the parents, were energized to fight for their rights and their program. But, like the parents, staffers ultimately became disillusioned and some quit the fight.

RECENT DEVELOPMENTS

In the time since we officially left the field, since our book was written, North Country Head Start's administration has taken complete control over real decisions, and the PC functions now *only* as a training ground. The PC that followed the one we describe in this chapter was completely uninterested in the issues that has so moved their predecessors. Meetings were, we are told, efficient but devoid of real substance. Reports of staff and adminstration were taken at face value and never challenged or questioned.

We had promised, at the beginning of our study, to tell the PC members what would be in the book we wrote. We had always kept in touch with the mothers we had come to know during the research, and many of them had read drafts of the book. We wanted, though, to share officially the results with the PC as we had promised.

However, when we contacted the current PC, the chair instructed us to make our presentation to the CAP board first. She said that if the board approved of it, then we could come to the PC. This deference was a huge change from the earlier PC's defiance. (We prepared a bland discussion of national trends for the board couched in highly obfuscatory language. While we would have told the PC parents the naked truth, we were not interested at that time in a public fight with the board, who had never wanted the study done. They were, though, quite satisfied, and the PC remained quite uninterested in hearing any of it.)

Further, more and more of the long-time staff have left the program. There are no longer advocates for parents' legitimate power on staff working to achieve it. Rather, the PC's rights and responsibilities are being explained to mothers by the very people who have carefully undermined those rights. A PC community representative who had been very critical of administration in our years in the field told us that she could not wait for her term to end. Watching the erosion of PC power had become very painful for her.

NATIONAL TRENDS: EMPOWERMENT VERSUS
MANAGERIAL ACCOUNTABILITY

It is tempting to dismiss these events as the result of poor administration of a wonderful program, as an anomaly. However, the increasing control demanded by the administration of North Country Head Start was not due solely to the specific personalities of the administrators. Nor are the events we detailed above random or isolated, as other chapters in this volume attest. These are specific effects of changes in the national discourse about "welfare" and in national politics of social service delivery.

Increasingly, social service agencies are bureaucratizing and instituting centralized policies and methods of cost control (Sosin 1986). According to the National Association for Community Action Agencies, a "large-scale effort to strengthen the role and management systems" of CAPs (1989, 5) was begun in the late 1970s. A U.S. Health and Human Services' report, "Creating a 21st Century Head Start" emphasizes strengthening "management practices at the local level." A major recommendation of this report was "increasing the emphasis placed on the *business practices* of the Head Start program, including the development of performance standards in the area of fiscal management," and "requiring minimal competencies for staff involved in financial and management related jobs" (30, emphasis added). Much farther down the list was "reinforcing the role of parents in the decision making process." There are now federal legislative initiatives to create better accountability and management (Takanishi and DeLeon 1994).

Much of this trend is in response to charges that "welfare" is administered by bloated bureaucracies that need to be drastically trimmed down. Further, in an era marked by punitive social service policies, administrators are eager to keep close tabs on money and personnel, either because they embrace those policies or because they hope to avoid negative and harmful scrutiny.

North Country CAP took these national-level trends and directives to heart, hiring an executive director with a background more business than social service. His mandate, which he *did* execute, was to bring more control, more discipline to the administration of Head Start. He was a professional manager with an emphasis on fiscal accountability, whose first allegiance is to organizational efficiency, even if at the expense of best practice in service delivery.

However, this businesslike behavior had the results described above: eventual frustration and withdrawal by parents from the potentially empowering mechanisms of Head Start. Parents exercising control democratically can be very messy and unpredictable. Parents refused to rubber-stamp new personnel policies; they refused to countenance some personnel decisions administration had made. Unpredictable policies and decisions are not compatible with tight fiscal discipline and hierarchical control. To enhance the latter, it is important that administration exercise the real power and the PC have only ceremonial power. In such a case, parents cannot be empowered, only frustrated.

Our discussion of administration's behavior should not be taken as signs of evil intent toward low-income parents or children. This is, unfortunately, not a story of one bad man or one county program gone awry. Administration was rather taking the conservative view of participation, a view that suggested parents needed to be trained by knowledgeable professionals, a view that rejects parents as able decision makers. This conservative view is consistent with a management philosophy stressing hierarchical accountability and efficiency, which are qualities increasingly emphasized at the national as well as the local level of social services. Within that view, administration *was* attempting to provide the training it deemed appropriate, but was not empowering mothers to train themselves or take charge.

Even under this conservative philosophy, Head Start may make a significant contribution to the lives of poor, rural women in the North Country. For most of the women the program touches, changes are not dramatic. Women do report that they have become better parents— results still possible with the conservative view of "participation" and a respectful staff. All these nondramatic changes make living easier for mothers, allowing them to find an easier path in their difficult lives.

More dramatically, though, sometimes women who have exercised real power have made changes in *structures*, rather than in themselves only. To be sure, these are limited changes to narrow, rather than broad-based, structures, to a single Head Start program, rather than to the abstract structure, *poverty*. Yet the changes are to those structures directly perceived and experienced by the women.

However, when mothers believe they have real power—or ought to have it—but then are impeded by administration in their attempts to use it, the result is training neither for self-improvement nor for empowerment, but rather for frustration and withdrawal. Because the performance standards for Head Start require parents to exercise authority over the program and parents know this—they have only to read 70.2—administration's failure to honor their *genuine* authority does harm, we conclude, that more limited "participation" cannot rectify. This is true not only for the mothers on the PC, whose powei is thwarted, but also for women who observe the process from the sidelines and for mothers now on staff. To all of them, it is just another display that they are incapable of power, that others remain in charge of their lives.

Note, then, that recent calls by conservative politicians for "personal responsibility" among those served by "welfare" can be answered by programs that give recipients genuine power over programs and, by extension, their lives. However, programs that continue to treat low-income people as incapable or unworthy of so taking charge will have the effect of creating further indifference among them. Empowerment, taking personal responsibility, requires overcoming that view of oneself and one's world engendered by oppressive forces (Collins 1991). Programs that only reinforce such a view cannot be empowering.

But, of course, empowerment is problematic precisely for that reason. People do begin to make changes to their lives and to the structures governing their lives. This can lead to direct challenges to existing power structures. Head Start *deliberately* brings poor parents together in the Policy Council and teaches them about power and using power in their own interests. Though those teaching seem to have lost their own fire for parent empowerment, here and in other localities, under the right circumstances, such groups could become the foundation of a grassroots movement for far-reaching social change. The right circumstances do not include autocratic, demeaning managers.

This is the potential for emancipating empowerment being lost as Head Start administration becomes more interested in hierarchical accountability, the potential for empowerment to extend to taking systemic, collective action.

REFERENCES

Ackelsberg, M. A. (1988). Communities, resistance, and women's activism: Some implications for a democratic polity. In Bookman, A. and Morgen, S. (Eds.), *Women and the politics of empowerment*. Philadelphia: Temple University Press.

Bunch, C. (1981 [1974]). The reform tool kit. In *Building feminist theory: Essays from quest*. New York: Longman.

Calabrese, R. L. (1990). The public school: A source of alienation for minority parents. *Journal of Negro Education* Vol. 59:148–154.

Collins, P. H. (1991). *Black feminist thought*. New York: Routledge.

Costello, C. (1987). Working women's consciousness: Traditional or oppositional?" In Groneman C., and Norton, M. B. (Eds.), *"To toil the livelong day": America's women at work*. Ithaca: Cornell University Press.

Fitchen, J. M. (1991). *Endangered spaces, enduring places: Change, identity, and survival in rural America*. Boulder, CO: Westview Press.

Fitchen, J. M. (1992). Rural poverty in the northeast: The case of upstate New York. In Duncan, C. (Ed.), *Rural poverty in America*. New York: Auburn House.

Fruchter, N. (1984). The role of parent participation. *Social Policy* (Fall), 32–36

Gordon, L. (1990). The new feminist scholarship on the welfare state. In Gordon, L. (Ed.), *Women, the state, and welfare*. Madison: The University of Wisconsin Press.

Greenberg, P. (1990 [1969]). *The devil has slippery shoes: A biased biography of the child development group of Mississippi (CDGM) a story of maximum feasible poor parent participation*. New York: MacMillan/Washington, D.C., Youth Policy Institute.

Joffe, C. E. (1977). *Friendly intruders: childcare professionals and family life*. Berkeley: University of California Press.

McAtee, A. (nd). *Family development: Empowering families to move out of poverty*. Washington, D.C.: National Association of Community Action Agencies.

Mink, G. (1990). The lady and the tramp: Gender, race, and the origins of the American welfare state. In Gordon, L. (Ed.), *Women, the state, and welfare*. Madison: The University of Wisconsin Press.

National Association for Community Action Agencies. (nd). *Media kit*.

Oyemade, U. J.. (1985). The rationale for Head Start as a vehicle for the upward mobility of minority families: A minority perspective. *American Journal of Orthopsychiatry*, Vol. 55, No. 4, 591–602.

Parker, F. L., Piotrkowski, C. S., and Peay, L. (1987). Head Start as a social support for mothers: The psychological benefits. *American Journal of Orthopsychiatry*, Vol. 57, 220–233.

Powell, D. R. (1982). From child to parent: Changing conceptions of early childhood intervention. *Annals AAPSS* Vol. 461, 135–144.

Reiner, M. B., List, J. A., and LaFrenier, P. (1983). An Evaluation of a Parent Education Program. *Studies in Educational Evaluation,* Vol. 9, 303–318.

Rosier, K. B., and Corsaro, W. A. (1993). Competent parents, complex lives: Managing parenthood in poverty. *Journal of Contemporary Ethnography,* Vol. 22, 171–204.

Sosin, M. (1986). Legal rights and welfare change. In Danziger, S., and Weinberg, D., (Eds.), *Fighting poverty: What works and what doesn't.* Cambridge, MA: Harvard University Press.

Takanishi, R., and DeLeon, P. H. (1994). A Head Start for the 21st century. *American Psychologist,* Vol. 49, 120–122.

U.S. Department of Health and Human Services. (1993). *Creating a 21st century Head Start: Final report of the advisory committee on Head Start quality and expansion.* Washington, D.C.: HHS.

Valentine, J., and Stark, E. (1979). The social context of parent involvement in Head Start. In Zigler, E., and Valentine, J. (Eds.), *Project Head Start: A legacy of the War on Poverty.* New York: The Free Press.

9

More Than a Job: Reflections of a Former Head Start Staff Member

Susan W. Geddes

The year was 1976—the bicentennial of the birth of our country, the year my second daughter was born, and the year my older daughter attended Head Start. What did Head Start mean to me then? It meant my child would meet children her own age to play with. It meant she would be more prepared for the demands of kindergarten the following year. As a young, tired mom, it meant catching up on some desperately needed sleep when the baby finally slept during the later morning hours. It meant a few quiet minutes to sort my frenzied thoughts, weigh my concerns about a failing marriage, and make some important decisions about our lives.

Is that what Head Start is supposed to mean? Yes, for some parents. But it could have been more. If my value system had not been permeated with a necessity for independence and a sense that I could rely only on self and family, if my way of thinking had not been clouded by shame, guilt, and fear about sharing personal concerns with an "outsider"—if, if, if—then Head Start could have been much more.

The year was 1991. Fifteen years had passed. Maturity had made me understand that "no woman is an island." Over the space of time, through desperation, I had learned that it is sometimes necessary to seek help from others. I had learned that there are vast resources available to help us survive the ills of the era. I had learned that healthy character does not mean being so full of pride that you never seek advice or assistance from the experienced. I knew there were

242

others out there in this isolated area still holding tightly to their personal values, suffering alone. I wanted to let them know they were not alone. I wanted to share with these sisters and brothers that it is okay to hold a helping hand as long as you do not forget to help carry your own weight. The door opened. A vacancy for a family worker at Head Start needed to be filled. I applied for the position and was hired. The training I received reassured me that there is a chance for the poor to move ahead. The feelings I experienced, the knowledge I gained through the period that followed reaffirmed a conviction that Head Start fills a gap in society not found elsewhere.

Muddling through reams of rules and regulations verified that Head Start is based on the need to build upon both the child's and the family's strengths, while overcoming or compensating for needs and weaknesses, to reach that family's desired goals. There lies a key—that family's desired goals, not the program's goals, not the government's goals, not the staff member's goals, but the family's goals.

Praise needs to be shared here for the foresight of those creating the original Head Start plan, and the inclusion in 1970 of the parents in the decision-making processes. The founders' awareness that parents basically want good things for their children and families relied on this belief in reaching family goals and thereby insuring that the goals of the program also could be reached.

So, what is Head Start supposed to be? It is supposed to be a warm, safe, educational and motivational environment for children and their families. It is supposed to be a method for expanding the horizons and knowledge of all members of the family so that children will learn not only during their time in the program, but also, through their families, during their whole lives. Head Start is supposed to be a place to cry, a place to heal, a place to learn how to move forward by using experience as a foundation and a stepping stone to success.

Is Head Start all these things? I cannot speak for all areas, but only from my limited experience in the remote northeast corner of New York. Yes, it is some of these things; no, it is not all of these things. There are wonderful, beautiful happenings at the centers in this rural area. Dedicated staff members create warm environments at the Head Start centers for children, their siblings, and their parents to feel welcome. Teamwork among the staff, volunteer parents, and community members makes possible events such as field trips, community speakers, sharing of knowledge about various resources, parent meetings to plan events for both children and parents, craft workshops, nutrition workshops, clothing swaps, job training, job and counseling referrals—the list goes on and on.

In many ways Head Start is successful, and yet there is an undercurrent not mentioned before. As history has played out, as society has changed, an air of business versus human services has pervaded this program, as it has so many other social service programs. Beneath the smiles of the Head Start teachers, teacher assistants, family workers, cooks, bus drivers, bus aides, and others whom the families meet daily lies the pain of a battle these workers must face every day. While such dedicated staff members share knowledge with Head Start parents about ways to become educated, skilled, and self-sufficient, these same workers earn a wage insufficient to meet their own needs. Many of these staff members must rely on social service programs themselves to make ends meet and provide subsistence for their own families.

Why do they stay? Many do not. Many workers become discouraged with their inability to move ahead, to provide for their families, and they move on to other jobs that can provide for their family needs. Some stay—those who have two wage earners and can afford to work at low wages, those who have not built the confidence to move on. Those who are so dedicated to the ideals upon which Head Start is based stay, ever hoping, ever fighting to improve the workers' status.

Over the past few years, in desperation, more and more of these hardworking individuals have banded together and turned to unions as a possible solution to their financial woes. Has it helped? In some locations, yes. But the service unions are new to our area. Management, enveloped in their bureaucratic positions, does not look kindly on this unwanted infringement on what they see as their domain of power. Poor contracts, harassment of workers, and an inability to air grievances have created a situation that is wearing down staff. The staff member can only remain motivated and cheerful so long under this pressure, and eventually the facade begins to crumble, affecting parents and children.

Policy Council, the main governing body of Head Start, which is made up of at least 50 percent parents, often has become embroiled in the staff-management differences. It does not take long for this type of negative situation to influence an entire program.

What is the solution? Communication, respect, understanding— many of the values Head Start staff impress upon the children—need to be implemented once again between frontline staff and management. Head Start is different from all other social programs in that parents are involved deeply in the decision-making process. This cannot be thrust aside, or we are no longer talking about Head Start. Management must be willing to share the power for Head Start to remain viable. And it is apparent in the document *Head Start in the 21st Century* that monies must be used to upgrade salaries and educate workers, goals must be set for promotion from within as well as for continuing to hire parents. Without these things, the basic concept of Head Start will be lost. Valuable staff will be elsewhere trying to earn a living wage, and society will suffer from the loss.

What does Head Start mean to me now, in 1996? It remains an impressive program battling to maintain its uniqueness for the good of all in an ever-changing society.

10

Personal Growth in Head Start

Wendy L. Kirby

I have chosen the following excerpts from letters, journals, reports, and class papers to comprise this chapter. I do not mean them to tell a complete story or to prove a particular point, but rather to give a sense of what my experiences with Head Start were and what they felt like at the time I was going through them. What you will see is that I have changed. In many ways, I have received an education. Although my knowledge has remained the same, the way I tell it has gotten more scholarly, as I hope will be apparent as the chapter progresses.

[From "Autobiography," covering times around 1990–91]

I was living in an unfinished basement. I had no running water, no toilet, cooked on a heating wood stove. I couldn't take it any more. I was trying to raise my children under these conditions, and things seemed hopeless.

Then I met Alan Kirby, my present husband. Alan is very supportive and accepted me with my children. My children love him, and he loves us dearly. Alan wanted me to join the Women's Auxiliary to the fire department he belongs to. I did. Things started looking up. Alan and I got married. We were all happy. Except for the finances.

I got dropped from assistance from welfare except food stamps and medicaid for the children. I did day care in my home for a while. Alan and I talked about one of us going to college. We needed to get an education to obtain a better job to support the family.

246

Then I got involved with the Head Start program. Head Start boosted my self-esteem so much. I became Policy Council chairperson. At the same time I was elected president of the fire department auxiliary. I became very active in the Head Start program and dropped the day care in my home. I started getting a very good education. Head Start offers a lot of education to their parents and tries to get them involved in the children's education. I became a very strong advocate for Head Start. I worked very hard for the program. I even traveled to Albany and Buffalo. It was worth every minute for that's how my self-esteem, along with my husband's support, got me to a point of wanting to go to college. One of my duties as Policy Council chairperson was to hold a seat on the Community Action Program (CAP) Board. What a fantastic learning experience! I found out [from my Head Start family worker that] I could get financial aid to go to college and became fascinated with going back to school. . . .

I started contacting people at the college. I wanted to make sure I could get financial aid. And now here I am. I have [two part-time jobs]. I have a wonderful and supportive family and many supportive friends. I am ready and waiting. I am at a teachable moment in my life and won't let it pass me by.

[From notes for a report to Policy Council (PC) on a conference, February 2–6, 1992]

I attended the National Head Start Association Winter Training Conference. It was a wonderful experience! I made new friends and shared many concerns of parents. The biggest concern of the parents' affiliate right now is the inadequacy of health care. The parents' affiliate is putting together a letter of concern to send to our senators and legislators. When I receive a copy of this I will need to collect signatures of supporting parents. I was told signatures are great, but it was made clear by one of the speakers that a registered voter carries much more power. I myself have to go get registered. When I do I will share information on how to go about it.

Another concern which needs our immediate attention is the School Readiness Act (S911). This is a call for action to mandate full funding for Head Start by 1997. We need this full funding, for example, to pay our teachers a competitive salary and to purchase or construct facilities, instead of renting. . . . Now the passage of this full funding bill will require a great deal of response from the Head Start community. That means us! There were letters given us on how to write and what to include in a letter of support to the bill. . . . I would like to write a letter of support for this bill for the Policy Council. I would also like to get a letter of support from each PC chairperson from each center and a letter of support from our director. These letters will make a difference. Remember what Head Start does for us. . . .

You as parents play an important role in Head Start. Parents must learn how to stand up for themselves and their children. No one affiliated with Head Start will criticize you for what you don't know. They will give you the guidance it takes to know. . . . When parents leave the Head Start program they should feel comfortable with the public school system and be able to express their feelings and thoughts in an effective manner.

[Notes from Report to Policy Council on a conference, May 10–13, 1992]

People, the trip I went on to Buffalo made me realize how important it is to work as a team. The parents sitting here today should be low-income people, right? I have talked to several people who say they *wish* things could be better. They *wish* certain things about welfare could change. Well, wishing about things will not make them change. You have to take *action*. If you sit back and let someone else take action for you they may not have the same ideas you have. You have to *educate yourself*. Look at the resources that are afforded in Head Start. The Looking at Life series showed us how to deal with our feelings about death. We had a class on first aid. We had a class on speech and hearing. We had a class on healing from sexual abuse. We have literacy volunteers who help people get GEDs or the help they need to get back to school. I asked for a class on how to vote. . . . You know how many people showed up? The speaker, the director of literacy volunteers, and myself! . . . People, wake up. Your voice counts, but only if you use it.

[Text of a speech for public speaking class, Spring 1994]

The Head Start program is one of the main reasons why I am in college today. The Head Start program brought about a confidence in me that had laid dormant for a long time. . . . Head Start reached me in a way that I would like to reach you to make you understand that *everyone* has a place in society. And children at a young age should be taught that. What I mean is we need to stop the detachments from society such as shunning Johnny Green because his family is poor [and thinking] "He probably won't amount to much anyway." Bull! [Whether] he will amount to something positive or negative to society depends on his surroundings. If we treat Johnny like he's nothing, he won't amount to anything. Head Start makes those surroundings a positive experience both socially and within the family. I would like to help the Head Start program as much as it has helped me. One way I hope to accomplish that is to get over this fear of talking to people, so that one day I will be able to stand before a crowd of people, particularly in Washington, and tell them a very emotional story about my life and how positively Head Start influenced it in hopes to insure that the program is supported so it may benefit others.

[Journal entry]
September 9, 1994

I had a very difficult day today with Head Start. We have been going through a process of job interviews. The person who I thought was best for the job, most qualified, and best for the transition the program is going through right now, was not the person who got the job. I had a hard time dealing with this because the agency is supposed to promote from within first and did not do this. They say that there is a better position in the future for this person, but there are no guarantees. I feel at this point that the director is being too particular. She is not giving people any chances! That's what this program is about. Take chances! What do you have to lose? The program suffers with no one to handle the position [and there's] someone who really wants to succeed in it.

[Journal entry]
October 5, 1994

I have come to an all-time low in my thoughts about Head Start. I am so tired of the agency using parents. They get parents' hopes up by enticing them with the thought that if they volunteer a lot, they may get a job with Head Start. (Even with the parents they know they won't hire.) I don't like how the Policy Council is manipulated. Example: they are supposed to be a part of management. They are only considered a part of management by management when management feels they have no choice but to comply with the performance standards. And when their signature and approval is needed for something, then they're only given half the information on the subject but expected to sign [and it's held over your head that if you don't sign] the program [will] suffer. You know the performance standards state quite clearly that parents are to be encouraged to volunteer but not used for staff shortages. This agency has always used parents for staff shortages, and now when it's getting harder for parents to be at the centers all day, the staff is feeling the pressure.

I hate seeing staff burdened with more and more responsibilities and not getting a raise; some work for minimum wage anyway. [The agency plays the staff and parents against each other. The parents were supposed to give added help to the classroom, not be the only help available.]

I don't understand my feelings about the tasks that the director assigns to me. (I feel like I am being used.) I never used to think that way. When I was given a task I felt proud that they would entrust me to do it. And when I was done I felt good about it. I can see how important it is to be positive about what you are doing. But also you have to feel positive about the people you are working for. My attitude has changed so much. I don't like it, but yet I can't change it. I guess it has a lot to do with the change in management style. When I first came to Head Start everyone built on the positive things about people, and it seemed sincere. They have become so false to me.

[Undated journal entry]

I often sit and wonder about things I've done in the past. I don't usually write about them though because I don't consider myself a good writer at all.

One thing I am sitting here thinking about tonight is that fact that I have returned to school. It was a scary feeling to return to school after being out for eleven years. I kept thinking, will I be able to keep up with work? Will I be even able to do college-level work? Well, I had it in my mind that some way somehow I would give it my best try. One thing I didn't think of was the family scheduling.

It has been hard trying to get homework done at home and maintaining the household at the same time. I have always been very attentive to my family, and now with school that has all changed. It's hard on me as well as the family. I don't like how the laundry and the dishes get so piled up because I am trying to do homework. I don't like how I feel when it seems that my two girls have spent more time at the baby-sitter's than with me. Yet I don't want to give up school. I know my family and I will be better off in the long run if I stay in school. I am so confused and don't know what to do sometimes.

[Journal entry]
October 6, 1994

This was an important meeting because this was the beginning of the investigation of matters of Policy Council being left out of [decision-making] processes, a turning point or should I say breaking point of how Policy Council wanted to be listened to and informed of things as they happened, as per 70.2, not after the fact.

Although parent participation and volunteering is to be encouraged, issue #47 from the Parent Involvement Institute in the Head Start bulletin states that you do not use parents exclusively as classroom volunteers or to alleviate staff shortages.

[Journal entry]
October 1994

During this time many questions were being presented to me about staff shortages. And management's solutions were to get parent volunteers.

Management was doing a lot of interviews at this time, but taking a considerable amount of time in making decisions on candidates.

October 20, 1994

I spoke to an administrator [about hiring bus aides], and she said we have to try and get parents to volunteer first. This brought to mind the fact that Policy Council had approved paid bus aides. Why not utilize some of these people in the centers that were having staffing problems?

[I asked again, and the administrator] replied that the union was holding up the paid bus aides. I told her I did not think this was true. I said I would find out what was going on. I asked another person about the matter who told me that the union would not agree to have paid bus aides. I sent a letter to the CAP director requesting to talk to him about the matter. He did not respond.

The union steward [came into the office], so I asked her about the paid bus aides. She said that the union rep was on her way in to the office. . . . She said there was no problem with this matter from the union.

Staff and parent morale was at low point. This effects children!!

It's hard not to dwell too much on the past, but you must ask yourself questions about all the resignations from positions in this agency. People do move on and better themselves, but even if it were for other reasons they surely would not state that in a resignation, especially if they still wanted to maintain a good relationship with the program. People also leave agencies because of change, but who in their right mind would want to leave an agency if this change was for the best? Maybe financially this program was changing for the best (for the CAP agency), but its philosophy was not. One of the reasons for Head Start's success was the strong philosophy of the program. Number one being its positive outlook on all people. The whole philosophy revolves around pointing out people's strengths not dwelling on their weaknesses. This was a changing thing at this time. People were also feeling that they were not being dealt with in a straightforward manner. [There were a flux of people leaving the agency at this time. Management was weeding its garden, pulling up gentle, beautiful flowers and leaving the weeds, thinking that it could ensure its own survival.]

There was talk of Head Start staff doing a peaceful demonstration. At this point I and a couple of other parents felt like management wasn't going to come through with any straightforward answers to anything, and with all the staff we were losing we figured we should at least stand behind these people. We didn't want to lose any more good people just because they wanted to be heard.

October 22, 1994

The demonstration was held. The wrong impression was made to the CAP Board because of it. Its intent was to indeed break the ice, get the board's attention, and get some problems solved. Not to insult the board members. The demonstration did not work as it was intended to. A lesson was learned. [The demonstrators were told, by program administrators that they should be ashamed of themselves for participating in the demonstration.] The lesson was not to be ashamed, but to be better prepared the next time. The people who demonstrated and the people who supported it are not ashamed and should not be ashamed! We were all taking a stand for something we believe in—Head Start!

October 25, 1994

This was the day of the CAP Board meeting. I was not prepared to go before the board and tell everyone's story of why they participated in the demonstration, but would have offered some information to clear up the misconceptions made to the board. The way I was treated on that day was disgraceful, and there were board members who were not happy with the way I was treated by the other board members.

Here I was, a parent of the Head Start program sitting among them, a person who three years ago wouldn't dare to speak up in front of people. I was a human being sitting there who deserved the same respect the board was demanding of me but definitely not all were showing to me.

October 31, 1994

Administrators terminated my internship with Head Start. For an agency that's supposed to move people up and out of poverty and build on family strengths and self-esteem, this action was a far cry from its goal. They stated that the internship was terminated because I did not subscribe to this management's philosophy. I didn't. I was a Head Start parent and believed in the Head Start philosophy.

[Presentation to CAP Board of Directors]
Page 1, Head Start Policy Council Introduction:

It may be hard for the Board of Directors to fully understand the scope of Head Start since there has been minimal training in this area and there are so many other programs under the umbrella agency. However, understanding the Head Start program is a requirement for funding to the CAP for the implementation of the Head Start program. "Parent involvement is the cornerstone of Head Start's past and future successes" (National Head Start Bulletin). It is one of the important tools used to empower families to achieve self-sufficiency. "The policy-making role of parents is the foundation of Head Start's unique success" (Report from the Parent Involvement Institute). Is it fair to say then that if the parents' role is not implemented as per federal law 70.2 by the CAP Agency, that it won't be the demise of the Head Start program, but the demise of the CAP's rights to funding for it? According to the Head Start Bureau, not only is 70.2 included in the performance standards but it carries the weight of the law (Public Law 90-22, December 23, 1967, Part B, Section 222, (I) (B)).

The Head Start Policy Council's goals are not to see the failure of any CAP agency. We know that they house the very programs that we utilize for our families. It would be like cutting off one's thumb. It is not impossible to function without it, but very useful to have it. So please do not misinterpret the actions of the Policy Council. Our goal is to maintain our rights and insure that parents, their children, and employees who directly affect our families are treated with the respect and dignity that they deserve.

As Head Start grows bigger and bigger there are a number of CAP agency directors that feel that the programs must be run as a business. This is fine if one keeps in mind that this is a HUMAN service agency and not a for-profit program. The reason for the emphasis is that people working in this program must be people who are willing to work and deal with what our society stigmatizes as lower class people; not to oversee them as in the roles of business, but to work with and nurture the people it serves; also not to try and save the agency money at the expense of the very people who founded this program or any others who have come on board since.

It is a goal of the Twenty-first Century Head Start to improve the quality of this program! In Head Start's very beginnings quality was a sacrifice to the cost of the Vietnam War, but Head Start withstood it and grew and grew. . . .

It is the knowledge of the parents who have previously served on [the] Policy Council and our community representatives that this agency is headed in the wrong direction for quality improvement internally. What is meant by that is: why would a woman who founded the beginnings of this program and has been with the program for twenty-eight years suddenly not meet the minimum qualifications for her job? Why would a successful teacher in the Head Start program for twenty-nine years not be capable of being the education coordinator? Why would a teacher and past Parent Involvement coordinator not qualify for the positions in this agency? Why wouldn't a past family worker, moved to an assistant teacher position and asking to be put back to family worker, not qualify for the position? Experience doesn't seem to count, but it's still a part of the job qualifications! Isn't it time to take a good look at the people who most directly affect the children being served and ask them for their opinion on what quality improvement should be about? The teachers, the family workers, the bus drivers, and cooks, the parents, the student interns, and volunteers who have day-to-day contact with families and children should know best the means to carry out their duties. . . . A [college] classroom is not going to teach you how to deal with people on a daily basis. It only teaches you the general aspects of human behavior.

[Journal excerpts]
November 28, 1994

Went to the Labor Dept. today on [a staff member's] behalf. I had to state to the judge what PC's role was and let him know what procedure should have been taken with her situation. I tried to explain why PC has a say, and someone helped me out by referring to 70.2. It was stated (by me) that we just had 70.2 training and the CAP Board had ultimate responsibility but not the final say. PC and the board must work together in joint decision making.

November 29, 1994

Down day. I had to go to the emergency room for a migraine.

November 30, 1994

Went to class today! Then went to the office to bring in the minutes.

December 3, 1994

It's 5:15 A.M. I have a lot on my mind. I've been up since 3:00. It's so amazing how I can analyze my dreams now. It seems like it's happened over night (great pun). It seems like I've always had weird dreams and didn't understand them. Even in reading about it in psychology I still didn't make the connection of how the mind plays out reality in a play (dream). The first dream I understood was a dream I had when it was the first time I ever fought back. It was a dream about an intruder breaking into my home, and when this person came down the hall and reached my room I went after him with a baseball bat. (Normally what would happen is the intruder would always come to me but then get to my children to use them to make demands. The dream never played itself out thoroughly enough after that to generalize.) This happened just after my taking a strong stand for the things I believe in. (Proper procedures in Head Start expected of parents but not done by management. I really want to make this program work the way it should. I see potential for a wonderful program just as its founders did. My program, this program, is not living up to its full potential.)

[Memo to Program Specialist for the district, February 9, 1995]

Please take note of the best-known consensual-style organization—the worker-managed system in Yugoslavia. Below I describe that organizational system and relate [it to] Head Start:

- Each enterprise (Head Start center) is viewed as "social property," temporarily governed by the workers (parents, staff, volunteers).

- By-Laws, overall policy—more than ten workers must formulate a worker council (center committee), which elects and may remove the management board and plant director (we need this implemented in order for the program to work correctly; somehow it got reworded and directed to staff). This is a form of checks and balances, to insure the goals of the program are met, and not to give dominance to one person's goals for the agency.

- Worker council sets overall "critical" policy while director and board run the day-to-day operation (sound familiar?).

This is the basis of performance standards and 70.2. I've never run across anything so much related to the philosophy of Head Start. Policy Council needs a say in the leadership of our program. You must realize that management is turning the agency into a pure bureaucratic system and this will be the demise of parent and community participation as it was intentionally meant to be implemented. It will also produce division of labor, "[the] dichotomy between intellectual work and manual work and between administrative tasks and performance tasks" (Iannello, *Decisions without Hierarchy*).

We need to pull together to save Head Start in this county. If things continue as they are, we will have another government agency that spends taxpayers' money on half an idea that only half works!

[In] organizations based on empowerment, members monitor themselves. In organizations based on power, there must be an administrative oversight function. Some of the expenditures of the oversight functions must be cut! The cost of conventional oversight will become too high and is not needed. Head Start needs to be on its own.

[Journal excerpt]
December 3, 1994

I had a conversation with the program specialist and expressed some of PC's concerns about our program and let her know that we wished to incorporate. She said that it could take two to three years. It could be a lengthy process, because both parties have to give consent, meaning that the CAP would have to agree to give up Head Start. And as it stands now PC doesn't have enough on the CAP to constitute taking the funding from them. Then we would also have to prove how we could run the program more effectively. This can be accomplished! I can't do it alone.

If this were my job it would be easy, but as it stands I am a mother of two young children who demand a lot of my time, and they deserve it, a full time student and work in the summer, plus there is Head Start which is a full time job. I should not have tried to take a class while doing an internship, but I never expected the internship to get so hard EMOTIONALLY as well as a lot of work (when it was first talked about it seemed so easy). It takes so much time from my family. I don't get paid, which would help relieve some other stresses, and it seems like the focus of the whole idea is so broad. I need to be organized and through the whole internship it seemed to get very disorganized for me. Too much was expected by Head Start. Some of this no doubt because they couldn't get rid of me from my elected position as Policy Council chairperson.

I can't imagine why I couldn't get focused. I don't know how I got 85s on my papers for PSY. I do know why I got 56s on two tests! How could my family put up with me. I would go from being okay to being a total BITCH. I yell at my husband on a regular basis!

December 13, 1994

I got the agenda for the meeting today. The meeting is tomorrow—excellent notice! I did see though that the postmarks don't match up. Looks like it was put through the agency mail machine Friday and then held till Monday.

Deember 14, 1994

Meeting, psychology final, union negotiations.

January 26, 1995

SAVI [mandated Head Start self-assessment validation instrument] training was given by me to the parents. I really enjoyed doing this. It felt great to give the parents information on how to use the SAVI forms and why it was important for the organization. I also enjoyed being able to stand in front of them as if it were a class, and I didn't feel uncomfortable. I was actually giving a class, and it felt great. I loved it. I think it also felt good to be doing something that was productive. This whole year PC has felt like it has been unproductive—not that it has been or not, just that that's how it feels.

February 1995

Things are getting too hectic. I can't handle going to school full time, being a mom to two children, a wife, working, and doing Head Start business. Head Start business has become extremely demanding. No matter what I try to do to make this agency run by its own rules, it doesn't work. The director of the CAP will do as he pleases no matter what laws are in place. As long as the funding source doesn't stand behind [the] Policy Council, what good are we?

March 21, 1995

I, Wendy Kirby, do hereby submit my resignation as Policy Council chairperson. I find it too difficult to effectively do my job when I am in a constant battle with management. When I came back to the program after my children had moved on, I knew it would be difficult but never dreamed it would be impossible to maintain the philosophy of Head Start. Head Start used to be a wonderful program for families. It is taking a major turn toward a daycare program. What the management team fails to notice is that this is not in compliance with the performance standards for a good reason. There have been many years of research that clearly state that the family must be developed together in order for Head Start contact to make a difference. Families must feel as though they make a difference to their community.

One of the most special things about Head Start is that it's supposed to be a collective decision-making program! That is how parents and staff alike feel motivated and dedicated to the program. Unfortunately this is now gone. . . .

Most of us, including the staff, come from families where punishment and ridicule were harsh. Head Start gave us hope and a new way to deal with punishment—don't dwell on the things done wrong, instead encourage the good in people and help correct the faults.

In the past year, [administrators] have ridiculed me more than I have ever been in my whole life. . . . To these administrators, I can only dedicate this psychological observation of Thomas Jefferson in 1785: "He who permits himself to tell a lie once finds it much easier to do it a second and third time, till at length it becomes habitual; he tells lies without attending to it, and truths without the world's believing him. This falsehood of the tongue leads to that of the heart, and in time depraves all its good dispositions."

This program has a beautiful little picture painted on the facade and inside is disheartening. This is not just my belief but other community members as well.

Parents and frontline staff, I wish you well. Keep your efforts combined for you are the heart of this program and the only thing left that represents what Head Start was all about. TAKE CARE AND GOOD LUCK.

I must say that I have a habit of analyzing every situation I encounter. I see that these excerpts do actually tell a story. However, it is not the whole story I would like someday to tell, of the good and bad experiences in Head Start, from the first day to the end in hopes to educate those concerned with policy making.

As I become more educated I am less willing to conform to the rules of society that I deem condescending to me or my children's future. One should not be proud to losing an internship, but I am! I refused to be a part of management's illegal practices. I could see past the immediate gains I'd get from conforming and acted for the betterment of my future.

I was a seed that planted itself in Head Start. In the beginning I was handled with care, nurtured, and loved. In response to that attention I grew prominent, but wilted here and there when degraded. But I regained my strength when provided with the proper nutrition—my first scholarship award. The award wasn't big, but the professor who made the introductory speech for it gave me the vigor I needed to endure the rest of my development. He said that his father may have come to this country a poor man, but the one thing that could not be taken away from him was his knowledge. This is true for me—as long as I possess the knowledge I have acquired I will use it to better my own as well as my family's lives. However, I need a more fertile environment in which to live than what has been provided. I hope, in time, society can be made more fertile for the gentle and beautiful plants this world has to offer. And fewer weeds will control and repress our growth, so the world may evolve as it should.

11

Developmentalism Meets Standardized Testing: Do Low-Income Children Lose?

Linda Spatig, Robert Bickel, Laurel Parrott, Amy Dillon, and Kate Conrad

INTRODUCTION

For nearly 30 years, Head Start has attempted to break the cycle of poverty in the United States by enhancing educational opportunities for low-income children of preschool age. Since 1992, thirty-two sites around the country have gone a step further by extending Head Start–like services to help children and their families "transition" smoothly into the elementary grades. In a two-county region of West Virginia, a state probably best known as an exemplar of Appalachian poverty, preliminary quantitative evaluation results of such a Transition demonstration program suggest that children who received Head Start and Transition services may not have gained ground academically.

Seeking explanations for these troubling results, we turned to in-depth qualitative data collected over a four-year period to supplement

Research for this chapter was funded by a grant from the Head Start Bureau of the Administration on Children, Youth, and Families. We are grateful to the many teachers who opened their classrooms to us and spent precious schoolday time talking with us. Also, we especially appreciate the staff developer profiled in this chapter. Her willingness to allow us to observe her work with teachers and to spend countless hours talking with us about her ideas made this writing possible.

the achievement test data on which the quantitative evaluation was based. Our examination led to no clear answers, but to some intriguing questions. Might there have been academic gains if the provision of health and social services had been more concentrated? Might the scores have been different if parent involvement activities had been more related to children's learning and development? These and other questions merit analysis.

In this chapter, however, we focus on questions related to the local project's staff development efforts with the children's elementary teachers. Historically, Head Start and other preschool programs have emphasized developmental, constructivist approaches to teaching and learning. Increasingly, such an approach has been accepted by early childhood educators in public school settings. At the same time, the use of standardized tests has increased at a startling rate (Kamii 1990), and it is possible that the two movements are incompatible (Stone 1996). We examine the dissonance created by these two movements in the context of the West Virginia Transition. Is the quantitative evaluation's reliance on standardized achievement measures inherently incompatible with the type of developmental, constructivist early childhood program encouraged by the local project? If so, is this incompatibility a disservice to Head Start and Transition programs and the children and families they serve? Perhaps even more important, is it possible that Transition inadvertently played a role in limiting educational opportunities of low-income children by seeking to optimize the development of each child irrespective of academic norms? If true, is this a disservice for low-income children who have limited means of gaining access to the dominant cultural knowledge that comprises standardized tests?

We want to be very clear that we are not championing standardized achievement testing and that we do not view the current societal focus on achieving ever higher test scores as an admirable, or even reasonable, goal for education. We also have concerns about the extent to which such tests are fair assessments of the knowledge of low-income and minority students. However, we recognize that standardized tests, whether or not we like them and the ways they are used, are a well-established feature of U.S. schooling and are tremendously powerful in opening or closing doors to high-status education, skilled and professional jobs, and other life opportunities. President Clinton's recent call for increased achievement testing suggests that confidence in and reliance upon this type of educational assessment is not abating. Thus, the questions we address here are not about whether or not standardized achievement testing is a good thing, but how best to work with low-income children in a context within which testing is a salient factor. While we certainly do not limit our aspirations for children to the realm of test scores, we also do not want them to be disadvantaged in this realm.

Head Start Transition in West Virginia

Head Start research has a long and controversial history. The unanswered question that recurs most frequently—Under what conditions are Head Start effects lasting?—provides a compelling rationale for programs such as the Head Start Public School Transition Demonstration Project (Transition). Transition is a national study, the purpose of which was to compare thirty-two different programs (each located in a different area in the United States) designed to assist low-income children make a successful transition into public school. To accomplish this goal, Transition demonstration projects were to provide low-income children and their families with continuous Head Start–like services through the first four years of public schooling. These services included comprehensive health and social services, parent involvement activities, and the provision of developmentally appropriate schooling experiences.

West Virginia as Context

It is not surprising that a Head Start agency in West Virginia was eager to become involved in the Transition program in order to help improve the academic and life chances of children. West Virginia's per capita income is among the lowest in the United States. Hannah (1995) reports high rates of poverty among West Virginia families. As of 1989, 26 percent of all children in West Virginia lived in poverty, compared to 18 percent in the United States as a whole. Nearly 40 percent of all students drop out before reaching the eighth grade (Bickel 1989). Only 32 percent of West Virginia's high school graduates enroll in a college or university, and the percentage of the state's population made up of college graduates is the lowest in the nation (Bickel, Banks, and Spatig 1991). Diversification of the state's economy has been slow to occur. Ongoing outmigration of native West Virginians in search of improved prospects for themselves and their families is a source of continuing concern (DeYoung 1988). Those who remain are, too often, the least well educated and most likely to be unemployed or underemployed.

Five demonstration schools and seven control schools were selected in a two-county region containing one of the state's largest cities as well as some of its most rural, isolated areas. Poverty levels in these schools were high. For example, in four of the five demonstration schools, between 70 and 80 percent of the students qualified for free or reduced-cost lunch. In an area of such great need, Head Start, as well as other programs designed to assist low-income children, is highly prized. But to what extent is Head Start actually succeeding in improving the life chances of its participants? A great deal of research has attempted to answer this question.

HEAD START RESEARCH

One crucial reason for the uncertain results of many Head Start evaluations is that, too often, they have been poorly conceived afterthoughts (Currie and Thomas 1995). The post hoc character of such endeavors has guaranteed that essential data would be missing, undercutting the best efforts of even the most sophisticated statistical analysis.

Furthermore, Head Start evaluations have been captives of methodological tradition. Quasi-experimental designs have taken near-exclusive precedence over other approaches. As a result, ethnographic research on Head Start, especially in relation to academic success, has seldom been done and rarely reported. Consequently, results of evaluations of Head Start and related endeavors are typically couched in the language of psychometric outcomes, especially achievement test scores, and less frequently, measures of social skills.

While some of the quantitative research on Head Start has been characterized by state-of-the-art sophistication, its very nature prejudges questions as to what Head Start can and should do. As is too often the case in quantitative research and evaluation, sophisticated statistical tools have been applied in the presence of very limited knowledge as to the concrete social nature of the programs being evaluated.

Evaluating the West Virginia Transition Demonstration Project

Design of West Virginia Transition's evaluation was intended to avoid these difficulties by assuring that data were available to permit the interpretable comparisons needed to assess the efficacy of the program. This included not only a set of more or less suitable outcome measures, but a useful complement of statistical controls, as well.

This endeavor, of course, entailed comparison of Head Start participants who also participated in Transition with Head Start participants who did not participate in Transition. The evaluation is even more informative, however, since we were able to include children who have *not* participated in Head Start. In effect, this enabled us to include Head Start participation as a categorical variable in our statistical analysis.

The Agency for Children, Youth, and Families (the federal agency that administers Head Start) and the national Transition evaluation coordinators determined which outcomes and measures were employed. Data collection began with the onset of the program and has proceeded in a well-organized fashion for the past three years. Sufficient, good-quality data on variables of interest are available to specify an informative quasi-experimental model to gauge not only the effectiveness of Transition but also of Head Start itself.

In addition, in an ambitious effort at triangulation, the traditional quasi-experimental work has been complemented by a sustained qualitative evaluation endeavor. Three full-time ethnographers, supervised by an experienced specialist in qualitative social research, have been on the job since early in 1992, involved in intensive documentation of program organization and functioning. They have spent hundreds of hours in schools and classrooms, observing and interviewing teachers and children; they have visited participants' homes to interview parents and children; and they have become a credible source of formative evaluation insights for program administrators and other staff members.

Of special interest here, the ethnographers and those in the conventional quantitative evaluation effort have begun to collaborate. Ethnographic material has been invaluable in filling in the programmatic "black box" and providing richly detailed contextual information concerning the experiences of Transition participants. Qualitative data provided insights that may help to further explain and illuminate the disappointing results of the quantitative evaluation.

From Kindergarten through Second Grade

The difficulties we are trying to explain are presented in tables 11.2 and 11.3. Using the independent variables described in table 11.1, we first tried to account for achievement differences among students when they entered kindergarten. The results of this effort are reported in table 11.2. Then, after the same children (with 16 percent

TABLE 11.1

Preschool/In-School Experience

HEADSTART	Head Start Participation, Scored 1 if Yes, 0 Otherwise
PRESCHOOL	Other Pre-School Participation, Scored 1 if Yes, 0 Otherwise
TRANSITION	Transition Participation, Scored 1 if Yes, 0 Otherwise

Student Characteristics

PRETEST	Achievement Test Score at Beginning of Kindergarten
GENDER	Child's Gender, Scored 1 if Male, 0 Otherwise
ETHNICITY*	Child's Ethnicity, Scored 1 if White, 0 Otherwise
CHILD HEALTH	Adult Respondent's Assessment of Child's Health, in Five Levels
SOCIAL SKILLS	Social Skills Scale Score, Thirty-Eight Likert Items with Three Responses to Each. (Cronbach's Alpha=.86)

Family and Household Characteristics

FAMILY INCOME	Family Income, in Twelve Levels
PARENTS' EDUCATION	Parent Respondent's Education Level, in Ten Levels
BOTH PARENTS	Parents Living in the Home, Coded 1 if Both, 0 Otherwise
PARENTING SKILLS	Parenting Effectiveness Scale Score for Primary Care Giver, Twenty-Six Likert Items with Six Responses to Each. (Cronbach's Alpha=.74)
PARENTS' HEALTH	Adult Respondent's Assessment of His/Her Health, in Five Levels
UNDER 18	Number of Children Under Age 18 Living at Home
OVER 18	Number of Adults Over Age 18 Living at Home

Contextual Factors

DISTRICT	School District/County, Scored 1 if Urban, 0 if Rural
COHORT	Scored 1 for Kindergarten in 1992, 0 for Kindergarten in 1993

*Only 27 students in the sample are black.

attrition) completed second grade, we did the same analysis once again.

The questions we were asking are obvious: in table 11.2, does Head Start make a difference in achievement test scores? In table 11.3, does either Head Start or Transition make such a difference? The answer to both questions is no.

Beginning Kindergarten

Table 11.2 reports three regression analyses with three different outcome measures, the Peabody Picture Vocabulary Test, the Woodcock-Johnson 22 Letter-Word Identification Test, and the Woodcock-Johnson 25 Applied Problem Solving Test. As the test names suggest, the first two are measures of verbal achievement, while the third is a gauge of basic math-problem-solving skills.

Which independent variables made a difference? The answer is, by now, all too familiar: socially ascribed traits, factors over which children, their families, and their schools have no control. Parents' education had a statistically significant and positive regression coefficient in each of the three analyses. The same was true for family income. Race worked to the advantage of the white majority group two times out of three.

In terms of these standardized measures, Head Start participation made no difference. In this data set, 58 percent of the beginning kindergarten children had been in Head Start. But the statistically nonsignificant Head Start coefficients indicate that participants are not gaining in ways that would show up on these tests.

These results are troubling for two reasons. First, they suggest that Head Start does not seem to work—at least in terms of these standard measures of achievement. Even with the Head Start variable incorporated into each regression analysis, socially ascribed traits—class and race—work much as we would expect in the absence of intervention. In fact, in analyses not reported here, we simply deleted the Head Start variable from each analysis to see what would happen, and the answer was nothing.

We initially took comfort in the statistically significant and positive findings for the relationship between social skills and achievement. In contrast to socially ascribed traits, here was a variable with a consistently positive effect on achievement which we may be able to do something about. Maybe Head Start works *through* social skills, indirectly affecting achievement.

TABLE 11.2
Regression Results—Cohorts 1 and 2

| | Unstandardized and (Standardized) Coefficients | | |
	PEABODY	WOOD22	WOOD25
	Beginning of Kindergarten		
HEADSTART	. −1.97	0.77	−0.38
	(−.07)	(.08)	(−.04)
PRESCHOOL	3.86	−0.45	0.41
	(.11)	(−.04)	(.04)
GENDER	−0.49	−0.16	0.46
	(−.02)	(−.02)	(.05)
ETHNICITY	10.14***	−0.44	1.76*
	(.19)	(−.03)	(.14)
CHILD HEALTH	−0.70	−0.03	−0.08
	(−.04)	(−.01)	(−.02)
SOCIAL SKILLS	8.58**	3.55**	3.36**
	(.15)	(.20)	(.21)
FAMILY INCOME	0.81*	0.58***	0.28*
	(.14)	(.32)	(.16)
PARENTS' EDUCATION	1.38**	0.53**	0.47**
	(.15)	(.19)	(.18)
BOTH PARENTS	1.29	−0.95	−0.66
	(.04)	(−.10)	(−.06)
PARENTING SKILLS	1.42	−0.07	−0.07
	(.05)	(−.01)	(−.01)
PARENTS' HEALTH	0.64	−0.16	−0.28
	(.04)	(−.04)	(−.07)
UNDER 18	−0.76	−0.09	−0.04
	(−.06)	(−.01)	(−.01)
OVER 18	1.41	−0.02	−0.03
	(.07)	(−.01)	(−.01)
DISTRICT	−3.56	−1.46**	−2.29**
	(−.11)	(−.16)	(−.26)
COHORT	0.04	1.02	0.54
	(.01)	(.11)	(.06)
ADJUSTED R–SQUARED	19.5%	16.2%	14.3%
	N=290	N=290	N=290

*P<.05   **P<.01   ***P<.001

When we ran our analysis with social skills as the dependent variable, the regression coefficient corresponding to Head Start was, in fact, statistically significant, but it was also *negative* (Bickel, McDonough, and Maynard, 1996). In other words, Head Start participation seemed to have a somewhat negative influence on social skills. However, since this was a rather weak statistical result, we would not read too much into this finding except to note that in terms of the measure of social skills used in this study (Social Skills Rating System, developed by F. M. Gresham and S. N. Elliott 1990), participation in Head Start did *not* make a positive contribution to participants' social skills.

Finishing Second Grade

Perhaps we should terminate the statistical analysis at this point. After all, one of the purposes of Transition is to maintain Head Start gains. But in this case the quantitative data provided no evidence of Head Start's efficacy in promoting measured achievement either directly or indirectly, through influencing factors such as social skills. However, perhaps Transition itself promotes measured achievement, even in the absence of Head Start effects. Examination of the regression results reported in table 11.3, however, indicates that this is not the case. The variables used are the same as those incorporated in the Head Start analyses, except that Transition participation and pretest score are added as independent variables and outcome measures are scores on tests administered at the end of second grade.

The results were no more encouraging than those reported for Head Start. Transition has a statistically significant regression coefficient in only one of our three analyses, and the coefficient is negative. Rather than risk oversimplifying one small, even if statistically significant, relationship, we conclude, much as with Head Start, that Transition has not affected measured achievement.

Predictably, there were strong positive relationships between pretest and outcome measures in each analysis. In view of this, it is also easy to anticipate that family income and parents' education did not show the analysis-to-analysis consistency we saw at the beginning of kindergarten. The emergence of gender effects in two of the three analyses is something we had not foreseen, but effects are quite modest. Pretest scores, in effect, overwhelm everything else. For our purposes, the most important findings were no Transition effects, and once again, no Head Start effects.

TABLE 11.3
Regression Results—Cohorts 1 and 2

| | Unstandardized and (Standardized) Coefficients | | |
	PEABODY	WOOD22	WOOD25
	End of Second Grade		
TRANSITION	−2.52*	−1.06	−0.29
	(−.11)	(−.05)	(−.03)
PRETEST	0.49***	1.00***	0.53***
	(.062)	(.48)	(.57)
HEADSTART	−0.33	−0.37	0.11
	(−.01)	(−.02)	(.01)
PRESCHOOL	1.68	−0.12	0.15
	(.06)	(−.01)	(.02)
GENDER	2.41*	0.17	0.99*
	(.11)	(.01)	(.13)
ETHNICITY	−1.58	−0.21	−1.39
	(−.04)	(−.01)	(−.10)
CHILD HEALTH	0.17	−0.17	0.07
	(.01)	(−.02)	(.02)
SOCIAL SKILLS	−0.05	−0.36	1.09
	(−.01)	(−.01)	(.07)
FAMILY INCOME	0.59*	−.01	0.27**
	(.12)	(−.00)	(.18)
PARENTS' EDUCATION	0.81*	0.64	0.12
	(.11)	(.10)	(−.05)
BOTH PARENTS	−1.26	1.96	−0.77
	(.06)	(.10)	(−.09)
PARENTING SKILLS	0.49	0.68	−0.45
	(.02)	(.04)	(−.06)
PARENTS' HEALTH	−0.60	0.02	0.22
	(.05)	(.00)	(.06)
UNDER 18	−0.46	−0.07	0.19
	(−.05)	(−.01)	(.06)
OVER 18	1.36	−0.68	0.22
	(.09)	(−.05)	(.04)
DISTRICT	0.95	1.69	0.35
	(.04)	(.09)	(.05)
COHORT	0.13	−1.37	0.45
	(.01)	(−.07)	(.06)
ADJUSTED R-SQUARED	51.8%	25.2%	43.9%
	N=243	N=243	N=243

*P<.05   **P<.01   ***P<.001

What's Going On?

Both Transition and Head Start itself, as time goes on, seem to produce costs rather than gains for participants, at least as far as measured by these standardized tests. What is going on here? The lack of achievement test advantages for Transition children may be related to the fact that the project encouraged teaching practices that are inconsistent with the standardized tests used to evaluate it and further, that such teaching practices may in fact be problematic for low income children for that very reason. Our argument in support of this line of reasoning draws upon the ethnographic research conducted throughout the program. The ethnographers were participant-observers in classrooms (grades K through 3 in the five project schools) and in staff development sessions for teachers. In addition, they conducted individual interviews with teachers and project staff involved in designing and implementing the staff development component. We turn first to the format and messages of Transition's staff development component.

THE STAFF DEVELOPMENT COMPONENT

Original Goals

One of four major goals of the West Virginia Transition project has been the provision of a "developmentally oriented program for children which focusses on children's strengths and most absorbing interests and does not adhere to a deficit curriculum" (grant proposal, 1991). The proposal goes on to list three strategies for implementing this developmentally oriented program which encourage teachers to: (1) be nonjudgmental observers and recorders of children in order to develop personalized programs for them, (2) share their knowledge about children with teachers in other grades as well as with other individuals and agencies who provide services to families and (3) assess each child's progress using the best child development knowledge and "document that growth and learning through narrative/descriptive data and samples of children's work."

In practice, the Transition staff development program included a variety of elements for teachers. Many teachers attended local and out-of-town conferences relating to developmentally oriented practices. Resource rooms established in each school served as lending libraries of developmentally oriented materials for teachers and parents to use with children. Ethnographers provided teachers with detailed field notes of classroom observations and teachers were encouraged to use the observational data as a basis for reflection on their teaching practices.

Most important to this discussion, though, are the series of local staff development meetings (four to seven per school year) that focused on reflective, child-centered teaching. These meetings served as the primary vehicle for communicating with teachers. Whereas only some teachers were offered or took advantage of opportunities to attend out-of-town conferences, and any one teacher's participation in classroom observations likely lasted for only two semesters, all Transition teachers were invited to attend the frequent staff development meetings. Thus we conclude that whatever messages teachers received from Transition were most likely received from these meetings, which were led by a visiting consultant with an extensive background in developmentally oriented early childhood education.

Meeting Format

The staff development consultant, Anna Bradley,[1] typically began the meetings by sharing her plans for the session and asking for additional ideas from teachers. For example, in a session in the third year of the project, "Anna began by saying she wanted to talk today about developmentally oriented practice and what that means. She said she also is hoping to talk today about some brain based research. She asked everyone if that was okay and nobody responded. She said she'd start out like that and then if they began to wiggle, she'd know it wasn't" (Meeting field notes).

Following this type of introduction, there was usually a period of relatively unstructured discussion. Depending upon the way Anna framed her comments and questions, teachers' responses consisted of either silence or comments addressing either specific children and concerns in their classrooms or more general issues. Anna alternated between asking questions designed to encourage teachers to think about their practice and expressing her own ideas about how children grow and learn, often supporting them by briefly mentioning various scholars, educators, research studies, and theories pertinent to the topic at hand.

Messages to Teachers

Based on observations of staff development meetings, interviews and conversations with Anna Bradley, and interviews with teachers, we identified five major overlapping messages to teachers about teaching young children. The messages are philosophically consistent with a constructivist approach to learning and development.[2]

1. Each child constructs her or his own knowledge through actively interacting with people and things.

2. It is the role of teachers and parents to facilitate these constructions by providing nonthreatening, stimulating environments with opportunities for active, meaningful exploration.

3. This facilitation should be informed by narrative, descriptive data obtained through observing and talking with children, not by textbooks and prescriptive curriculum guides.

4. The effectiveness of this facilitation should be evaluated by the teacher who is continuously reflecting on her own practice, not by standardized testing of children.

5. As the teacher engages in studying children, providing opportunities for their learning, and reflecting on the entire process, she is constructing her own knowledge about teaching and learning.

Each Child Constructs Knowledge

The entire series of staff development messages rests on the notion that each individual creates or constructs his or her own knowledge. The idea is that children (or learners of any age) can and must do the learning themselves, by actively engaging with meaningful aspects of their environment. This cannot be done to or for them. Anna referred to the ideas of John Dewey: "There's nothing new about it. We go back to Dewey. In a sense, we're reclaiming the naturalness of children's learning."

Teachers were encouraged to think about their teaching practices in relation to this view of learning that focuses on the facilitation of a stimulating, meaningful learning environment for children, rather than on the transmission of information. "[Anna] said what she is really trying to do is to get teachers to think about [the difference between] instruction, where you teach, dictate or lead the student, and construction, where the child adds to his own knowledge. . . . There is no such thing as teaching, only providing opportunities for learning" (Meeting field notes). Similarly, teachers were urged to help children be in control of themselves and their learning by effectively setting the stage for students to take their own learning forward.

Teachers and Parents[3] Facilitate Learning

Anna saw teachers as facilitators of learning rather than as direct instructors. She encouraged them to interact with children in a manner that would enable them to create their own knowledge. For example, she discussed the art of questioning in a way that "leads kids to create their own knowledge," commenting, "Children know *how* to think; we just have to ask good questions." Also, she cautioned against imposing on children, recommending that children play a major role in classroom decision making. She suggested involving children in curricular and pedagogical issues by asking kids what they want to know, engaging them in dialogue about "things that are meaningful to them," and allowing them to participate in setting their own goals and standards, making up their own daily schedule, and deciding what goes in their own portfolios. Along the same lines, Anna argued that children should be encouraged to become self-disciplined by being responsible for their own behavior. For example, she once suggested to a teacher who used time-out as a behavior management technique that she consider allowing children to decide when they were ready to return to the group.

Just as important as teachers, to Anna, was the environment teachers created in their rooms. She exhorted teachers to "set the stage" for learning, and said, "Your classroom can become your assistant teacher." She advocated an environment full of choices and opportunities for exploration and discovery—an environment that is not overstructured, and one that provides a great deal of freedom for students to create knowledge.

Anna encouraged the use of learning centers to facilitate exploration and learning. She mentioned having learning goals for the centers, but also talked about the value of having teachers "just put stuff out and see what happens." Anna recommended using materials where the form is not prescriptive—for example, wooden blocks, art materials such as paints and clay, and kitchen utensils rather than worksheets and dittos. "You need to use sand. You need to use a lot of water. You need to use lots of science activities that they can discover. And cooking.... Any way you want to do it, but they need free movement and a lot of appropriate activities for their age level and their development.... I think any class that you do a lot of ... sitting still and you do a lot of paperwork, and run off sheets, is not a developmental kindergarten" (Interview).

Know Your Children

According to Anna, the effective facilitation of learning ultimately rests on the teacher's knowledge of child development generally and, even more important, on her knowledge of the particular children in her classroom. By carefully observing and talking with her students, the teacher can gain the knowledge needed to create an environment—a curriculum—that is personalized for those particular children. Transition teachers were encouraged to use this approach rather than to conform to prescriptive curriculum guides.

Anna wanted teachers to observe and study the children in their classes and use what they learned "to create curriculum that's personalized for children," curriculum that focuses on children's "strengths, interests, and passions." In the original grant proposal, Anna described a "child study" process where teachers would be asked to volunteer to select a child who interested her to study in depth. Teachers would study and describe the child in terms of a list of "multiple perspectives":

A. The child's stance in the world: gesture, posture, inflection, rhythm, energy.

B. The child's emotional tenor and disposition: tone, expressiveness, intensity, range, pattern.

C. The child's mode of relationship to other children and to adults: attachments, variations, consistency, quality, and range.

D. The child's activities and interests: modes of engagement, pattern of involvement, range, intensity.

E. The child's involvement in formal learning: modes of approach, interest, patterns or involvement.

F. The child's greatest strengths and most absorbing interests.

G. The child's areas of greatest vulnerability.

Anna emphasized the importance of *describing*, rather than *judging*, children in this process, cautioning teachers not to try to "psych kids out," but simply to watch and listen to them, attending to and recording only what is directly observable.

Anna contrasted this emphasis on studying children and developing personalized curriculum for them with more content-oriented approaches to curriculum. She advocated focusing on the child rather than the content, saying that "content-driven approaches have failed in early childhood" and recommending that teachers "put content aside and focus on the child." She was particularly opposed to what she called "canned curriculum," suggesting instead that teachers "do what is right for each child."

Along the same lines, Anna seemed to prefer a focus on "life skills" rather than on academics in the early school years. She argued that teachers are pushed into teaching reading, writing, and other subject matter instead of teaching social skills such as how to get along with people. According to Anna, teachers try to teach advanced curriculum to kids too soon. "Learning to read is not hard. We make it difficult by trying to teach it too early and [we] confuse kids." This "push-down" curriculum results in school failure for young children. "A lot of children aren't successful in school because they're not ready for the material they're expected to learn. . . . If the content is too far ahead of the kids, the kids will pull out due to fear of failure" (Meeting field notes).

Anna asserted that ultimately, we need to ask ourselves: "What is important for young children to know? What is worth knowing?" According to Anna, the answer to those questions often comes back to the life skills. "The biggest thing to me that's worth knowing is how to get along with each other, how to respect yourself and respect others. . . . The second thing that's important—and the criterion for me would be: 'Is everything you teach related to what the kid is doing outside of school and are you taking everything outside of school and enriching it and enhancing it in school?' " (Interview).

In addition, we determine what is worthwhile for children to know by observing and listening to them. They will let us know what is important to them. "On the other hand, . . . it's different for each child. . . . Knowing what's worth knowing really means listening to the child and extending what he's interested in. We're back to strengths and absorbing interests. . . . What's worth knowing is something that you really want to know. In your gut level, you want to know it. And that means, back again to knowing the child, to know what for him is worth knowing" (Interview).

Reflect—Question Your Practice

Anna called on teachers to reflect on their own teaching practice and its meaningfulness to children. Along these lines, she urged teachers to be critical consumers of educational knowledge, advising them not to believe all the research they read, not to "buy every pig in a poke," and to examine and question educational "fads." She extended this advice to her own ideas: "Nothing I say is absolute gospel."

Anna frequently championed the value of reflection in general, saying things such as "The unexamined life is not worth living." She used and advocated asking questions as a vehicle for reflection, encouraging teachers not to be threatened by questions because "the questions are as important as the answers," and "it is the questions that open doors for options for change."

For Anna, the ultimate goal of reflecting is to study and "analyze your own teaching" to see how it could be improved. She invited teachers to test ideas in their classrooms, to become researchers. In addition, she urged teachers to ask themselves three questions: "Why am I doing this? What is it teaching? What other ways are there to do it?" In this way, teachers would be able to "see how [their] teaching stands up to what [they] believe, . . . to [their] philosophy of teaching." Acknowledging the difficulty of this kind of honest self-evaluation, Anna called on teachers to have the "courage" to analyze their teaching.

Construct Your Own Knowledge about Teaching

Anna believed it was important to treat teachers the same way she asked them to treat their students, in other words, to "demonstrate the process" by allowing and encouraging them to construct their own knowledge. For example, she commented, "If I don't want [teachers] to be prescriptive with kids, I can't be prescriptive with them." Similarly, she commented to a group of teachers at a staff development meeting, "The grant never intended to change your teaching. You bring about change yourselves." In accordance with this, she strongly supported teacher autonomy, maintaining that teachers need to "set their own goals" and "find their own way," rather than being pressured to accept particular teaching ideas and strategies.

It was not uncommon to hear Anna assert that teachers' knowledge and wisdom gave them the right to teach in whatever way they best saw fit. Contending that "teachers know best about curriculum," "know what's right for their classroom," and "know more than they think they do," she argued for giving teachers "carte blanche, [and] they'll do what's best for their students." In Anna's view, Transition teachers did not have this kind of autonomy. "You're not autonomous. You've got to have freedom to teach where you want to, when you want to, and how you want to." She attributed the lack of autonomy to a widespread and unwarranted lack of trust in teachers in U.S. society. Anna urged teachers to stand up for themselves and their beliefs about teaching and learning. She encouraged them, "trust your feelings," "be brave enough to call people on things you don't agree with," "argue your point, say you don't agree," and "talk back to administrators."

Teacher Responses to Staff Development Messages

Even if Transition teachers overwhelmingly embraced and practiced the constructivist ideas discussed in staff development meetings, it is debatable whether these practices would translate to increased standardized test scores, especially in the short term. Before discussing this in greater detail we turn briefly to the issue of how teachers actually responded to the messages of Transition's staff development.

Classroom observations and teacher interviews suggest less than full endorsement and use of the developmental practices Anna stressed. Many teachers exhibited varying levels of resistance to the meetings themselves, some of which had to do with the involuntary nature of their participation in the project (Parrott, et al. 1993). Some felt criticized when Anna spoke out against teaching practices they employed. Also, many teachers objected to the fact that meetings consisted primarily of general discussions of philosophy rather than new ideas and "something useful" to take back and try in their classrooms.

However, virtually all Transition teachers valued the staff development meetings as opportunities to get together with their professional peers—other early childhood teachers—to "talk with other adults," to "vent," to use each other as a support system, and, when possible, to get new teaching ideas from each other. Furthermore, some teachers responded favorably to the constructivist messages about learning and development. In some cases, teachers primarily responded by reflecting on their practice in a new way; in other cases, they made modifications in their teaching as well. It is these changes in thinking and practice that deserve closer scrutiny because of their relevance to our concerns about the possible relationship between staff development messages and test scores.

Changes in Thinking

Interviews with teachers suggest that Anna was successful in her attempts to encourage teachers to reflect on their practice. Again and again, many teachers talked about the way their thinking was influenced by Transition. One teacher found herself wondering what Anna would do in a particular situation. She said she might not always do what Anna would do, "but it makes me stop and think and question some of the practices I've been doing."

Another teacher spoke about considering whether or not there are other ways to accomplish her teaching goals. "You might not agree with [Anna], but it makes you think. If it does nothing more than make you think, that's a good thing to do. To rethink what you're doing, maybe 'Is this the only way? Is there another way?'"

Teachers also examined their ideas about curriculum and instructional practices. For example, one teacher reflected about using pencil and paper tasks such as workbooks in teaching young children. She found the staff development sessions helpful in keeping her "in constant check" about whether her teaching methods were child oriented. "I think Anna kind of called a lot of attention to it, you know, and you think you're in constant check. . . . We'll mention something at the meeting, and it will make you think, and you go back and [ask yourself] 'Do I really do that in my classroom? Should I be doing that?' I think it's probably kept me reflecting through the year" (Interview).

One teacher explained how she learned from other teachers, as well as Anna, and considered their ideas in light of her own students and her own philosophy.

> I like hearing everybody's philosophy, because I have my own thoughts, but nothing is engraved in stone. You know, I mean, especially Anna. Because everything that she says, even if I don't agree with it 100 percent or if I'm sitting there thinking, "That sounds good, but that would not work at my school with my particular class," I see the logic in it. And like I said in the other meeting, it just . . . makes me question, "Why am I doing this? What is the benefit for these kids?" (Interview)

Some teachers described changes in their thinking about classroom management. For example, one teacher responded to Anna's request to critique a staff development meeting by saying that the discussion about time out had particularly interested her. She touched off an exchange that illustrates the reflective thinking Anna encouraged:

[The teacher] said she used time-out for 16 years and now was wondering why. She said that teachers fall into a trap where they're in a room with a closed door and they use things that work. She said often teachers aren't reading, but they're experimenting to see what works for them, and she said time-out worked for her. Anna said the fact that it works is not an argument for time-out; there must be more rationale. [The teacher] said she is thinking that her own time-out is not working. She said she sends the same children every day, so she guessed it wasn't working for these children. Anna beamed and said, "Isn't that what a good staff development program does for you? It makes you reflect about some of the things you are doing." (Meeting field notes)

Changes in Practice

Sometimes the changes in thinking resulted in changes in classroom practices. For example, teachers reported being less structured and more child centered in their classrooms. "My teaching is more child-centered. . . . Before, there were certain things that I thought they should know. And I think I treat each child a little bit differently instead of just putting them all in one mold and making sure they all know exactly the same thing."

When asked for an example of something she had previously thought her children needed to know, she responded: "When I was structured we would sit down every day and go over the alphabet or we'd sit down and write, and that part of the structure is gone. [Now] they're just kind of writing on their own. It's not like it has to be made exactly this way. It's kind of their own development." Asked what prompted that change, she responded: "From the meetings we've had with Anna. You know, I've just looked at my teaching and brought a [few] other teaching [ideas] into it. [Also], talking with other kindergarten teachers and [hearing about] things they've done. I've used some of their ideas. So I think that's made me a better teacher" (Interview).

Along the same lines, some teachers began giving children more choices and greater freedom to explore. One teacher, who described herself as less strict and more flexible and "loosened up" as a result of Transition staff development, began to look at playtime as "more constructive." She described how she now likes to provide children with materials, such as a set of dominoes, and just observe their play.

I like to just sit when they just play for the object of just playing. Take these [dominoes] and do whatever. I give no instructions. I say, "Here they are." I like to listen to the interaction between the kids. . . . I like to listen to how they work out things, who tends to be the boss . . . or who tends to sit back and not get involved. . . . [Now] I think that is something more than just . . . goofing around. . . . But I never would have done that before. I've gotten away from, "This is the way it is and that's the way you're supposed to do it," and it comes from this [Transition staff development] I'm sure. (Interview)

Not all teachers were pleased with the results of allowing children greater freedom.

Instead of giving them specific things to play with, we've given them more choices. And I've let mine move around the room instead of staying at a certain table for so many minutes. I'm not as strict [as a result of] hearing Anna talk. And I'm not comfortable with that situation. I was more of a structured teacher. They had some free time, but I'm giving them more opportunity to interact with each other. . . . I think there's good about the way I taught before, and I think there's good about letting them have more time where they can just socialize—[time] when the teacher's not telling them exactly what to do. (Interview)

Another teacher became more comfortable with "not being in total control of the lesson" while the children are working together in small groups and letting children move around more interacting with each other.

Some teachers spoke about modifying their expectations of young children. A second-grade teacher, for example, described how she had changed some of her instructional methods. "I found out they're not supposed to be able to do that! Six- and seven-year-old kids cannot look up [at the board] and see something and then transfer it to paper. It's difficult for them to do. So, I don't try to make them do it anymore" (Interview).

Summarizing Teachers' Responses

Clearly, some teachers responded to Transition staff development experiences in ways that are consistent with original project goals. They observed children more and made an effort to allow for greater freedom and choice for children in the classroom. Also, many engaged in serious reflection about their teaching practice as a result of participating in the meetings with Anna. However, teachers did not talk about the individual construction of knowledge or about themselves as facilitators of these constructions, language used above to describe the major staff development messages to teachers. Most likely teachers did not speak in these terms because the staff development messages were not presented to them in that manner. As noted earlier, the sequence of messages was *our* construction. When Anna spoke with teachers, she did not talk in terms of any particular list of messages or objectives. The discussions were much more informal and loosely structured.

Nevertheless, we believe the staff development program clearly promoted a developmental and constructivist approach to early childhood education. Whereas teachers' responses to staff development messages varied, quite a few had favorable reactions to the messages and modified their thinking, and in some cases their teaching practice, in relation to them.

DEVELOPMENTALISM MEETS STANDARDIZED TESTING

Those who tried to move their thinking and/or practice in a more developmental, constructivist direction faced a dilemma. They felt increasingly pressured to teach to the state-mandated standardized tests at the same time they were being urged by Anna to disregard the tests and do what they knew was best for children. Anna spoke again and again about an inherent contradiction between standardized testing and developmentally oriented/constructivist ideas about teaching and learning, especially in the early elementary grades. Anna argued that standardized tests are "contradictory to what we know about developmentally oriented teaching and may be detrimental to young children and their learning." She believed such tests often resulted in the premature labeling of children as low achievers. In addition, she felt that teachers under the gun to raise test scores begin "teaching to the tests," a process that encourages children to look for right answers (the "right answer syndrome"), rather than to freely explore and construct meaningful knowledge.

Anna also contended that serious philosophical reflection, in conjunction with the study of children, was superior to standardized testing as a means of assessing teaching and learning. She frequently and strenuously criticized the use of standardized tests with young children, maintaining that the tests are not valid indicators of what children know. Anna contended that teachers, especially those who make good observational records of children, can "tell us more about what each student knows than the tests can. . . . I don't think [the test is] the least bit valid. . . . A teacher could probably have told you within the second month of school exactly what that kid knows. . . . Now are teacher's judgements erroneous? Sure. But more erroneous than standardized measures? Absolutely not. You know, because they're going to factor in everything else" (Interview).

Because of her strong beliefs about the inconsistency of standardized testing and developmentally oriented practice in early childhood education, Anna was disturbed and embarrassed by Transition's nationally mandated standardized testing of children in grades K through 3. She also opposed the state-mandated testing of children using the CTBS (California Test of Basic Skills) and the West Virginia STEP test, and on a number of occasions, she urged teachers to resist standardized testing. "Anna told the teachers they have a choice. . . . 'You [either] (1) say I can't do anything about it and so I'm going to leave it the way it is, or (2) [you] fight.' She said she sees the teachers as fighters. . . . She said the teachers could tell right now what the kids are going to make on those tests so why are we wasting the time? She said the teachers 'need to start fighting these things' " (Meeting field notes).

Teachers shared Anna's aversion to standardized testing and struggled with what they perceived as a conflict between some aspects of a developmental program and state and county requirements or policies. Several teachers reported that even though ideas from staff development fit with their own philosophy of teaching, they felt pulled to meet county or state requirements to teach certain things in certain ways and to assess with standardized tests. As one teacher explained, "It kind of pulls you apart because the county wants you to have this, this, and this, and Anna's saying, 'No, this, this and this—that's what you should be doing.' "

This conflict intensified during Transition's fourth year as children entered third grade, when state-mandated standardized achievement testing intensified. One third-grade teacher asked, "If you're doing all these developmentally appropriate things for each child, what do you do when it's CTBS time?" Two schools, in particular, were under extreme pressure from their counties to increase test scores. In one case, teachers reported being "verbally attacked" for low scores and instructed to do "whatever it takes to get the scores up." As a result, teachers made significant modifications in their teaching, focusing on the content and format of the CTBS. As one teacher explained: "All we did the first half of the year was drill and skill. We drilled skills. We pounded it into them. . . . Our goal was to bring up the CTBS scores and that's what we did. . . . We were given [by a district supervisor] a list of vocabulary words that would be on the CTBS. . . . Those became our spelling words" (Interview).

Teachers who most keenly experienced the tension between what they perceived as contradictory pushes for a developmental, constructivist approach on the one hand, and the push for higher standardized test scores, on the other, felt caught in the middle. They often felt frustrated, overwhelmed, and/or less and less in control of their teaching.

SUMMARY AND CONCLUSIONS

A developmental approach is not necessarily inconsistent with standardized testing. It is possible that children who are provided with stimulating, appealing environments, rich with opportunities for exploration and learning of all kinds, will be autonomous learners *and* eventually will make high scores on standardized tests. However, this is not a likely outcome of the way teachers experienced developmental, constructivist ideas in the context of Transition's staff development meetings.

Ideas typically were discussed in the absence of specific suggestions and guidance about how to apply them in the classroom. Moreover, when teachers requested more specific information about classroom application, Anna typically responded by explaining that this project is about "whys, not about how-tos." As noted above, she believed it unwise to be prescriptive with teachers when she was asking them not to be prescriptive with their students.

In addition, ideas often were discussed very briefly, with many truisms or brief comments about a line of research or a theory thrown out in quick succession. It was rare for one idea or set of ideas to be pursued deeply and extensively, with teachers engaging actively in the process. As a result, teachers found it difficult to integrate the ideas and apply them in their classrooms. One teacher described it this way: "We've had . . . bits and pieces of what we could use with our kids. But . . . nothing seems to gel. It's a little bit here and a little bit there. . . . I guess I'm going back to the idea that we need . . . more structure as far as what will help us to have the foundation so that we can do more in the classroom itself. We just get so much . . . and I don't know that . . . [it all] sticks or that you can use it. . . . And too much of it is lecture, and it's not real world" (Interview).

Teachers who, despite the pressure of standardized tests and the lack of strategies for applying developmental and constructivist ideas in the classroom, modified their teaching as a consequence of the staff development did so in ways that resulted in less structured, more relaxed, comfortable environments for children, but they may not have provided a highly challenging environment intellectually. The teachers described changes that, in most cases, seemed to demand less, rather than more, from children academically. Without specific guidance about how to facilitate particular kinds of learning in a way that at the same time promotes children's autonomy, some teachers tended to leave children free to do what they would with materials, games, and so on. The result of this seemed to be greater freedom and autonomy for children, but less progress in terms of developing skills and understanding concepts. This may not be unique to Transition. For example, Stone (1996) argues that developmentalism, and its "most recent expressions . . . in developmentally appropriate practice and constructivism," discourages teachers and parents from "asserting themselves" or intervening with children. "Developmentalism gives rise to a disabling hesitancy and uncertainty about how or whether adults should attempt to influence children. It strongly suggests the possibility of harm, but it offers no clear guidance as to a safe and effective course of action" (para. 55).

We agree with Kostelnik (1993) that developmentally appropriate practice does not *necessarily* mean an unstructured program with minimal teacher guidance, nor does it *necessarily* mean low academic expectations for children. Kostelnik argues that the essence of developmental practice involves respecting each child as an individual and using all we know about "how children develop and learn" in planning "content and strategies" for them in early childhood programs. Calling the idea that "academics have no place in a developmentally appropriate program" a "myth," she asserts that developmentally oriented teachers should play an active role both in planning and in working directly with children in the classroom in an effort to *accomplish particular learning goals*. However, the nature of the planning and teaching is informed by teachers' knowledge of how children learn and grow. In Kostelnik's notion of a developmental perspective, children do not learn "less," they learn "better" as a result of receiving a "solid foundation of academics within a context of meaningful activity."

This line of thinking is not new. Dewey (1958) emphasized the importance of parents and teachers taking account of the developmental needs of children, but also playing an active role in structuring a way of satisfying those needs.

> Let me illustrate from the case of an infant. The needs of a baby for food, rest, and activity are certainly primary and decisive in one

respect. Nourishment must be provided; provision must be made for comfortable sleep, and so on. But these facts do not mean that a parent shall feed the baby at any time when the baby is cross or irritable, that there shall not be a program or regular hours of feeding and sleeping, etc. The wise mother takes account of the needs of the infant but not in a way which dispenses with her own responsibility for regulating the objective conditions under which the needs are satisfied (37–38).

Dewey did not believe that such regulation was an infringement of the baby's freedom. Along the same lines, while acknowledging that "traditional education tended to ignore the importance of personal impulse and desire," Dewey was critical of teachers who hesitated to actively guide their students' learning.

Guidance given by the teacher to the exercise of the pupils' intelligence is an aid to freedom, not a restriction upon it. Sometimes teachers seem to be afraid even to make suggestions to the members of a group as to what they should do. I have heard of cases in which children are surrounded with objects and materials and then left entirely to themselves, the teacher being loath to suggest even what might be done with the materials lest freedom be infringed upon. Why then even supply the materials, since they are a source of some suggestion or other (84)?

Whereas Dewey acknowledged the harm done by teachers who "abused their offices" by dictating to children, he criticized progressive educators for failing to recognize the importance of the teacher playing an active role, especially in terms of selecting and organizing subject matter. He did not advocate a single course of study for all progressive schools; however, he felt that progressive educators had neglected to attend to the importance of the "orderly development toward expansion and organization of subject matter."

[U]p to the present time, the weakest point in progressive schools is in the matter of selection and organization of intellectual subject matter. . . . [T]he basic material of study cannot be picked up in a cursory manner. Occasions which are not and cannot be foreseen are bound to arise wherever there is intellectual freedom. They should be utilized. But there is a decided difference between using them in the development of a continuing line of activity and trusting to them to provide the chief material of learning (95).

Of course Dewey strenuously objected to the way traditional educators "ladled" out "doses" of previously organized knowledge. However, as the excerpts above illustrate, his experiences with progressive schools and teachers led him to advise educators, even those committed to a progressive or developmental perspective, to keep in mind the intellectual and academic goals of schooling. "When education is based in theory and practice upon experience, it goes without saying that the organized subject-matter of the adult and the specialist cannot provide the starting point. Nevertheless, it represents the goal toward which education should continuously move (103)."

Clearly Dewey, and more recent scholars such as Kostelnik, advocated teaching that is informed by knowledge of children as well as a knowledge of subject matter and how to organize and introduce it in ways that are meaningful to children in the present, but also will move them toward more extensive knowledge and understanding of the subject matter. The Transition teachers, however, understood developmentally oriented teaching in a way that downplayed the importance of traditional subject matter, focusing instead on spontaneous learning, which would emerge as children interacted freely with each other and with stimulating materials. While Anna undoubtedly agreed with Dewey and other developmentalists cited here, and while she clearly believed that teachers and parents should facilitate children's learning, what she stressed most in this facilitation was creating an environment with opportunities for children to explore freely in order to create their own knowledge. Accordingly, Transition teachers who talked with us about how the program affected their thinking and practice explained it in terms of giving young children more freedom and providing a less rigid classroom structure generally, rather than in terms of accomplishing any particular subject matter or learning goals for children.

This is consistent with Stone's (1996) argument that, despite what Dewey and others might have said or written, in practice, developmentally oriented teachers may be inclined, even encouraged, to play a relatively inactive role, to do little more than arrange the learning environment in a way that is conducive to optimal development which should occur almost naturally. "From a developmentalist perspective, if opportunity and conditions conducive to developmental advancement have been maximized, the developmentally guided teacher or parent has done all that can safely be done" (para. 59). Stone asserts that developmentalism encourages teachers and parents to lower their expectations of student achievement. "Given that developmentally appropriate teaching and parenting is intended to fit current developmental status and given that efforts to exhort or otherwise induce advancement beyond the child's developmentally governed potentialities are considered risky at best, teachers and parents are given to understand that expecting too little is a much better choice than expecting too much" (para. 59).

Whereas Transition staff development messages paralleled Kostelnik's concern with respecting each child as an individual, they did not stress the teacher's role in guiding children toward *specific learning goals*. By de-emphasizing "how-tos," or specific ideas about applying a developmentalist, constructivist approach in their classrooms, the program may have unintentionally encouraged teachers to lower their academic expectations.

What about the low-income children the Transition project is designed to benefit? Despite the sincere good intentions of project designers and staff, it seems that the children may be losing something in this situation. Current social circumstances in the United States are characterized by an unprecedented emphasis on standardized testing as a means of assessing one's knowledge and abilities, even in the early elementary school years. In this context, it may be unwise to advocate for developmental, constructivist education for low-income children who often have limited means of gaining access to the dominant cultural knowledge that comprises standardized tests.

We agree with Apple (1982) and Cornbleth (1990) that knowledge is not value-free, nor is it distributed equally. Higher SES individuals receive more high-status knowledge than those from lower SES. Along the same lines, Delpit (1993) opposes the de-emphasis of basic skills in the orientation of "white liberals who advocate a child-centered approach" to teaching literacy. According to Delpit, members of minority cultures want their children to learn the "discourse patterns, interactional styles, and spoken and written language codes of the dominant culture so they can succeed" (285). Without this knowledge, the children will be forever handicapped despite the good intentions of "white liberals attempting to be nice to minority students."

Kozol (1972) articulated a similar position in his critique of free schools that downplayed the importance of math, English, and other traditional subject matter in the schooling of poor, urban young people. He contrasted privileged youth, with financial and social supports as protection, who could afford not to comply with alienating expectations of schools and society, with poor children who did not have this luxury. In order to survive, poor children had to adapt, to a certain degree, to the "present conditions of the system." Then, as now, standardized achievement testing was an important aspect of those alienating expectations and conditions. "To show a poor . . . kid . . . how to make end runs around the white man's college-entrance scores— while never believing that those scores are more than evil digits written on the sky—to do this, in my scale of values, is the starting point of an authentic revolution" (53).

However, is it fair to subject low-income children to the "drill and skill" rote learning of basic skills associated with teaching to standardized tests? This is the kind of instruction low-income children have received in low-tracked groups and classes in traditional programs— a form of what Freire (1973) called "banking education," where teachers make deposits of information into their passively receptive student-banks. We agree with him that low-income children may be losers in this scenario as well. Like Anna, we believe that knowledge is socially constructed and that the learner must be the *starting point* of effective teaching. However, we would urge educators, perhaps especially those working with low-income students, also to stay focused on the *intellectual and academic goals* of education; to remember Dewey's comments about organized subject matter as the "goal toward which education should continuously move."

We are not claiming in this discussion to have explained the low achievement-test scores that provoked and concerned us. We continue to believe that a variety of factors, programmatic and otherwise, contributed to these outcomes. Rather, we have drawn upon our ethnographic data to explore the possible dissonance between the unparalleled expansion of standardized testing and the growing movement in early childhood education toward a developmental, constructivist approach to teaching and learning for all children. We believe this issue merits serious consideration by Head Start and other programs that attempt to increase life opportunities of low-income children.

NOTES

1. The staff development consultant's name has been changed to protect her privacy.

2. The series of messages is our own construction. Anna did not develop this list of messages, nor were they ever presented in this fashion to teachers. We developed the list as a result of combing through pages and pages of field notes and transcripts. We showed our first draft of the messages to Anna and modified it in response to her suggestions.

3. Whereas the messages to teachers are highlighted here, Anna maintained that parents were critical of this facilitation process.

REFERENCES

Apple, M. (1982). *Education and power.* Boston: Routledge & Kegan Paul.

Bickel, R. (1989). Opportunity and high school completion. *Urban Review,* Vol. 21, 251–261.

Bickel, R., Banks, S., and Spatig, L. (1991). Bridging the gap between high school and college in an Appalachian state: A near-replication of Florida research. *Journal of Research in Rural Education,* Vol. 7, No. 2, 75–87.

Bickel, R., McDonough, M., and Maynard, S. (1996). No effects to fade: Head Start in two West Virginia counties. Huntington, WV: College of Education and Human Services, Unpublished.

Cornbleth, C. (1990). *Curriculum in context.* New York: Falmer.

Currie, J., and Thomas, D. (1995). Does Head Start make a difference? *The American Economic Review,* Vol. 85: 341–361.

Delpit, L. (1988). The silenced dialogue: Power and pedagogy in educating other people's children. *Harvard Educational Review,* Vol. 58, 280–298.

Dewey, J. (1958). *Experience and education.* New York: Collier Books.

DeYoung, A. (1988). Dropout issues and problems in rural America with a case study of one central Appalachian school district. Unpublished paper, Lexington: University of Kentucky.

Freire, P. (1973). *Pedagogy of the oppressed.* New York: Continuum.

Hannah, K. (1995). *West Virginia women in perspective 1980–1995.* Charleston: West Virginia Women's Commission.

Kamii, C. (1990). *Achievement testing in the early grades: The games grown-ups play.* Washington, D.C.: National Association for the Education of Young Children.

Katz, L. (1994). Child development knowledge and teacher preparation: Confronting assumptions. Paper presented at the Annual Conference of the Midwest Association for the Education of Young Children, Peoria, IL.

Kessler, S. (1991). Early childhood education as development: Critique of the metaphor. *Early Education and Development,* Vol. 2, No. 2, 137–152.

Kostelnik, M. (1993). Developmentally appropriate programs. *ERIC Digest.* Washington, D.C.: ERIC Clearinghouse Products.

Kozol, J. (1972). *Free schools.* New York: Houghton Mifflin.

Parrott, L., Spatig, L., Dillon, A., Conrad, K., and Campbell, B. (1993). The value of teacher reflection in enhancing developmentally appropriate practices: An early childhood case study. Presentation at the 2nd National Head Start Research Conference, Washington, D.C.

Stone, J. (1996). Developmentalism: An obscure but pervasive restriction on educational improvement. *Education Policy Analysis Archives*, Vol. 4, No. 8. [On-line]. Available epaa:internet.

12

A Bumpy Transition from Head Start to Public School: Issues of Philosophical and Managerial Continuity within the Administrative Structure of One School System

Stacey Neuharth-Pritchett and
Panayota Y. Mantzicopoulos

The renewed interest in the efficacy of publicly supported early childhood intervention has highlighted the need to focus on the processes that promote children's successful transition to public school. While findings from small, nongovernment, early education model programs suggest that early intervention has lasting effects for children (Barnett 1993; Berrueta-Clement et al. 1985; Lazar et al. 1982), the data from publicly funded early intervention efforts demonstrate less promising results (McKey et al. 1985).

Specifically, studies on the impact of Head Start indicate that children experience immediate cognitive gains that begin to decline one year after Head Start (McKey et al. 1985). This steady fade-out of gains has been attributed to the lack of continuity in the programmatic and philosophical orientation between agencies that deliver the Head Start program and the traditional public school systems (Zigler and Styfco 1994).

The impact and magnitude of programmatic discontinuity has not been documented empirically in the Head Start literature. Moreover, much of the evidence on publicly funded programs, designed to address the transition to school (i.e., Project Follow-Through), has been less promising, methodologically weak, and difficult to interpret (House et al. 1978). Inadequate documentation of the underlying school context factors affecting the conditions of program implementation was one of the many errors identified in that research. This drawback also has plagued the Head Start efficacy literature and has made it impossible to ascertain why some programs are more efficacious than others.

With respect to Project Head Start, the absence of systematic data on how public school contexts sustained the effects of early intervention efforts is particulary hard to justify because the project claimed neither philosophical nor programmatic compatibility with public school systems. In fact, as Woodhead (1988, 451) noted, "bypassing practices common in the public school system was viewed [by the originators of Head Start] as an important first step in helping the disadvantaged child."

Few would debate that continuity plays a critical role in the growth and maintenance of developmental outcomes. As it applies to the early schooling process, the relevance of continuity may be gleaned from research on (a) children's transition to school (Love et al. 1992); (b) early intervention models with a follow-on school component (e.g., Reynolds 1994); and (c) the quality of public schools attended by former Head Start children (e.g., Lee and Loeb 1995). This small body of work supports the inference that programmatic continuity has positive effects on children's achievement and school adjustment (Reynolds 1994). In addition, it suggests that economically disadvantaged children in the public schools are more likely to experience discontinuities and to encounter less positive staff attitudes than do children from higher socioeconomic backgrounds (Love et al. 1992). That public school factors introduce discontinuities that interfere with the sustenance of gains made by children during the Head Start year has been asserted recently by Lee and Loeb (1995). These investigators examined school-level variables and concluded that former Head Start children were much more likely to end up in public schools of low quality "where achievement levels are lower and the climate is not academically stimulating, where poverty is concentrated; in schools that are unsafe and that are characterized by less harmonious relations between staff and students" (Lee and Loeb 1995, 73–74).

Preliminary data from our longitudinal study on Head Start children's transition to public school (Mantzicopoulos and Neuharth-

Pritchett 1995) offer a related perspective on issues of programmatic discontinuity. However, unlike Lee and Loeb (1995), who examined global indices of school climate and quality at the middle school, we were interested in providing a micro-level view of the administrative and ideological workings behind a Head Start/Public School Transition Intervention project. We undertook this task in the context of a larger research effort intended not only to focus on outcomes but also to recognize and document the underlying complexities of program implementation efforts. We believe that the data from the analyses of in-depth interviews reported in this chapter provide valuable information, especially in light of policy analysts' powerful claim "that the consequences of even the best planned, best supported, and most promising policy initiatives depend finally on what happens as individuals throughout the policy system interpret and act on them" (McLaughlin 1987, 172).

Specifically, this study was guided by the notion that individuals' beliefs and interpretations are fundamental components that underlie program implementation efforts. Consistent with this framework, we examined the perceptions of administrative personnel in a school system funded to implement a comprehensive Head Start/Public School Transition intervention. We expected that issues of continuity would be particularly salient because (a) the Head Start program was housed in and operated by the public school system and (b) the transition intervention was implemented through a period of administrative change in the school system. Within this dynamic, evolving context we explored how groups of administrators, who assumed responsibility for implementing the intervention at different stages, (a) viewed the philosophical roots of the program and the goals guiding program implementation and (b) described the administrative structures and policies that supported the day-to-day operation of the intervention.

METHODOLOGY

Context/Environment

This study was conducted in a midwestern school system housing twelve elementary schools. In 1990, the school system, in response to meeting the needs of the rising numbers of economically disadvantaged students, received funding to operate a Head Start program. In 1991, the interest to support the connection between the Head Start program and the elementary schools within the system led to a successful application for a Head Start/Public School Transition Demonstration Project.[1]

In the fall of 1991, Head Start Transition personnel worked in tandem to develop programs in three randomly selected transition demonstration elementary schools. Because Head Start contracts are usually granted to community agencies rather than to school systems, this school-based Head Start site had the unusual opportunity to establish smooth and continuous experiences for children and their families as they moved from Head Start into their kindergarten year and the early elementary grades.

While the Head Start program and the Transition program were under the same leadership from 1991 to 1994, three separate upper-level administrations served the school community since 1991. Citing radical change in the school system and a differing philosophy regarding the education of economically disadvantaged young children, the director of the local Transition project resigned her position in August of 1994. A new project director was hired at that time and was charged with coordinating the components of the Transition program. One year later, as a result of a new policy to centralize the school system's social service department, the Transition social service component was placed under the direction of a central office administrator.

Participants

Interview data were gathered from both public school and Transition program administrations who had direct responsibilities either in the formation of the program or in its administration during some part of the program's tenure. Data collected during the spring of 1994 (pilot test) and 1995 provided preliminary evidence that highlighted the need for assessing the perceptions of upper-level administrators. In the spring of 1996, the authors completed a third round of interviews that solicited information from all of the program and public school administrators who were involved with the Transition project. Because data collected during the spring of 1995 contained valuable insights for a more thorough understanding of the implementation of the project, we chose to include in our analyses all interview data collected from administrators during 1995 and 1996. Overall, participants are categorized into three distinct subgroups: (a) school district administrators; (b) building-level administrators; and (c) transition program administrators/coordinators.

School District Administrators

Interviews were conducted with top school district administrators who were ultimately responsible for the successful implementation of the Transition program in the school district. Seven individuals comprised this group. The social service director was interviewed over two years because, in addition to her responsibilities with the school district, she also was responsible for the social service component of the Transition program during the 1995 data collection period. In an effort to centralize school services and avoid service duplication, the social service director had direct supervision duties for frontline Transition social service providers. Other members of this group included the school superintendent, the assistant superintendent, two former assistant superintendents, the staff development director, and the elementary curriculum director.

Building-Level Administrators

Three principals were interviewed about their views of the Transition program. All three principals had held their respective positions prior to the program's implementation. Their experience as principal ranged from twenty-three to thirty-four years. Each of these participants was interviewed both in the spring of 1995 and the spring of 1996. One assistant principal also was interviewed in 1996 as he had assumed direct line responsibilities in 1995 for the Transition program in his building.

Transition Program Administrators/Coordinators

Over the course of the Transition program's implementation, a number of different individuals had facilitated the delivery of the program. The program structure was designed with an overall director facilitating interactions between Transition program coordinators (e.g., parent involvement, social services) and the school's central administration. Data from the parent involvement coordinator and the social service coordinator were analyzed for this report. Specifically interviewed were the current project director, former project director, the Head Start director, two former parent involvement coordinators, and the former social services coordinator.

A Scheme for Viewing Project Participants' Orientations

The sections above provided a general description of the traditional roles of the participants in this investigation. However, to orient the reader to the temporal and ideological framework of our data, we provide a classification of the participants based on analyses reported in the "Results" section. As table 12.1 shows, the first group of administrators, who initially conceptualized and directed the program, included individuals who reported beliefs and practices consistent with the Head Start orientation. Members of this group viewed Transition as a process that would enhance the continuity of experiences for children and families as they made the transition to the public school. An enabling approach to management was described as most appropriate for facilitating this group's mission.

Over the course of the program's tenure, significant changes in the school system's central administration resulted in personnel and philosophical changes to the Transition program. Three years into the project, personnel new to the school system and the Transition project, staffed the supervisory positions. The initial group of Transition program administrators either left their positions or were replaced. At that time, the Transition project, characterized by the new administration as an entity of its own within the school system, was directed to align itself with the new school system administrative policies. The new group of school administrators was comprised of members who saw the ultimate goal of all intervention programs in the school system to be that of academic achievement. Focus was not placed on the translation of Head Start philosophies and practices but rather on how well the Transition project fit with and facilitated the new "school system" philosophy. The leadership style of this group of administrators was described as hierarchical.

Nestled between the previous two groups of administrators were a few administrators who had been involved with the program from its inception. Wavering in commitment to either of the two previous groups, this group of individuals saw situational merit in both the earlier and the new administrations' orientations. The members of this group were building-level principals. Their approach to management was that of merely facilitating the program within their respective buildings.

Interview Protocol Design

An interview protocol was developed with both open- and close-ended questions beginning with the 1992 through 1993 pilot data collection. Data analyzed from this pilot investigation were utilized to refine or augment questions for interview participants. A revised protocol was

TABLE 12.1
Classification of Administrators on Philosophy, Instruction,
and Management Dimensions

	Initial Group	Intermediary	Final Group
Philosophy	Head Start Orientation	Direct Service Model	Academic Orientation
Instructional Beliefs	Developmentally Appropriate Practices	Developmentally Appropriate Practices and Traditional Approaches	Drill and Practice
Management Style	Enabling	Situationally Dependent	Hierarchical

pilot tested in 1994, and a final version was developed in 1995. Each of the participant groups was asked a core set of questions that centered around the following seven themes: (a) overall perceptions of the Transition process (i.e., philosophy, approach, and program goals); (b) strengths of the Transition process; (c) obstacles and barriers to program implementation; (d) communication issues; (e) training issues; (f) curriculum and classroom management issues; and (g) implementation of Transition practices. Additional questions were added for the auxiliary staff coordinators to solicit specific information about the services offered in each area (e.g., parent involvement, social services). The interview format also encouraged the respondents to provide, whenever possible, specific examples that reflected their views and experiences.

Procedures and Analyses

All interviews were conducted in the offices of the respondents by personnel trained in qualitative interviewing practices. Interviews were audio taped for later transcription, coding, and analysis. Extensive field notes were taken for three individuals who did not give consent for audio taping. A completed transcription, compiled from field notes, was then sent to each of these participants for verification. During the analysis stage, interview transcripts were coded for the major themes presented in this chapter: (a) beliefs of the underlying philosophy of the program; and (b) beliefs concerning appropriate management or administrative styles.

Consistent with the work of Erickson (1986), transcripts were inductively coded for the major themes presented in the paragraph above. Concurrently, we searched for discrepant cases. Two separate coders were employed to verify the existence of an assertion in the data. Every effort was made to protect the anonymity of the participants. Specific statements from transcripts were selected to provide support for assertions made in this paper. Characteristic examples from these data are also provided to allow the reader to examine the evidentiary value of the assertions (Erickson 1986).

RESULTS

Philosophical Principles Guiding Program Implementation: Overview

In analyzing each interview protocol we discovered that the respondents' implicit assumptions about the philosophical underpinnings and goals of the Transition program formed themes that were embedded in much of the discussion on most aspects of the program. Information about the program's vision and principles was obtained from responses to questions asking the participants to reflect directly on the philosophy and goals of the program as well as from responses to all other topics addressed throughout the interview.

A holistic examination of the transcripts suggested the presence of three global philosophical orientations about the mission and goals of the Transition program. These orientations, supported by representative quotes, are outlined in Table 12.2.

One group of responses emphasized the program's alliance with the Head Start principles. From this perspective, the program was viewed as an extension of the Head Start philosophical orientation in the public schools. A second group of responses referenced the provision of services as the major impetus behind efforts directed at helping at-risk children and families succeed in school. This set of responses acknowledged neither the specific principles underlying the rationale for services nor the interconnectedness of the services provided.

A third set of responses identified academic achievement as the ultimate objective of all project activities. Represented in most of these responses was the notion that the provision of services would free disadvantaged children from the multiple problems that interfered with their academic progress. Only two respondents within this

TABLE 12.2

Representative Quotes on the Philosophical Principles Underlying the Transition Program

	Head Start Model	Direct Service Model	Academic Model
Overall Program Philosophy	*Ecological Emphasis* One [goal] would be the child and maintaining their academic and social and emotional growth through those early years. Another would be the involvement of the parent and the child's education and a growing awareness of the roles that the parents play in the lives of their children. And then, I suppose the family as a whole I see as the main focus because you cannot deal with children in an isolated way. To be really effective, you have to involve the entire family. *Extending the HS Philosophy to Enhance Programmatic Continuity* Those were the major goals, to create a whole, one of the reasons we called it "Bridges" was because we felt like we were bridging a lot of gaps in our [school] program and in the home program, and certainly bridging from Head Start into a regular schooling program at some time. We kind of looked at that as an all-inclusive thing. There was a lot of coordination, linking, connections to Head Start. Head Start never lost that connection; trying to keep those Head Start philosophies . . . I do the best I can to relay those values and try to train new staff, my staff in particular, about Head Start philosophies and looking at everything, every component, not just social services or not just education.	*Goal is Direct Service Provision but Underlying Philosophy is Not Clear* The Transition process in our school gives adult supervision to children who may be at risk. So we have a lot of adults other than just their teachers working with those kids to see them through the school year. And we have a full time nurse/nutritionist, a parent involvement coordinator, a two social workers, social providers. And they provide the extra support needed for various families, so children are more successful educationally. Having the extra adult manpower here . . . Full-time nurse is wonderful. The social workers are able to deal with student problems, the extra baggage they bring to school every day and help them concentrate more on their studies by alleviating some of the other pressures of the day. This frees up the teacher so the teacher can do more teaching. Right now everybody is uncertain about where things are headed. . . . We don't know what kind of direction we are going with what. . . . The staff is barely keeping up, and sometimes it's like drowning.	*Lack of Clarity on Program Goals Necessitates a Refocusing Effort on Academics* I don't think that school staff really understood the program. . . . I don't think they understood what the goals were. . . . One of the things I believed happened, we got into the program without articulating to anyone what it was about. I think the philosophy varies from building to building. . . . We have been asking some serious questions for two years, and this year we really tried to get back to understand that it's the academic achievement that is supposed to be our focus. I am sure that is real well defined in some people's minds. The final result of education has to be academic skill development. The philosophy itself is to help kids in terms of the academic focus by using support people from the standpoint of parent involvement and the five different "hubs" as we call it to support the teacher in the classroom . . . our whole emphasis . . . we took it as a big wheel and the teacher was the hub and out of this was the spokes and that was our support people . . . so it was developed from our teacher hub.

TABLE 12.2 (continued)

	Head Start Model	Direct Service Model	Academic Model
Approach to Services	*Service Linkages/Integration* Because [parent involvement and social service staff] work together so much of the time. Really we have collaborated that way where we are in tune to each other.	*Hierarchical Approach with No Acknowledgment Service Integration* What I have seen is that you dive in and here's the top person and here's the person under that and here's how it goes and who's under . . . . It would be nice to see [how the components fit together], because my feeling is that we need to overlap in some way. We have job descriptions for each area. Maybe that is what you are looking at as a model. "Here is what you are expected to do; here is what you are expected to accomplish; here might be some ways that you can do it."	*The Focus of Services Should be in Support of Academic Achievement* The regular program, the transition program, the hot lunch program—all of those have to be focused together, but the overriding issue has to be that the major function that the school can accomplish, that no one else is charged with, is the academic development of the child. We can have parents involved, we can do a lot of things, but if we cannot improve academic achievement so that students can function better then we are probably not achieving much success.

TABLE 12.2 (continued)

	Head Start Model	Direct Service Model	Academic Model
Parent Involvement	*Family Empowerment through a Family-Focused Approach* What we tried to encourage is that you take the parent where they are and work with them. . . . so you just got to take her where she is and just keep encouraging her. So parent involvement can be so much. . . . It's really exciting to see them grow and take new avenues. Another goal was certainly to get more parent involvement, and that of course is a part of Head Start and was certainly part of what we wrote into that grant. Parent involvement not in terms of so much of being in the school, although that was a part too, but more in terms of helping them grow as parents . . . acting as an advocate for them. I feel the best way is to go into their homes and to work on their turf. I think we probably still don't realize how much we talk differently and walk differently. . . . And we still create an aura of suspicion and looking down at and not accepting wholly when they walk onto our turf. But when we walk onto their turf, we tend to be more like them, and that is the thing that I found to be so much more successful.	*Parent Involvement = Parent Presence* I have mixed emotions when we start getting this push, you know, right now there is a big push to let these parents in here. Sometimes we are coming across as a bit pushy. Parent involvement—get parents in for "meet the teacher night," get them [parent involvement workers] in the home demonstration learning games, [and] . . . tell families of the services so they feel a strong support there. *Parents Need Modeling Experiences from Experts:* But if you approach the parents from an academic way: "We're promoting reading at home, and this is a puppet that we'd like to share with your family, we'd like you to read this book to your other children maybe at home. It might really model to the parents a way of reading aloud because many of the parents probably weren't read to as children, so this might be a way of modeling to the parents how to read aloud to your children.	*Parent Involvement = Parent Presence* What we want to do is get the parent involved in the assistance of the classroom teacher where they can come in and help with bulletin boards where it allows the teacher and the academic assistant to spend more time on the academics. It is taking up the clerical time, for maybe running copies, those kinds of things. *Parents Need Direct Guidance about School Expectations* In terms of instructing the children from low income, there would have to be a baseline set up with the parents. We have to establish ourselves as a learning institution with that parent and as we start over, let them know that we are generally interested in working with them and their child. *Lack of Clarity on what Constitutes Parent Involvement* We were unclear on what we were supposed to do with parents. Teachers are mixed with it.

TABLE 12.2 (*continued*)

	Head Start Model	Direct Service Model	Academic Model
Instruction	*Emphasis on Child-Centered Practices (DAP)*	*Both Child-Centered and Teacher-Directed Instruction Are Appropriate*	*A Basic Skills Orientation*
	It is to move the teachers toward learning more about how to deal with children and families at risk, how to make their classrooms me child-centered, how to increase the amount of active, participatory learning in the class-room—more development appropriateness. That was really what it was. Also meeting individual learning styles and needs of the children.	All children benefit from traditional didactic instruction, but to what extent would depend on the child. DAP would probably play a role in children's academic achievement, but to what extent, I didn't know.	All children benefit from direct instruction, whereas no child benefits from DAP. DAP lowers academic achievement and gives children a false sense of success in the classroom.
		I don't know if DAP is better than didactic instruction. All kids learn in different ways. Some kids would be most comfortable in the traditional classrooms. Others are more comfortable in the DAP room. It probably takes a combination to get the best level of education out of kids.	All the research that I'm seeing with at-risk kics says that maybe the cooperative learning approach isn't working very well, that maybe some more intense basic instruction with a lot of writing is the best way to go. . . . The fact is, whether a kid knows his multiplication tables or not has everything to do with how well he does in math.
	We were looking at how [teachers] would learn more about developmentally appropriate curriculum and getting away from first graders doing dittos and kindergartners doing dittos to me of the developmentally appropriate curriculums. We did a lot with High scope because we felt that curriculum did indeed address those issues and we brought some people in from the Wright Group because their whole thematic use for things and their use of language as a foundation for all kinds of learning.	*Inconsistency between Transition Program Expectations and School System Mandates* There is little time for training teachers with a philosophy that is consistent with the grant, not an imposition of the school system's philosophy. The administration misinterprets DAP. I think that the teachers agree with the interdisciplinary approach or the integrated language approach. I think they disagree with the testing. So those things are inconsistent with what teachers have to do in the school system.	As we have looked at all students, we feel that there is a certain structure that is needed in the school setting. The school system's evaluation of children's achievement impacts children's instructional approaches. Teachers understand what proficiencies are required and conduct activities appropriately. There is validity in that kind of [standardized] assessment.

TABLE 12.2 (continued)

	Head Start Model	Direct Service Model	Academic Model
Does the Transition Program Fit within the School System?	*Transition and School System Goals Are Incompatible* Well, I thought it fit well there at one time. I really don't know that it fits in now. The original administration that supported the grant saw and approved the direction of [the] grant [this administration does not]. It was supposed to be so that everyone is under the same umbrella, but I think that school system policies and procedures are being implemented more than the philosophies of the Head Start Transition project. With the Head Start philosophies in mind, I don't see the program driven very much in that direction at all. I don't see it community networked or based. I don't see social service providers being in the picture at all. There will not be that person that is the link between home and school and community, unless it is the counselor. Basically that is behavior counseling in the building. I don't know what the parent involvement components will be like. To make school family friendly, and I don't see it going in that direction right now. I think they [the new administration] see parent involvement as the educated parent with degrees.	*Transition and the School System Are Complementary* Well, this revolves around the same theory. That with the extra people and the extra adults here to service children with needs who are having problems the teacher has more time to focus on other things. They [services] are working together fine. The [Transition] people are well accepted here. I don't think they are working at odds against each other. I think our teachers in any school system here will tell you "You can no longer teach." Kids come with so many problems that they have to have the resources to help them. How it fits in is that we try to provide that link to them (the teachers). I don't know that there has been a conflict. I think it (the program) has been accepted. Whether it was accepted graciously or not I don't really know. I can only speak for this school. That staff here has really accepted the transition program to help kids. We are going to try to do everything we can to try to help kids while the program is here. I don't know how it's taken in other buildings. The view of the [school system] is to provide children with a well rounded education. The goals for the Transition program should fall under or be included in that umbrella. The goals for Transition should be no different than that of [the school system]: To provide children with a well-rounded education.	*Aspects of Transition's Service Components May Be Compatible with the Goals of the School System* If there is not an academic growth component it doesn't and it won't [fit with our programs]. We look to expand social services, but we are looking pretty hard at this and saying, "Is it going to make a difference, or isn't it?" The business we are in, in public education, is clearly defined as that of educating students and helping students achieve. If we provide all these programs and there is no academic advantage, then I think we have missed a great opportunity and something has to change about it. The service component fits [with the school system's philosophy]. We have some real concerns over the academic component. DAP is not consistent [with our goals]. Yes it fits with our plan. We have proposed as part of the program to provide, for example, additional social service providers, persons to do that. We have talked about providing additional health services through nurses. That all fits in with, although not to the extent that transition provides this kind of services. The school system did not fully adopt some of the philosophies that were simply presented to transition workshops without the school system adopting them and espousing that particular philosophy. It fits to a tee. There are a lot of things being planned as support areas [in the school system]. Some of the things we are doing right now. I would think it fits in very well. I would think our philosophy is to bring all of our students to greatest potential.

category voiced a perspective that elaborated on the value of linkages across the program components. Much like the first group of respondents, these two participants stressed the need for a conceptual model that would serve as the guiding principle for the Transition program. However, unlike the first group (who used Head Start as their frame of reference), these two respondents' conceptualizations focused on the school system as the starting point.

Head Start Philosophy as the Guiding Principle

The responses of six individuals clearly indicated that the Head Start philosophy formed the foundation for the Transition program. All of these participants had been involved with the program from the beginning. However, none of the respondents had been part of the Transition intervention staff in the 1995 through 1996 academic year. Two of the six respondents had retained their involvement with the Head Start program, while the remaining four had resigned their administrative positions.

The analysis of these six transcripts indicated much consistency in the views expressed both across participants and within each individual protocol. Asked about the program's philosophical orientation, the respondents stated that Transition was conceptualized as an extension of the Head Start model in the public schools. Comments suggested that these participants shared an ecological view of development. Specifically, responses in this area stressed that the child should not be viewed in isolation from his or her family and recognized that a major program goal was the development and maintenance of links between families, schools, and communities. Other characteristic remarks highlighted the importance of promoting programmatic and philosophical continuity beginning at Head Start and continuing through the public school. Additional statements emphasized the need for interrelationships across program components whose ultimate goal was to enhance child and family development during the school years. The respondents also commented on the importance of developing an appreciation of and sensitivity to the diverse perspectives of the families being served by the program. Frequently stated were the goals of family development and empowerment. It was thought that these goals would be best facilitated by approaching families from "their turf." Furthermore, parent involvement was seen as multidimensional. It was often defined as including (a) parent presence in the schools; (b) a greater awareness of family goals; (c) an effective integration of families within the community; and (d) mechanisms through which families would be increasingly "tuned-in" to the school culture.

Four of the six respondents had direct involvement with the educational component of the program and commented extensively on the application of developmentally appropriate instructional practice (DAP) through the early school grades and on the importance of educational continuity. The comments suggested a strong belief in the value of DAP for the education of young children. Also conveyed was a sense of excitement and appreciation for the opportunity, provided by the grant, to promote staff development in the early grades. Intense teacher training through direct involvement in the classroom, group seminars for teachers, and meetings with Transition teachers were planned. These activities were in support of efforts to move away from teacher-centered instruction by emphasizing classroom practices that were sensitive to children's individual interests and unique needs. The use of meaningful materials, integration of curriculum through thematic instruction, and cooperative learning techniques were endorsed by this group of respondents.

Asked about the match of the Transition program and the public school system, five of the six respondents expressed significant concerns about the extent to which the transition program "fit" within the new administrative structure and its goals. Committed to the Head Start philosophy, these individuals questioned whether Transition, within the new administrative framework, would serve as the medium that would boost the school system's sensitivity and responsiveness to the diverse needs of children.

Transition as a Direct Service Model

Included in this group of respondents were six individuals: three principals and three program administrators who joined the staff immediately after the appointment of the new school system administration. Their responses described the Transition program's philosophy in terms of the delivery of extra services in the public schools. Although there was no clear articulation of the interconnectedness of the components, there was recognition that the services alleviated much of the tension that was previously placed on teachers and principals. Moreover, the services were thought to be helpful in "fixing" many of the problems that children brought to school and that interfered with school learning. Absent from these transcripts was a clear set of principles underlying the service provision. For example, although there was some recognition that the social service personnel served as supportive adults for parents, the transcript analysis indicated that five of the participants did not communicate a clear view of how these personnel approached family development. One of the participants, however, noted that the approach to social services had "a child focus" and later in the same transcript, the model of family development was defined as having a "family systems" focus.

Additional comments acknowledged that a program function was to help parents understand and work within the school system's expectations. However, the comments conveyed a focus on being directive rather than facilitative. Specifically, the protocol analysis suggested that the respondents viewed family, child, and teacher development from a school-system perspective. Concurrently, the goal of "meeting the needs of the whole child," referenced in two of the transcripts, was not internally consistent with other comments also made, within the same transcripts, about the program's guiding principles.

Parent involvement was thought to be an important program goal, but it was frequently defined as parental presence in the schools. Furthermore, the transcripts revealed a theme of promoting family involvement by instituting activities thought, by the program (not the families), as appropriate for enhancing family literacy and development. These protocols, as a group, reflected little awareness of the family's perspective or dynamics and conveyed a view of parents as ineffective individuals who needed guidance mostly in the form of direct modeling experiences.

A number of comments made by the six respondents indicated that little integration occurred across the transition program components. Specific statements in three of the six protocols clearly suggested that there was little to no communication or interaction between the social service, parent involvement, and health/nutrition components. One respondent in particular expressed strong concern over the lack of service integration and the narrowly defined roles of social service and parent involvement personnel. Moreover, that individual expressed discomfort over the new mandate of "pushing" parents to be present in various school functions without regard for their special circumstances or needs.

Four of the six respondents made extensive comments on instruction without, however, making reference to the importance of instructional continuity though the elementary school years. All four were aware of the transition program's emphasis on developmental appropriateness and stated that a strength of the approach was its emphasis on active learning with meaningful materials. Although DAP was cast in a positive light, the comments revealed no real sense of commitment to this practice. When asked to reflect on the merits of traditional didactic instruction vis-à-vis a child-centered, DAP approach, three respondents voiced no particular commitment to either approach. Rather, each approach was viewed as having merits for children. However, the fourth respondent gave a more comprehensive view that placed into perspective many of the incidental comments of the other three participants. Specifically, that individual attributed the program's inability to move to full DAP implementation within the school system to (a) the lack of support for the practice from the school system's central administration; (b) insufficient time for training; and (c) teachers' skepticism about the effects of child-centered practices on standardized achievement test results. All four respondents stated that teacher training had decreased, compared to previous years. This was a direct result of a school system mandate to minimize loss of instructional time by keeping teachers in the classroom as much as possible. Transition teacher meetings across and within schools were also discontinued, and there were no efforts from the education coordinator to facilitate teacher development by working with individual teachers within their classrooms. All four interviewees noted that the education coordinator primarily provided materials and scheduled inservice workshops.

Asked about the Transition program's fit within the school system, five of the six respondents viewed the program as fitting very well within the school system's orientation. One respondent's comments were less specific and described the atmosphere within the school system as negative toward the program: "I think it's just a general feeling that whatever there has been hasn't worked the way they wanted to see it work, so that one half is cold and the other half is just . . . they haven't really come out and said what we're going to do."

The Program Must Enhance the School's Academic Function

Five participants reflected on the program's philosophy and goals by commenting on the extent to which they enhanced the school's main function of promoting academic achievement. These respondents were school-system administrators who had been involved with the operation of the project for the last two years. Their responses clearly stated that the Transition program's philosophy was neither well defined nor well understood in the school system. This lack of understanding, coupled with a perceived lack of academic gains for Transition program children, led to a need to reconsider the goals of the program within the school system's structure. It was believed that successful implementation would result only if the program's tenets were reconceptualized within the school system's ultimate goal of enhancing academic achievement. Thus, the philosophical framework presented by these individuals was neither child nor family centered. Rather, it had a school-system focus that was fully geared toward enhancing academic achievement as measured by the state-mandated standardized achievement test. Within this focus, one respondent stated that the goals of the program were to provide enrichment experiences for those children who came from deprived backgrounds. Along these lines it was emphasized that, in the process of correcting the children's deficits, schools must safeguard against lowering their expectations. It was pointed out that lower expectations were often the result in the process of attempting to accommodate the needs of children from low-income backgrounds.

Two respondents presented a well-conceptualized and integrated system of service delivery that viewed the teacher as a central figure (a "hub") in a wheel. The interconnected services were represented as spokes in the wheel that supported the hub, thus creating a force that propelled the child on the road to achievement: "The wheel is turning, and the whole thing is coming down here to academic achievement . . . and that is how the wheel, through all of this, will move the child down the road . . . "

In discussing family involvement, the respondents commented on the importance of parents being made aware of the school system's expectations. However, only one participant addressed comprehensively the many functions of parent involvement and the school's efforts at getting the parents involved with literacy both at home and in the schools. Despite the recognition that the school must work at establishing positive bonds with families for program success, there was little acknowledgment of modifications needed in the school system to address the diverse needs of families.

The academic focus presented by these five interviewees permeated the discussion, and as a result a number of comments were made on instructional practice. Three respondents viewed DAP as a thoroughly ineffective instructional approach that was of little relevance and value to students, teachers, and the school system. These respondents emphasized that direct drill-and-practice approaches were most appropriate and most likely to enhance achievement outcomes. Moreover, standardized achievement testing was promoted as a reliable and necessary method for evaluating and improving instruction. Although it was recognized that standardized tests "drove" instruction in the school system, there was little concern or discomfort accompanying that realization.

A dissenting viewpoint was voiced by the fourth respondent, who stated that DAP (characterized as active, cooperative learning) had many merits and added that it was a practice particularly appropriate for educating children from low-income homes. In contrast to all other responses within this group, this respondent felt that traditional, didactic instruction had positive effects only for children who came from middle-class homes and already functioned well academically: "Needless to say, the ones who thrive in a traditional classroom environment would probably be the more higher academic and social." This individual and the fifth respondent de-emphasized the need for standardized achievement testing in the early grades and expressed concerns over an excessive reliance on test results to evaluate young children.

The responses of this group about the compatibility of the Transition program with the goals of the school system were mixed. Three individuals strongly argued that the educational approach promoted by the program was inconsistent with the school system's goals and direction. All respondents, however, noted that the service components (social service and parent involvement) were worth pursuing, as long as the evidence supported their positive effects on student achievement.

Management Styles

Three distinct perspectives emerged from the transcript data with regard to administrative style. One group of administrators identified themselves with an enabling approach to school management. Composed of all but one of the individuals who began the Transition program, this group administered the project until the end of the third year of implementation. The fourth and fifth years of the program were directed by a second set of administrators who adhered to a hierarchical orientation to management. Involved with the program from its beginning, a third group of administrators adhered neither to the tenets of the enabling nor to the hierarchical approach to management. Building principals comprised this group of participants who varied their management approaches to meet the expectations of either the enabling or the hierarchical administrators in particular situations.

Differences among participants' perceptions were evident in two major areas that included: (a) hierarchical versus enabling structure of control of the program; and (b) organizational membership. Data presented in the following sections reflect the perceptions of the change in administration and its overall impact on the program.

Hierarchical versus Enabling Structure of Control

Pervasive throughout the interview transcripts was the division of participants' views regarding the management of an early intervention program. Data from the enabling group suggested acknowledgment of the belief that school reform was a difficult and lengthy process best promoted by inclusion of key stakeholders. Administrative practices were based upon a supportive environment that facilitated roles and provided staff members with autonomy. Frequent comments described the program as a "bridge" for the gaps that existed between school and home, as well as between Head Start and the regular schooling program. As one participant stated: "There was a lot of coordination, communication, linking, connections to Head Start. Head Start never lost that connection, trying to keep those Head Start philosophies."

Communication as a means to articulate the goals of the program and maintain the philosophy of Head Start was of the utmost importance to these administrators. Lateral rather than vertical communications existed between people of different ranks and promoted sharing information and advice as opposed to instructions or decisions. Consultation was the preferred communication model as a means to facilitate the collaboration and coordination of the components perceived as necessary ties that bound the program together. As one administrator commented: "Any type of major school reform that would occur, I think will take open-minded people to lead and choice to follow. I think leadership in school systems tends to be very close-minded and . . . I think open-minded, cooperative, empowering types of leadership, when you are involved in change tend to be the most effective. Choice and reward to follow. Schools aren't set up that way."

Finally, emphasis was placed on appreciating diversity in the needs of children and families by acknowledgment of (a) the novelty of translating this type of project to the public schools; and (b) the need to identify and foster the most effective practices to guarantee successful outcomes of the program.

At the other end of the management continuum, during the later stages of program implementation, the hierarchical administrators described their management approach as a structure of control, authority, and top-down communication. A solid chain of command and communication existed from which all information was disseminated. Participants commented that there was little tolerance for information concerning program implementation dictated to the school system from outside sources.

Unlike the sharing approach to communication emphasized by the enabling administrators, information concerning the formative outcomes of the program was filtered through the lens of the hierarchical administrative viewpoint. Consistent with the organizational literature on self-serving causal attributions (Bettman and Weitz 1983), this group of administrators tended to attribute successful organizational performance to internal organizational actions and unsuccessful performance to external participants in the project.

During the fourth and fifth years of the program, from the project director to the frontline service providers, control was maintained by established and monitored restrictive procedures and guidelines. Operations and working behaviors were strictly governed by the instructions and decisions issued by superiors. Duties and positions were both formalized and centralized to diminish the number of individuals who were able to make autonomous decisions. Such structures were reported to cause delays in the service delivery for children and families as well as employee dissatisfaction:

> It is just specifics and detail management that slowed the process down, checking things over or requesting things, when in the past we would just go do it and get it done and report back what we have done. There was a lot more requesting in the new director's management style. There was a lot of prior supervision that the project director required. So making decisions representing the Transition project, you just couldn't go out and do that generally. So some things probably did not get done because of the process, less creative initiative I think. The whole structure got more rigid. It is not flexible, it is not parent focused, it is school-system focused. I would use the words *micro-managed*, and in some instances *intimidation*.
>
> The atmosphere in the school system in general is fear at all levels. People do not feel free. People look around to see who is around them before they do things.

Data from the third group of respondents suggested referral of responses to other administrators as a means to mediate the conflict of publicly stating an opinion on an issue. Transcript data indicated that this group of administrators (a) made few comments about district policies that affected their buildings and (b) revealed little insight as to how comprehensively the Transition program was managed in their respective buildings. Analysis of transcript data did not illustrate a strong consistent alliance of this group of administrators with either the enabling or hierarchical administrators. Rather, alignment with either of those two groups was situationally dependent.

This group of participants described control of the program as pertaining to an individual principal's respective building. Abundant communications regarding the operation of the program did not exist within the data provided by this group of administrators. When asked to comment on the impact of a particular practice or belief, most often the response was "I don't know. You have to ask them." Indications of the powerlessness of this group of individuals to have a lasting impact on the Transition project were apparent. One principal stated: "Well, as principal, I have the final word. I mean, legally. So, but they don't do anything that's not legal, so it means I don't have to worry about that. But I have the final word. Well, OK, I let them create the programs, what not, and I just give the OK or not give the OK."

Organizational Membership

Diverse perspectives on organizational membership were gleaned from participant responses. Commitment to the project's tasks and its expansion was highly valued within the enabling management perspective. Emphasis was placed on facilitating the program as one viable solution to assisting economically disadvantaged children and families upon transition into the public school. Members of the enabling group of administrators saw themselves as catalysts of school change. The goal was to mold an environment within the public school system in which low-income children and families could thrive. This goal meant that the program and its staff must adhere to this goal of continuity and stability both in effective services and in retention of personnel to accomplish this task. Retention of members in this enabling group of administrators was solidified by each member's respect for others and development of a network of support for staff and their respective duties.

Although an enabling framework among project personnel was well entrenched during the first three years of the program, changes in the school's central administration during the fourth and fifth years of the project promoted another view of organizational membership.

Insistence on loyalty to the administrative policies and obedience to superiors was characteristic of the hierarchical view of management.

After the change in the school system's central administration and the Transition project director, very little input was either solicited or welcomed from Transition staff. School administrators sought to control the program from every angle. Transition staff members perceived that they were given the opportunity to promote the thinking of the hierarchical administrators or face punitive action (i.e., demotion, termination). Evidence for this finding is found in the following quote: "The new administration tended to want to get rid of people from the old guard and get their own people in place. Ultimately, I felt that as long as I was someone who had been chosen by the old guard, that I would never please them in a way that a new person could, even if we did the exact same thing, it would be someone that they chose and someone they wanted and that it would work better."

Transition staff members were caught between the ideals of the project, serving children and their families, and the fear of losing their position within the school system. One participant remarked, "It really killed me to be in a circumstance where I knew what I really needed to do, yet I did not have the autonomy."

DISCUSSION

This investigation provides insights into the philosophical beliefs and managerial orientations of public school and Transition program administrators in a site with a Head Start/Public School Transition Project. Differences in beliefs concerning (a) the philosophical roots and goals of this intervention program and (b) the administrative processes and structures in one school system strongly support the need to explore the social context in which early intervention programs operate.

Our data indicate that the Head Start philosophy is incongruent with the more typical hierarchical structure of school administration and that this incongruence may have an impact on the experiences of children and families. Specifically, in each of the major themes examined in this chapter, fundamental differences emerged in the beliefs of groups of administrators. These differences, described by the participants as disruptive and dissonant, may be the cause of significant discontinuities in the service delivery process.

The findings of this investigation are consistent with the literature on school change and school reform that suggests that reform strategies often fail because (a) the change process is uncontrollably complex and, in many circumstances, unmanageable and (b) efforts fail to address fundamental reform and the associated development of new collaborative cultures among participants (Fullan 1993). Our study illustrates that key stakeholders in the transition process vary in their opinions about the complexity of school change. It is suggested that the group of individuals with the most perceived power and control in the school system promote the view that the transition program is one that furthers the school's academic function, rather than one of interconnected service components as a means to the same end. Given that teacher or staff motivation is contingent on the attitudes of school administrators (McLaughlin 1990), individuals who work on the front line of the program may be reluctant to commit to the ideals of the original philosophical orientation mirroring Head Start. In addition, the managerial styles of the upper-level administrators are likely to promote the compliance of project personnel to the established hierarchical system of management.

Historically, schools have been incorrectly perceived as malleable structures (Sedlak and Schlossman 1985). Efforts to improve the performance of schools without changing either the way in which they are organized or the controls to which they respond set up comprehensive intervention programs for failure (Chubb 1988). As our data indicate, change is a dynamic process that depends on a variety of local factors that are also dynamic in nature. Specifically, in this study, the initial group of Transition program administrators was supported by school-system administrators in the development of a perspective that strived for consistency with the federal goals for the transition intervention. In addition, these individuals formed a cohesive group upholding the belief that the introduction of the Head Start model in the public schools would, over time, serve as a powerful catalyst for systemic change. Conversely, the new administrators who "inherited" the transition program voiced strong objections about the merits of the philosophical origins of the program. Moreover, with few notable exceptions, they expressed disconnected views of the principles underlying the service delivery components and of the interconnectedness of the components to form a coherent whole. Focusing on academic achievement as the defining role of public schools, this group of administrators discussed change from a mechanistic perspective. However, this approach to change negates the ecological focus of the transition intervention and does not provide a culture that maximizes the likelihood of institutionalization. The reported incongruities in stakeholders' perspectives accounted not only for a lack of cohesiveness and direction in the school system's approach to program implementation but translated into perceptions of negative interactions among staff members that could further create a culture of failed implementation. Within this context, the focus of the intervention gradually shifted from an effort to establish a culture in which the program could be successful to a struggle for control of the program.

Studies of comprehensive school reform (Easton 1991; Taylor and Teddlie 1992; Wehlage, Smith, and Lipman 1992) suggest that interventions do not bring about fundamental change because the basic policies and practices of school systems are so entrenched that change does not occur. Our findings are consistent with these observations. Schools that are successful in their attempts at school reform are those schools that perceive themselves as having a mission. Further, leadership in successfully reformed schools is more pedagogical and less managerial (Chubb 1988). This investigation clearly indicates that the culture of this school system did not accommodate the philosophy or practices of Head Start as a means to promote continuity for children. Instead, the leadership diverted attention from this new school culture by imposing new rules governing school practice and monitoring compliance with those rules. Autonomy of staff members was lost through the hierarchical governance style that was characteristic of the most recent administration. Consequently, a focus on mutual adaptation of project goals with the institutional setting was not present within this school system.

The perspectives shared by our respondents highlight the dynamic and complex interplay of local factors and have direct implications for the successful implementation of an educational innovation project. The results of this study thus underscore the need for evaluations of early intervention efforts to include examination of contextual factors to explore adequately the hypothesis that it is the lack of philosophical and programmatic continuity that influences outcomes for children. Critical examination of context will provide the key for understanding the efficacy of the Head Start Transition experience.

NOTE

1. This effort is aimed at providing answers about the efficacy and feasibility of federally funded early intervention in the public schools. Funding was provided in the fall of 1991, by the Department of Health and Human Services, to thirty-one sites around the country that would "implement a coordinated

and continuous program of comprehensive services for low-income children and their families" (Federal Register 1991, 31818) beginning at Head Start and continuing through elementary school. In the fall of 1992, following one year of planning, projects funded through this initiative began to provide services to Head Start children and their families. To avoid mistakes of past research, the design of the study focused on previous Head Start attendees in randomly selected demonstration and comparison public schools. Demonstration schools were to implement transition activities targeting continuity in the key areas emphasized by Head Start (i.e., continuity in educational programming through the application of developmentally appropriate practices in the early grades, parent involvement, health and nutrition services, and social services).

REFERENCES

Barnett, W. S. (1993). Benefit-cost analysis of preschool education: Findings from a 25-year follow-up. *American Journal of Orthopsychiatry*, Vol. 64, No. 3, 500–508.

Berrueta-Clement, J. R., Schweinhart, L. J., Barnett, W. S., Epstein, A. S., and Weikart, D. P. (1985). *Changed lives: The effects of the Perry Preschool Program on youths through age 19*. Ypsilanti, MI: High Scope.

Bettman, J., and Weitz, B. (1983). Attributions in the board room: Causal reasoning in corporate annual reports. *Administrative Science Quarterly*, Vol. 28, 165–183.

Chubb, J. E. (1988). Why the current wave of school reform will fail. *The Public Interest*, Vol. 90, 28–49.

Easton, J. (1991). Decision making and school improvement: LSCs in the first two years of reform. Chicago, IL: Chicago Panel on Public School Policy and Finance.

Erickson, F. (1986). Qualitative methods in research on teaching. In M. C. Wittrock (Ed.), *Handbook of Research on Teaching*. (3rd ed.). New York: Macmillan.

Federal Register, Vol. 56, No. 133, July 11, 1991, 31818–31841.

Fullan, M. (1993). *Change forces: Probing the depths of educational reform*. New York: Falmer Press.

House, E. R., Glass, G. V., McLean, L. D., and Walker, D. F. (1978). No simple answer: Critique of the Follow Through evaluation. *Harvard Educational Review*, Vol. 48, No. 2, 128–169.

Lazar, I., Darlington, R. Murray, H., Royce, J., and Snipper, A. (1982). Lasting effects of early education: A report from the Consortium for Longitudinal

Studies. *Monographs of the Society for Research in Child Development*, Vol. 47, Nos. 2–3, Serial No. 195.

Lee, V. E., and Loeb, S. (1995). Where do Head Start attendees end up? One reason why preschool effects fade out. *Educational Evaluation and Policy Analysis*, Vol. 17, 62–82

Love, J. M., Logue, M. E., Trudeau, J. V., and Thayer, K. (1992). *Transitions to kindergarten in American schools*. Final report to the Office of Policy and Planning, U.S. Department of Education. Portsmouth, NH: RMC Corporation.

Mantzicopoulos, P. Y., and Neuharth-Pritchett, S. (1995). *A progress report on Cohort 1 first grade children and families: 1993–1994*. Technical report. West Lafayette, IN: Purdue University, Department of Educational Studies.

McKey, R. H., Condelli, L., Ganson, H., Barnett, B. J., McConkey, C., and Plantz, M.C. (1985). *The impact of Head Start on children, families, and communities*. DHHS Publication No. OHDS 85-31193. Washington, D.C.: U.S. Government Printing Office.

McLaughlin, M. (1990). The RAND Change Agent Study revisited: Macro perspectives and micro realities. *Educational Researcher*, Vol. 19, No. 9, 11–16.

McLaughlin, M. W. (1987). Learning from experience: Lessons from policy implementation. *Educational Evaluation and Policy Analysis*, Vol. 9, No. 2, 171–178.

Reynolds, A. J. (1994). Effects of a preschool plus follow-on intervention for children at risk. *Developmental Psychology*, Vol. 30, No. 6, 787–804.

Sedlak, M. W., and Schlossman, S. (1985). The public school and social services: Reassessing the progressive legacy. *Educational Theory*, Vol. 35, No. 4, 371–383.

Taylor, D., and Teddlie, C. (1992). Restructuring and the classroom: A view from a reform district. Paper presented at the annual meeting of the American Educational Research Association, San Francisco.

Wehlage, G., Smith, G., and Lipman, P. (1992). Restructuring urban high schools: The New Futures Experience. *American Educational Research Journal*, Vol. 29, No. 1, 51–93.

Woodhead, M. (1988). When psychology informs public policy: The case of early childhood intervention. *American Psychologist*, Vol. 43, No. 6, 443–454.

Zigler, E., and Styfco, S. J. (1994). Is the Perry Preschool Project better than Head Start? *Early Childhood Research Quarterly*, Vol. 9, 269–287.

13

Inspiring Delusions: Reflections on Head Start's Enduring Popularity

Jeanne Ellsworth

During the months when I was reading manuscripts for this book, candidate Bill Clinton was boasting in his re-election campaign to have increased the number of children in Head Start by some fifty-thousand. A drop in the bucket, to be sure, hardly worth boasting about, but more amazing was that a candidate for public office anywhere in the nation at this time would mention, let alone brag about, increasing the numbers of people served by a War on Poverty program. Currently, the social welfare policies of the 1960s are the target of ridicule and vitriolic attacks. But, of course, Clinton was not going out on a limb with his boast—he surely knew that many, probably most, of his listeners would be pleased. Among poverty programs, Head Start is different. It is and has been tremendously popular with the general public as well as among members of both political parties, even some of the most miserly and conservative; it has been claimed more than once that "everybody likes Head Start."[1]

My personal experiences with Head Start confirm this. I have been involved with Head Start as an academic and as a volunteer, and for the past few years this involvement has consumed a fair amount of my professional energies—from late 1992 through mid-1995, I was regularly in and out of Head Start offices and centers, serving on committees, reading and writing reports, organizing student interns, working and talking with staff, parents, children, and administrators.

Even through difficult times, some of which are detailed elsewhere in this volume, I was struck by a fierce loyalty to Head Start—a love, really, for *the program*, if not for every regulation, every individual, every policy or practice.

I am intrigued, if not surprised, by the fact that a social program is so consistently applauded and supported despite virtually no consistent evidence that it has or ever will achieve its goal of moving families out of poverty, despite a public and political climate of increasing hostility toward "welfare" and poverty programs. Head Start certainly has not ended poverty in the United States or even put a dent in it. Individuals, though often dramatically impressed by the program, do not always reap its putative benefits of social mobility. At least two women I met through Head Start talk fondly of their children's good times at Head Start, and now their grandchildren's.

Of course, I am not naive enough to suspect that Head Start's reputation has been gained through research that clearly demonstrates that Head Start "works." Certainly there is a mountain of research on the program, literally hundreds of independent, sponsored, and commissioned research studies, dissertations and theses, and reviews and meta-analyses—a body of scholarship that varies widely in methodology, scope, and quality, but generally fails to offer decisive evidence of Head Start's benefits. Given the traditional relationship of research to programming, it should not be surprising that this literature has had limited influence on the funding or operations of Head Start. Neither are the many and complex findings widely or well known outside the academic and research quarters. But there are persistent claims that Head Start is successful and worthy of great admiration.

What is the nature of Head Start's enduring appeal, its privileged place among "welfare" programs in the public imagination? My work with Head Start provided some insider views of the program and predictably has also brought me to read a great deal about it—beginning, of course, with that large body of academic and research literature, which I reviewed with interest. I also have learned a great deal about Head Start's public image in publications such as *Time, Newsweek, Life, Reader's Digest*, and *Look*—even a few pieces in *Parents, Good Housekeeping*, and *Seventeen*—"supermarket" publications. As part of another project, I came upon a third fascinating literature, the transcripts of congressional hearings on Head Start, providing another look at the reputation and claims of the program. Beyond the academic volumes, Head Start certainly has public and political personae which were illuminated for me by these other literatures.

What follows are my observations on some aspects of Head Start's perennial appeal, based on the literatures, my experiences, and my own personal perspectives. I can see, as have others, that Head Start has a warm and attractive look and feel, because it serves innocent children. But the appeal of dewy-eyed youngsters did not shield AFDC (Aid for Families with Dependent Children) or SSI (Supplementary Security Income). Head Start is popular because its premises about children's school performance fit our deepest cultural beliefs about education and poverty. Part of the appeal, too, comes from the ways in which Head Start supports the "othering" of the poor, while at the same time deflecting criticism and attracting a substantial group of supporters. In fact, I think that Head Start has gained an appeal powerful enough to derail any serious discussions about whether it works (not to mention what "works" might mean). Among all the sad and disgraceful stories about poverty, Head Start's charm and reputation can inspire us to believe that something (something important, grand, and powerful) is being done, but I believe this amounts to inspiring sad and disgraceful delusions.

APPEALING TO THE EYE, HEART, AND MIND

Head Start almost certainly appeals to the U.S. public because its aims are seemingly irreproachable; it offers a simple home remedy for the most endearing and innocent of the poor, little children. Forwarding such an appealing program, indeed, was the intent of planners and OEO officials, as Greenberg and Kuntz make clear in other chapters of this volume. It is, indeed, a very "pretty" program. (Early [1965–69] publicity for Head Start included photos of wide-eyed or shy or giggly youngsters, working and playing in wholesome, but not extravagant, surroundings.) And there are human interest stories or vignettes such as the following which provided warm, happy-ending feelings to associate with Head Start:

> At the outset of another Head Start class, a diminutive four-year-old boy was shut off behind a wall of hostility; he was surly to the teachers and aggressive toward the other children. One day he brought a knife to class and thereafter had to be frisked each morning. But somehow the patience of the Head Start teachers and the example of his contemporaries had a civilizing effect on him. Four weeks after the program started, when he bumped into another youngster, he said, "Excuse me." By the time the program ended, he was relaxed enough for the discipline of a regular school.[2]

Enrolled in a Head Start course at a Lower East Side school called *Escuela Hispana*, Hector for days was tearful and forlorn. But in time he learned that clay can be made into shapes, and a round, purple thing is a plum and tastes sweet. He learned to take part in counting games and to button buttons. Most important, he learned that teachers could be trusted friends. Simultaneously, Head Start gave Hector a medical check-up and began impressing on his Puerto Rican–born mother the essential fact that home is an extension of school. All this has put Hector one leg up from zero. When he reaches first grade he may have become a receptive, participating boy.[3]

While such stories celebrated Head Start, the rest of the War on Poverty came under intense fire even as early as its first anniversary in 1965. In addition to administrative "boondoggles," there were reports of drunkenness, sodomy, prostitution, knifings, theft, and vandalism in connection with other programs, rendering the photos and stories of children all the more appealing in contrast.

Of course, children *are* adorable, and photos and stories about them are just as charming to me as anyone. But there are subtler messages, too. From 1965 through 1967, Head Start's first two years of operation, the popular periodicals I was reading published some forty-five photos (among thirteen articles) of Head Start children. The portrait of Head Start programs that emerges is clearly a segregated one, with mostly black children as the central characters. Six photos depict scenes of four or more children—all of those children (approximately fifty-five children total) are black; of the thirty-seven children appearing singly or in photos with two or three children, twenty-eight are black, four are white, and two are Latino (as identified in captions or text). Of the twenty-three teachers appearing in the photos, thirteen are white and ten are black—white staff are in charge of a number of the black children, but no black staff member appears with white children. It is unlikely (but not impossible) that the photos were chosen purposefully to avoid depicting integrated scenes, and it is true that Head Starts were and are very often racially segregated. Whatever those circumstances, though, the image is one of segregated, mostly black programs. For predominantly white, middle-class readers in the tumult of the civil rights era, this must have been a comforting picture—a lovely program in which poor minority children are aided through the beneficence of the middle class, but not by bringing them into *their* nursery schools or *their* neighborhood day cares.

"Selling" Deficit Theory

Along with the pretty pictures, though, there was substance, in the form of a scientifically enunciated view of poverty—deficit (or cultural deficit or cultural deprivation) theory. In my experiences with Head Start, the public schools, and teachers, I am regularly astonished, even now, at the strength and depth of attachment to assumptions connected with deficit theory. Beginning education students, for example, largely ignorant of educational theory, can nonetheless recite the basic premises of deficit theory, as if they have been raised on it— and, in some respects, they have. The media, popular culture, pop psychology, the public imagination, and political arguments about poverty are saturated with it.

Back in the 1960s, it seems that the inauguration of Head Start was one of the vehicles for the transmission of this "new" knowledge to the general public and policy makers. Of course, the basic premises of deficit theory were not really new. Child savers of many eras have located a range of social problems in parental incompetence.[4] But the ideas were newly clothed for the postwar era, in the sophisticated garb of science. Congressional committees in the 1960s apparently were fascinated with the concepts of deficit theory. Benjamin Bloom's assertions about the development of intelligence appear over and over in Head Start congressional hearings from the late 1960s. Senator Walter Mondale presented Bloom's thesis in 1969 as having been the basis for the development of Project Head Start:

> We know that the beginning years of life are the most important for a child's intellectual growth and for his social, emotional, physical, and motivational development. We know, for example, that about 50 percent of an individual's intellectual development takes place between conception and age 4, another 30 percent between ages 4 and 8, and only about 20 percent between ages 8 and 17. These early years are the formative years—they are the years in which permanent foundations are laid for a child's feelings of self-worth, his sense of self-respect, his motivation, his initiative, and his ability to learn and achieve.[5]

These statistics about the pace of intellectual development had been presented a number of times to congressional committees, and the mentions and questions they attracted suggest a certain captivation with the notion.

Another key element of the theoretical argument for Head Start was that during this critical period, those "formative years," poor parents were not providing the proper environment in which their children would develop intellectually, psychologically, or socially. Based on and joined with the medical model of early health and nutritional intervention, the Head Start foundation was, "We know beyond a doubt that unless infants and young children receive adequate nutrition, health care, and intellectual stimulation, their potential is severely compromised, and the cycle of poverty is perpetuated."[6]

Finally, in order to buy the Head Start idea, one must be convinced that these regrettable circumstances can be remedied, in this case not by unpopular income redistribution plans or radical social change, but simply by providing some compensatory education for children and by changing the way women in poverty bring up their children. Bloom testified that "when mothers are helped to find effective ways of teaching, reading, and playing with their children," those mothers "stimulate their children's development [, and] they also develop through this process a closer relation with their children."[7] In describing research wherein tutors worked with children and their mothers for an hour a day, four or five days a week, a Dr. Schaefer reported to a congressional committee significant successes, including the case of one mother who "decided to tutor the younger child in the family while the tutor tutored the older child and that younger child began to speak in sentences at 14 months."[8]

The popular print media introduced the American public to these small miracles, as illustrated in these excerpts from articles published in 1965:

[Head Start] aims to make . . . underprivileged children of 4, 5, and 6 more prepared for school next fall, if only by showing them how to hold a pencil and giving them some square meals. The individual attention and assurance these children get is something altogether new for most of them and can make all the difference between learning something and not.[9]

The project puts kids of four, five and six into child development centers, where under close personal attention they will be encouraged by simple successes to avoid the spiral of failure that often starts with school's first day. They will have medical and dental care, free meals. Their parents will be counseled at home, urged to help the kids by such easy steps as reading to them and telling them stories. . . . "The greatest difficulty these children have is in language," explains [pediatrician] Robert E. Cooke. . . . "Other children are taken into laps, held, read to and shown pictures. At first they don't get

much—only emotional value. The deprived child, without this exposure, never gets the emotional reassurance of the words and
pictures." . . . Children who had never held a fork sat at tables for a
breakfast.[10]

Such reports surely resonated with the widely approved idea that
school failure and poverty are the result of personal failures, in this
case, parents' failures. As Mimi Abramovitz has pointed out, the United
States has long harbored a pointed distrust of the ability of poor women
to raise their children competently.[11] And, by looking to the "deprivation" created when parents' language and habits are deemed substandard, cultural deprivation theories can be very effective in deflecting
attention from issues of privilege and in supporting faith in the myth
of an open competitive system in the United States. The complemen-
tary optimism about public schooling as a "panacea" made Head Start
a sure winner. In short, cultural deprivation theories had a very comfortable fit for Americans.

Rarely does sociological theory get such play in the mass media.
And deficit theory has proven hardily resistant to competing theories
and serious attacks from many quarters. Clearly it has moved beyond
its status as social theory to entering the realm of common sense, folk
wisdom, cultural myth. What sets Head Start apart from other social
programs, perhaps, is that a folk wisdom has developed that *supports*,
even celebrates, the program, while most other "welfare" programs
have been attacked by another set of cultural myths whose latest forms
emerged in the eighties. New "common sense" about "family values,"
personal responsibility, and the end of racism and sexism, for example,
have heaped censure, blame, and ridicule on most other means-tested
programs.

DEFINING THE "OTHER"

Classifying families (and all people, ideas, things) as either "good" or
"bad," superior or inferior, has a firm foothold in American culture,
long absorbed with making polarizing judgements.[12] Another notable
ingredient in Head Start's popularity, I believe, is that the concepts
and language used in describing Head Start serve to define families in
poverty as inferior and other. In the 1960s the middle-class public had
been more or less "awakened" to the existence of poverty in the United
States. Exposés such as Michael Harrington's *The Other America* and
Edward R. Murrow's television documentary "Harvest of Shame"

brought American poverty to the American living room. As Gunnar Myrdal observed, the public became aware of an "ugly smell rising from the basement of the stately American mansion."[13] Head Start, though certainly not single-handedly, helped the public construct images of "the poor" as other, that is, to locate the source of the smell in homes unlike their own and symbolically, if not always physically, distant.

The processes of "othering" have been defined as serving "to mark and name those thought to be different to oneself" and must be understood as part of the development and maintenance of patterns of domination and subordination.[14] In the language and texture of descriptions of Head Start and its foundations, we can view the "co-production" of two prototypes—middle-class, white families and those others who are poor and often nonwhite. Returning to my observations about the photographs included in Head Start coverage, the association with African Americans is clearly part of this process. In addition, in excerpts previously quoted, the reader is invited to hear (if he or she has not already) the subtle messages about "these children" who are not held on laps or read to, who have not held a pencil or a fork, whose relationships with their parents are not particularly "close." While characteristics like these are certainly dispersed throughout the population (is it really so odd for four year olds not to have held a pencil, eaten efficiently with a fork, spent time away from home, or tasted a plum?), in the context of othering, they take on new and significant meaning as definitive of substandard parenting. Consider the following excerpts from congressional hearings, noting (a) the juxtaposition of characteristics of medical pathology and poverty, (b) the uncloaked association with African Americans, and (c) the contrasts to middle-class children:

> The enormous effect of experiences in early childhood can be best appreciated by brief reference to less known work carried out a number of years ago by Hampson, Hampson, and Money in our department at Johns Hopkins. The psychologists and psychiatrists studied children with abnormalities of external sex organs caused by chemical changes during pregancy [sic]. Their studies clearly showed that the way in which these children were handled by parents established the concept the child had of himself as a male or female, independently of his genetic sex or even of his physical appearance. This concept was established within the first 2 years of life and the individual is fixed in this pattern for the balance of his life regardless of efforts later even though these may be extremely intensive. It is

not surprising, therefore, that less fundamental characteristics such
as attitudes toward success, ability to concentrate, to abstract, and to
verbalize may be impaired even more by inadequate experiences in
the early months and years of life.[15]

What we have learned about these children is that because of many
difficult life experiences, the press of crowding and of confusion,
these young children have been actively inhibited in their language
experimentation. They have been actively repressed in their efforts to
learn for themselves. They have been punished with rather striking
violence, not because of cruelty but because this has been the tradition handed down from years and years of punishment practices,
probably going back into the slave period. It is not surprising, then,
that when these children approach maturity, violence is a way which
they understand: it is a method of achieving. It is also not surprising
that they have little motivation to succeed, they have little ambition
in academic affairs, and that they have serious deficiencies that involve the use of language and language concepts.[16]

These families live in very crowded circumstances. They frequently
have a number of children. The mother in a small middle-class family, for example, is very actively interested in each word her child
speaks because this is a great accomplishment. But in a large poor
family setting a noise becomes an enormous distraction and it is very
difficult for the mother to take the time to encourage the child to use
language. [17]

The message is that "these children" are *not* like "our children";
their experiences are not like ours; they are other than our own children, our sisters and brothers, our neighbors' children. This is perhaps
most vivid in articles intended to recruit young women as volunteers
in the program. "These children," "these people," are exotic and unknown. It is difficult, we are told, to even imagine what they are like:

We were told about the background and home life of many of the
Head Start children and were shown poverty as something more
than lack of money. To a child, we learned, it may be a missing
parent, living with six brothers and sisters in a one-room apartment,
a mother so preoccupied with her own terrible troubles that she literally cannot speak a loving word. . . . I listened carefully to every
word, but deep down I didn't believe that the lives of these children
could really be so tragically different from all that was familiar to me.
Surely people were exaggerating. But they weren't.[18]

We have met those people and they are quite real to us: Children who can't afford to pay 15 cents to go swimming. And when given the chance to go free, can't go because they have nothing to swim in. Others who wear suits that don't fit and are styled for ten years ago. Adults who can't cook good meals with the surplus food given to them, because they can't read recipes. Adults who lost money because they don't know enough basic math to count change.[19]

They can't sing London Bridge, they can't draw, they can't build castles in the sand. Because they may not know what a song is, or a crayon, or a sandbox. They may never have seen a book or held a flower. . . . Perhaps it's hard for you to imagine children learning from such commonplace things—teaching your little brother to sing "Row, row, row your boat" is easy, isn't it? But try teaching the same song to a child who doesn't know what rowing is, who has never seen a boat or a stream! [20]

People who are poor are thus defined as "other," as remote and separate. At the same time, the identity and superiority of middle-class child-rearing habits are more clearly defined by contrast.

DEFLECTING CRITICISM AND GAINING ALLIES

In the optimistic 1960s, these others were considered eminently salvageable, especially the children. And Head Start was quickly proclaimed the area of greatest hope in this regard. The rest of the War on Poverty was considered a failure almost before it got fully under way. Reported were "countless charges of nepotism, malfeasance, and administrative fiddledeedee, of demeaning interagency squabbles in the capital and squalid scandals in the boondocks."[21] But Head Start was largely exempt from such criticism; in the coverage of the problems and controversies, just two short paragraphs were included that mentioned difficulty in a Head Start program. Those paragraphs, appearing in a brief 1966 *U.S. News and World Report* piece, referred to the case of the Child Development Group of Mississippi (sponsors of Mississippi's Head Start project). For Head Start in Mississippi, this conflict was intense;[22] in retrospect, for the War on Poverty, it was symbolic of dramatic changes in poverty policy and power structures; as national news in popular magazines, however, it was another blip on the screen of War on Poverty attacks.

Head Start was portrayed as nearly innocent of administrative scandal and also as a nearly unqualified success. As early as the close of its first short summer session, Head Start had been declared a success in the popular media. *Reader's Digest* reported that Head Start had "made an auspicious beginning at one of the most inspiring tasks an enlightened nation can undertake: launching its youngest and most-needy citizens on an upward spiral to personal fulfillment and the good life."[23] *Time* announced, "No campaign in the war on poverty has been fought with more zeal,"[24] and in a subsequent article, it was declared that Head Start had "proved the poverty program's best success."[25] All this was written long before it reasonably could have been "proven."

I think Head Start's popularity, its unassailable status in our culture, has kept it relatively exempt from anything but the most mild and sporadic criticism. To be sure, there have been controversies about Head Start's effectiveness. There have been periodic rounds of "serious questions," "uncertainty," and "sobering" conclusions. But an aura of faith is also evident as time and again, critics prove themselves willing to put "tests and statistics aside."[26] As one congressional witness explained,

> I think a lot of research—you have to excuse me, I am not really knocking professionals, but professional people don't live in the areas where they make their researches in so all this research is a lot of figures and numbers on paper. And what we need, we need more money to run these types of programs, because, we already know they are working, because you have to communicate with people, parents, participating in this type of thing.[27]

Research traditionally has been brushed aside in the face of testimonials and sheer faith in the wisdom of the program. I am astonished that the 1970s Westinghouse study, generally cited as central in Head Start's history, was not covered by the newsmagazines at all. That first national-scope, large-scale comparative study stirred considerable controversy in Washington and among Head Start and War on Poverty insiders. It was considered, according to the sitting president of the National Head Start Association, "a slap in the face."[28] But it was not news in the popular magazines; and even in congressional hearings, there was considerable resistance to its conclusions, apparently because they flew in the face of what was becoming commonsense wisdom about the successes of the program. In the words of Senator Walter Mondale, "One of the things that always strikes me about Westinghouse type of studies is that their results so often conflict with the judgment of people experienced in the program. I have rarely talked to educators or Headstart teachers or parents of children in Headstart who weren't delighted. They think it is working, they think it is helpful. The child is doing better. But then these studies come up and say, 'We don't see any progress.' "[29]

And, correspondingly, an increasing amount of time at congressional hearings on Head Start has been given over to testimonials from proud or grateful parents, community members, and, later, graduates. As one reporter observed, people involved with the program are "enthusiastic almost to the point of euphoria."[30] These Head Start "rooters," as they were called, give life-story testimonies that are often presented emotionally and received enthusiastically (if patronizingly). An abridged example (which was interrupted four times by applause):[31]

Ms. Phetteplace: This is my third year as a Head Start parent. . . . I was not at all prepared for the comprehensiveness of the program or the transformation that my life was about to take. In my work with the local program and the State, regional and national associations, I came to realize that Head Start was offering me an opportunity to piece together my bruised life. . . . We have learned that no matter what our background before Head Start, we now have a safe, nurturing environment in which to sort out our lives to provide a healthy existence for our families. . . . I am not sure what path my life is going to take in the near future, but I am sure it will be rich with opportunity and confidence gained through my Head Start experience. Thank you.
[Applause.]
Chairman Martinez: You just got a standing ovation, do you know that?
[Laughter.]
Ms. Phetteplace: Amazing what a few tears will do, huh?
Chairman Martinez: Maybe I should start crying, huh?

My own experiences confirm the sincerity and enthusiasm of Head Start fans. In fact, their fervor often has impressed me as almost cultlike. And, of course, it has the essential ingredient of gratefulness, proving the ultimate "worthiness" of the population served by Head Start.

While the Head Start rooters agree on the program's merit, in public and political conversations, we hear from time to time that Head Start works, then it does not, then it does, then it does not—the ups and downs characteristic of any love affair, I suppose. Cycles of concern are expressed: expecting IQ gains was naive, so social and emotional gains should be prioritized; program standards and assessment and monitoring must take center stage; add-ons (e.g. Follow-Through or Home Start) would increase or maintain gains; that staff training should be increased; and, most recently, tight business management will be expected for "quality control" or, in order to be effective the program simply must start earlier, with younger children. There will continue to be such currents, particularly in the context of welfare "reform." But there will probably emerge no definitive proof that Head Start "works" in the terms it claims to work, and there will continue to be claims such as a recent one that Head Start is "a miracle solution" for children.[32] Recently I was startled to see a report in the Wall Street Journal that claimed IQ gains for children through early intervention of the Head Start variety,[33] which seems to me to bring the issue full circle, back to the first claims of the pediatricians and psychologists of the 1960s.

But these new claims, new frills on the program, new hopes, are unlikely to be viewed any more skeptically or thoroughly than has been the case in the past. In short, I believe that for the public and policymakers, it simply does not matter any more whether Head Start will have a significant influence on children's academic achievement or families' social mobility. Head Start has indeed gained, if not earned, the status of cultural icon.

I am not arguing here that in the absence of proof of increased achievement scores, Head Start is a failure and/or should be abandoned. And what's wrong with Congress being swayed by moving testimonials? I've heard a few testimonials myself, in interviews and conversations, and I have been deeply moved by them. I am convinced that some people benefit greatly from the program. I did myself, through the opportunity to work with a number of extraordinary women. And I suppose that the search for "effects" must continue, since neither Congress nor the public is likely to support the program for the same reasons that middle-class parents support their own nursery schools and preschools—as an enriching experience for their children and/or a stimulating, safe, attractive, and well-staffed place for their children to stay while they work. But the rationale for the program and the attendant cultural myths of equal opportunity and cultural deficit are also beneficiaries of the faith in Head Start. And if we continue to support the program because it "works" in these terms (no matter the validity of that claim), we are also cementing even more firmly these conventional beliefs about poverty. I am concerned that our love for Head Start, with its cheery and reassuring face, can "inspire delusions." Those delusions are dangerous because of their capacity to divert attention from the barbarities of increasing poverty among children. And they lead us all toward the kind of self-congratulation that President Clinton employed in bragging about his "achievements" in terms of Head Start enrollment.

NOTES

1. This phrase, or variations on it, has been used repeatedly. See, for example, "Can Johnson Win His Other War?" *Look* 31 (June 13, 1967): 26–37; "Everybody likes Head Start," *Newsweek* 113 (February 26, 1989): 49–50; Valora Washington, and Ura Jean Oyemade Bailey, Project Head Start: Models and Strategies for the Twenty-First Century (New York: Garland 1995).

2. "A Head Start for America's Youngsters," *Readers Digest* 88, (April, 1966): 156–63.

3. "A 'Head Start' for a Boy in a Cubby," *Life* 59 (September 24, 1965): 91–92.

4. Detailed in Beth Blue Swadener, and Sally Lubeck, eds., *Children and Families "At Promise": Deconstructing the Discourse of Risk*. (Albany: State University of New York Press, 1995).

5. August 4, 5, and 6, 1969, Hearings before the Subcommittee on Employment, Manpower, and Poverty of the Committee on Labor and Public Welfare, United States Senate, 91st Congress, First Session on S. 2060 to provide for an expanded Head Start child development program, Part 1, p. 15. References to Bloom's statistics are made in a number of places in the transcripts of these hearings—Dr. Cooke was questioned about them in his testimony, as was Bloom himself. Later in the 1969 hearings, Senator Gaylord Nelson refers to Bloom's assertions about the development of intelligence as "statistics I have seen in a number of places" (18).

6. Ibid., 15.

7. Ibid., 77.

8. Ibid., 96.

9. "What Poverty 'War' Is About," *Life* 59 (July 16, 1965): 6.

10. "Fast Start for Head Start," *Time* 86 (July 2, 1965): 64.

11. Mimi Abramovitz. *Under Attack, Fighting Back: Women and Welfare in the United States* (New York: Monthly Review Press, 1996).

12. See, for example, Conrad Arsenberg, and Arthur Neihoff. "American Cultural Values," in C. Arensberg and A. Niehoff, eds., *Introducing Social*

Change, Hawthorne, NJ: Aldine de Gruyter, 1971); Adolph Reed, Jr., 1992. "The Underclass as Myth and Symbol: The Poverty of Discourse about Poverty," *Radical America* 24 (1): 21–40.

13. Quoted in Mark I. Gelfland, "Elevating or Ignoring the Underclass," in R. Bremner, G. Reichard, and R. Hopkins, eds., *American Choices: Social Dilemmas and Pubic Policy Since 1960*. (Columbus: Ohio State University Press, 1986), 4.

14. Lois Weis, 1995. "Identity Formation and the Processes of 'Othering': Unraveling Sexual Threads," *Educational Foundations* 9 (1): 17–33.

15. February 10, 1970. Hearings before the Subcommittee on Employment, Manpower, and Poverty of the Committee on Labor and Public Welfare, United States Senate, 91st Congress, First Session on S. 2060, To provide for an expanded Head Start child development program, Part 2, 341.

16. Ibid., 345.

17. Ibid.

18. B. L. Wilkinson, K. Hamilton, and S. Wolf, "Come Take My Hand," *Seventeen*, (December, 1965): 98–99.

19. "A Southern Girl's Diary of Discovery," *Look* 29 (July 13, 1965): 107–13.

20. "Project Head Start," *Seventeen* 24 (May, 1965): 218–19.

21. "The War within the War," *Time* 87 (May 13, 1966): 25.

22. For a complete account of the conflict, see Polly Greenberg, *The Devil Has Slippery Shoes: A Biased Biography of the Child Development Group of Mississippi* (Washington, D.C.: Youth Policy Institute, 1969/1990).

23. Irwin Ross, "A Head Start for America's Youngsters," *Readers Digest* (April, 1966): 156–63.

24. "What 'Sonny' Learned," *Newsweek* 67, (February 21, 1966): 87.

25. "The War within the War." *Time* 87, (May 13, 1966): 25–29.

26. "Not Enough Head Start?" *Newsweek* 68, (November 7, 1966): 100.

27. August 4, 5, and 6, 1969. Hearings before the Subcommittee on Employment, Manpower, and Poverty of the Committee on Labor and Public Welfare, United States Senate, 91st Congress, First Session on S. 2060 to provide for an expanded Head Start child development program, Part 1, 66.

28. Quoted in Edward Zigler, and Susan Muenchow, *Head Start: The Inside Story of America's Most Successful Educational Experiment* (New York: Basic Books, 1992), 72.

29. February 10, 1970. Hearings before the Subcommittee on Employment, Manpower, and Poverty of the Committee on Labor and Public Welfare,

United States Senate, 91st Congress, First Session on S. 2060, To provide for an expanded Head Start child development program, Part 2, 357.

30. "Not Enough Head Start?" (November 7, 1966). *Newsweek* 68, 100.

31. February 10, 1994. The administration proposal for Head Start reauthorization: Joint hearing before the Subcommittee on Children, Families, Drugs, and Alcoholism of the Committee on Labor and Human Resources, United States Senate, and the Subcommittee on Education and Labor, House of Representatives, 103rd Congress, Second Session on examining Head Start and the administrations' plans for expanding and improving it, 22.

32. Linda S. Thompson, "Head Start Program a 'miracle solution.' " *AfroAmerican* November 25, 1995, A, 5:1.

33. Rochelle Sharpe, "To Boost IQs, Aid Is Needed in First 3 Years," *Wall Street Journal* April 12, 1994, B, 1:6.

14

Hope and Challenge:
Head Start Past, Present, Future

Jeanne Ellsworth and Lynda J. Ames

The chapters in this book seem to tell widely different stories and yet tell the same story in different ways: Head Start promises so much and seems, in some ways, mostly anecdotally, to yield so much. And yet there is precious little that we can hold on to, point to, as *unequivocal* proof of Head Start's achievement and success.

Head Start's beginnings were full of hope—the programs would break the "cycle of poverty" for innocent children; Head Start would empower parents; it would invigorate the community; it would be a key weapon in winning the War on Poverty. But we have seen that Head Start has not done or been any of that, at least not consistently or extensively, at least not that we can demonstrate conclusively. There seems to be, thirty-some years into the program, more in the way of challenges than there are hopes fulfilled. In the chapters of this book, we have learned something about what has diminished those hopes.

The first hope was that the children would flourish, would come to scramble after and achieve the American Dream. This was the hope that Lady Bird Johnson and other poverty warriors likely had. But no one, really, has ever tried to establish the connection between a summer or a year in Head Start and conventional success for individuals, much less the connection between Head Start and the defeat of poverty. As Spatig, Bickel, Parrott, Dillon, and Conrad tell us, research on Head Start's effects was very quickly focused on quantifiable gains in IQ or other standardized achievement scores. Other quantitative research analyzed the effect of the program on children's probabilities of being held back a grade or needing special education programs later. All of this research merely assumes, rather than demonstrates, that successful education *will* lead to success in American capitalism—a most problematic assumption.

That focus has generated a veritable industry among quantitatively oriented psychologists who came to dominate the research on Head Start. All of that research, though, has shown us little about Head Start—except that one year's worth of preschool does not increase IQ scores, at least not over the long term. The assumption and focus *did* help to distract researchers from looking at other, more fundamental consequences of Head Start involvement (or the lack thereof). That is why the chapters in this book seem so path-breaking—they are.

However, even if IQ scores did increase, even if Head Start did improve educational outcomes, would the War on Poverty be won? Spatig, Bickel, Parrott, Dillon, and Conrad say no. A key reason that the hope and the promise of Head Start to defeat poverty have not been realized is simply that the cause of poverty lies less in individual deficiencies of education and ambition than in the social structures of capitalism, patriarchy, and racism. Head Start *might* fix the former, but it cannot scratch the surface of the latter. As Greenberg argues, as Mickelson and Klenz conclude, and as all of us believe, the social structures of poverty cannot be altered by a preschool program for a few poor kids, even with educational programs aimed at their parents, too. We are beginning to know, even, that very specific job training programs for adults will not end their poverty or poverty in general (Friedlander and Burtless 1995; Rose 1995). There are too few jobs in the United States that pay wages adequate to support a family. Further, there are too few opportunities for poor, for nonwhite, for female children or parents to achieve "success" in this country of widening inequality, increasing racism, and mundane misogyny. Sexism, racism, professionalism, and the sheer force of structural poverty rob Head Start of its hopeful promise.

As Kuntz and Greenberg each explain, part of the original promise behind the War on Poverty was the opportunity for the poor to *re*structure society as they saw fit, through "maximum feasible participation." Herein was the actual potential to end poverty, the potential for community organizing and action, as Saul Alinsky put it, the potential for "a deep, hard-driving force striking and cutting at the very roots of all the evils which beset the people" (1946, 154). Such a

potential never existed in merely teaching poor children colors and
numbers before they got to kindergarten. As we have seen in the
chapters of this book, though, little is left of that broader promise of
empowerment.

Indeed, Head Start's promise to empower parents—mothers—was
broken almost as soon as it was made. Women and women's activities
were perceived as apolitical by nature, and thus women's empowerment was seen as neither possible nor desirable. Kuntz tells us that
women's activism in Head Start never made the "news" sections of
local black newspapers in Minneapolis in the 1960s because it was
women's activism about children. Women were simply not seen as
political actors, even in their own communities.

Neither were/are mothers taken as legitimate partners in action
by the professionals running Head Start programs. Spatig, Parrott,
Dillon, and Conrad show us how mothers' attempts to participate in
the 1990s are being channeled into busywork, not empowering control. Mickelson and Klenz show us that the mothers are being trained,
not in control and management, but in how to be better parents—this
is their proper role. Mothers saw through this patronization and
disempowerment, though, as Ames and Ellsworth show us and as Kirby
explains from her experience. Yet, even armed with that insight and the
control codified in Head Start regulations, mothers have remained largely
powerless to realize the promise of genuine empowerment. Sexism has
served as an important barrier, a huge challenge to hope.

From the beginning, too, Head Start's potential to empower those
it serves suffered from an association with "other," with poor people,
with people of color. This fact helps account for the patronization
displayed by professionals and policy makers to mothers and other
community members from the beginning. Indeed, as Hamilton, Hayes,
and Doan show us, most of the participants of Head Start nationwide
are people of color. Relatively greater proportions of eligible children
in minority communities are served than is true for majority poor
children.

Like kindergartens and the settlement houses before it, Head Start's
programs are aimed, in large part, at teaching "other" parents how to
fit in, how to become "American," white, middle-class. The strong
presumption, as Greenberg argues, is that these others are defective in
character or at least in human capital preparation. Defective parents
must be fixed, first, and the fixing process itself is the empowerment.
Much energy and attention is spent on the fixing of individuals, and
not much is spent on more politically empowering actions. And the

very assumption of deficient others contradicts the assumption and hope of the poor restructuring society as they see fit.

These issues are perhaps most clearly seen in Inoway-Ronnie's study and Quintero's reflections on her experiences. The promise to parents that they could control the program is broken by apparently well-meaning Head Start workers bent on training mothers and children to accept and live according to white, middle-class standards—in spite of the fact that the families do not have the material or cultural resources to do this. Ironically, the parents' aim, as Inoway-Ronnie shows us, is exactly to fit in, to become "American"—or at least to have their children fit in as Americans. Even so, the methods the parents chose to achieve that aim are rejected by the (mostly) white Head Start staff. Even this small power promised to parents is denied.

Furthermore, the children are not learning very much that is positive about their own cultures or about other, nonmajority cultures. Hamilton, Hayes, and Doan demonstrate that many, if not most Head Start programs treat "multiculturalism" in a very superficial way. So the children are neither learning pride in themselves and their culture, nor, according to parents, learning enough about fitting in to the majority culture to be successful.

A most powerful challenge to the promise of Head Start is this very notion that professionals know better than lay parents and that teaching and learning occurs from staff to mom and child, and never vice versa. The need for professionals to guard their status and their control is seen in many of the chapters of this book. This need is clearly reinforced by the nature of the parents and children: poor, female, of color, other.

Greenberg tells us that this was an issue from the very beginning. Professionals of various political and academic stripes jockeyed for dominance in the formulation of Head Start policy (as well as other War on Poverty programs). Many of the developers were quite convinced of their ability to define what parents and children needed and were equally convinced of their right, even obligation, to do so. Few were interested in hearing from recipients about what was wanted or needed.

Head Start programs operating thirty years later continue to suffer from such attempts at professional control and the consequent disempowerment of recipients. Ames and Ellsworth show us that professionals controlled, unremarkably, the Policy Council, the very heart of the hope for parents' power. Spatig, Parrott, Dillon, and Conrad show clearly that parents were not seen as partners, but as servants of the professionals. Parents were enlisted not to design effective curricula or policies, but to help with day-to-day classroom chores for teachers who would design their own curricula, thank you.

Neuharth-Pritchett and Mantzicopoulos demonstrate the effects of management styles on the potential for meaningful parent involvement. Like Ames and Ellsworth do, they show us that concerns about professional, "tight" management are incompatible with Head Start's commitment to remaining a flexible and permeable program. The experiences of former Head Start staffers Geddes and Kirby make clear the negative effect on staff—and thus on parents and children— of these management styles.

In spite of the largely unfulfilled hopes for empowerment, in spite of the challenges posed by social structures of power, Head Start was and remains well loved. Ellsworth shows us that negative research findings—either the kind documented in this book or the more usual kind showing small and temporary IQ gains—and the lack of robust positive findings have had little to no effect on the public perception, via the popular media, of Head Start. One reason, perhaps, is that the promise *is* very compelling (for the reasons Ellsworth outlines). We want to believe the program does good, damn the evidence.

So, given what we have learned from these chapters, why is it that many of us, the authors, continue to value Head Start? Why, moreover, do we recommend continued and expanded funding of the program?

We asked ourselves this question, beginning at a conference in Montreal in November of 1996 (the American Education Studies Association). A number of the contributors to this book participated in a panel discussion of our chapters. Afterward, we held an open conversation on the questions above among ourselves and the "audience." We later continued this conversation on-line with all contributors.

For several of us, the answer lies in the fact that many mothers and children love the program. In several of the chapters in this book, women have said they enjoy the programs, social and instructional, that Head Start offers. Whenever parents have been asked about Head Start, including during congressional hearings, there is strong support from mothers. For their own reasons, not necessarily the ones we expect, mothers do value Head Start.

One issue here is that the things families take from the program are not easily measured, certainly not in quantifiable terms. Given the dominance of quantitative methods in the evaluation of Head Start, we have not been able to "see" the impact, the positive impact, Head Start has had on families. Kathy Hayes suggests that we should be questioning not Head Start, but our instruments or our expectations. Hence, what may be needed is not to abandon Head Start, but to conduct more thorough, more sensitive analysis. Current negative findings, those in this book and elsewhere, should not be used to dismantle the program.

Eden Inoway-Ronnie, in our on-line discussion, makes the point that, since Head Start was designed to be responsive to local concerns, effectiveness must be evaluated locally. Large-scale, multisite studies are inappropriate because the specifics of programs and aims differ across localities. Yet, many policy analysts cling to a multisite, statistical design and thus inevitably miss the varying, difficult-to-measure positives.

Those varying goals may not include the elimination of Poverty, capital "P." They may not include increases in individual IQ scores. They may, as Inoway-Ronnie shows in her chapter, instead include simply better fitting in with American society. Personal goals of mothers (developed a priori or ex post facto) may not be focused on fulfilling the American Dream, but may, as Ames and Ellsworth discuss, focus on being better able to discipline children or on gaining a measure of self-respect. Local programs may be found quite successful in these terms, if we evaluate them in the right ways.

However, a member of our AESA audience and several of us raised another issue. Head Start easily can be seen as a status-quo preserving program. There is an emphasis, as we have seen, on conventional achievement and "fixing" "disadvantaged" children and parents to so achieve. If they do not get fixed or if they do not achieve, there is additional blame. They were deficient in the first place in a fair society; then they had an extra helping hand with Head Start and still failed in a more-than-fair society.

Further, as Jeanne Ellsworth argued on-line, Head Start may be doomed to low quality, as long as it remains cheap and does not rock the boat. After all, it is "other people's children" who are being served here. The children of policy makers (senators, representatives, presidents) do not attend Head Start. If Head Start sounds nice and appears to the public as beneficial, it serves its purpose—which is not necessarily to raise test scores and certainly not to end poverty. It *seems* to address intractable problems.

In the end, this line of argument goes, Head Start may be worse than nothing at all. Kathy Kuntz (on e-mail) told us that a student responded to her discussion of the history of Head Start by calling the program "a cruel joke." "To him, the idea of giving [a] five year old a year-long experience in a warm and caring environment and then sending that child to the public schools of Chicago or Detroit was inhumane."

Head Start does very little to change the world of inhumane, in-human schools or workplaces or street corners. It is not "striking and cutting at the roots of all the evils." Maybe we should abandon it. Certainly we have worried that this book might be taken as an argu-ment to do just that. And yet, as several of us have pointed out, what else have we got? Kathy Kuntz says, "Instead of attacking the in-equalities inherent in our educational system, OEO created a cute Band-Aid—Head Start. The Band-Aid has managed to draw some attention to the problem but in itself it is a wholly inadequate solution. Further, it may inhibit a real solution since it gives the illusion of addressing the problem. Does this mean we should remove it and let the bleeding begin in earnest?" Kuntz goes on to describe two women who had experienced severe life troubles. Their troubles were made bearable, the women could get through the troubles only because of Head Start support. "I'm immediately confronted with the vision of those two women and their children. Yeah, it's a Band-Aid and a crummy one at that sometimes. But I'm not willing to remove it." Despite the severe challenges we have documented, there *is* still the hope.

At this time, the future of Head Start is unclear. Congress passed and President Clinton signed welfare "reform" legislation, and the states are beginning, as we write, to implement it. The legislation calls for various limits on eligibility for public assistance and calls for re-cipients to "work"—as though raising children was not work. Sympa-thy for the poor and desire to end poverty through government programs are sentiments only rarely found in the public discourse. Indeed, public money for programs benefiting the *middle* class—fund-ing for public higher education, Medicare—is being cut at every level of government. Paying for a Head Start program serving all eligible children seems unlikely this summer of 1997. Further, of course, there is an acceleration of the forces we have identified as harmful to Head Start—bureaucracy and professionalism.

Nevertheless, we see this book as the beginning of a project to pinpoint how programs like Head Start *do* help to improve people's lives. We need to know what works, when, how, and for whom. We need more policies and more political activism to put such knowledge to work, and we need to target not just the Band-Aid, but the roots of the evils that beset us. In the mean time, though, we must not let "the bleeding begin in earnest."

REFERENCES

Alinsky, Saul D. 1946. Reveille for Radicals. Chicago: University of Chicago Press.

Rose, Nancy. 1995. *Workforce or Fairwork: Women, Welfare, and Government Work Programs*. New Brunswick, NJ: Rutgers University Press.

Friedlander, Daniel and Burtless, Gary. 1995. *Five Years After: The Long Term Effects of Welfare-to-Work Programs*. New York: Russell Sage Foundation.

Contributors

Lynda J. Ames is associate professor of sociology at State University of New York, Plattsburgh. She has written on women in the workplace and pay equity. Most recently, her focus has been on poverty among women in rural New York, and she has begun a study of poor women's access to health care and antiviolence services. She lives happily in a tiny hamlet on Lake Champlain with her partner and menagerie.

Robert Bickel is professor of education leadership at Marshall University in Huntington, West Virginia, where he teaches courses in statistics, research methods, and the social foundations of education. His recent publications concern dropping out, adolescent pregnancy, social distress among rural adolescents, and dubious conventional wisdom regarding parental involvement. He is currently engaged in research on early adolescent pregnancy and in a local-level evaluation of a post–Head Start education intervention.

Kate Conrad earned degrees in anthropology and education from the University of Cincinnati and a master's degree in anthropology from the University of Kentucky. In addition to having been a classroom teacher, she worked for five years as an ethnographer on a qualitative research team studying the West Virginia Head Start to Public School Transition Demonstration Project.

Amy Dillon has had firsthand experience with Head Start by attending Head Start in place of kindergarten and also by having a mother who was a classroom aide in the program for several years. Amy has a B.A. in elementary education and an M.A. in reading education and has taught in preschools and public schools. She has worked as a qualitative researcher for the past five years in the Head Start/Public School Transition Demonstration Project in West Virginia.

Henry M. Doan is currently with the Administration on Children, Youth, and Families (ACYF) of the U.S. Department of Health and Human Services. Dr. Doan is specializing in research and evaluation studies to assess national programs for children, youth, and families. He holds a Ph.D. in social psychology and has had more than twenty-five years of experience teaching, conducting, and managing research at the college level. Prior to joining ACYF, Dr. Doan was at Adelphi University, Long Island, New York, where he was founding director of institutional research and special assistant to the president. He has conducted seminars on cross-cultural communication to federal agencies and various professional organizations for many years.

Jeanne Ellsworth is an associate professor at the Center for Educational Studies and Services at Plattsburgh State University of New York, where she teaches courses in social foundations of education. She was a community representative on a Head Start Policy Council from 1992 through 1995. Her research interests include education for poor children, education as charity, and teacher education. She lives with her family in the Adirondacks.

Susan W. Geddes worked for fifteen years in the insurance field, for four years in the parent involvement/social services area of Head Start, and is now employed as an office manager in a new fund-raising business. She enjoys singing and writing songs, writing poems and stories, and spending time with her granddaughter.

Polly Greenberg was a staff member at the Office of Economic Opportunity in Washington, D.C., working for Jule Sugarman during the months Head Start was being created and Sugarman was administering it into nationwide existence. For two years she was among a group of activists who lived and worked with black parents in Mississippi in the mid-1960s to bring Head Start to thousands of youngsters and to mobilize communities in a quest for human and civil rights. She remains an advocate for the poor and for children everywhere and currently is with the National Association for the Education of Young Children in Washington, D.C.

Patricia A. Hamilton is the Vice President of Cygnus Corporation, located outside of Washington, D.C. in Rockville, Maryland. She has conducted numerous studies and authored many reports and articles on early childhood development, teacher training, special education, minority and disadvantaged populations, and parent involvement. A former Montessori teacher, speech pathologist, and school administrator, she received her doctorate in education from the George Washington University.

Katherine Hayes, senior associate at Juárez and Associates, is an educational anthropologist and research methodologist. She has designed and implemented numerous ethnographic studies for specialized populations and has studied multicultural Head Start programs, workplace literacy for immigrant women, basic education in Guatemala, and adolescent educational experiences. She has directed qualitative cross-cultural studies about health maintenance organizations, youth and drug use, parent involvement in primary schools, Head Start parent attitudes, aging, prenatal care, nutrition, and interrace relations in the wake of the 1992 Los Angeles riots. She teaches qualitative methods and educational anthropology courses at the University of California at Los Angeles.

Eden Inoway-Ronnie is a postdoctoral research associate at the University of Wisconsin-Madison. She conducted an ethnographic study of two ethnically and racially diverse Head Start classrooms. Her current research interests include the study of intergroup relations, ethnically and racially diverse school contexts, teachers' work, and the schooling experiences of Asian Americans.

Wendy L. Kirby is a student at Plattsburgh State University of New York, working toward a degree in psychology with a minor in sociology. She is a wife and the mother of two girls, ages eight and ten, both of whom attended Head Start. She worked in the Head Start program as a substitute teacher's aide, substitute cook, bus aide, and any other position that needed filling. She became Policy Council chairperson and served in that capacity for three years. She has worked for the Champlain Valley Technical School with children and disabilities for the past five years. She is presently working for a union that represents nonprofit organizations. She would like to use her education to educate policy makers for the betterment of all people in our society, particularly the poor.

Mary Trotter Klenz is currently the president of the League of Women Voters of Charlotte-Mecklenburg, North Carolina. She is the chair of the North Carolina statewide grassroots campaign to repeal the state's sales tax on food. She received her M.A. in sociology from the University of North Carolina at Charlotte in 1993. Her research interests include issues of public policy and tax fairness.

Kathryn R. Kuntz is a project manager at the Energy Center of Wisconsin where she works with educators and low-income advocates to design and implement programs promoting energy conservation. She has an M.A. in U.S. history from the University of Wisconsin, Madison, and participated in the development of one of Head Start's experimental Comprehensive Child Development programs between 1989 and 1992.

Panayota Y. Mantzicopoulos is an associate professor of educational psychology at Purdue University. Her research focuses on the development and education of young children. She is currently the research director of a Head Start/Public School Transition Demonstration Project.

Roslyn Arlin Mickelson is professor of sociology and adjunct professor of women's studies at the University of North Carolina at Charlotte. She received her Ph.D. from the University of California, Los Angeles, in 1984 and completed a postdoctoral fellowship with the Bush Program for Child Development and Social Policy at the University of Michigan, Ann Arbor. She has published widely on the political economy of education, especially about the ways that race, class, and gender shape educational processes and outcomes. With funding from the National Science Foundation, she is currently investigating the academic and equity consequences of corporate involvement and leadership of local school reform.

Stacey Neuharth-Pritchett is an assistant professor of elementary education at the University of Georgia. Her research specialties center on the contexts of early intervention and children's transitions to school. Her involvement with Head Start was as the research coordinator for one of the Head Start/Public School Transition Demonstration projects.

Laurel Parrott's love for qualitative research was sparked and nurtured during her five-year stint as an ethnographer on the staff of the West Virginia Head Start to Public School Transition Project. She is currently involved in qualitative research on the Rural and Urban Images: Voices of Girls in Science, Mathematics and Technology Program for the Appalachia Educational Laboratory, Inc., in Charleston, West Virginia. She has a master's degree in elementary education.

Elizabeth P. Quintero is an associate professor of early childhood/ elementary education at the University of Minnesota, Duluth. Her doctorate is in curriculum and instruction with a major in early childhood education and a minor in bilingual education. Her dissertation research focused on literacy development in bilingual preschoolers in a bilingual Head Start program in El Paso, Texas. She has worked with several Head Start programs beginning in the 1960s and currently spends as much time as possible at Copeland Head Start in the Harborview Housing Project in Duluth, Minnesota, which serves bilingual Hmong and Laotian families in Head Start and family literacy programs.

Linda Spatig is an associate professor at Marshall University (Huntington, West Virginia) where she teaches courses in educational foundations and qualitative research. From 1992 through 1997 she led an ethnographic research team in the study of a Head Start to Public School Transition Demonstration Project. Her scholarly work addresses schooling and social inequalities.

Index

African Americans, 39n. 44, 117, 149–51
American Indians, 49n. 71, 149–51
Asian Americans, 149–51; perspectives on learning English, 177. *See also* Southeast Asians

bilingual children, 144–65, 167–95, 200–18; biliteracy and, 203–5; home languages of, 152–53; language instruction for, 146, 177–79; use of language by, 156, 212, 213–14. *See also* cultural diversity, multiculturalism
Bloom, Benjamin, 322, 323
business-style management in Head Start, 134, 214, 237–39, 254

Child Development Group of Mississippi, xii, 18, 22, 33, 34, 46n. 106, 69, 71n. 10, 229, 327
community action, Head Start as, xi–xiii, 1–59
Community Action Agencies. *See* Community Action Programs
Community Action Programs, 3, 10, 24–25, 29, 43n. 83, 222; opposition to, 5, 11; relation-

ship to Head Start, 10, 116–17, 253
conferences, parent participation in, 133–35, 247–48
constructivism, 209–10, 272–77; minority/poor students and, 287–88
Cooke, Dr. Robert, 6, 17, 24, 44n. 87, 56, 323–24
critical perspectives, described, x–xi
cultural capital, 75, 114–15, 137–39
cultural deprivation, 4, 322, 324. *See also* deficit theories
cultural diversity, child development theory and, 210; child-rearing and, 208–9, 225; extent and nature of, among Head Start children, 148–54, 167; Head Start principles for responding to, 188–89, 202–3; immigration and, 167–68, 195n. 1; influence on beliefs and values, 168, 184, 189–90, 202–3; lack of, among Head Start staff, 154–57; need for further research on, 164–65; parent involvement and, 162–64, 168; recruiting for, 162. *See also* multiculturalism

349

curriculum approaches in Head Start, 169, 194–95, 261; diversity and, 188–89, 211–12; in family literacy programs, 203–5; in transition project, 270–71; parents and, 191–95, 196n. 8. *See also* constructivism; developmentalism; Developmentally Appropriate Practice (DAP); High/Scope

deficit theories, viii, 31, 113, 220, 322–24
Department of Health, Education, and Welfare, transfer of Head Start to, 23–27
developmentalism, 281–88, 270
Developmentally Appropriate Practice (DAP), 182–83, 209–12, 284, 305, 307, 308–9
Dewey, John, 272, 284–87
dropping out of school, xi, 67, 80–81

Elementary and Secondary Education Act, 15
employment and career opportunities in Head Start, 19–20, 135–37, 139, 243
empowerment, xiii, 20, 31, 58, 67–70, 204–5, 219–39, 256, 304, 336

family literacy projects, 200–16; goals of, 204–5; risk-taking in, 215–16
Follow-Through, 14. *See also* transition programs
functionalist perspective, 74–75
funding, 10, 27
fundraising by parents, 92, 122, 130–31

gender issues, 17–23, 42n. 71, 63–65, 119

High/Scope curriculum approach, 167–95; bilingual students and 185–86; bilingual parents' perceptions of, 176–80; defended by teachers, 180–84; described, 169–70
Hispanic Americans, 117, 149–51; in family literacy programs, 203–5; parental authority, 212–14

income eligible children, percent enrolled in Head Start, xvii n. 4, 70n. 1, 150
I.Q., ix, 4, 26, 44n. 87, 71n. 8, 330, 334–45

Job Corps, 3, 41n. 64, 54, 55, 57, 70n. 4
Johnson, Lady Bird, vii, 8–9
Johnson, Lyndon B., vii, 2, 8, 54

Kennedy, Robert F., 52

Latino/a children and families. *See* Hispanic Americans

maximum feasible participation, 2, 53, 54, 59, 60, 335
media attention to Head Start, 8, 14–15, 21–22, 25, 29–31, 57, 320–21, 323–24
mothers, as deficient, 32, 306, 323, 324; as synonymous with parents, 63, 179, 221–22; as volunteers, 91–94; case histories of, in West Virginia, 79–87; self-esteem, 227–28, 247, 248–49, 257

Moynihan, Daniel Patrick, 19, 41 n. 67
multiculturalism, definitions of, 145; Head Start guidelines on, 145–46; health services and, 160–61; holidays and, 158–59; in Head Start classrooms, 157–60; materials for, 159–60; research on, 145; social services and, 161–62. *See also* cultural diversity

Nixon, Richard, 23, 44 n. 87
non-English speaking children and families, 156–57, 160–61, 202, 213–14

Office of Child Development (OCD), 23–24, 26–28, 30–34
Office of Economic Opportunity (OEO), xi, 2–27, 32–33, 54; opposition to, 5, 11, 23, 57–58
Office of Education, transfer of Head Start to, 11–13
othering, 324–27

parent activism, examples of, 14–15, 21–23, 29, 206–7, 230–34, 247–48, 252
parent education, as part of family literacy programs, 204–5; concepts of, for Head Start, 7, 16–17, 31, 50, 60, 78, 220, 247–48; in transition project, 90–91, 94–98; informal, 223–26
parent governance groups, 14–15, 28, 29–30, 78, 111–40, 228–36; agendas for, 98–100, 123–24; empowerment and, 115, 230–32; limited power of, 98–100, 122–33, 138–39, 192–93, 232–36, 249–51; mandated roles for, 116; role in budgeting, 98–100, 126–27, 229; role in hiring and firing, 125–26, 229, 249
parent involvement, 73–108, 111–40, 219–39; among low-income families, 73–74, 77, 107, 112; among minority families, 162–64, 191–93; as socially reproductive, 104–8, 112, 113, 122–33; educational advantages of, for children, 74, 100–4, 107, 113; in transition program, 87–101; personal gratification from, 89–90, 91, 100, 104, 329, 338; recruiting parents for, 88–90; theoretical rationale for, 74–75, 112–13, 256–57; visions of, for Head Start, xiii, 7, 16–17, 28–29, 31, 50–51, 58–63, 74, 76–77, 111–13, 115, 191–92, 252, 219–21, 253–54
popularity of Head Start, 5–6, 21, 24, 32–33, 41n. 64, 62, 318–33
poverty, awareness of, in U.S., 52; images of, 6, 66; rates, 51–52, 81, 149; income guidelines, 108n. 3
public schools, parents and, 67–68, 206–7, 226; relationship of Head Start to, 10–13, 20–21, 25–26, 28, 58, 180–81, 292, 313–16; reform in, 313–16; standardized testing in, 261–62, 281–83, 287–88, 308–9; teachers, 278–81, 286–87, 305, 307. *See also* transition projects

race/racism, 6, 14, 52, 65, 39n. 44, 42 n. 71, 119, 266, 321
reproduction theories, 114–15
research on Head Start, ix–x, 61, 263, 292, 319, 334–35, 338–39; Kirschner report, 27; Perry Preschool Project, 170; Westinghouse study, 25, 26, 32, 44n. 87, 328–29
restricted linguistic codes, 112, 114–16, 137–38, 140

70.2 (Head Start Performance Standards section), xiii, 28, 115–16, 191–92, 229, 253, 255
Shriver, Sargent, 5–6, 8, 9–10, 11–12, 14, 32, 33, 35 n. 13, 54, 55, 56, 59
Southeast Asian Americans, family literacy programs and, 203–5; Hmong, 171, 196 n. 10; individuality and, 188–89; response to Head Start curriculum, 176–80; social relationships, 189–90. *See also* Asian Americans
staff, Head Start, salaries, 244–45, 247, 250; unionization, 234–36, 244

Sugarman, Jule, 17–18, 59, 61–62, 70n. 3

transition programs, 73–108, 260, 262, 291–315, 315–16n. 1; administration of, 309–13; influence on public school teachers, 227–31; parent involvement in, 304–5, 306; philosophical principles of, 298–309; staff development in, 271–77

volunteers, 18–19, 55–56, 59, 64; misuse of, 93, 250, 251

War on Poverty, 2, 23, 50, 51, 53–54, 56, 145, 327; roles of women in, 17–18; support for, from educational establishment, 12
Women, as volunteers, 17–18; in history of early childhood education, 35n. 13, 63–64; roles of, in Head Start design, 63–65. *See also* mothers

Zigler, Edward, 4, 22, 24–25, 26–27, 28, 30, 31, 32, 56, 57, 70n. 7